Women in European Culture and Society

Women in European Culture and Society: A Sourcebook includes a range of trans-national sources which encompass the history of women in Europe from the beginning of the eighteenth century right up to the present day. Including documents from across Europe, from France and Germany to Estonia, Spain and Russia, organised in a broad chronological spread, the diversity of the sources included in the book is unique – including many never translated into English before. Deborah Simonton offers detailed interpretive introductions that analyse and contextualise the sources.

A central feature is the exploration of how women operated within gendered worlds and used their skills and abilities to shape and claim their own identities and to engage with how they contributed as practitioners to shaping European culture and society. With over 200 sources, the book allows us to 'hear' women's voices as they articulate their understandings of their worlds and helps to capture a sense of women's motivations, options and choices as they understood them – allowing readers to focus on either a period or a theme and providing a comparative resource.

Ideal for use on its own or as a companion volume to Simonton's other major work, *Women in European Culture and Society: Gender, Skill and Identity since 1700*, this sourcebook is an invaluable collection offering vivid first-hand accounts of women's lives.

Deborah Simonton (FRHist) is Associate Professor at the University of Southern Denmark and leads the Gender in the European Town Network. Her publications include *Women in European Culture and Society: Gender, Skill and Identity since 1700* (Routledge, 2010) and *The Routledge History of Women in Europe since 1700* (Routledge, 2006), as well as the forthcoming *Female Agency in the Urban Economy: Gender in the European Towns, 1640–1830*, co-edited with Anne Montenach (Routledge, 2013) and *Women in Eighteenth-century Scotland*, co-edited with Kate Barclay (2013).

'A wonderful collection, giving students access to over 200 sources by and about European women from c.1700, and highlighting the rich diversity of their experiences. Particularly valuable is the large selection of materials from countries often omitted in European sourcebooks.'
Elizabeth Ewan, *University of Guelph, Canada*

'*Women in European Culture and Society: A Sourcebook* is a particularly welcome collection both because it covers a lengthy period and because it is genuinely European in scope, allowing for comparisons and contrasts and providing evidence of continuity and change in women's history. The introductory focus on historiography and method, and the chronological and thematic structure, with its overlap and echoes of voices between chapters, make this an especially useful text for teaching not only specialist areas but also European survey courses.'
Jane McDermid, *University of Southampton, UK*

Women in European Culture and Society

A Sourcebook

Deborah Simonton

Routledge
Taylor & Francis Group

LONDON AND NEW YORK

First published 2014
by Routledge
2 Park Square, Milton Park, Abingdon, Oxon OX14 4RN

and by Routledge
711 Third Avenue, New York, NY 10017

Routledge is an imprint of the Taylor & Francis Group, an informa business

British Library Cataloguing in Publication Data
A catalogue record for this book is available from the British Library

Library of Congress Cataloging in Publication Data
Women in European culture and society from 1700 : a sourcebook / [edited by] Deborah Simonton.
pages cm
Includes bibliographical references and index.
1. Women–Europe–History–Sources. 2. Women–Europe–Social conditions–Sources. 3. Europe–Civilization–Sources. I. Simonton, Deborah, 1948–
HQ1587.W664 2013
305.4094–dc23
2013019587

ISBN: 978–0–415–68438–5 (hbk)
ISBN: 978–0–415–68440–8 (pbk)

Typeset in Bembo
by Keystroke, Station Road, Codsall, Wolverhampton

This book is dedicated to Eve

Contents

Figures

Acknowledgements

This book derives from my own work with primary sources with students and the experience of writing the survey *Women in European Culture and Society: Gender, Skill and Identity from 1700*, which it partners. It has also relied on a great deal of good will and support from so many people that many will remain nameless. You know who you are and I thank you.

I am especially thankful for the everlasting patience, support and insight of Eve Setch and Vicki Peters of Routledge, who helped shape this book by their persistence, thoughtful questions and encouragement. They have been pragmatic and always compassionate throughout the process. Eve's involvement, understanding and enthusiasm have always felt personal and I appreciate her dedication – and humour. I also am so grateful to Laura Mothersole of Routledge, who patiently and persistently obtained an enormous number of permissions, and for her advice in this fraught process.

Many people gave generously in helping to find and/or translate materials or in checking my translations. I am extremely appreciative for the help and patience of Martin Solgaard Andersen, Katie Barclay, Hanne Con, Carol Gold, Mieke van den Berg Walch, Trine Vesti Hansen, Ulla Ijås, Henna Karppinen, Theresa McClintock, Elina Maines, Anna Mazanik, Linda Masson, Margaret Ross, Anne Montenach and Kristine Vestergaard Nielsen. Martin, in particular, deserves a medal for translating both Danish and German, virtually 'on demand'. I appreciate the generosity of Lynn Abrams for sharing unpublished transcripts of two of her Shetland interviews and Callum Brown's in sharing the transcripts of the Scottish Women's Oral History Project. For help with images I am grateful to Tiina and Liis Jääger, Lauri Suurmaa, Kim Downie of Aberdeen University Library and Kirstin Halla Baldvinsdottir of the National Museum of Iceland.

Friends have been an important part of my writing and thinking. Some are also colleagues in women's and gender history. I am especially grateful to Katie Barclay, Elaine Chalus, Marjo Kaartinen, Nina Koefoed and Anne Montenach for personal and professional sustenance, and to my sister Kemille Moore for always being at the end of a Skype call. Katie Barclay and Andrew Newby read and made important suggestions and comments, especially Katie, who took her editor's eye to this. Nina Chatelain and Helle Lundgaard also gave it a 'trial run' and I appreciate the time and trouble they took to give me a student's-eye view. I am enormously grateful for all the support, but also I remain culpable for the final product. I wish to acknowledge the support also of the Gender in the European Town Network – while this sourcebook was unrelated to our network activities, its understanding and enthusiasm were a tonic when this project became overwhelming.

My ultimate appreciation goes to David Hastie. Not only did he type out many of the sources, check messy scanned texts and cope with French when he is only a learner, but he exhibited more tolerance and patience than he thought he had. As always, he celebrated the end of it.

The publishers would like to thank Lynn Abrams, Mary McAlpin, Tiina Jääger, Doug Scott, Callum Brown, the University of Aberdeen, Myriam Benraad, the University of Chicago Press, Wiley-Blackwell, Yale University Press, Random House, Amsterdam University Press, the Arkiv der Sozialen Democratie und Bibliothek, the University of Nebraska Press, Basic Books, Springer-Verlag, Berghahn Books, the Irish National Archives, Mohr Siebeck, Rowohlt, Princeton University Press, Roderick Stackelberg, Sally A. Winkle, Karl Dietz, Berg Publishers and the Finnish Archive for their kind permission. Whilst every effort has been made to trace copyright holders, this has not been possible in all cases. Any omissions brought to our attention will be remedied in future editions.

Introduction

This sourcebook originated while I was working on *Women in European Culture and Society: Gender, Skill and Identity*. In striving to find and explore women's voices, I encountered many gaps and frustrations. My aim then, as now, was to explore the history of women in Europe from the beginning of the eighteenth century and to push beyond national studies to create an integrated view of three hundred years of women in Europe. A central goal is to explore how women operated within gendered worlds and used their skills and abilities to shape and claim their own identities, and to engage with how women contributed as practitioners to shaping European culture and society. Concentrating on the period from 1700 to the present reflects an account of 'modern Europe', situating the French Revolution and the 'Victorian' woman in the longer historical context. It also embeds the twentieth century into its historical context, which helps to identify its 'difference' but also recognises the importance of continuities that permeate this longer period.

The biggest problem was to find primary sources from across Europe to reflect this agenda. This book is intended to be an important addition to the existing corps of sourcebooks, many of which are out of date or limited to specific periods, issues or nationalities. In particular, it meets students' and lecturers' need for a broad range of accessible documents. The book is organised chronologically, following the structure of *Women in European Culture and Society*, with internal repeating themes, which assist in visualising chronological periods as well as reading across themes. Thus, it benefits from a structure that allows lecturers and students to focus on a period or a theme and acts as a comparative resource.

The volume has a broad geographic coverage, and many of the materials are translated from the original language. This is significant, since many European languages remain unintelligible to most of the rest of Europe and much of the English-speaking world. So readers gain access to material they might otherwise not have access to, or may be unable to read. The volume focuses primarily on Western Europe, but the increasing publication of Eastern European materials in English provides access to more of Europe. This is particularly important, since primary material on Eastern, Nordic and Southern European women often is not captured in existing source books, and frequently this is precisely the material which students and lecturers find it hard to access – and read. If some nations or regions are not as well covered as specialists would like, this is partly due to the difficulty of finding the originals, and in the case of some southern regions, women's writing is either limited or not necessarily directly attributable to the themes here.

Certainly there are many good sourcebooks, in English and other languages, and the growth of the Internet and the increasing digitisation of material has given us far greater access to sources than ever before. All sourcebooks, this one included, are limited by space, editorial decisions and which themes and issues are given priority. This is to be expected; time also plays a part, since historical research interests and agendas change: where 'rights' has long been a fundamental issue, personal experience and emotions now play a much larger part in the questions we pose and seek to answer. Several European-wide and a few 'national' documentary studies can be found in the 'Further Reading' at the end of this volume, and students and scholars would be well served to draw on them.

The Internet presents a somewhat different set of issues. One of its main drawbacks is, of course, that it is so vast that students have a quixotic journey to find appropriate materials. Many students have difficulty understanding what primary material is, and the Internet blurs this so that they frequently are simply more confused. They also struggle to identify what is 'reliable' material, especially when confronted with a number of 'snippets' and schools history sites, which present digested gobbets. Dedicated teaching websites (e.g. Minerva, Blackboard, WebCT) go some way toward resolving this, but are extraordinarily demanding on lecturers' time, and the issue of permissions restricts uploading material. Lecturers too find the web daunting at times. Searching is not always easy or transparent, and web addresses change, or disappear, with dizzying frequency. In the final analysis, a great deal remains untranslated.

The increasing digitisation of large collections or groups of sources is a positive and important development in historical scholarship. It has certainly helped many academics and their students. Of significance to women's history is the steady growth of online collections from across Europe, with notable examples including Aletta (International Archives for the Women's Movement) from the Netherlands, KVINNSAM (Kvinnohistoriska samlingarna, Centre for Studies in Women's History) from Sweden, and GenderInn (Women's and Gender Studies Database) from Germany. The FRAGEN database relates to the second-wave European feminism throughout the European Union (including Croatia and Turkey). These materials demand language skills, but they hold the promise of being able to probe unexplored terrains and to act as a further incentive to engage in the interdisciplinary and multi-national agenda of women's history. Digitisation has also opened up collections like ECCO (Early English Collections Online) and the British Newspapers project of the British Library. Yet, for smaller institutions, perhaps ones that are not largely English speaking, these collections can be too expensive and remain inaccessible, a factor I deal with daily.

Editorial decisions

Limitations of space, and ultimately of cost, mean that difficult editorial decisions are necessary. From an original body of over four hundred enticing items, the final selection was cut virtually in half. Non-English-language materials are an essential core of this collection and are of particular importance to an English-speaking audience, so that sometimes an English-language source is omitted in favour of others. So some 'favourites' may be missing, or are shorter than one would like. This process meant that many delightful or interesting accounts had to be left out. But by exploring the Further Reading, other sourcebooks and the web, readers can pursue further research, follow up longer versions of those included and look for others to complement them.

The sourcebook is based on a mix of shorter and longer extracts, which gives a flavour of the discussions and views of women while allowing deeper penetration into some documents to flesh out the arguments, experiences and language of women more explicitly. The structure of the book allows themes to be studied in their own time, but also to be read across the sections, following themes across time; so, for example, singletons can be traced throughout the period. Notably, section boundaries necessarily blur since women's lives are multi-faceted. Thus, women better known as novelists may turn up commenting on women's rights. Others known for their art or social position turn up as mothers, like Käthe Kollwitz and Suzanne Necker. Others like Aldeheid Popp comment on their working lives, political activism and support for other women, thus reappearing in multiple sections. The selection process has deliberately prioritised the female voice, but men make an appearance when their influence was such that it was warranted, especially men telling women how to behave and run their lives, like practical Joachim Campe, controversial Jean Jacques Rousseau and witty Gustave Droz.

The introductions have been kept deliberately brief. First, this is to give scope for readers and lecturers to shape materials to their own uses and frameworks, not to prejudge documents but to keep the door open for various approaches and interpretations. Second, the volume aims to encourage the reader to develop the skills required in reading and understanding sources. This is a central part of understanding history and how historians read the past. It also enables a personal and intellectual engagement with the voices of the past, and specifically women.

This volume was created as a partner to *Women in European Culture and Society: Gender, Skill and Identity*, and although each volume also stands alone, it was a deliberate decision to create parallels so as to enable easy cross-referencing and to link sources to the discursive text. A fundamental decision in writing the original volume was to create a chronological organisation that allowed for blurring of the traditional boundaries of historical time. This was reflected in the chapter structure, and has an impact on this sourcebook in that the sources are numbered by 'Part' not by chapter, in order to retain the ideas inherent in the original structure. As I wrote then, 'Women's history is not a single narrative and it does not always work chronologically.'

Using sources

Sources are the 'bread and butter' of understanding history and can be read on many levels. One issue is that they are almost always mediated, by having been 'kept', either in printed form or through archival practices. Often, as here, they have been 'selected' and edited, so that the editor has made decisions. But also, my inclinations and interests inevitably shaped what this volume contains. Language plays a part as well, because what historians and students can read – and understand – is limited by their linguistic ability. In this sourcebook, most of the translations are mine, or mine with help from colleagues and former students. It has been a primary aim to translate as accurately as possible, of course, but also to retain the tone and flavour of the original. We also need to acknowledge that even sources in English may not be in a language that is familiar today. Here too the original has been retained, even where the language is that of an illiterate servant or an early eighteenth-century Scotswoman. So, reading sources often requires access to a good dictionary, and one which gives historical usage is a real bonus, like the full *Oxford English Dictionary*, fondly known as the *OED*, and now widely available online.

Defining sources

Primary sources are, strictly speaking, first-hand sources, and are the evidence from which historians extract clues, whereas secondary sources, defined at their most simple, are second-hand materials, usually based on primary evidence and research. This simple definition is contentious within the historical community, but works as a broad guideline. Thus, primary sources are in one sense the 'raw material' of history. They are the closest we will come to the past; they are the 'original traces' of the people we want to know and understand.

But they are not the history itself. They are laden with potential but must be read, understood and contextualised to realise their possibilities. They are also limited in that one source tells only one story – and probably part of one at that. So they have to be read together, and situated in context. They also have to be interrogated. There is a mythical notion that sources give us historical 'truth', but not so. People are notoriously poor witnesses even when they intend to be or assume they are being reliable. And consciously or unconsciously, writers and other producers of evidence did so steeped in their own 'baggage' of class, gender and values. Thus, certainly read them for content – and the pleasure that the voices of the past give us – but also with a critical mind.

Historical evidence comes in a variety of different forms, and as our views of history have changed from a fixation on politics and state archives, the range of materials employed by historians has also expanded. Reflecting approaches that draw on other disciplines like art, music, anthropology, sociology and economics, history has developed a much broader reach and employs materials from a wider spectrum of possibilities.

The most obvious is the array of written and printed material, which dominates this book. They may be documents concerning legal, domestic or business matters, produced for a practical purpose at the time, not with historians in mind, such as legal deeds, contracts between business partners, assessments of income tax or codes of law like the ones here on marriage. Many local and national administrative records, from parish records to census materials, also fall into this category. There are also personal documents that were intended to be private, such as letters or diaries, of which several are utilised here. Letters nominally were between the author and the recipient, but also secretaries and friends assisted in writing, and letters were often shared in close circles. In any case, the author almost inevitably shaped the content for her audience, and if she knew it might be read by others, this would also influence what she wrote as well as its tone.

Some diaries, and even letters, were intended for publication. Epistolary writing was a style of literature, and some 'letters' were in fact literary constructions, even if reporting what the author saw or experienced. Lady Mary Wortley Montagu wrote letters on her travels which, despite her statements to the contrary, were clearly intended for publication: she edited and organised them before handing them to a friend who arranged publication. Similarly, memoirs might have been nominally private – written for family members, for example – but often they were intended for publication, or the author imagined that they might be published. Mary Sommerville therefore scrupulously did not write about her personal life because she did not believe it was anyone's business, although she wrote a detailed memoir, published by her daughter. In this case Somerville deliberately excluded material, and we know from later editions that so did her daughter. And famously, Jane Austen's sister, Cassandra, deleted and obliterated sections of Jane's letters relating to family affairs. So a healthy scepticism is an important tool for the historian, while 'reading between the lines' is an art.

Narratives of events in which the writers were concerned or interested are a common form of primary source and figure significantly in this sourcebook. They are subject to all the caveats above and, like anything meant to be published, they definitely come from the author's point of view. Tracts, manuals and various forms of propaganda, from apparently straightforward childcare manuals to Nazi publications on women, have more overt agendas and are never neutral. Neither are speeches, advertisements, newspaper editorials or parliamentary debates. Newspapers and magazines fall into the slightly grey area of sources. Reportage is usually based on evidence itself and therefore might seem to be a secondary source. But these are a key form of historical artefact and are usually treated as primary sources giving a window into the past like other primary sources. And, logically, they need to be treated with the same sort of scepticism and critical mind as any other production.

Physical objects made or adapted by humans form another group of sources. These include fields, roads, houses, castles, churches and gravestones. They could be musical scores, sketches and drawings, or a finished work of art. The study of material culture has enlisted the help of fabric, patterns, design, dresses, hats and gloves, pottery, porcelain, silverware, tables, chairs – the list is endless. Catalogues like those of the furniture maker Chippendale, for example, give a priceless glimpse into the ways the people of the past lived – or wished to. As we moved into a more technologically adept age, then film and sound recordings offer a different lens into the past. But the basic rules still apply: all sources have to be met with a critical approach.

Interrogating the source

Before moving further, it is important to point out that historians are at different stages in their 'skill set'. The young pupil or student may be approaching sources for the first time and therefore will have few tools at hand to explore them and will not be able to probe into their depths in the same ways we expect a senior student, a postgraduate, a researcher or experienced historian to do. The discussion which follows should give some guidance useful to many, but do not be intimidated if you have little experience – it takes time to become proficient. Indeed, the uncertainty created by primary sources, their very slipperiness, can lead to debates among historians who read them differently and make alternative interpretations. So it is also useful to remember that there is no single way to understand a source.

Working with sources is a form of forensic science, and the historian is a detective unravelling clues and contextualising sources as she interprets and works to understand them. Take nothing at face value, and keep an open mind and be prepared to adapt your views as you discover more and gain fuller insight. This requires slow, careful reading of the written material, with the use of a dictionary where necessary. Then there are questions to ask yourself as you read it – and I use the word 'read' in a broad sense, since some materials, as I have said, are not written.

Start by identifying who made the source. If it is unsigned, is there any evidence which enables you to make a probable guess about the author? What do we know about the producer that might help our understanding of the source? It is helpful to know when and where it was produced. If no date is given, check for any internal clues to help solve the problem. Often the date of publication is not the date of origin, which you may have to seek elsewhere.

It is also important to identify exactly what the source is and to think about how this affects our 'reading' of it. So, identify what the purpose of the source was. Why was it created? What was its original function? And related to this, who was its intended audience? Did the author intend to publish it, or not? It is useful to take this further and think about how contemporaries might have understood it. Note also the kind of perspective the producer adopts. For contemporary narratives, it is important to think about the following as well: did the writer observe the matter for him or herself? If not, from where did s/he get the information? How reliable was the other source? And think about whether the author seems to be a good observer, able to understand and record what s/he saw and heard. Remember, of course, that this does not mean neutrality, since all observers instinctively select what they see and hear, with or without intention. To answer these questions you will probably have to do some research since not all of these answers can be gleaned from the source itself – even if it has been extracted and introduced.

The interpretative process

Once you have established these basics, you move on to the interpretation of the source. From your reading, you should note: What questions does this source raise? What don't we know about it? What other information do we have about this document or object? Now you begin to dig deeper, and probably will have to rely on other reading to help you build up the context in which the source operates. You will want to know if other evidence corroborates it and also what it says – and what it does not say. Thinking like this can help to open up the source and relate it to others.

The historical context is also important, so, where possible, compare sources, asking if they say similar or different things to other sources of the period or place. Does it cohere with other evidence from the period and with other information in other histories? Sometimes our knowledge of an event rests on one document only. A historian needs to cross-check the evidence to see if sources agree or whether one source is strongly prejudiced. It might be useful to look at how other historians have used the same document, especially if it is a well-known one, such as Rousseau's *Émile* or Wollstonecraft's *Vindication of the Rights of Woman*. Of course sometimes this is not easily possible, simply because the document has not been widely used, such as the Finnish and Scottish advertisements in this sourcebook. However, looking at the treatment of similar materials can be enlightening in 'reading' sources. So think about what other sources might help to answer questions, and what else we need to know in order to understand the evidence in a specific source.

Provenance

For a deeper understanding of any primary source, an appreciation of its provenance is important. This is more than just knowing when and where it was produced, but leads us to think about it as artefact, as object. For example, why was it preserved? So much of the material of the historical past is ephemeral, so knowing why and how an item was preserved enhances our knowledge and comprehension of it. We also have to know if it is genuine, authentic. That is, is it really from the time, by the author and the type of document that it purports to be. Even a 'fraud' can be useful, but knowing if it is 'real' or not can affect the way that we read the document.

Then, we identify whether the source is in its original form, or whether it is a reproduction that has been transcribed, printed or even produced as facsimile. The documents in this sourcebook come from a combination of originals, as in a printed first edition of Wollstonecraft's *Vindication*, transcribed, like most of the letters, or digitised, like Parliamentary debates. Some are later inscriptions of speeches or documents. So the question that arises is how have these been changed in the process; have they been altered or edited? Clearly those in this book have been edited, although the intention was to stay as true to the original as possible. But think about the route that such sources might travel, from handwritten letter to printed version, which may have also been edited. Stages in publication may also have altered them. So what problems might these pose for a historian? For example, the female farmworker's testimony included in this sourcebook was from interviews conducted by male committee members selected by the British Parliament, and they or a scribe wrote them down, reported to Parliament and printed them in Parliamentary Papers which we can read in facsimile, and sometimes in digitised form as well in a variety of edited and extracted versions.

Translation inevitably affects a source. So in addition to the route that it might have travelled from the producer's hand to reader, translation adds another layer to the process. Clearly most translators aim for accuracy, but they are also products of their own time and place. For example, for some of these sources translations by Americans and British translators varied, probably to address different national audiences; translations from the early twentieth century varied from recent ones, and some translations can be essentially revisions, for example, of Simone de Beauvoir's *Le Deuxième Sexe*. So we need to recognise that translations are interpretations of the originals, by the translator.

In many respects, transcribed texts are fundamentally also translations, often with normalised spelling and grammar and 'deduction' of unclear words. Thus, these become interpreted versions of the text. As with translations, they may also pay heed to the conventions of the recipient language. Sometimes language is modernised, for example. In transcribing handwritten text to print, some meaning can be lost or changed. Handwriting can often reflect the writer's emotional state – particularly useful in reading diaries or personal letters – but obviously is lost in translation. Marginalia, scribbles, crossings out are also usually lost. Walter Scott wrote with no punctuation, so his various publishers and editors have had a challenge to punctuate his novels, with the result being quite different flavours in published editions.

The act of editing and selection also changes the original. A simple example comes from newspapers, where stories and advertisements are plucked from their original positions. This can also happen with digitisation when it produces text without the embellishments and placement of the text. Thus we do not read them in the same way that the contemporary reader would have; we do not see what is next to them, and whether the story or advertisement is buried or prominent.

Use of language

The way that language is used and interpreted is ultimately important to our understanding of sources. We need to be alert to the fact that different words or phrases mean different things to different audiences. Words do not have the same meaning over time and between different communities. They are open to multiple readings, dependent on the context in which they are read, by whom and for what purposes. These sources, for example, have a different purpose if read in the context of women's history – which is what is intended – than if, for example, they were part of a study of gender and war, or family life or imperial policy. The subtleties of language and the nuances of reading affect how we interpret and use our materials.

Often sources simply do not tell historians what they want to know about the past. The text of a speech may be relatively straightforward in that it is probably what was said – within the context of corrections and reproduction, as discussed above. But to understand why the speaker said those words in a particular way – like the Hartford speech of Emmeline Pankhurst – or to make points about its political importance, we use our reason and inference. So we move from the source to conclusions about its functions and levels of meaning. We contextualise it, which means reading other things to put it into perspective, and therefore we interpret and evaluate it in terms of its role as a historical statement and historical insight.

Recognising prejudice

'Prejudice' is laden with strong connotations. But it really means preconception, prejudgement, predisposition, partiality. It can also mean bias, bigotry, intolerance. So, examine who wrote the document and see if it is likely that the author would hold a preconceived view. For example, middle-class men, and women too, of course, might well adopt values like thrift and cleanliness which could make it difficult to understand the situation of a labouring farmwoman. This does not mean that these men disliked the women, nor does it make their account worthless. It does mean that the reader has to be aware of these possibilities and interpret the source accordingly. So, in reading a source, ask if the author shows any clear prejudice for or against any of the people or events in the document. If so, can you recognise it and see how it would affect the account? This does not necessarily mean that prejudice is always present. It also means 'shades of grey', in that partiality may be present, but not bigotry, for example.

Prejudice often makes itself plain by the nature of the words used by the writer. For example, an action is called foolhardy – it is condemned; courageous – it is praised. A politician is labelled tenacious – s/he is approved of; stubborn – s/he is disapproved of; Communists are 'Reds'; Conservatives 'exploit' workers in prejudiced writings. These are 'coloured' words that shade or distort an account. A good case in point is the torrent of responses to Margaret Thatcher's death that flooded the social networking sites, newspapers and reportage in April 2013. Prejudice can also be shown by generalisation from individual cases. For example, a few Social Democrat politicians are revealed as 'unconcerned' for their constituents' interests; therefore all Social Democrats are condemned as such. Some nations or races are praised or approved of on a basis of limited first-hand experience – 'all Germans are hardworking', etc. Thus, careful reading and thinking about the use of language and the background of the producer aid in identifying prejudice and partiality.

And finally

The basic approach to reading and using primary sources, whether compiled in a volume like this one, located in an archive, printed in a diary or auto-biography, or even a film or interview, is the same. Adopt a critical attitude to the source, thinking of who, when, where, why, for whom, and how much, if any, prejudice is shown. Think about the route that the source took to your own hands and examine what this source can tell you and what it cannot say about the past – and what else you need to do to gain the fullest understanding that you can.

Part I

Rights of man
and duties of woman

Prelude: women's identity in eighteenth-century culture

Intellectually, the Enlightenment shaped the eighteenth century with its concentration on the social contract, rights of man, the importance of Nature, Reason and perfectibility, which influenced thinking about individuals, state and society. Attitudes towards 'woman' were ambivalent, and notably drew on older Judeo-Christian ideas that depicted woman as temptress and lustful, as well as employing an Enlightenment notion of a 'natural' woman cast as a domestic creature but with a special role as mother, responsible for the proper education of young children.

At the end of the century, Olympe de Gouges and Mary Wollstonecraft represent two clarion voices of the Enlightenment and the debate on women's rights. Writing from different perspectives, they epitomised feminist criticisms of woman's allocated place in European society. De Gouges wrote in response to the *Déclaration des droits de l'homme et du citoyen* [Declaration of the Rights of Man and Citizen, 1791], which she closely parallels. Claiming equal rights, she imagined a vision of the political landscape where women, like men, had rights and responsibilities under the law. She was executed on the guillotine for her stringent advocacy of women's rights in 1793, at the height of the 'Terror' of the French Revolution. Wollstonecraft, in contrast, focused on the operation of Nature and Reason and on education and gendered expectations in constructing masculinity and femininity. Thus she argued for women's equal right to reason and to a rational education which would enable her to realise her capacities, to achieve virtue and make her a suitable companion to man, and not his insipid sexual slave.

1.1 *Declaration of the Rights of Woman*, Olympe de Gouges

Déclaration des droits de la Femme et de la Citoyenne (Paris, 1791), 5–13.

Preamble

   Mothers, daughters, sisters, representatives of the nation, ask to be constituted as a national assembly. Considering that ignorance, forgetfulness or contempt of the rights of woman are the sole causes of public misfortunes and governmental corruption, [we] have resolved to set forth in a solemn declaration the natural inalienable and sacred rights of woman: so that this declaration, being constantly before all members of society, shall remind them continually of their rights and duties; so that the actions of women's and men's power can be compared at any moment with the aim of any and all political institutions and thus be more respected; so that the complaints of citizens, based henceforth upon simple and incontestable principles, shall tend to the maintenance of the constitution, morality, and happiness of all.

In consequence, the sex, which is superior in beauty as in the courage or maternal sufferings, recognises and declares, in the presence and under the auspices of the supreme Being, the following rights of woman and the citizeness.

First article
Woman is born free and remains equal to man in rights. Social distinctions may be founded only on public utility.

II
The aim of every political association is the preservation of natural and inalienable rights of woman and man: These rights are liberty, property, safety and especially resistance to oppression.

III
The principle of all sovereignty resides essentially in the Nation, which is nothing but the union of woman and man: nobody, no individual can exercise authority that does not emanate expressly from it.

IV
Liberty and justice consist of restoring all that belongs to others, so the exercise of natural rights of woman has no limits except the perpetual tyranny with which man opposes them; these limits must be reformed by laws of nature and reason.

V
The laws of nature and reason prohibit all actions injurious to society: whatever is not prohibited by these wise and divine laws should not be obstructed and no one can be constrained to do what they do not require.

The law should be the expression of the general will; all Citizenesses and Citizens must contribute either personally or through their representatives to its formation; it should be the same for everyone: all Citizenesses and Citizens, being equal in its eyes, should be equally eligible for all honours, positions and employments, according to their capabilities, and without other distinctions than those of their virtues and talents. . . .

VII
No woman is excepted; she is accused, arrested and detained in cases determined by law. Women like men obey this rigorous law.

VIII
The law should only establish strictly necessary punishments and no one can be punished except by virtue of a law established and promulgated prior to the crime and legally applied to women.

IX

Any woman being declared guilty, law should exercise complete rigour.

X

No person shall be harassed for fundamental opinions, woman has the right to mount the scaffold; she must equally have the right to mount the rostrum, provided that her demonstrations do not disturb public order established by law.

XI

Free communication of thoughts and opinions is one of the most precious rights of woman, since this liberty assures the recognition by fathers of their children. Any Citizeness can freely say I am the mother of a child that belongs to you, without being forced by a barbaric prejudice [against unmarried mothers] to hide the truth, except in response to the abuse of this liberty in cases determined by law.

XII

The guarantee of the rights of woman and the Citizeness requires a usable power; this safeguard should be established for the benefit of all, and not for the particular benefit of those to whom it is entrusted.

XIII

For maintenance of public authority and expenses of administration, the contributions of woman and man are equal; she takes part in the *corvées* [forced labour], in all painful tasks; she also must have the same share in the allocation of positions, employments, responsibilities, honours and in industry.

XIV

Citizenesses and Citizens have the right to decide, either for themselves or through their representatives, the necessity for public contributions. Citizenesses can only accede to them on admission of an equal share, not only of wealth but also of public administration, and to determine the amount, basis, collection and duration of tax.

XV

The mass of women, joining men as taxpayers, has the right to hold any public agent accountable for his administration.

XVI

Any society, in which the guarantee of rights is not assured, nor the separation of powers determined, has no constitution; the constitution is void, if the majority of individuals who constitute the nation have not cooperated in its drafting.

XVII

Property belongs to both sexes whether united or separated; it is for each an inviolable and sacred right; no one may be deprived of it, since it is a true patrimony of nature, except when public necessity, legally established, obviously dictates it, and under the condition of a just and advanced indemnity.

Postscript

Woman, wake up; the tocsin of reason sounds throughout the universe; understand your rights. The powerful empire of nature is no longer surrounded by prejudice, fanaticism, superstition and lies. The torch of truth has dispersed all the clouds of folly and usurpation. Enslaved man has multiplied his strength and needs recourse to yours to break his chains. Become free, he has become unjust to his companion. Oh, women, women! Women, when will you cease to be blind? What are the advantages that you have received from the revolution? A scorn more marked, a disdain more overt? During the centuries of corruption you only reigned over the weakness of men. Your empire is destroyed; what is left to you then? The conviction of the injustices of man? The reclamation of your patrimony, founded on the wise decrees of nature; why should you fear such a beautiful enterprise? . . . Are you concerned that our French legislators, correctors of that morality, long attached to political practices no longer in fashion, will only repeat: women, what is it that is common between you and us? Everything, you respond. . . . courageously apply the force of reason to their vain pretensions of superiority; unite under the banner of philosophy; deploy all the energy of your character, and you will soon see these haughty men, not servile adorers crawling at your feet, but proud to share with you the treasures of the Supreme Being. Whatever barriers oppose you, it is within your power to free yourselves; you have only to want to.

1.2 *A Vindication of the Rights of Woman*, **Mary Wollstonecraft**

3rd ed. (London: J. Johnson, 1796), iii–xvi, 1–10.

To M. Talleyrand-Périgord . . .

Contending for the rights of women, my main argument is built on this simple principle, that if she be not prepared by education to become the companion of man, she will stop the progress of knowledge, for truth must be common to all, or it will be inefficacious with respect to its influence on general practice. And how can woman be expected to co-operate, unless she know why she ought to be virtuous? Unless freedom strengthen her reason till she comprehend her duty, and see in what manner it is connected with her real good? If children are to be educated to understand the true principle of patriotism, their mother must be a patriot; and the love of mankind, from which an orderly train of virtues spring, can only be produced by considering the moral and civil interest of mankind; but the education and situation of woman, at present, shuts her out from such investigations. . . .

Consider, . . . whether, when men contend for their freedom, and to be allowed to judge for themselves, respecting their own happiness, it be not inconsistent and unjust to subjugate women, even though you firmly believe that you are acting in the manner best calculated to promote their happiness? Who made man the exclusive judge, if woman partake with him the gift of reason?

In this style, argue tyrants of every denomination from the weak king to the weak father of a family; they are all eager to crush reason; . . . Do you not act a similar part, when you FORCE all women, by denying them civil and political rights, to remain immured in their families groping in the dark? . . . the more understanding women acquire, the more they will be attached to their duty, comprehending it, for unless they comprehend it, unless their morals be fixed on the same immutable principles as those of man, no authority can make them discharge it in a virtuous manner. They may be convenient slaves, but slavery will have its constant effect, degrading the master and the abject dependent. . . .

Besides, whilst they are only made to acquire personal accomplishments, men will seek for pleasure in variety, and faithless husbands will make faithless wives; . . . now that more equitable laws are forming your citizens, marriage may become more sacred; . . .

The father of a family will not then weaken his constitution and debase his sentiments, by visiting the harlot, nor forget, in obeying the call of appetite, the purpose for which it was implanted; and the mother will not neglect her children to practise the arts of coquetry, when sense and modesty secure her the friendship of her husband.

But, till men become attentive to the duty of a father, it is vain to expect women to spend that time in their nursery which they, 'wise in their generation,' choose to spend at their glass; for this exertion of cunning is only an instinct of nature to enable them to obtain indirectly a little of that power of which they are unjustly denied a share; for, if women are not permitted to enjoy legitimate rights, they will render both men and themselves vicious, to obtain illicit privileges. . . .

INTRODUCTION . . .

I have sighed when obliged to confess, that either nature has made a great difference between man and man, or that the civilization, which has hitherto taken place in the world, has been very partial. . . . The conduct and manners of women, in fact, evidently prove, that their minds are not in a healthy state; for, like the flowers that are planted in too rich a soil, strength and usefulness are sacrificed to beauty; and the flaunting leaves, after having pleased a fastidious eye, fade, disregarded on the stalk, long before the season when they ought to have arrived at maturity. One cause of this barren blooming I attribute to a false system of education, gathered from the books written on this subject by men, who, considering females rather as women than human creatures, have been more anxious to make them alluring mistresses than rational wives; and the understanding of the sex has been so bubbled by this specious homage, that the civilized women of the present century, with a few exceptions, are only anxious to inspire love, when they ought to cherish a nobler ambition, and by their abilities and virtues exact respect. . . .

In the government of the physical world, it is observable that the female, in general, is inferior to the male. The male pursues, the female yields – this is the law of nature; and it does not appear to be suspended or abrogated in favour of woman. This physical superiority cannot be denied – and it is a noble prerogative! But not content with this natural pre-eminence, men endeavour to sink us still lower, merely to render us alluring objects for a moment; and women, intoxicated by the adoration which men, under the influence of their senses, pay them, do not seek to obtain a durable interest in their hearts, or to become the friends of the fellow creatures who find amusement in their society. . . .

My own sex, I hope, will excuse me, if I treat them like rational creatures, instead of flattering their FASCINATING graces, and viewing them as if they were in a state of perpetual childhood, unable to stand alone. I earnestly wish to point out in what true dignity and human happiness consists – I wish to persuade women to endeavour to acquire strength, both of mind and body, and to convince them, that the soft phrases, susceptibility of heart, delicacy of sentiment, and refinement of taste, are almost synonymous with epithets of weakness, and that those beings who are only the objects of pity and that kind of love, which has been termed its sister, will soon become objects of contempt. . . .

I wish to show that elegance is inferior to virtue, that the first object of laudable ambition is to obtain a character as a human being, regardless of the distinction of sex; and that secondary views should be brought to this simple touchstone. . . .

The education of women has, of late, been more attended to than formerly; yet they are still reckoned a frivolous sex, . . . It is acknowledged that they spend many of the first years of their lives in acquiring a smattering of accomplishments: meanwhile, strength of body and mind are sacrificed to libertine notions of beauty, to the desire of establishing themselves, the only way women can rise in the world – by marriage. And this desire making mere animals of them, when they marry, they act as such children may be expected to act . . . Surely these weak beings are only fit for the seraglio! Can they govern a family, or take care of the poor babes whom they bring into the world?

1   Intimate worlds

Self, sex and family

On woman

Many writers took on the task of defining woman during the Enlightenment, but in many respects Jean Jacques Rousseau had one of the deepest impacts. His views on the role of woman, while deeply misogynistic, also captured much of the Enlightenment validation of motherhood and reflected newer ideas on children and their upbringing. The extract on *Sophie* captures these two threads. Catherine Macaulay was only one of many who responded, in her *Letters on Education*, as did Mary Wollstonecraft, in *A Vindication of the Rights of Woman* (1.2) and Charlotte Nordenflycht (1.57).

1.3 Sophie, or Woman

J. J. Rousseau, Émile, ou de L'education (La Haye: Jean Néaulme, 1762), V, 1–29.

But for her sex, a woman is a man; she has the same organs, the same needs, the same faculties. The machine is the same in its construction; its parts, its working, and its appearance are similar. Regard it as you will the difference is only in degree.

Yet where sex is concerned man and woman are unlike; each is the complement of the other; . . . In the union of the sexes each alike contributes to the common end, but in different ways. . . . The man should be strong and active; the woman should be weak and passive; the one must have both the power and the will; it is enough that the other should offer little resistance.

When this principle is admitted, it follows that woman is specially made for man's delight. If man in his turn ought to be pleasing in her eyes, the necessity is less urgent, his virtue is in his strength, he pleases because he is strong. I grant you this is not the law of love, but it is the law of nature, which is older than love itself.

If woman is made to please and to be in subjection to man, she ought to make herself pleasing in his eyes and not provoke him to anger; her strength is in her charms, by their means she should compel him to discover and use his strength. . . .

The Most High has deigned to do honour to mankind; he has endowed man with boundless passions, together with a law to guide them, so that man may be alike free and self-controlled; though swayed by these passions man is endowed with reason by which to control them. Woman is also endowed with boundless passions; God has given her modesty to restrain them. . . .

The consequences of sex are wholly unlike for man and woman. The male is only a male now and again, the female is always a female, or at least all her youth; everything reminds her of her sex; the performance of her functions requires a special constitution. She needs care during pregnancy and freedom from work when her child is born; she must have a quiet, easy life while she nurses her children; their education calls for patience and gentleness, for a zeal and love which nothing can dismay; she forms a bond between father and child, she alone can win the father's love for his children and convince him that they are indeed his own. What loving care is required to preserve a united family! And there should be no question of virtue in all this, it must be a labour of love, without which the human race would be doomed to extinction.

The mutual duties of the two sexes are not, and cannot be, equally binding on both. Women do wrong to complain of the inequality of man-made laws; this inequality is not of man's making, or at any rate it is not the result of mere prejudice, but of reason. She to whom nature has entrusted the care of the children must hold herself responsible for them to their father. No doubt every breach of faith is wrong, and every faithless husband, who robs his wife of the sole reward of the stern duties of her sex, is cruel and unjust; but the faithless wife is worse; she destroys the family and breaks the bonds of nature; when she gives her husband children who are not his own, she is false both to him and them, her crime is not infidelity but treason. . . . a thief who is robbing his own children of their inheritance. . . .

Thus it is not enough that a wife should be faithful; her husband, along with his friends and neighbours, must believe in her fidelity; she must be modest, devoted, retiring; she should have the witness not only of a good conscience, but of a good reputation. In a word, if a father must love his children, he must be able to respect their mother. For these reasons it is not enough that the woman should be chaste, she must preserve her reputation and her good name. . . .

When once it is proved that men and women are and ought to be unlike in constitution and in temperament, it follows that their education must be different. Nature teaches us that they should work together, but that each has its own share of the work; the end is the same, but the means are different, as are also the feelings which direct them. . . . women are always exclaiming that we educate them for nothing but vanity and coquetry, that we keep them amused with trifles that we may be their masters; we are responsible, so they say, for the faults we attribute to them. How silly! What have men to do with the education of girls? What is there to hinder their mothers educating them as they please? . . . Who is it that compels a girl to waste her time on foolish trifles? Are they forced, against their will, to spend half their time over their toilet, following the example set them by you? Who prevents you teaching them, or having them taught, whatever seems good in your eyes? Is it our fault that we are charmed by their beauty and delighted by their airs and graces? . . .

To cultivate the masculine virtues in women and to neglect their own is evidently to do them an injury. . . . If you are a sensible mother you will take my advice. Do not try to make your daughter a good man in defiance of nature. Make her a good woman, and be sure it will be better both for her and us.

Does this mean that she must be brought up in ignorance and kept to housework only? Is she to be man's handmaid or his help-meet? . . . No, indeed, that is not the teaching of nature. . . . On the contrary, nature means them to think, to will, to love, to cultivate their minds as well as their persons; she puts these weapons in their hands to make up for their lack of strength and to enable them to direct the strength of men. They should learn many things, but only such things as are suitable.

1.4 Catherine Macaulay responds

Letters on Education (London: C. Dilly, 1790), 218–22.

Among the most strenuous asserters of a sexual difference in character, Rousseau is the most conspicuous, both on account of that warmth of sentiment which distinguishes all his writings, and the eloquence of his compositions: but never did enthusiasm and the love of paradox, those enemies to philosophical disquisition, appear in more strong opposition to plain sense than in Rousseau's definition of this difference. He sets out with a supposition, that Nature intended the subjection of the one sex to the other; that consequently there must be an inferiority of intellect in the subjected party; but as man is a very imperfect being and apt to play the capricious tyrant, Nature, to bring things nearer to an equality, bestowed on the woman such attractive graces, and such an insinuating address, as to turn the balance on the other scale. Thus Nature, in a giddy mood recedes from her purposes, and subjects prerogative to an influence which must produce confusion and disorder in the system of human affairs. Rousseau saw this objection; and in order to obviate it, he has made up a moral person of the union of the two sexes, which, for contradiction and absurdity, outdoes every metaphysical riddle that was ever formed in the schools. In short, it is not reason, it is not wit; it is pride and sensuality that speak in Rousseau, and, in this instance, has lowered the man of genius to the licentious peasant. . . .

The situation and education of women is precisely that which must necessarily tend to corrupt and debilitate both the powers of mind and body. From a false notion of beauty and delicacy, their system of nerves is depraved before they come out of the nursery; and this kind of depravity has more influence over the mind, and consequently over morals, than commonly apprehended. But it would be well if such causes only acted towards the debasement of the sex; their moral education is, if possible, more absurd than their physical. The principles and nature of virtue, which is never properly explained to boys, is kept quite a mystery to girls. They are told, indeed, that they must abstain from those vices which are contrary to their personal happiness, or they will be regarded as criminals both by God and man; but all the higher parts of rectitude; everything that ennobles our being, and that renders us both innoxious and useful, is either not taught, or taught in such a manner as to leave no proper impression on the mind. This is so obvious a truth . . .

But the most difficult part of female education is to give girls such an idea of chastity, as shall arm their reason and their sentiments on the side of useful virtue. For I believe there are more women of understanding led into acts of imprudence by the ignorance, the prejudices, and the false craft of those by whom they are educated, than from any other cause founded either in nature or in chance. . . . with an unfortunate bias on her mind, she will fall a victim to the first plausible being who has formed a design on her person. . . . as I intend to breed my pupils up to act a rational part in the world, and not to fill up a niche in the seraglio of a sultan, I shall certainly give them leave to use their reason in all matters which concern their duty and happiness, and shall spare no pains in the cultivation of this only sure guide to virtue. . . . I shall intimate, that the great difference now beheld in the external consequences which follow the deviations from chastity in the two sexes, did in all probability arise from women having been considered as the mere property of the men; and, on this account had no right to dispose of their own persons: that policy adopted this difference, when the plea of property had been given up; and it was still preserved in society from the unruly licentiousness of the men, . . . I shall observe, that this state of things renders the situation of females, in their individual capacity very precarious; for the strength which Nature has given to the passion of love, in order to serve her purposes, has made it the most ungovernable propensity of any which attends us. The snares, therefore, that are continually laid for women, by persons who run no risk in compassing their seduction, exposes them to continual danger. . . That, for these reasons, coquetry in women is as dangerous as it is dishonourable. . . . if women had as much regard for the virtue of chastity as in some cases they pretend to have, a reformation would long since have taken place in the world; but whilst they continue to cherish immodesty in the men, their bitter persecution of their own sex will not save them from the imputation of those . . . severe satirists on the sex.

Educating girls

Girls' education was at the centre of debates about women's place in society, as well as about education for the middle and labouring classes. The school rules below are typical of community and private efforts to provide education for girls of these classes. Great Yeldham School in Essex was established to teach deserving poor girls basic education and the habits and skills of industrious work. Local people, like patrons Mr and Mrs Way, established a variety of schools, not all of which taught only 'charity' children. Copenhagen Daughters' School was typical of many endowed and private day schools where curricula varied little, with an emphasis on reading, perhaps writing and arithmetic, and the ubiquitous needlework. Note the emphasis on cleanliness and good behaviour captured in both sets of rules.

Numerous women had an imperative to learn, but struggled to gain access to materials, learning and support. This was a recurring theme well into the twentieth century. Some gained a practical or academic education at home, like Charlotte Dorothea Biehl. Fathers often acted as mentors to girls wanting more than a basic education, but just as often they constrained them. Biehl became one of the first female Danish writers, producing moralising stories, plays and her autobiography, from which this extract comes.

1.5 Industry School

Great Yeldham, Girls' Industry School Minute Book, 1789–1798, D/P 275/28/2, Essex Record Office.

All Girls may be admitted into this School, who are past eleven Years old, and have been admitted into the Sunday-School, and shall be recommended by the Trustees of that School.

The Scholars are to be at the School every Day, (except Sunday, Christmas Day, and Good-Friday,) at nine o'Clock, with clean Faces and Hands, and Hair combed. They are there to sew and to knit; and every Day the Mistress is to hear each Scholar read in the NEW TESTAMENT, in SELLON'S ABRIDGEMENT, or TRIMMER'S SERVANTS' FRIEND. They are to continue at School 'till Two o'Clock.

Every Saturday the Scholars are to say the Church Catechism to the Mistress, the last Thing before they go from School.

Every Sunday the Scholars are expected to attend Divine Service at Great Yeldham Church ONCE, and twice when their Parents can spare them. The same on Christmas-Day and Good-Friday.

Every Monday the Scholars are to say to the Mistress the Collect of the Day before, the last Thing before they go from School.

No Scholar is to stay away from School, without letting the Mistress know the Reason before-hand, in order that Mr. or Mrs. WAY may be told thereof.

Any Scholar staying away from School to go Hop-picking, will be turned out of the School.

No Gown or other Cloaths lent by Mr. or Mrs. WAY to any Scholar, is to be worn any where but in the School, except by particular Leave . . . and if any Scholar be discharged or taken away from the School before the End of four Years, such Gown or other Cloaths are to be returned . . .; but those Scholars who continue four Years, are to have for their own, the Cloaths which may have been so lent them.

The Scholars are allowed to bring any Work of their own to the School, provided it be clean, and they shall have Needles and Thread given them to use upon such Work; but no Work, when once brought into the School, can be taken out again before it be quite finished in the Manner directed by Mr. or Mrs. WAY.

If any Work be done in a slight or improper Manner by any Scholar, the Mistress is particularly ordered to make such Scholar pick it out, and do it all over again.

Every Scholar may be continued in the Industry School four Years, if deserving thereof. Each of them will be required during the last three Years to take in Turn of six Weeks at a Time to clean the Mistress's House and the School-Room, to dress the Mistress's Victuals, and to do all other Household Work for her throughout the Day, (Sundays excepted) and the Mistress will find such Scholar in Victuals and Drink during the six Weeks she is so employed. . . .

When two or more Scholars belong to one Family, they will be allowed to attend School by daily turns; but when either of them is upon the House-work, she must attend every Day as usual.

Each Scholar will be allowed to stay from School one Day in each Week, to help wash for her Parents home, except the Girl who shall be upon the House-work.

Six weeks Holidays are allowed during Harvest, Gleaning, and Hop-picking.

1.6 Bourgeois girls' school

Skole-Reglement før Lærlingerne i Døttre-Skolen, Døttre-Skolens Board, 1 November 1791, Copenhagen City Archives, Arkivserie ID=17144.

1   On their way to and from school they ought not to dawdle or engage in any sort of immodesty; they should be in school just before the hour of 9 in the morning and 3 in the afternoon.
2   Their clothing ought to be clean and in order; their hair ought to be neat and combed, their face and hands washed.
3   In each class they are to sit in their assigned places, be attentive and proper; never except . . . with the headmistress's permission, leave the room or go to other classrooms, and not to occupy themselves with things which can hinder their own, not to mention their classmates' attention, nor waste time with gossip.
4   They need to provide themselves with books, writing materials, drawing materials and what is used in their needlework classes, keep them in good order and when they do not need them any more, put them back in their proper place.
5   During teaching, they are not to cluster around the teacher, nor to talk with her, and not ask questions which distract others' attention, break the flow of teaching and waste precious time.

6 When teachers ask questions, they are not to answer in place of others, but quietly wait their turn.

7 When a teacher corrects them, they are not to allow the slightest opposition nor defiance, nor to involve themselves in the matters of others, and certainly not to let the student who has been corrected hear the slightest teasing or criticism.

8 Students should be kind to one another, but not be too intimate.

9 When teachers write in the gradebook, students are not to hang over them and try to coax a sign of approval and not to complain about grades others receive.

10 When a child cannot come to school due to sickness or other cause, her parents or guardian should inform the headmistress in writing, or by a reliable person in order to prevent inaccurate accounts.

11 Should a child contract a contagious disease, she ought not to be sent to school . . . she will immediately be sent home and will not be allowed to return until she is completely cured.

12 It is the particular job of the two female teachers to ensure that the above rules are completely carried out by the students, without the slightest exception, and that any negligence shall be noted in the gradebook.

1.7 Home education

Charlotte Biehl, *Mit Ubetydelige Levnets Løb*, 1787 (Copenhagen: Museum Tusculanum, 1986), 65–70, 72.

[Soon] I could read until my immense reading pleasure remarked itself, I even turned to reading Scripture before I could write a letter, to reading every filthy sheet I found.

My Grandfather who called it an innocent predisposition supported me wholeheartedly, and in the years he was alive he gave me a great number of Danish and German animated books, Holberg's comedies, and the History of Denmark. . . . I took my doll Toey, who had been killed more than several times . . . and threw it into a corner in the loft, put my Books in the cupboard and put the key in my pocket. Every time my grandfather gave me a book he had to listen to my detailed descriptions of its contents and I asked him about the things I did not understand as he was privy to my most private thoughts. The Greek and the Latin in Holberg's writings he also had to explain to me, . . .

'What good could it do to you', he said, 'You do not wear trousers and so cannot become a professor.'

'Yes, but it is so very disagreeable not to understand a book fully and so you must let me learn in the summer.'

'I have promised you to teach you to play your aunt's piano and to write, how much more do you want to learn little girl?'

'Everything', I answered and crawled up onto his lap and put my arms around his neck. 'I shall be so hard-working that you will care for me even more, for if you do not teach me, your girl will not learn anything.'

'Here you have my promise, he said, as long as God lets me live I will teach you everything you desire to learn.' Who was now happier than I know. . . .

I chatter far too long about my childhood years, but please excuse and forgive me, as this was the only time of my life which I recall with pleasure. The rest filled me with bitterness. . . .

My grandfather had hardly been dead two months before my father made it the worst sin for me to read, and assured me that if he found me with a book in my hands he would whip me. . . . My mother asked him what reasons he had against me reading once my day's work was completed? But he answered that it was enough reason that he did not wish it. Had he sentenced me to live on bread and water, it would have been less painful to me, in fact I would rather do without food than my books.

Transitions

Marriage was the goal of most women, and the period between childhood and adulthood was a fraught time for many young women – and their parents. To wish to be courted, to hope for a proposal were never far from most girls' thoughts. In the first extract a Scottish father writes to his daughter about a proposal, and takes the opportunity to share some advice with her. Clearly he values her judgement and his advice is full of common sense, even if he dwells on her responsibilities and not on those of her future husband. Writing from Ireland, the Countess of Portarlington scarcely disguises her glee that one of her impecunious daughters has received a proposal. The letter is replete with surprise, pleasure and, indeed, concern about her remaining girls. Henriette Herz has given us a detailed and revealing portrait of her non-existent courtship, betrothal and wedding. As a fifteen-year-old Jewish girl, we see her romantic ideas about engagement and marriage, but also her anxiety and fear. Marcus Herz was older than she, but promised her a happy marriage, which it was. She also went on to host one of the most successful intellectual salons in Berlin. 'Domestic occurrences' presents a glimpse into the darker side of adolescence for women. A labouring girl was accosted by a man of some 'quality' and, given the difference in standing and power, things could well have turned out differently. That the newspaper described the story with some hilarity obscures the real danger that such an encounter represented.

1.8 A father's advice

Robertson of Strowan to his daughter Margaret, 23 May 1755, National Archives of Scotland, GD155/851.

My dear Meggy, as you are now past the tender and thoughtless age wherein children are and must be used, with authority and constraint, but of experience sufficient to direct your conduct thro' the perplexities of a turbulent and vicious world allow me to give you some general hints that may be of use to you in the future course of your life. . . . tho' perhaps you cannot as yet conceive how tenderly I have loved you ever since you came into the world, and how anxiously I have study'd to promote your happiness. You know very well and perhaps sometimes grudged my severity to your little faults but on time you will look upon this as the greatest demonstration of my affection. . . .

You are desired in marriage by a gentleman who knows you have no fortune, what do you think are his motives for making this proposal, or of his parents agreeing to it . . . it is probable indeed he see something agreeable in your person, but that is not the main point. It is this, he himself has been brought up in the path of honour & virtue, in which he resolves to persist. He has a favourable opinion of your temper & education & as the greatest friendship proceeds from a resemblance of manners, he expects to find in you an agreeable companion for life – I hope he will not be disappointed nor have I the least cause to suspect it. You have often heard what was right, you have had your mothers example before you, & I thank God you have a moderate share of commonsense, & I may be allowed to tell you for once, that you advance in discretion as in years; but alas those years are so few & your experience so little, that I am afraid I shall be forced to give you another half sheet of such thoughts and directions as I think may be of use to you,

. . . promote the happiness of everyone we are concerned in. . . . preserve your mind in a calm, chearful & benevolent disposition, this is the proper soil for all virtues, both social & divine; whereas the mind that is soured ruffled or exasperated at every cross accident, disappointment or contradiction is like a troubled sea that threws up dirt & mud, uneasy & unhappy in itself, vexing and troublesom to everyone about it; . . .

In all your conversation with mr — let your countenance & tone of voice, as well as your words express your affection & regard, & if you happen at any time to differ from his opinion in small matters, propose your sentiments mildly by way of getting information, & not by downright contradiction & in general avoid disputes with every one. . .

Let Mr — be your principal confident, if there is anything vexes or disturbs you, for which you imagine there is any remedy, communicate it to him; let him never [hear] it at second-hand. & if anyone propose to tell you a secreat with a caution that you are not to communicate it to Mr — you may answer with a smile, that you can keep nothing from Mr — & so you'll be free of many impertinent tattles, . . . – tho' to be sure you'll hear many things not withy repeating to him or any one else, on the other hand if mr — intrusts you with a secret, let neither father or mother, brother or sister every hear of it. In short as man & wife are said in scripture to be one flesh so ought they to be one soul; no separate views or separate interests in prosperity or adversity in sickness or in health.

. . . love of neatness and order is not to be laid aside when you are married, on the contrary you must double it, . . . the husband is always the person most offended.

Grave and serious countenance be confined to your closet & retirement . . . chearfulness is absolutely necessary in youth, decent & engaging in advanced years & charming in old age . . . it is not necessary to be always talking. . .

tho you are about to leave my family, you are ever to have the same place in my affection – my daughter & mr —'s wife claims a double regard. I pray God you may be a comfort to him, & the instrument of happiness to his family . . . your most affectionate father

1.9 A daughter's proposal

Alice Georgina Clark, ed., *Gleanings from an Old Portfolio*, Vol. 3 (Edinburgh: Private, 1898), 68–70.

Lady Caroline Dawson, Countess of Portarlington to Lady Louisa Stuart
Cheltenham, 28th November 1800

You will be surprised when I tell you I do not know how long Caroline may keep the name of Dawson, as she has had a very agreeable proposal which she is inclined to accept. It is now time to tell you his name is Parnell, Sir John's eldest son, and if I were sure he would like her and make her a good husband, it is the match of all others I would have wished, as I have known him from a child, have a great regard for all his family and connections . . .

He is remarkably handsome, very sensible and well-informed, and of a very active mind; he was at Abbeyleix when we were there . . . He did not seem to observe my girls and has always been more reserved to them than was natural, considering they used to play together as children. We thought all the admiration he had met with in Dublin had made him conceited and that he was too fine to take notice of my shy, timid girls. . . . He says he has but a very small income independent of his father, but you know I cannot expect any great things for my daughters, who have so little to bring to a family. I can't tell you how happy this event would make me if I could think he had taken a fancy to her. . . . Poor Caroline does not know what to think of it, she is so surprised, and indeed so are we all, for they have never been asked to think of *husbands*. Louisa and Harriet are as much children in their way as they were five years ago, and poor Car was only in the world for the small space of two months . . . and she, not being forward or used to the ways of *town misses*, made very few acquaintances. If I dispose of her I believe I shall be tempted to bring out Harriet and Louisa together, as Harriet is more grown up in her person than Louisa, but she is very awkward, and it may take that off. The Duchess of Gordon admired Louisa, but I think Harriet will be thought the best-looking. Caroline is certainly the least, so therefore it shows it is mere luck and not beauty that attracts husbands! I think I shall be very vain of my son-in-law if Henry Parnell becomes so, and I shall long to introduce him to you.

Adieu, my dear sister. My mind is so occupied with this unexpected event I can think of nothing else.

1.10 Betrothal and wedding

Henriette Herz, *Ihr Leben und ihre Erinnerungen*, ed. J. Fürst (Berlin, 1850), 21–26.

[1779] And who is the man who has been assigned to me – I asked hastily. – You told me Marcus Herz, a respected doctor. I had seen him sometimes with my father, but he was more observant than communicative with me, and also at his window, because he lived near us, . . . I only remember that I had a childish joy to become a bride, whether precisely this man's bride, I know nothing. I vividly pictured myself as I walked out led by a groom, how I would get nicer clothes, and above all, when I was married, a hairdresser. . . . I calculated the way ahead and the likelihood of an increase in my pocket money, which amounted to only two pennies a month now. What more could I ask? –

I waited impatiently for the day of the engagement, which the aunt had betrayed to me in confidence. She had also told me that my father would ask if I was satisfied with his choice, which flattered me very much. – The longed-for day arrived. The morning passed, and the forenoon, I was not told, I was not asked anything. We sat down to dinner, dish after dish was set before us, still no word. At last my father finally said, 'My child, who would you rather marry a doctor or a rabbi?' My heart beat powerfully. I replied that I was satisfied with what he would decide for me. But soon I reflected that my good father, moreover, was a doctor himself, and certainly would come to see him, and added: 'I would certainly prefer a doctor.'

. . . after lunch, I opened up to my mother that I would be engaged in the evening to Doctor Marcus Herz, . . . She then gave me a long speech, which struck me at the moment as very inopportune and very boring, but I still listened from filial piety, and not without benefit for me because it contained some good teaching, which I remembered later, and certainly stood me in good stead. . . . and at last she recommended to me her marriage as a model for mine. And in fact, there never was a happier one.

In the evening the company assembled in my parents' rooms. I was alone in another. According to the former, and perhaps still, custom of the Jews, the bride only came into the circle of family and guests after the marriage contract had been drawn up by the notary, and they had been asked in advance for their indisputable consent. Uneasily, in anxious expectation I sat in my finery. I was burning with anxiety. I could not help have a premonition of the fatal step. . . . I jumped from my seat, and walked up and down. I came over in front of the mirror, and for the first time I appeared more than pretty to me. The redness of the cheeks gave my dark eyes an even higher gloss, the little mouth was more graceful than usual and the apple-green and white striped silk dress and black feather hat, were excellent on me! – Many years have passed me by, but the youthful, animated face, that moment, the whole form, are as vivid to me that I could paint it.

At last the door opened, and the notary, followed by two witnesses, entered. I tried to hold still, I wanted to appear calm, but I do not think I succeeded. For I know that asked about my consent, my yes! I could only stammer. Soon after, my groom kissed my hand and led me to the company. I knew little more of him than that he was a physician and scholar. That he had little of any lover in my novels, I could see. He was fifteen years older than me, small and ugly, . . . But I pushed everything to the back that could be disturbing to me, because I saw my parents so very bright, so very happy, still loving each other, as usual. . . .

My fiancé, so much older than me, and a general practitioner, a German scholar and a scientific writer, even older than his years, treated me as a child, and what annoyed me most, speaking of me, he called me: the child. However, I was still, but since I was a bride I did not want to hear it, and least from my fiancé. When walking with him, we did not have much to talk about, although I was often in his company. At that time he came to us almost every evening to play cards . . . I had no map, but knew I had to sit next to him. . . . and I was bored to death. –

At last the wedding day. – Many, many years have passed since then, and yet I still recall almost every moment of the morning of that day. – After a restless night I awoke with a feeling of infinite sadness. The thought of my family, especially leaving my father tore me. . . . At some other time I would be pleased at the beautiful, rose-studded gown of white satin, which was soon brought to me as my wedding dress! I looked at it indifferently, let me get dressed mechanically and consecrate it with my flowing tears. The bridegroom came, the guests assembled, my mind was just on my family. Soon as the time drew near for the ceremony, I had to try to speak once more to my father. I succeeded. My love found at that moment no other expression than in the pleading, accompanied by hot tears. . . . [He] hugged me, crying, and beckoned me to go, saying in a choking voice: 'Child, break not my heart' – I'll hear those words until my last breath! – God has answered his blessing. I went to meet a rich, yes, a beautiful life. –

It was the first December of the year 1779. In the courtyard, on which stood the canopy under which I was married according to Jewish custom, there was a lot of snow. . . . I was again put on display for the first time to my pain. Everything was winter.

The next morning the fifteen-year-old newlywed sat alone in her room. I had not yet seen anyone as a married woman. A thousand conflicting emotions flooded me. How gladly I would have had words, as far as I could, with my loved ones in my father's home! I also thought they certainly thought of me! . . . Finally, I hear footsteps, coming from the staircase. They are men's footsteps. Certainly my father! – The door opens. – As a long-cherished wish is granted at the wrong time. It is the hairdresser.

Women going it alone

Many women did not marry, up to 25 per cent in some regions. Their motivations varied widely, and certainly some may not have had the chance. Others, however, saw singleness as a conscious decision. These women made

DOMESTIC OCCURRENCES.
A B E R D E E N.

YESTERDAY the Revd. Mr. Occum, the Indian Mi·nifter, preached in this Place to a verv crowded Audience.

2. The Article in our laft Domeftick Occurrences, concerning the Baptifm of the Earl of Errol's Son, was premature; the Ceremony having been delayed for fome time.

3. The following adventure happened in this county fome time ago: A young gentleman riding into town, accofted a girl who was leading a cow on the road, and would fain have perfuaded her to retire with him behind the dyke.——He difmounted accordingly, and leaving his horfe upon the road, took her in his arms. The lafs, who was more tenacious of her virtue than he expected, gave him fo fmart a reception, that after throwing him on the ground, fhe adminiftered the ordinary fchool-difcipline with a very heavy hand. At length, on the apperance of fome perfons on the road, he was fuffered to go: which he did with fo much precipitation, that he forgot to take his hat and whip: and to avoid being feen, took a round about road, fo as to make it dark before his arrival in town. The heroine picked up and carried home with her the trophies, which have never yet been called for.

4. Some time ago, a young man in this place undertook, for a wager, to lift a boll of malt, which was to be laid upon him, he lying on the ground. He gained his wager, but at the expence of his life; for he was directly feized with a fpitting of blood, which carried him off in a few days.

5. Infirmary Collections· Aberdour, 2l. Crimond, 1 l. 15 s. 8d. three farthings; Bourtie, 1 l. 5 s. Daviot, 5 l. all for 1767. A donation from a gentleman in Aberdeen, 5 l.

Arrived, The Three Brothers, Gibbons; the Speedwell, Bomftade; the Duke of Gordon, Wood; the Mermaid, Craik; the Ally, Thomfon; all from London; the Three Brothers, Simfon, from Sunderland; the Charles, Gibbons, from Campvere.

Sailed, The James, Morrifon, for London.

Figure 1.1 The risks of the road, *Aberdeen Journal*, 29 June 1767

a decision not to marry. Charlotte Biehl rejected her first proposal because she did not feel her suitor had spent sufficient time getting to know her. She later forswore marrying altogether. Her account illustrates the thinking of women who ultimately decided to marry only for love. The *Gentleman's Magazine* also suggests the innkeepers from Poplar, London took on a same sex–partnership for similar reasons, but their motives are not clear, and may hide deeper reasons to deliberately choose to live together.

1.11 Choosing singleness

Charlotte Biehl, *Mit Ubetydelige Levenets*, 73, 75, 76**.**

A man of thirty something years, more beautiful than hideous, with a fairly good fortune, in an esteemed position, and known by all as a worthy and competent government official did by coincidence see me in my elaborate negligee a few days after my fifteenth birthday. This image made a remarkable impression on him. . . . [His attentions] would have flattered any young woman's vanity whose thinking ability was more fleeting than mine, and that mine was less so, was more due to my circumstances than any hard work on my behalf. I had never socialised with anyone but those who were much older than myself, my parents were often the youngest after myself in all the parties we attended. This had dampened the flighty and inconsiderate tendencies of my age in me, made me ponder over things and not set my eyes upon the shining façade or to be fooled by the wrapping. . . .

   This understanding combined with numerous examples I had read about resulted in me considering marriage from a very serious point of view and the woman's responsibilities to be very important, and since my mind could not think this at all pleasant without a large measure of devoted love, I concluded that it was most necessary that the wife must love her husband dearly for them to be happy. . . . I knew how perishable beauty is and so did not desire to be loved for the sake of it, and as the exterior alone had imprisoned my suitor and he had not taken time to get to know my tendencies and way of thinking before expressing his intentions, I did not value his love.

1.12 Innkeepers

'Historical Chronicle, 1766, Tuesday 10 July', *The Gentleman's Magazine*, XXXVI, 339.

A discovery of a very extraordinary nature was made at Poplar, where two women had lived together for six and thirty years, as man and wife, and kept a public house, without ever being suspected; but the wife happening to fall sick and die, a few days before she expired, revealed the secret to her relations, made her will, and left legacies to the amount of half what she thought they were worth. . . . the pretended husband, . . . at first endeavoured to support her assumed character, but being closely pressed, she at length owned the fact, accommodated all matters amicably, put off the male and put on the female character, in which she appeared to be a sensible, well-bred woman, although in her male character, she had always affected the plain plodding ale-housekeeper. . . . Both had been crossed in love when young, and had chosen this method to avoid farther importunities.

Marriage law

Codification of law was an important Enlightenment agenda, a process begun in the late seventeenth century. Through regulation of betrothal and marriage, the state shaped gender and confirmed or established the outline of sexual relations. The tone of the Danish Law of Christian V shows a sense of marital equality, operating to keep people together, while protecting individuals against specific injustices. The same tone can be found in the later Prussian Code; however, it also echoes the view that women left their parental homes for marital homes and by doing so granted rights over their persons and bodies to husbands. The most explicit view of women subsumed in marriage is Blackstone's famous comment that 'the husband and wife are one person in law'. While the French Code Civile clearly retained the husband's overlordship in marriage and home, there are signs of flexibility in female legal identity that are not apparent in English law. The Code Civile applied to more areas of Europe than did the others, as a result of Napoleonic conquests, while the Danish and Prussian codes suggest the impact of Protestantism that accepted a woman's individual right of responsibility to God.

1.13 Danish law

Kong Christian den Femtis Danske Lov, 1683 (Copenhagen, 1856) III, Chapter XVI, 494–523.

On Marriage

Article 1

Whoever wants to take a wife, must ask for her from her parents or true guardian, though with her agreement and desire.

2

If she married without the consent of her legal guardian, then he may keep her goods, while she lives, if he wants.

3

Secret engagements shall not be honoured, if they occur without the consent of parents or legal guardians. However, if the parents or legal guardian have no legitimate or legal reason to forbid the marriage, then their prohibition or any obstacle they may make, will not hold.

4

If a guardian keeps a maiden unmarried, after her eighteenth year, for his own benefit, when she conveniently could have been married, then her other relations and friends must complain to the authorities, who shall see that justice is done.

5

Engagements entered into during a state of drunkenness, shall not be upheld, nor if they are entered into during the party's minority, which is under twenty for a man, and for a woman under sixteen years, nor shall they be upheld if one is not competent or rational. . . .

7

If a husband or a woman who live together as married agree to marry someone else as well as those who accept such an engagement, they shall go to public confession and be punished with the forfeiture of their property, if they have any, otherwise the man shall be sentenced to a long period in irons, the woman to the Workhouse.

8

If a husband sleeps with another woman while he is married, he may not marry that woman after his wife's death. Neither may a wife, who sleeps with another man, marry him after her husband's death. . . .

Reasons, why married people may separate:

1   Fornication. However, the person who is the complainant shall legally summon the defendant in court and convincingly prove it. It is not enough that the defendant admits to this, because it often happens that many lie so that one can be free of the other, . . . 3. If a Danish man's wife is raped, then she shall not, because of this rape, be separated from her husband, because the victim should not be punished, but rather the perpetrator. 4. If a man, after having found his wife fornicating, seeks her in bed, then he dismisses his charge against her, but if she does this a second time and he stays away from her, then he can accuse her and be divorced from her; and she may not remarry without the King's special permission, and that after three years' passage and she shall have careful witnesses that she has conducted herself honestly and in a Christian manner during that time, but she may not marry or remain in the same parish, county or city in which the innocent party lives. The same applies if a wife finds her husband fornicating. The innocent party is free immediately to remarry, once the divorce is finalised.

2   Desertion, when the one party without any convincing reason or permission from the other, leaves the second party and travels away . . .

3   Impotence, when one is incompetent for marriage, shall the person with this flaw wait three years and seek advice if it can be helped if they had this problem before the marriage, and if nothing helps, then there shall be a divorce. But if the problem comes after the wedding, then it shall be borne as any other circumstance which can befall married people.

1.14 Germanic law

The Frederician code: or, A body of law for the dominions of the King of Prussia (London: J. Richardson, 1761), I, 37–39

TITLE VIII
Of the rights of the husband with regard to his wife; and of those of the wife with regard to her husband, acceding from the family-state.

§1

AS the domestic society, or family, is formed by the union of the husband and wife, we are to begin with enumerating the advantages and rights which result from this union.

§2

The husband is by nature the head of his family. To be convinced of this, it is sufficient to consider, that the wife leaves her family to join herself to that of her husband; that she enters into his household, and into the habitation of which he is the master, and grants him rights over her body, with intention to have children by him to perpetuate the family.

§3

Hence it follows, judging by the sole light of reason, that the husband is master of his own household, and head of his family. And as the wife enters into it of her own accord, she is in some measure subject to his power; whence flow several rights and privileges, which belong to the husband with regard to his wife.

For,

1) The husband has the liberty of prescribing laws and rules in his household, which the wife is to observe.
2) If the wife be defective in her duty to her husband, and refuse to be subject, he is authorised to reduce her to her duty in a reasonable manner.
3) The wife is bound, according to her quality, to assist her husband, to take upon her the care of the household affairs, according to his condition.
4) The husband has the power over the wife's body, and she cannot refuse him the conjugal duty.
5) As the husband and wife have promised not to leave each other during their lives, but to share the good and evil which may happen to them; the wife cannot, under pretext, for example, that her husband has lost his reason, leave him, without obtaining permission so to do from the judge.
6) For the same reason, the wife is obliged to follow her husband, when he changes his habitation; unless, a) it has been stipulated by the contract of marriage, or otherwise . . . or, b) unless it were for a crime that the husband changed his habitation, as if he had been banished from his country.

§4

The wife likewise enjoys certain rights and privileges with respect to her husband. For,

1) As it is in quality of an assistant that the wife enters into the family with her husband, she ought to enjoy all the rights of the family. Thus she carries her husband's name and arms, she partakes his rank, she is under the same jurisdiction as he, &c. These advantages are continued to her even after her husband's death, as long as she remains a widow.

2) The husband is bound to defend his wife, as well before the judge as elsewhere; wherefore also he may appear in a judicature for her, without a letter of attorney, provided he give security, that she shall ratify what he does.

3) The wife hath the power of her husband's body, who cannot refuse to pay her the conjugal duty, when he is not prevented by sickness or other accidents.

4) By virtue of these engagements, the husband cannot, without committing adultery, have criminal correspondence with another woman.

5) Neither can he separate from his wife, without very important reasons.

6) The wife succeeds to an equal portion with her children in her husband's effects; unless by contract of marriage, or other settlements, the succession be otherwise regulated. . . .

7) The husband is obliged to maintain his wife according to his rank and condition, whether he took her without dowery [*sic*], or she lost her fortune after her marriage.

8) In these cases he is also obliged to bury her at his own charge.

1.15 Husband and wife

William Blackstone, *Commentaries on the Laws of England* (1765–1769), Edward Christian, ed., 4 vols (London: A. Strahan, 1809), I, 442–5.

By marriage, the husband and wife are one person in law: – that is, the very being or legal existence of the woman is suspended during the marriage, or at least is incorporated and consolidated into that of the husband: under whose wing, protection, and *cover*, she performs everything . . . in our law-french a *feme-covert* . . . or under the protection and influence of her husband, her *baron*, or lord; and her condition during her marriage is called her coverture. Upon this principle, of an union of person in husband and wife, depend almost all the legal rights, duties, and disabilities, that either of them acquire by the marriage. . . . For this reason, a man cannot grant anything to his wife, or enter into covenant with her, for the grant would be to suppose her separate existence; and to covenant with her, would be only to covenant with himself: and therefore it is also generally true, that all compacts made between husband and wife, when single, are voided by the intermarriage. A woman indeed may be attorney for her husband; for that implies no separation from, but is rather a representation of, her lord. And a husband may also bequeath anything to his wife by will; for that cannot take effect till the coverture is determined by his death. The husband is bound to provide his wife with necessaries by law, as much as himself; and if she contracts debts for them, he is obliged to pay them: but for anything besides necessaries, he is not chargeable. Also if a wife elopes, and lives with another man, the husband is not chargeable even for necessaries; . . . If the wife be indebted before marriage, the husband is bound afterwards to pay the debt; for he has adopted her and her circumstances together. If the wife be injured in her person or her property, she can bring no action for redress without her husband's concurrence, . . . neither can she be sued, without making the husband a defendant. . . .

THE husband also (by the old law) might give his wife moderate correction. For, as he is to answer for her misbehaviour, the law thought it reasonable to entrust him with this power of restraining her, by domestic chastisement, in the same moderation that a man is allowed to correct his apprentices or children; for whom the master or parent is also liable in some cases to answer. . . . But, with us, . . . this power of correction began to be doubted: and a wife may now have security of the peace against her husband; or, in return, a husband against his wife. Yet the lower rank of people, who were always fond of the old common law, still claim and exert their ancient privilege: and the courts of law will still permit a husband to restrain a wife of her liberty, in case of any gross misbehaviour.

1.16 Napoleonic law

Code Napoleon; or, The French Civil Code (Paris: 1804).

CHAPTER VI. Of the respective Rights and Duties of Married Persons.

212   Married persons owe to each other fidelity, succour, assistance.
213   The husband owes protection to his wife, the wife obedience to her husband.
214   The wife is obliged to live with her husband, and to follow him to every place where he may judge it convenient to reside: the husband is obliged to receive her, and to furnish her with every thing necessary for the wants of life, according to his means and station.
215   The wife cannot plead in her own name, without the authority of her husband, even though she should be a public trader, or non-communicant, or separate in property.
216   The authority of the husband is not necessary when the wife is prosecuted in a criminal matter, or relating to police.
217   A wife, although non-communicant or separate in property, cannot give, alienate, pledge, or acquire by free or chargeable title, without the concurrence of her husband in the act, or his consent in writing.
218   If the husband refuse to authorise his wife to plead in her own name, the judge may give her authority.
219   If the husband refuse to authorise his wife to pass an act, the wife may cause her husband to be cited directly before the court of first instance . . .

220   The wife, if she is a public trader, may, without the authority of her husband, bind herself for that which concerns her trade; and in the said case she binds also her husband, if there be a community between them. . . .

226   The wife may make a will without the authority of her husband.

Husbands and wives

Like Charlotte Biehl, Frenchwoman Manon Phlipon carefully considered the qualities of the man she married, and her memoirs illustrate the working and affectionate relationship that grew up between them. Jane Aiken's letter to her daughter, English writer Laetitia Barbauld, similarly demonstrates the deep affection that many husbands and wives shared. Comparing these to Rousseau and Wollstonecraft and to marriage law helps to demonstrate how lived experience could both differ from and accommodate the ideological constraints and opportunities of the time.

   Of course, not all marriages were happy, and while divorce and separation were difficult some women faced lives of discord and often physical violence. These were not limited to the labouring classes. Thus, Madame Rapaly was told that she 'can and must' appeal against the previous judgment which had quashed her case, to the King, the supreme justice.

1.17 On marriage

Manon Roland, *The Private Memoirs of Madame Roland*, 1793, Edward Gilpin Johnson, ed. (Chicago: AC McClurg, 1901), 351–3.

At length I became the wife of a man of genuine worth, who loved me more in proportion as his knowledge of me increased. Married thus with my own full consent, I found nothing to make me repent of the step; I devoted myself to him with a zeal perhaps more ardent than discreet. . . . I have not for a moment ceased to behold in my husband one of the most estimable of men, to whom I deem it an honour to belong; but I have often been sensible of a certain lack of parity between us, and felt that the ascendency of a somewhat masterful character, added to twenty years of seniority, rendered one of these superiorities too great. If we had lived in solitude, I should have had many disagreeable hours to pass; had we mingled much in the world I might have been loved by some whose affection, as I have learned, might touch me too deeply; I plunged, therefore, into work with my husband – an excess which also had its drawbacks, since he soon grew so accustomed to my aid as to be unable to dispense with it.

   . . . I acted as his secretary and corrected his proofs. I performed these tasks with a humility that I cannot help smiling at when I recollect it, and which was incongruous enough in a mind so cultivated as mine; but it proceeded from the heart. I revered my husband so frankly that I supposed he knew everything better than myself; and I so dreaded to see a cloud upon his brow, and he was so set in his opinions, that it was not until long afterwards that I gained assurance enough to contradict him.

I was then taking a course in Botany and Natural History; those were the recreations with which I relieved my labours as housewife and secretary; . . . and perceiving that my husband's delicate health did not accommodate itself to all kinds of cookery, I took it upon myself to prepare such dishes as suited him best.

. . . my constant care of him had its results, and this proved a new tie between us. He loved me the more for my devotion, I him for the services I had rendered.

1.18 Mourning a husband

Jane Aikin to Anna Letitia Aikin Barbauld, in *Memoir of Mrs Barbauld*, Anna LeBreton, ed. (London: G. Bell & Son, 1874), 20–3.

Jan. 1st, 1781.
My dear Child,

It is a considerable alleviation of the heavy stroke that is fallen upon me that I have children who were sensible of the worth of their excellent father, and I believe sincerely lament the loss of him, and tenderly sympathise with their afflicted mother, let us mingle our tears and pay that best tribute of honour and love to his memory, the imitating his virtues. I am indeed greatly afflicted, and the few remaining days of my pilgrimage will be sorrowful, oh! may it be that sorrow by which the heart is made better! . . . my whole life has been a life of mercies; my union with your dear father was a constant source of happiness; very few couples have lived so long together; peace and plenty crown'd our days, we saw our children brought up, saw them virtuous, esteemed, beloved, and comfortably settled in the world; and when increasing infirmities no longer permitted my dearest partner to labour in his Lord's vineyard, he was called to receive his reward, and has left a name behind him that will reflect an honour on his latest posterity. On his account we ought to rejoice, his constitution was so worn that had he continued longer, his sufferings would probably have been greater than his enjoyments, let us therefore say from our hearts, the Lord gave, the Lord has taken away, blessed be the name of the Lord.

. . . t'is a satisfaction to me that I never left him from the time he was seized till I closed those eyes which were the light of my life. Your brother saw him expire, and was affected as a son ought to be; he and your sister have shewn me every attention and tenderness, and press me to live with them. I have not yet determined how I shall dispose of myself, but if upon mature consideration I have reason to think that it will be neither inconvenient nor disagreeable to them, it seems the most eligible asylum I could chuse. Was I to continue in my present solitary situation, I believe I should sink under it. Pray for your poor

mother, that I may attain to a calm submission to the divine will, and so live that I may again meet with the dear partner of my soul in that happy world where all tears shall be wiped away, and there shall be no more death.
I am ever your affectionate Mother,
  Jane Aikin

1.19 Seeking separation

Mémoire à consulter, de Paulus-du-Mesnil (Paris: 1737).

La Dame RAPALY asked the Council if she can lodge an appeal against the Judgment of the Parlement of 24 April 1736, which dismissed her application for separation of body & home.

Madame Rapaly was married at age 16, her parents arranged the engagement against the most vigorous resistance on her part.

After many stormy periods, she was forced to appeal for separation of body & home for the safety of her life.

Her complaint contains the most serious incidents, as Mr. Rapaly has specifically agreed in the memoirs printed for his defence, that not only do they outweigh the separation, but also they would be worthy of an exemplary punishment if they were real.

This is a woman knocked to the ground, dragged by her hair, trampled by her husband, and torn from his arms almost dying and bathed in blood, by her Household, Tenants, Neighbours who hurried [in response] to her cries.

Mr. Rapaly, agreeing the atrocity of these facts and that they were more than sufficient for the separation, has formally denied all. He claimed that it was a comedy played out, (his words) and that the abuses his wife accused him of were all impostures & slander.

Experts on childcare

Throughout Europe, experts, often male, wrote detailed practical manuals on childcare. Like those below, these shared Enlightenment views on the significance of childhood years. They combined philosophical ideas that shaped childrearing practices, like the importance of breastfeeding and the primary role of mothers as caregivers, with practical advice on health. William Buchan admonishes women to follow Nature in tending to their children, and is highly critical of those who choose to hand their children to others to raise. Bernhard Faust wrote his manual specifically for use in schools, and its overt didacticism utilises a catechism of questions and answers. Notably, however, both also assign childcare responsibilities to fathers, indicative of a growing idea of refined masculinity which accepted familial responsibilities, but also echoing an older value system that saw fathers and not mothers as the primary caregivers.

1.20 Parenting

William Buchan, *Domestic Medicine* (London: A. Strahan, 1790), 1–6.

Nothing can be more preposterous than a mother who thinks it below her to take care of her own child, or who is so ignorant as not to know what is proper to be done for it. . . .

We mean not, however, to impose it as a task, upon every mother to suckle her own child. This, whatever speculative writers may allege, is in some cases impracticable, and would inevitably prove destructive both to the mother and child. Women of delicate constitutions, subject to hysteric fits, or other nervous affections, make very bad nurses: and these complaints are now so common, that it is rare to find a woman of fashion free from them . . .

Almost every mother would be in a condition to give suck, did mankind live agreeably to Nature: but whoever considers how far many mothers deviate from her dictates, will not be surprised to find some of them unable to perform that necessary office. Mothers who do not eat a sufficient quantity of solid food, nor enjoy the benefit of free air and exercise, can neither have wholesome juices themselves, nor afford proper nourishment to an infant. Hence children who are suckled by delicate women, either die young, or are weak and sickly all their lives. . . .

A mother who abandons the fruit of her womb, as soon as it is born, to the sole care of an hireling, hardly deserves that name. A child, by being brought up under the mother's eye, not only secures her affection, but may reap all the advantages of a parent's care, though it be suckled by another. How can a mother be better employed than in superintending the nursery? This is at once the most delightful and important office; yet the most trivial business or insipid amusements are often preferred to it! A strong proof both of the bad taste and wrong education of modern females. . . .

Were the time that is generally spent by females in the acquisition of trifling accomplishments, employed in learning how to bring up their children; how to dress them so as not to hurt, cramp, or confine their motions; how to feed them with wholesome and nourishing food; how to exercise their tender bodies, so as best to promote their growth and strength . . . mankind would derive the greatest advantages from it. But while the education of females implies little more than what relates to dress and public shew, we have nothing to expect from them but ignorance even in the most important concerns. . . .

But the mother is not the only person concerned in the management of children. The father has an equal interest in their welfare, and ought to assist in every thing that respects either the improvement of the body or mind. . . .

Their negligence is one reason why females know so little of it. Women will ever be desirous to excel in such accomplishments as recommend them to the other sex. But men generally keep at such a distance from even the smallest acquaintance with the affairs of the nursery, that many would reckon it an affront, were they supposed to know any thing of them. Not so, however, with the kennel or the stables . . . yet would blush were he surprised in performing the same office for that being who derived its existence from himself, who is the heir of his fortunes, and the future hope of his country.

1.21 Attending infants

Bernhard Christoph Faust, *Catechism of Health: For the Use of Schools, and for Domestic Instruction* (London: C. Dilly, 1794), 23–36.

45   *What does the little helpless infant stand most in need of?* The love and care of his mother.
46   *Can this love and care be shewn by other persons?* No. Nothing equals maternal love.
47   *Why does a child stand so much in need of the love and care of his mother?* Because the attendance and nursing, the tender and affectionate treatment which a child stands in need of, can only be expected from a mother.
48   *How ought infants to be attended and nursed?* They ought always to breathe fresh and pure air; be kept dry and clean, and immersed in cold water every day. . . .
50   *Is it good to swathe a child?* No. Swathing is a very bad custom, and produces in children great anxiety and pains; it is injurious to the growth of the body, and prevents children from being kept clean and dry.
51   *Is the rocking of children proper?* No. It makes them uneasy, giddy, and stupid; and is therefore as hurtful to the soul as to the body.
52   *Do children rest and sleep without being rocked?* Yes. If they be kept continually dry and clean, and in fresh air, they will rest and sleep well, if not disturbed; the rocking and carrying about of children is quite useless. (Observation. As the human soul in a state of infancy is disturbed by rocking, carrying about and dancing, such practices ought to be considered as dangerous and erroneous. The mother ought to play with the child in an affectionate and gentle manner; ought to give it frequent and bland exercise, and instil gradually into its mind a knowledge of such objects as attract its notice.) . . .

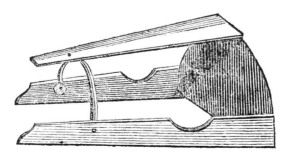

Figure 1.2 Aruccio, Italian device for protecting suckling infants in bed with mothers

56 *Is it necessary or good to give children composing draughts, or other medicines that tend to promote sleep?* No. They cause an unnatural, and, of course, unwholesome, sleep; and are very dangerous and hurtful.

57 *How long must a mother suckle her child?* For nine or twelve months. (Observation. In fact the child ought to be suckled till it has two teeth in each jaw. Some children are suckled for two or three years; a practice not only erroneous, but hurtful both to mother and child.)

58 *What sort of aliment is prejudicial to the health of children?* Meal–pap, pancakes, and tough, heavy, and fat meats.

59 *What harm do they do?* They obstruct the bowels; and children's bellies get, by those indigestible meals, hard and swelled.

60 *What food is most suitable for children?* Pure, unadulterated new milk, and thin gruel; grated crusts of bread; or biscuit boiled with water only, or mixed with milk. . . .

62 *What is in general to be observed with regard to the feeding of children?* That they be regularly and moderately fed, and their stomachs not loaded with milk or other things. It is, therefore, necessary to prevent people from giving children sweetmeats, or food out of season: the feeding of the child ought to be entirely left to its mother.

63 *Do affectionate careful mothers act right when they take their infants with them to bed?* No. It is dangerous and hurtful; children ought, therefore, to lay by themselves. . . .

64 *Is it necessary to keep infants very warm?* No. They must not be kept too warm.

65 *Is it good to cover their heads?* By no means; it causes humours to break out. (Observation. From the hour of birth the head of a child ought to be kept uncovered. Mothers will find that, even in the coldest night, when they lay their hands on an infant's head, it is always warm.) . . .

85 *What ought we further particularly to observe with respect to children?* That children be suffered to exercise their bodies and minds in company with each other in the open air.
(Observation. Parents ought not only to be present at the exercises and amusements of their children, and guard them from all dangers and injuries, but they ought also to encourage them, and lead them to all that is good and becoming, by their own virtuous example.)

86 *Ought female children to receive the same education as boys in their infancy?* Yes; that they may at a future period enjoy the blessings of perfect health as well as men.
(Observation. The most pernicious consequences to the rising generation flow from separating female children, at the earliest period of their existence, from male children; from dressing them in a different manner, preventing them from taking the same kind of exercise, and compelling them to lead a more sedentary life.)

Mothers and children

We now accept that mothers in the past loved their children, and the impact of Enlightenment attitudes, which placed more attention on the child, coupled with enhanced 'mothering', was felt especially among the educated classes. Susanne Necker, *saloniste*, describes her feelings at the birth of her daughter, and her insistence on breastfeeding captures the Rousseauean ideal, which was becoming embedded in bourgeois thought. Similarly, Caroline Schlegel Schelling, like Necker, shared the anxiety and fear that mothers felt as the time of delivery approached, while both found the birth process horrifying. Elizabeth Vigée-LeBrun speaks of the pleasure and joy in watching her daughter grow up, sharing her feelings on this close relationship. In the final extract, Mary Doe was tried for infanticide. Her voice is silent, but she had the support of neighbours who note that she behaved modestly, shifting blame to her father. The interrogation process was typical, and her acquittal was not unusual, especially as she had made preparation for the birth.

1.22 Susanne Necker on childbirth

Pierre Kohler, *Madame de Staël et la Suisse* (Paris: Librarie Payot, 1916), 28–31.

22 April 1766, to Mme de Brenles:
   I confess that my terrified imagination fell far short of the truth. I was for three days and two nights in the torments of the damned, Death was at my bedside; she had as satellites a species of men more terrible than the Furies, invented expressly for the sole purpose of making decency shudder and revolting nature. The word *accoucheur* still makes me tremble in horror! And I would have expired in his infernal claws if the fatal injuries he caused me had not finally forced them to fetch a *sage-femme*. . . . The revolting details of childbirth had been so carefully concealed that I was as surprised as I was horrified, and cannot help but think that most women make very foolhardy vows; I doubt whether they would voluntarily go to the altar to swear that they will allow themselves to be broken on the wheel every nine months, come what may. But extreme tenderness can withstand extreme pain, and I felt it more than anyone.
   11 June 1766, to Mme de Brenles: I nurse [her] myself and despite your suspicions, it is a great success.
   September, to Élie Reverdil: I was determined [to nurse] up to three and a half months; [but] nature failed, denying the milk at the moment I fell into a languor. I am fine now and my little one is much better with a large Flemish woman; I do not lose sight of her; she is very pretty and eager to chat.
   November, to Mme Brenles: [I did not give up without] bitter sorrow [having] overcome all the pains and all the sufferings of this state for nearly four months. . . . [But] my little girl was weakening before our eyes, and me too. It took a long time to tame my stubborn enthusiasm.

1.23 Caroline Schelling on childbirth

Georg Weitz, ed., *Caroline Schlegel Schelling, Briefe* . . ., 2 vols (Leipzig 1871), trans. Doug Stott, http://www.carolineschelling.com/volume-1-index/letter-57/.

Clausthal, 22 June [17]85

Your husband is a false prophet, my dear Luise, and your own wonderful example seduced me into entertaining false hopes. . . . Closed up in my room here for two full weeks against the foul weather and the fear of contagion, I experienced in anticipation not only certainly all the joys, but also all the afflictions of motherhood – until at last the day came that would make me, too, a mother, albeit amid a thousand prolonged sufferings and fearful anxiety. The final moments strained my powers to the limit, for I feared the baby was already dead – . . . And then there was an all-too-brief moment of joyous exhilaration that spread throughout the entire house – my husband beside himself now that the lives of his wife and child had been saved, . . . and I, enjoying it all. I fell into a slumber from which I awoke barely conscious, followed by 14 horrific days and nights spent in a violent nervous fever during which, despite an overwhelming urge to sleep, I could not even close my eyes without being immediately roused by convulsions and frightful hallucinations; a time when Böhmer often feared for my very life and I for my own mind, of whose confused state I was most sadly aware; when I everywhere saw only sadness, when even my precious child did not gladden me apart from the gloomy satisfaction I took, leaning over it, in being able to weep! So weak was I in body and soul that I shrank equally from both rest and activity. – But it is over, and I thank God for having rescued me through the enormous efforts of my husband, for whom my respect and tenderness have doubled as a result of the countless demonstrations of his own during this episode and as a result of the steadfastness from which he never wavered, not even during the most acute danger. I have recovered only very slowly, and it has only been during the past few days that I have once again felt completely healthy. . . . Gustav turned into an Auguste, [daughter, not a son] and this charming creature silently requests through her goodness and beauty that everyone be satisfied with her after all; and as far as I am concerned, I would much prefer a daughter – for whom a mother's heart doubtless beats more sympathetically and with whom I can certainly begin having a relationship much earlier. And the father? – ah, he was only too happy to forget the original choice!

1.24 Mothers and daughters

The Memoirs of Madame Vigée Le Brun, trans. Lionel Strachey (London: Grant Richards, 1904), 22, 70–71.

[1780] I will not attempt to describe the transports I felt when I heard the first cry of my child. Every mother knows what those feelings are. . . .

[At] Posilipo. . . . In the evenings I walked on the seashore; I frequently took my daughter, and we often remained sitting there together until moonrise, enjoying the salubrious air and the gorgeous view. This was a rest for my daughter after her daily studies, for I had resolved to give her the best education possible, and to this effect I had engaged at Naples masters of writing, geography, Italian, English, and German. . . .

My daughter had attained the age of seventeen. She was charming in every respect. Her large blue eyes, sparkling with spirit, her slightly tip-tilted nose, her pretty mouth, magnificent teeth, a dazzling fresh complexion – all went to make up one of the sweetest faces to be seen. . . . A natural dignity reigned in all her person, although she had as much vivacity of manner as of

Mᵐᵉ VIGÉE LEBRUN.

Figure 1.3
Elizabeth Vigée Le Brun and her daughter, self-portrait

mind. . . . But what enraptured me above everything else was her happy disposition for painting, so that I cannot say how proud and satisfied I was over the many advantages she commanded. I saw in my daughter the happiness of my life, the future joy of my old age, and it was therefore not surprising that she gained an ascendancy over me. When my friends said, 'You love your daughter so madly that it is you who obey her,' I would reply, 'Do you not see that she is loved by every one?' . . . I was not invited without her, and the successes she won in society were far more to me than any of my own had ever been.

1.25 Infanticide

Trial of Mary Doe, December 1733 (www.oldbaileyonline.org, version 6.0, 23 January 2011, t17331205–20).

Mary Doe, was indicted for the Murder of her Male Bastard Infant, by strangling and choaking it with both her Hands, on the 29th of October last.

Frances Crook, Midwife. On the 30th of October, I was sent for to the Prisoner, and found she had been delivered of a Child. She said, something (she knew not what) was come from her, but it was no Child. I ask'd her, what she did with that which came from her? She said she did not know where it was. I told her it signify'd nothing to deny it, for I was sure she had had a

Child, and therefore a Child I would find. Then she confess'd that it was a Man Child; but said it was born dead, and that her Father took it from her, but she could not tell what he had done with it. Her Father coming in I told him his Daughter had been Deliver'd – Deliver'd! says he, Ay, so she has – of a Sir-Reverence. Those were his Words, begging your Worship's Pardon. I saw so much by his Behaviour towards the Prisoner . . . that in short, I told him, I believ'd he was Father to the Child, as well as Grandfather; and that he had done my Business, and deliver'd her himself before I was sent for. So he went out, and I examin'd the Prisoner, and she declar'd to me, that her Father had lain with her, and that she never had to do with any other Man but him. On the 2d of November following, the Prisoner's Mother gave me a Note . . . it was said, that the Child was wrapt up in an old Curtain, and laid in among some Horse-litter . . . and there it was found. I saw no Marks of Violence upon it; but I believe it bled to death for want of proper Help. . . .

Mary White. The Prisoner and her Father and Mother liv'd in a Room in my House for many Years; her Father is a Journeyman Carpenter, and her Mother went out a Washing. The Prisoner, as far as ever I saw, always behaved herself prettily and modestly, tho' at last, poor Creature, she happen'd to be with Child, and she was deliver'd in my House. . . .

Court. Do you think she was so weak that she could not [call out], or that she was under any Surprize, and her Labour came so suddenly that she had not Time to call for Assistance?

M. White. I know nothing as to those Things, but here is a Waistcoat proper for a young Child, which found in a Waistcot Box in her Room, and she said she had provided it for that Purpose; and she told me her Father took the Child from her – poor young Creature – she's hardly Sixteen – her wicked Father has ruin'd her. . . .

Susan Glover. I have known the Prisoner two or three Years; I always took her for a good-natur'd, inoffensive, modest Girl, and I was extreamly startled at the News of her having had a Child; I talk'd with her about it – she complain'd of her Father for deluding her, and said she had indeed had a Child, but that her Father took it from her, and she did not see it more. There were no Marks of Violence on the Child, and I believe it might bleed to death thro' her Ignorance and want of proper Help.

2   Community spaces

Keeping house

The most important work for most women of all classes was keeping house. Despite a perception of female frailty, these women were vigorous, vigilant and meticulous housekeepers, just as Zedler charged the German Haus-mutter. His tone is one of esteem, and there is little doubt that women commanded respect and managed their homes with authority, and often with tact. It was clearly their domain and perceived as a key element in the household partnership. Women of the middle and upper classes usually had housekeepers, as Lady Grisell Baillie did, but their correspondence and housekeeping books make it clear that they knew, in great detail, what tasks had to be completed and when, and usually the best way to do them.

1.26 Haus-Mutter

Johan Heinrich Zedlers Grosses vollständiges Universallexicon aller Wissenschafften und Kunste (Leipzig: 1731–1754), XXII, 907.

The House-mother is the householder's helper, [and] therefore the other main person in a household, without whom it is not easy to keep good order and maintenance. . . . she is, as wife and mother, seen in relation to the domain and its upkeep, but she is also important as the woman of the house and as its commander.

It is constantly demanded of her that she is god-fearing, modest and affable and as comfortable in this, as other Christian virtues, that she is a good example to the servants and other people employed under her . . . and that she does not permit various superstitions . . .

She should attend to all the needs of her people in due time, in sickness and on other occasions give proper advice and action, and the wages for service [should] not be held back under some apparent excuse, or not paid at all. She must also be domestic; she should therefore acquire everything that is necessary, or, as much as is possible prepare on her own, and put it in storage at the right time, maintaining a correct list with no subtractions and additions, keeping things conveniently stored and properly used, as well as keeping all items in a usable condition in the kitchen, cellar and storage-vaults, and over this [she should] have detailed supervision.

She should finally also give herself over to order, so that she, at the proper time and in the appropriate circumstances, not starting with the last thing first, can keep everything in the expected condition, most notably that the beds are diligently attended to, the clean laundry kept in places [safe] from rot, mice and other damage, that damages may be mended in time, with an unwearied diligence and vigilance . . . so that everything she at once undertakes is properly completed [not] . . . superficially conducted.

Where a household keeps cattle, she must frequently visit the stables, and check that everything is being well kept, pleasant, clean, the food not wasted, or misused and all grimy things should be noticed.

1.27 Directions for the housekeeper

The Household Book of Lady Grisell Baillie, 1672–1733, Robert Scott-Moncrieff, ed. (Edinburgh: University Press, 1911), 278–80.

To get up airly is most necessary to see that all the maids and other servants be about their proper business. a constant care and attention is required to every thing that there be no waste nor any thing neglected that should be don.

The dayry carefully lookt after, you to keep the kie of the inner milk house where the butter and milk is, see the butter weighted when churn'd, and salt what is not wanted fresh, to help to make the cheese and every now and then as often as you have time to be at the milking of the cows.

Keep the maids closs at their spining till 9 at night when they are not washing or at other necessary work, weight out to them exactly the soap, and often go to the wash house to see it is not wasted but made the proper use of, and that there be no linnen washt there but those of the family that are alowed to do it often see that they waste not fire either in the wash house or Landry and that the Landry be kept clean.

Take care that the Cooks waste not butter, spices, nor any thing amongst their hands, nor embasel it, and that the kitchin fire be carefully lookt after and no waste, let it be getherd after diner and the cinders thrown up that non be thrown out, neither from that nor by the Chamber maid.

Make the kitchin maid keep all the places you have lookt up very clean, also the kitchin, Hal and passages, and see the Cook feed the fouls that are put up right and keep them clean or they can never be fat nor good.

To take care the house be kept clean and in order, help to sheet and make the straingers beds, that the beds and sheets be dry and well aird. get account from the chamber maid of what candles she gets from you for the rooms and see there be no waste of candle nor fire any where.

Keep the kie of the cole house but when it is wanted to get out coals, but be sur it be always lockt at night, that the Turf stack be not tred down but burnt even forward. let them fill all their places with coals at once, that the kie be not left in the door. . . .

As every thing is weighted to you give out nothing but by weight. . . .

The servants sheets is changed once a munth.

One week the body linnin is washt, the second week table and bed linnin . . . the third week the landry maids must be keept closs at spining and at all times when they have not other necessary business, such as Hay and Harvest and the Barn which the dairy maid goes to when she has a moments time for it . . . the dairy maid, house maid and kitchin maid always to spine when they are not otherways necessarily imployd which they will often pretend to be if they are not diligently lookt after and keep to it. . . .

All the scim'd milk that can be spaird after serving the family or when cheese is not made of it, to be measurd and sent to Grisell Wait who sells it and accounts for it, or gives it away to such poor people in the toun as I give her a note of. but non of them to come about the doors for it.

Take care there be no hangers on, nor santering odd people come about the house, but those that have business. . .

See that every one keeps what is in their charge in there proper stated places, then nothing will be out of order, or to seek when wanted, nor any hurry.

In general to keep all the servants in order, with some authority and make them obay you and do their duty without feed or favour to any, and to look after every thing with the same care and faithfulness as if it was your own, then few things can go wrong. if diffident or ignorant of any thing, ask derections from me.

Labouring women

The vast majority of women came from the labouring classes, where work was not a choice, nor was it necessarily regular; in a family setting it was usually unpaid and juggled with family and housekeeping commitments. Mary Collier's poem, written in response to Stephen Duck's *The Thresher's Labour*, which lauded men's work and belittled women's, shows precisely this variety and uneven character of women's work. Plebeian poets, like Collier and Luisa Karsch, were fashionable in the eighteenth century, and both benefited from patronage. Here, however, in Collier's poem and Karsch's autobiographical letter to her patron, Sulzer, we see the labouring lives such woman faced. This is echoed in Arthur Young's comments on women in rural France during one of his agricultural tours in 1787. William Hutton also observed and commented on women workers, on female nail makers in the Black Country near Birmingham. Note the tone of these two extracts and contrast them with the letter from an Essex servant writing home.

1.28 Rural women

Mary Collier, *The Woman's Labour: an Epistle to Mr. Stephen Duck* (London: private, 1739), 8–14.

> For my own Part, I many a *Summer*'s Day
> Have spent in throwing, turning, making Hay;
> But ne'er could see, what you have lately found,
> Our Wages paid for sitting on the Ground.
> 'Tis true, that when our Morning's Work is done,
> And all our Grass expos'd unto the Sun,
> While that his scorching Beams do on it shine,
> As well as you, we have a Time to dine:
> I hope, that since we freely toil and sweat
> To earn our Bread, you'll give us Time to eat.
> That over, soon we must get up again,
> And nimbly turn our Hay upon the Plain;
> Nay, rake and prow it in, the Case is clear;
> Or how should Cocks in equal Rows appear?
> But if you'd have what you have wrote believ'd,
> I find, that you to hear us talk are griev'd:
> In this, I hope, you do not speak your Mind,
> For none but *Turks*, that ever I could find,
> Have Mutes to serve them, or did e'er deny
> Their Slaves, at Work to chat it merrily. . . .
> What ! would you lord it quite, and take away
> The only Privilege our Sex enjoy?
>
> WHEN Ev'ning does approach, we homeward hie,
> And our domestic Toils Incessant ply:
> Against your coming Home prepare to get
> Our Work all done, our House in order set;
> *Bacon* and *Dumpling* in the Pot we boil,
> Our Beds we make, our Swine we feed the while;
> Then wait at Door to see you coming Home,
> And set the Table out against you come:
> Early next Morning we on you attend;
> Our Children dress and feed, their Cloaths we mend;
> And in the Field our daily Task renew,
> Soon as the rising Sun has dry'd the Dew.
>
> WHEN Harvest comes, into the Field we go,
> And help to reap the Wheat as well as you;
> Or else we go the Ears of Corn to glean;
> No Labour scorning, be it e'er so mean;

But in the Work we freely bear a Part,
And what we can, perform with all our Heart.
To get a Living we so willing are,
Our tender Babes into the Field we bear,
And wrap them in our Cloaths to keep them warm,
While round about we gather up the Corn; . . .

We must make haste, for when we Home are come,
Alas ! we find our Work but just begun; . . .
You sup, and go to Bed without delay,
And rest yourselves till the ensuing Day; . . .
Our Toil and Labour's daily so extreme,
That we have hardly ever *Time to dream*.

THE Harvest ended, Respite none we find;
The hardest of our Toil is still behind:
Hard Labour we most chearfully pursue,
And our, abroad, a Charing often go: . . .

WHEN bright *Orion* glitters in the Skies
In *Winter* Nights, then early we must rise; . . .
While you on easy Beds may lie and sleep,
Till Light does thro' your Chamber-windows peep.
When to the House we come where we should go,
How to get in, alas! we do not know:
The Maid quite tir'd with Work the Day before,
O'ercome with Sleep; we standing at the Door
Oppress'd with Cold, and often call in vain,
E're to our Work we can Admittance gain:

But when from Wind and Weather we get in,
Briskly with Courage we our Work begin;
Heaps of fine Linen we before us view,
Whereon to lay our Strength and Patience too;
Cambricks and Muslins, which our Ladies wear,
Laces and Edgings, costly, fine, and rare,
Which must be wash'd with utmost Skill and Care;
With Holland Shirts, Ruffles and Fringes too,
Fashions which our Fore-fathers never knew.
For several Hours here we work and slave,
Before we can one Glimpse of Day-light have;
We labour hard before the Morning's past,
Because we fear the Time runs on too fast.

AT length bright *Sol* illuminates the Skies,
And summons drowsy Mortals to arise;
Then comes our Mistress to us without fail,
And in her Hand, *perhaps*, a Mug of Ale
To cheer our Hearts, and also to inform
Herself, what Work is done that very Morn;
Lays her Commands upon us, that we mind
Her Linen well, nor *leave the Dirt behind:*

Not this alone, but also to take care
We don't her Cambricks nor her Ruffles tear;
And *these* most strictly does of us require,
To save her Soap, and sparing be of Fire; . . .
Now we drive on, resolv'd our Strength to try,
And what we can, we do most willingly;
Until with Heat and Work, 'tis often known,
Not only Sweat, but Blood runs trickling down
Our Wrists and Fingers ; still our Work demands
The constant Action of our lab'ring Hands.

NOW Night comes on, from whence you have Relief,
But that, alas! does but increase our Grief; . . .
Tho' we all Day with Care our Work attend,
Such is our Fate, we know not when 'twill end.

1.29 Into a life of labour

Anna Luisa Karsch, 'Autobiographical Letter to Sulzer', *Erster brief, Zeitgenossen. Ein biographisches Magazin für die Geschichte unserer Zeit.* Series 3, 3/18 (1831), 3–10.

1st September 1762

   My mother handed me over into the service of a burgess' daughter so that I could practise sewing under her guidance. I was eager to learn, for in one summer I had command of the various skills of the seamstress. . . . one day a splendid hunting coach stopped in front of our house. I saw my [former] teacher despite the crimson taffeta-lined fur she wore. She jumped down from the carriage, came toward us with the vivacity of an Amazon, hugged my mother, and asked me to be her companion. I leave her eloquent plea unrecorded; suffice it to say that she was persuasive and I had to make myself ready for the journey that same evening. I, like a young Spanish damsel with a head full of adventures, agreed to everything.

   I kissed my mother and was proud to ride off on such a beautiful sled. . . . In the first weeks I was fed abundantly, but after that, I suffered from lack of everything. Famine had descended on the land due to flooding in the fields.

People feared impoverishment; my share of bread was given out in little bites. My mistress, provoked by bad treatment from her husband, took vengeance on me. I was to be her servant, yet my age of twelve years did not give me enough strength for the job. Drawing water and pushing a wheelbarrow of corn up to the mill was my daily work. It pleased my benevolent Creator to test me early in the school of patience so that in the future I would submit to more harrowing trials without a murmur.

[She married shortly after her stepfather's death, which had left her mother ill, with five children and without the means to make a living.]

My husband did not ask about my paternal inheritance before our marriage. He had refrained out of an affected high-mindedness, but in time I realised that my dowry had been too small for him. Our natures did not harmonise at all; my rich melting heart, my tenderness, and his desire for riches were too different for a happy fraternity to be possible. My only solace lay in the books which the shepherd boy still provided me; . . . Now, however, my days were laborious; either I used a carding board, preparing prickly tufts of wool for the spinner, or I incessantly turned a small wheel by hand to wind yarn on to for the swiftly rotating weaving spool.

. . . My genius lay buried under a pile of stones, my arduous daily toils. Yet, nothing could smother this divine spark in me completely.

1.30 Poverty and toil

Arthur Young's Travels in France During the Years 1787, 1788, 1789, Matilda Betham-Edwards, ed. (London: George Bell and Sons, 1909), II, 10, 53, 82, 85; IV, 46.

The 22d. Poverty and poor crops to Amiens; women are now ploughing with a pair of horses to sow barley. The difference of the customs of the two nations is in nothing more striking than in the labours of the sex; in England, it is very little that they will do in the fields except to glean and make hay; the first is a party of pilfering, and the second of pleasure: in France, they plough and fill the dung-cart. . . .

Pass Payrac, and meet many beggars, which we had not done before. All the country, girls and women, are without shoes or stockings; and the ploughmen at their work have neither sabots nor feet to their stockings. This is a poverty, that strikes at the root of national prosperity: . . . Women picking weeds into their aprons for their cows, another sign of poverty I observed, during the whole way from Calais. – 30 miles. . . .

The vintage itself can hardly be such a scene of activity and animation as this universal one of treading out the corn, with which all the towns and villages in Languedoc are now alive. The corn is all roughly stacked around a dry firm spot, where great numbers of mules and horses are driven on a trot round a centre, a woman holding the reins, and another, or a girl or two, with whips drive; the men supply and clear the floor; other parties are dressing, by throwing the corn into the air for the wind to blow away the chaff. Every soul is employed, and with such an air of cheerfulness, that the people seem as well pleased with their labour, as the farmer himself with his great heaps of wheat. The scene is uncommonly animated and joyous. . . .

Take the road to Pezenas. . . . – At supper, at the table d'hôte, we were waited on by a female without shoes or stockings, exquisitely ugly, and diffusing odours not of roses: there were . . . two or three mercantile-looking people that prated with her very familiarly: . . . at the poorest and remotest market village in England, such an animal would not be allowed by the landlord to enter his house; or by the guests their room. – 32 miles.

The 12th. Walking up a long hill, to ease my mare, I was joined by a poor woman, who complained of the times, and that it was a sad country; demanding her reasons, she said her husband had but a morsel of land, one cow, and a poor little horse, yet they had a *franchar* (42 lb.) of wheat, and three chickens, to pay as a quit-rent to one Seigneur; and four *franchar* of oats, one chicken and 1f. to pay to another, besides very heavy *tailles* and other taxes. She had seven children, and the cow's milk helped to make the soup. . . . This woman, at no great distance might have been taken for sixty or seventy, her figure was so bent, and her face so furrowed and hardened by labour, – but she said she was only twenty-eight.

1.31 Nailers of Birmingham

William Hutton, *History of Birmingham* (Birmingham: Thomas Pearson, 1795), 116–7.

When I first approached her [Birmingham], from Walsall, in 1741, I was surprized at the prodigious number of blacksmiths shops upon the road; and could not conceive how a country, though populous, could support so many people of the same occupation. In some of these shops I observed one, or more females, stript of their upper garment, and not overcharged with their lower, wielding the hammer with all the grace of the sex. The beauties of their face were rather eclipsed by the smut of the anvil; or, in poetical phrase, the tincture of the forge had taken possession of those lips, which might have been taken by the kiss. Struck with the novelty, I inquired, 'Whether the ladies in this country shod horses?' but was answered, with a smile, 'They are nailers.'

A fire without heat, a nailer of a fair complexion, or one who despises the tankard, are equally rare among them.

1.32 A servant writes home

Colchester, St Leonards, Overseers, Essex Record Office D/P 245/18/6, 1783.

I wish you would write a Littel ofenr for I have no body to speak to and I can not wright so often as i would because my place is so heavy and I have not time to wright I have nobody to do nothing for Me and I have not mended but three pairs of stockings since I have been at my place I hope these Lins will meat you alle in good health as I am at present bless God for it for I conclude with my duty to you my Love to brothers, sisters.

Artisans

Women carved out a niche in the needle trades, building on their acknowledged role as needlewomen, but also their interest and knowledge about fashion. Many served full apprenticeships, were well trained and frequently developed profitable businesses and good reputations. Mercier describes the fashion sense embedded into the shop of a Parisian 'marchande de mode' or fashion merchant, albeit with a sarcasm which shows that he does not entirely approve. The *Book of Trades* is more neutral, with its goal of describing trades to aid parents and young women in choosing a craft. Throughout Europe, needlewomen came into conflict with tailors, nominally a male artisan trade with its privileges and rights. For the most part, women moved into sewing women's clothes, especially making the much less tailored mantua. Ebenezer Bain describes how women gained access to mantua making in Aberdeen, as well as the restrictions and obstacles put in their way. Inevitably, the tailors grudgingly gave way, as they did across Europe. Widows often held specific rights to trade, but the extent of their entitlements depended on the discretion of each guild, as the passage from the tailors' regulations in La Rochelle indicates.

1.33 Fashion merchants

Louis-Sébastien Mercier, *Le tableau de Paris* (Hamburg and Neufchatel, 1781), I, 290–3.

There is no one as serious as a fashion shopkeeper, selling puffs and putting hundredfold meanings into flowers and gauzes. Every week you can see a new form and shape of hats. In this line of business, the invention makes its author famous. Hems and seams receive a profound and heartfelt respect for the happy geniuses that make the advantages of their beauty and figure vary. What is spent on fashion today exceeds the expenses of the table and that for horses and carriages. The unfortunate husband can never calculate to what price these changing fantasies will climb; & he will need swift resources to fight off these unexpected whims. He thinks he will be singled out and pointed at, if he does not pay these superficial people just as precisely as he pays the butcher or the baker.

It is in Paris that the inventors in this area decide the laws of the universe. The infamous doll, the precious model, deck themselves out in the newest fashions; finally, the inspiring prototype passes from Paris to London every month; & from there it will spread its grace to all of Europe. It will go to the

North and to the Mediterranean; it will penetrate as far as Constantinople & Petersburg; & the fold that a French hand has folded will be repeated by all the nations, who are but mere observants of the taste displayed in the Rue Saint-Honoré! All this indeed very silly! But custom, carrying an unwavering sceptre, decides everything, orders everything, there is no answer to these words; one says, one does, one thinks, one is clothed as it says.

1.34 Lacemakers and milliners

The Book of Trades, or Library of the Useful Arts, 1804 (London: Tabart & Co., 1806), II, 40–50.

The LACE-MAKER is . . . busily engaged in her work in the open air, which even in this country is no uncommon sight during the summer months.

Lace is not woven, and of course it requires in the operation neither warp nor woof. It is made of silk or of thread, which is wound on little bobbins, made of bone or ivory, about the thickness of a skewer: hence the name bone-lace. The pattern, to which the lace is to be made, is drawn on paper or parchment, pricked with pin-holes, and then put on the pad or cushion which the woman holds on her knees. All the ends of the thread are first fastened together, and the lace-maker twists them variously, over and under each other, round the pins, which are stuck into the holes in the pattern: these pins they remove from one part to another, as their work goes on; and by these means are produced that multiplicity of eyes, or openings, which give to lace the desired figures.

Lace Maker.
London, Publish'd by Tabart & Co Aug 11 1804

Figure 1.4 The Lacemaker

For this operation much art and ingenuity are not necessary: it is, however, very tedious work; and when the thread is fine, and the pattern full and complex, it requires a degree of patience which can rarely be expected in persons of easy circumstances. Lace-making, therefore, is consigned to the hands of indigent women and young girls, who, by their skill and dexterity, raise the value of materials, originally of little worth, to almost any sum. But the time required to produce this beautiful manufacture is always in proportion to the value of the work; so that after all, little money is earned in the business.

THE MILLINER
The business of a MILLINER, and the articles which she makes up for sale, are very well displayed in the plate. In the window of

the shop are exhibited hats, caps, and bonnets; a cloak, a muff, and a fur tippet; while the milliner herself is busily employed at her counter in making up a hat. The boxes on the floor are intended either to send home her work when finished, or they are meant to hold some of the articles belonging to her trade; as feathers, artificial flowers, muslin, gauze, crape, &c. The drawers in the counter are usually devoted to ribands of different widths, colours, and prices; thread, laces, &c.

In the milliner taste and fancy are required, with a quickness in discerning, imitating, and improving upon the various fashions, which are perpetually changing among the higher circles.

Figure 1.5 The Milliner

1.35 Seamstresses and tailors

Ebenezer Bain, *Merchant and Craft Guilds a History of the Aberdeen Incorporated Trades* (Aberdeen: J. & J. P. Edmond & Spark, 1887), 256–8.

On 30th May, 1717, a deputation was appointed to meet with a Rachel Baxter anent a petition she had presented craving liberty for mantle-making; and after consultation the following minute was adopted:

The trade hereby grants libertie to the said Rachel Baxter for mantuamaking allenarly within the said burgh, and admittit, and hereby admits, her free in this incorporation for that effect (with and under the restrictions following) that she shall neither take to be prentiss nor employ in any work either within or without doors as servants but only women, and that these women servants, or prentisses, shall be feed or entered in the same way and manner as the other prentisses or servants in the said tailor trade agreeable to their constant practice and constitution; second, that she shall have only the privilege of mantua-making, and no ways make stays, or import the same to sell from any other place, and that the traid's clerk shall be employed to draw her indentures with her prentisses and agreements with any servants who are to be still subject to the rules of the traid in such cases, for payment of ane certain sum of money for banqueting money to the boxmaster of the tayliour traid of this burgh, which is accepted of by them for her freedom in the tayliour traid, as above expressed, and this besides of her expenses due and quarterly penny as use is in such cases; and it is hereby declared that thir presents to be no precedent to any woman in tyme coming, and the said Rachel Baxter obliged herself to implement the haill premises as above expressed, and for that end subscribed thir presents. (Signed) Rachel Baxter. . . .

7th November, 1728. The Trade, taking to their consideration that the number of the women mantua-makers in this burgh is very much increasing, and that the same is a great hurt and prejudice to this Trade, do therefore statute and ordain that every woman who for the future shall be tollerate to work at mantua-making by the Trade, shall pay yearly to the boxmaster of this Trade for such tollerance the sum of twenty-four shillings yearly, without any mitigation or defalcation whatever.

1.36 Tailors' widows

Reglemens et statuts des maistres tailleurs d'habits, marchands drapiers et chaussetiers de la ville de La Rochelle (La Rochelle: P. Mesnier, 1753), 19.

XX. Item. And the Widows of the said masters received & tested by master-piece for & during their widowhood will be allowed to have that trade kept & exercised in their homes by a boy who had been accustomed to work that said business [who] shall also have to make the pieces of work good & honestly according to the said Statutes & to take an oath in front of the said Mayor and the said masters overseers will also visit the said house, to report any abuse which takes place, which said widow shall be punishable as other masters according to the Statutes, & (we) ordain that the said Sworn Masters henceforth inviolably will observe & keep the current Statutes & Regulations & their successors will do the same in the future on the detained (contained) & declared penalties.

Businesswomen

Many women operated both large and small businesses across Europe. A sample of advertisements from Aberdeen in Scotland and Åbo (Turku) in Finland show how such women used business language and acumen to establish and maintain business reputations. They claimed elegance, intimated well-run businesses and addressed the polite circles of their society. They also recognised the importance of patronage, not only from customers but also from benefactors and those who wielded power and sources of potential income, like town councils. Thus Susan Trail, co-proprietor of the *Aberdeen Journal*, petitioned the Council for all the rights and privileges available to a well-run and aspiring printing firm, while Maria Augustin did so to continue her father's merchant firm – while he was still alive. Daniel Defoe, a great proponent of commerce and trade, insisted on tradesmen's wives knowing enough to operate a business, though he never saw them as businesswomen in their own right. Many women did wish to take up business opportunities for a wide range of reasons, and working in business families, as Maria Claessen and Ann Buchanan did, showed the value of a competent wife when husbands were away, and the strength and weaknesses of family connections in providing openings for women. Buchanan's correspondence also gives us a glimpse of what happened when things went wrong.

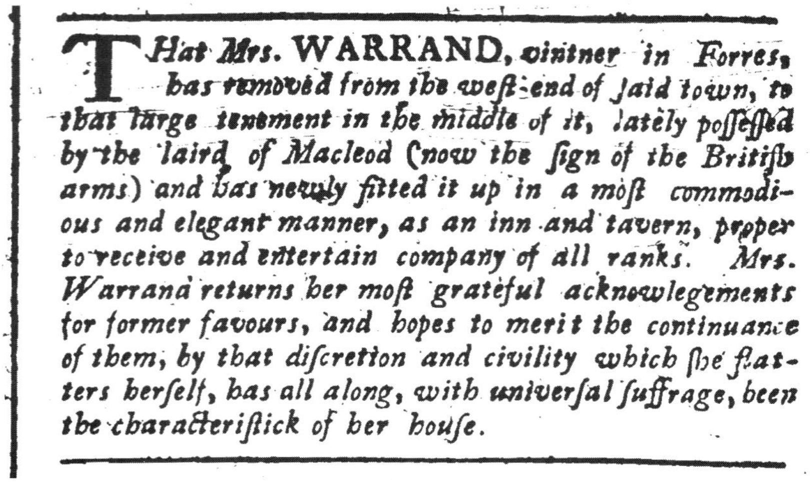

*T*Hat *Mrs.* WARRAND, *vintner in Forres, has removed from the west-end of said town, to that large tenement in the middle of it, lately possessed by the laird of Macleod (now the sign of the British arms) and has newly fitted it up in a most commodious and elegant manner, as an inn and tavern, proper to receive and entertain company of all ranks.* Mrs. *Warrand returns her most grateful acknowlegements for former favours, and hopes to merit the continuance of them, by that discretion and civility which she flatters herself, has all along, with universal suffrage, been the characteristick of her house.*

Figure 1.6 Mrs Warrand, innkeeper, *Aberdeen Journal*, 1 August 1758

Advertisements.

*T*Hat Miss ISABELLA MORISON, at her Lodgings in the East-side of the Gallowgate, near the New Street, Aberdeen.— Teaches young Ladies all Kinds of Millinary Work, to cut out and make up for themselves, Clokes, Bonnets, Hats, Capes, Ruffles, Handker-chiefs, Stomachers, Sleeve-knots, &c. and will al-low the young Ladies to make up their own Mil-linary Work gratis, and see it properly executed in the neatest and most fashionable Manner. She will give them three Hours Attendance every Day, either from ten to one o'clock in the Fore-noon, or from three to six in the Afternoon, at the Rate of five Shillings per Month. Miss Morison also takes in all Kinds of Millinary Work and Childbed Linen, upon the most reasonable Terms.

N. B. Miss Morison served an Apprentice-ship of five Years at London, and has settled a proper Correspondence there. She hopes her Cus-tomers will find her properly qualified.

Figure 1.7 Isabella Morison, milliner, *Aberdeen Journal*, 18 September 1769

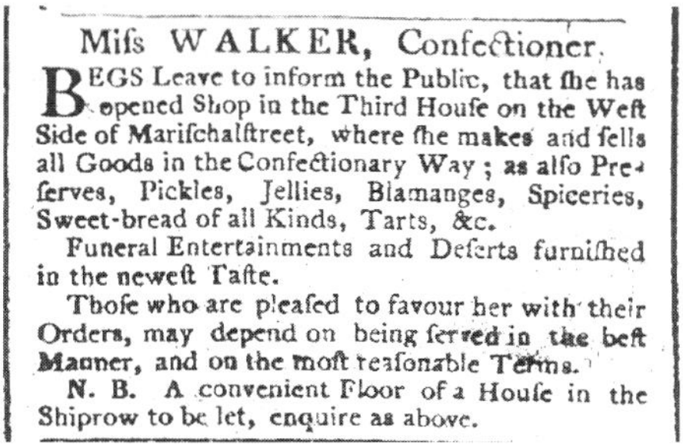

Mifs WALKER, Confectioner.

BEGS Leave to inform the Public, that fhe has
opened Shop in the Third Houfe on the Weft
Side of Marifchalftreet, where fhe makes and fells
all Goods in the Confectionary Way ; as alfo Pre-
ferves, Pickles, Jellies, Blamanges, Spiceries,
Sweet-bread of all Kinds, Tarts, &c.
Funeral Entertainments and Deferts furnifhed
in the neweft Tafte.
Thofe who are pleafed to favour her with their
Orders, may depend on being ferved in the beft
Manner, and on the moft reafonable Terms.
N. B. A convenient Floor of a Houfe in the
Shiprow to be let, enquire as above.

Figure 1.8 Miss Walker, confectioner, *Aberdeen Journal*, 2 September 1783

1.38 Finnish businesswomen

Åbo Tidningar, National Library of Finland, The Finnish Historical Newspaper Library, 1771–1890, http://digi.lib.helsinki.fi/sanomalehti/secure/main.htm.

28 August 1797
  A respectable woman from Stockholm offers to the Inhabitants of the Town a fine service by means of teaching Clavier playing and making hairstyles and finery. The address should be left at the Baker's widow Öhman at the corner of Rytorget; leave also the information whether there is a Clavier in good condition.

11 December 1797
  A respectable woman recently arrived here from Stockholm wishes to receive work of making dresses and other clothes, and also educating children if that is wished for. Address will be received on Tavastgatan at number 42, ask for Mrs Lindeström.

24 January 1791
  Novelties from Stockholm have recently arrived: Women's modern flower kaftans and bonnets, as well as straw hats and ordinary kaftans are found in the shop of Mrs. Alleen inhabitant of Luostarikortteli.

Eva Falck's Hotel and Restaurant
17 February 1802
  The owner of the Brinkkala Mansion by the Great Square in this town, who has handed it over to become a safe and comfortable lodging for foreigners as well as notable domestic travellers, has asked the undersigned, who has the honour of serving the incoming guests, to advise: from now on the rooms will be kept warm during the cold seasons, the rooms are equipped with the necessary furniture of chairs, tables, bureau, mirror, writing desk, attractive and

clean beddings, etc. and other essential equipment in the house. Especially I assure you that I will serve well the travellers and Gentlemen and Ladies, who wish to eat and drink at the house, with food and all kinds of refreshments they wish for and in exchange for the most reasonable reimbursement; also that the rent which is stated in writing and which must be shown at the owner's request, will not be exaggerated. Turku the 9th of February 1802. Eva Falck.

10 March 1802

Mlle Eva Falck informs all the gentlefolk, who would frequently visit a well-equipped restaurant and who understand the necessity of a public gathering place for all honest people of both sexes, that in the Brinkkala Mansion by the Great Square she will serve ladies and gentlemen with food, tea, refreshments, balls, assemblies, picnics, dress parties etc.

She thinks that everyone knows what a responsibility a housewife has to carry in the case of having a party at home, therefore a great amount can be spared when it comes to costs.

The small fee she will charge cannot in any way be compared to the costs and troubles that a housekeeper gets from a number of unnecessary rooms, furniture, porcelain, glass, tables and tablecloths, serving, laundry, etc. which are rarely used for others than strangers, and which will almost be avoided, as long as this service [in the Mansion] is maintained.

Her reliable behaviour and her stylish service manners will convince every one, who wishes to give her a chance to serve, of the pleasure and the real benefit her restaurant intends.

The Ladies, and the Gentlemen, who do not smoke, are served in several rooms, which are closed to the smokers. Turku the 1st of March 1802.

1.39 Susan Trail at the *Aberdeen Journal*

Aberdeen City Archives, *Town Council Register*, Vol. 63 (26. Oct. 1763–21 Sept. 1773), 5 September 1764.

Petition to the Council

This said day anent the petition given in to the honourables the Magistrates and Council . . . by Susan Trail Widow of the deceased James Chalmers Printer in Aberdeen for herself and in name and behalf of James Chalmers her eldest son Humbly shewing That the said James Chalmers their Petitioner's husband having lately died, their Petitioner designed along with her said Son to carry on the Printing business as formerly done by her husband, and for that purpose had retained in the service all the Journeymen and Apprentices formerly employed by him. That as the said deceased James Chalmers served their Honours and the Town of Aberdeen for a great many years preceding his death in the Office of Printer and as she hoped with general approbation and that said James Chalmers her Son was not only regularly bred to the Business with his father but also for several years past had been at London, and other places

JAMES CHALMERS,

Son of the deceafed *James Chalmers*, Printer,

Begs Leave to acquaint the Public,

THAT he is juft arrived from London, and carries on the Printing Bufinefs in all its Branches, in Conjunction with his Mother.— They have got a neat Affortment of BEAUTIFUL TYPES, from the Foundery of the ingenious Meff. Caflon at London : And their Employers may depend on being ferved in the moft neat, correct, and expeditious Manner.

They take this Opportunity of returning their unfeigned Thanks to the Gentlemen of the Town and County of Aberdeen, for their Favours to the late Mr. Chalmers, They humbly hope for the Continuance of them, of which it fhall be their conftant Endeavour to fhew themfelves not unworthy.

They intend to ftand Candidates, at the next General Election, for the Place of Printer to the County, an Office which Mr. Chalmers enjoyed for 28 Years with univerfal Approbation, and hereby follicit the Votes and Intereft of the Electors, which if they fhall be fo happy as to obtain, it fhall be their unwearied Study to fhew their Gratitude by the ftricteft Attention and Obedience to their Orders.

The ABERDEEN JOURNAL will continue to be regularly publifhed as formerly.—Its Friends may be affured, that neither Pains nor Expence will be fpared to render it both *Entertaining* and *Ufeful :* particularly by a *well-digefted Collection of News*, of the *Frefheft Intelligence*, and a judicious Selection of fuch *Effays, Hints*, or *Propofals*, as more immediately relate to the *Commerce, Manufactures, &c.* of North Britain : without omitting fuch entertaining Anecdotes, *&c.* as fometimes appear in the London and Edinburgh Papers.

Figure 1.9 Trail and Chalmers advertisement, *Aberdeen Journal*, 15 October 1764

in England prosecuting and improving himself in the same and designed in a short time to return to and carry on the Printing business along with their Petitioner in this place, She humbly hoped their Honours would be pleased to prefer her said Son to the Office of Town's Printer and all the profites and Emoluments thereto belonging as formerly enjoyed by her husband more especially as several of her own and well as her husband's Progenitors were long Residenters in this City and had the honour to fill some of the highest public Offices thereof, . . . They unanimously Granted the desire of the same And Elected and Choised the said Susan Trail and the said James Chalmers her Son Jointly and the longest liver of them to be Town's Printers in place of the said deceased James Chalmers, And Granted to them the whole profites and Emoluments belonging to the said Officers formerly enjoyed by the deceased James Chalmers they always keeping proper and well qualified servants for carrying on the Business.

1.40 Daughter and father

City of Turku Central Archive, The City Court, annexed documents, 1790–1792, 13 October 1790.

The Noble Mayors and the Honoured Magistrates and the Elders of the Town

Since my dear father, shopkeeper Matias Augustin, who has served in this town as a Burgher for forty-six years, has reached a high age and with it has aches and pains, he was forced to renounce his recognition, on which he was given a certificate by the Noble City Administrative Court on the 16th of last April. The Highly Respected Mayors and the Honoured men of the City Administrative Court and especially the Elders of the Town are well aware of the fact that the shopkeeper's supplies of iron, salt etc. which my dear father has in the course of time acquired and bought cannot be deposed or sold at a profit at once, but it takes time and care so that the loss will not be heavy and hard.

The enclosed testimony of my dear father confirms how I have for altogether fifteen years during his old age obtained the supplies and alone managed the shop and run the business. In addition to this there is a copy of the merciful order by his Royal Majesty who on the 19th of last February declared me plenipotentiary.

On these grounds and because my dear father cannot in his old age bear a considerable loss on the purchased goods, I am forced in the most humble way to plead to The Noble Mayors and the Honoured City Administrative Court and the Elders of the Town that against a specific yearly fee I am allowed to sell the store of supplies which still may be left and which would in any event be my dear father's burden.

Because no one can say that he would be wronged I take pride in the happy desire that in relation to my dear father's burden of being a Burgher for many years in this respect wins The Noble Mayors and the Honoured City Administrative Court and the Elders of the Town favourable consent and with respect continues to be so.

Your most humble servant
Maria Augustin

1.41 Absent husband

Maria Elisabet Claesson to ship captain Petter Claesson, Turku Provincial Archives, Archive of Petter Claesson, Biographica 5c, number 64.

Turku 7th December 1781
My dearest darling
   Although in my last to you on the 23th I promised no more letters until I have got the delight from you, my own darling, that you have arrived safely to Bordeaux . . . I also fear that my dreams and premonitions say something very different. May God almighty protect me from any unfortunate news regarding you, my own darling. . . . so my darling don't hide anything from me but let me know, because I don't want nor can hide anything from you my own darling.
   Captain Sjöman was here . . . and I paid him 909 daler for the cargo and expenses and 2 pieces of cotton fabric, which I and Mrs Strandhem are interested in and she took 8 lod of every sort of spices for which I had the money earlier from her.[1] The cloth we had woven I brought home and according to my accounting it would cost 16 daler per aln, so I have taken wool for 4 daler per lispund and I had 2 skålpund and got 32 aln, for which there is a sample. Then I and Mrs Strandhem had fabric woven so I have 13 aln of which I am sending you a sample so that if you would like a piece of clothing for yourself, let me know. I can get it for 24 daler per aln, the work will cost 10 daler, so I paid 90 daler because he previously had 230 daler. . . .
   My dear husband be good and buy me a big umbrella so that Majalisa can have my old one, it is a little worn-out for me. I have no others news than Eskolin owns 1/8 share of a new ship . . .
   Finally I wish you, my trusted darling, the protection of the God Almighty, with the warm greetings to you from me and our dear children. I will close myself in your affectionate love and will be yours forever until my death's moment, my dearest devoted love.

Maria E. Claesson

1.42 Female partnerships

Murray of Polmaise Collection, Stirling Council Archives, PD189.

Ann Buchanan to Jannie Muschet, her shop in the Luckenbooth, Edin.
22 Mar 1757
My D[ea]r Jannie,

I had the Favour of yours this day eight days and is glad to see business is going on so well with you, I think you need make no apology for not writing me, as I flatter myself it is not out of any indifference to me that hinderd you

I return you my most sincere thanks for your ready agreeing in taking me in partners with you, & your beloved spouse; I indeed look on it as a favour that I never can repay O how happy will I be my dr with you both and I hope you shall have no reason to be otherwise with me – I had a letter from — Buntine Last week where she tells me that Mama and Grandpapa is very well pleased with the proposal and is willing to give as much credit as is needed; so I hope there is no fear of my getting Employment as I have so many relations; for there's all the Kier folk, Lady Helen Colquhoun; Lady Grace Campbell; Mrs Smalet and many my Dr that is needed to name – they were told at home that it was Lady Polmaise that first made the proposal of taking me in with you; so in case they be writing anything of it to you; Don't say any thing that it was myself; I will long for the time when I shall be with you; now my Dear, as you'll have your house furnished with everything, and no doubt will have laid out a good deal of money; you and Cicy will think what I will doe in that case. . . . kind compliments to you and Cicy.

And believe ever to be Janny your sincere friend and much obliged Servant

Extracts from Mrs Lindesay (Cicely Murray) to her brother John, January 1758

10th. With your letter has let me see [what] sort of person (Miss Muschet) I had such a friendship for us put so much confidence in . . . the writer [lawyer] that is to be employed on my acct to pursue ye accts must go to Miss Muschet for all ye accts owing to ye copartnery while I was in it. I know she will put him off by telling she has not time just now to make out ye accts, but I beg you will order him to demand ye Books so as he may make out ye accts & her liable for payment.

13th. I have writ ye Dr (Murray) a long letter & told him my mind vy freely how I think Janny Muschet has used me, tho I don't doubt by but he will be put in the right. She has the art of making things appear very different from what ye really are.

23rd. Never has there such ingratitude as I have met with from Janny Muschet. As to her making it a loss to me, yt I think she cannot do, for at ye inventory she took ye goods all off my hand . . . I have sent you Miss's (Muschet) pretty letter I got this day, wch I cannot say was worth ye postage. . . . I now heartily regret Anny's being in business with her . . . I think my friends should make no secret how I have been used by her, so as none may go on my acct.

Ann Buchanan, 10 February 1758, to Dr Murray at Polmaise
Dear Sir,

I'm extremely sorry to give you the Trouble of this, as I know it will be very disagreeable to you . . . But Sure if you had known the Way I have been in Since I came to Town, and the Reflection and Work Miss Muschet is pleased to make, you woud not Blame me so much as perhaps you may now Doe; throu the Influence of her, I really Don't know what she means By her Behaviour to me; I have done all that is possiable I can for the Business, But I fancy she imagined when I came that I was to run and serve her; in everything Even to the making ready her Meat and putting on her fire in the morning, She thinks herself on a quite Different footing with me then she was with Mrs Lindsay for she behaves to me as I were far below her, and that I should not go out of the Door without asking her lieve; . . . She could find no Objections to my work; now she tells me I have been a manifest loss to the Business, But in what shape she wont condescend upon But that if the Company makes things meet it will be more than she Expects, for we are out a 150£ per Annum which by the by I Don't See how she makes it out So much; But let that goe as it will, it should Be the Least of my Care; for Some Comfort And peace in the world is all I want, So Im now resolved tho I should lose Every halpenny that I have put in, not to be any longer in this Disagreeable Way, now Dr Sir Don't be Angry for it's a thing I cannot help, . . . I shall only say if the Business Depends upon her Sewing or Mine Either; it won't be much Worth; but I fancy Miss thought she was to sit as a fine Lady And Do nothing But Derect; . . . I make no doubt But the Blame will be laid Upon Me; as her and Mrs Lindsay liv-d so well together, . . . So beging pardon for this Im with all gratefulness to you for the many favours receive-d

Your aft Niece And Humble Servant

1.43 Wives and business

Daniel Defoe, *Complete English Tradesman* (London: Rivington, 1726), 348–58.

[P]ride is, indeed, the great misfortune of tradesmen's wives; for, as they lived as if they were above being owned for the tradesman's wife, so, when he dies, they live to be the shame of the tradesman's widow. . . .

I would have them have the opportunity put into their hands, and that they may make the best of it if they please; if they will not, the fault is their own. But to this end, I say, I would have every tradesman make his wife so much acquainted with his trade, and so much mistress of the managing part of it, that she might be able to carry it on if she pleased, in case of his death; if she does not please, that is another case; or if she will not acquaint herself with it, that also is another case, and she must let it alone; but he should put it into her power, or give her the offer of it.

First, he should do it for her own sake, namely, as before, that she may make her advantage of it, either for disposing herself and the shop together, as is said above, or for the more readily disposing the goods, and getting in the debts, without dishonouring herself, as I have observed, and marrying her 'prentice boy, in order to take care of the effects – that is to say, ruining herself to prevent her being ruined.

Secondly, he should do it for his children's sake, if he has any, that if the wife have any knowledge of the business, and has a son to breed up to it, though he be not yet of age to take it up, she may keep the trade for him, and introduce him into it, that so he may take the trouble off her hands, and she may have the satisfaction of preserving the father's trade for the benefit of his son, though left too young to enter upon it at first. . . .

I am not for a man setting his wife at the head of his business, and placing himself under her like a journeyman, . . . I say, it is not this kind, or part, that I would have the tradesman's wife let into, . . . so much, of the trade only as may be proper for her, not ridiculous, in the eye of the world, and may make her assisting and helpful, not governing to him, and, which is the main thing I am at, such as should qualify her to keep up the business for herself and children, if her husband should be taken away, and she be left destitute in the world, as many are.

Midwifery

Midwives had a long-established tradition, yet this arena was highly contested as medicine became more professionalised, and consequently masculinised, in many parts of Europe. The *Encyclopédie* rehearses many of the criticisms of midwives, denigrating their skill and experience. However, women recognised the value of qualifications and licensing. Elizabeth Nihell, a practising midwife, wrote her midwifery manual precisely because she understood that not all women had appropriate training. At the same time, she was quite clear that the advent of men in the profession was not a solution and pointedly commented on their errors and abuses. A concern with untrained and unskilled midwives also informs the petition by French *accoucheuses* requesting that their qualifications and licenses be respected. The last word belongs to Catharina Schrader, a Frisian midwife, who recorded her experiences in her meticulous diary. Through her voice we can hear the seriousness with which she and many others undertook their vocation.

1.44 Woman–obstetrician

Denis Diderot, Pierre Tarin, 'Accoucheuse', *The Encyclopedia of Diderot and d'Alembert Collaborative Translation Project*, trans. Sonja Boon (Ann Arbor: Scholarly Publishing Office of the University of Michigan Library, 2006), http://hdl.handle.net/2027/spo.did2222.0000.659 (accessed 15 February 2012), Vol. 1 (1751), 85.

Woman-Obstetrician, a woman who makes a profession of delivering babies. Skilled woman-obstetrician. More commonly referred to as Midwife. . . .

I feel obliged to declare, in the interest which any honourable man must take in the birth of citizens, that, pushed by a curiosity natural to a thinking individual – the curiosity of experiencing the birth of man after having seeing him die numerous times – I took it upon myself to visit one of those Midwives who produces students and who receives young people who are looking for instruction in the matter of birthing, and that I witnessed there instances of inhumanity which would be almost unbelievable, even among barbarians. These Midwives, in the hope of gathering around them an ever larger number of spectators, and by consequence paying spectators, announce through their emissaries that they have a woman in labour whose infant will surely arrive against nature. One rushes up; and in order not to deceive the wait, the Midwives replace the infant back into the woman, and instead make it come out by its feet. I would not dare to state this fact, if I had not previously been witness to this numerous times and if the Midwife herself had not had the imprudence of admitting to this in front of me after all her assistants had departed. Therefore, I invite those who are responsible for attending to the disorders which occur in society to keep their eyes on these women.

1.45 A midwife strikes back

Elizabeth Nihell, *A Treatise on the Art of Midwifery* (London, A. Morley, 1760), i–xvi.

The truth is, that my very natural and strong attachment to the profession, which I have long exercised and actually do exercise, created in me an unsuppressible indignation at the errors and pernicious innovations introduced into it, and every day gaining ground, under the protection of Fashion, sillily fostering a preference of men to women in the practice of midwifery: a preference first admitted by credulous Fear, and admitted without examination, upon the so suspicious recommendation of those interested to make that Fear subservient to their selfish ends. . . .

Read the men-writers on this art, and you will find interspersed in most of them, amidst the most flagrant proofs of their own ignorance of it, reproaches to that of the midwives, too just, perhaps as to some, but shamelessly absurd in them, who to that ignorance substitute their own subtilities of theory, which, when reduced to practice, are infinitely worse than any deficiency in some particular female-practitioners; being mostly, in truth, fit for nothing so much, as to prepare dreadful work for their instruments. But if they so falsely exalt their own learning above the ignorance of women; they have their reason for it. They seek to drive out of the practice those who stand in the way of their private interest: that private interest, to which the public one is forever sacrificed under the specious and stale pretext of its advancement. Can it then be wrong in any of our sex and profession to endeavour, at least, to justify ourselves, and to undeceive the public, of the ill and false impressions which have been given it of our talents and ability? . . .

I Own however there are but too few midwives who are sufficiently mistresses in their profession. In this they are some of them but too near upon a level with the men-midwives, with this difference however in favour of the female practitioners, that they are incapable of doing so much actual mischief as the male-ones, oftenest more ignorant than themselves, but who with less tenderness and more rashness go to work with their instruments, where the skill and management of a good midwife would have probably prevented the difficulty, or even after its coming into existence, prove more efficacious towards saving both mother and child; always with due preference however to the mother. . . . it is even easy to refute the pretentions and sistem of the instrumentarians, in which I shall note here only three essential defects.

The first, in that the origin of the men, insinuating themselves into the practice of, has absolutely no foundation in the plea of superior safety, and, consequently, can have no right to exact so great a sacrifice as that of decency and modesty.

The second, for that they were reduced first to forge the phantom of incapacity in the women, and next the necessity of murderous instruments, as some colour for their mercenary intrusion. And, in truth, the faculty of using those instruments is the sole tenure of their usurped office.

The third, their disagreement among themselves about, which are the instruments to be preferred; a doubt which, the practices tried upon the lives and limbs of so so many women and children trusted to them, have not yet, it seems, resolved, even to this day.

1.46 Accoucheuses

Archives municipales de Grenoble, FF 46 (19 octobre 1755) (folio 359v°–360v°).

To Monsieur the General Lieutenant of the city, districts and suburbs of Grenoble humbly pleads Demoiselle Claire Bourgeois, the wife of sieur Pierre Vincent, tailor of suits, Marie Ravet wife of sieur Balthazard Vincent and Jeanne Charpy, wife of Pierre Perier, tailor of suits, all three mistress wisewomen midwives received by letters of last 16 September represent that they have been examined by the lieutenant and syndic of master surgeons sworn in this town and consequently received their title of wisewomen midwives sworn to this town of Grenoble; but as they know that a quantity of women without names, without titles, without abilities, and without morals are meddling in the births of this town, putting children at risk and doing illegal business, and not knowing the art of childbirth, which is in fact quite difficult; even more so is the theory than the practice, [they] maim or let the children perish and the mothers; the supplicants are interested in not being confounded by the aforementioned pretended midwives who have no names and [the supplicants want to] benefit from their exclusive privileges in the town of Grenoble and its suburbs.

For these reasons we ask you Monsieur, presenting to you the afore-mentioned letters and certificate, letters and patents by His Majesty from 23 May 1752 . . . suppressing all women who have not fulfilled two years of apprenticeship, who are not of age, who are not received and appointed to fulfil the functions of midwives either publically or in private in individual houses, in their apartments or in other places whichever may be the pretext, even without paying, nor [can they, without apprenticeship and appointment] take in pregnant girls or women to their homes and let them give birth there, at a fine of 500 livres of amendments for informing Your authority, and the order that you will kindly give, all that is here mentioned should be read, published and posted up in every place necessary and [that is at] justice's hand.

To be presented to the King's prosecutor in Grenoble this 18 October 1755

Having seen the documents brought by the supplicants and their present request, We require that it shall be forbidden for all women who are neither appointed nor received to fulfil the functions of midwife publicly or in private, neither in their apartments nor at any individual's house even without paying, to take into their homes any girl or pregnant woman to let them give birth there at the fine of 500 livres amendments and at exemplary punishment and in the case of contravention should be informed to the seat of authority [and] on the information given we shall decide what they deserve, let us request for the better of the public that the present request and the order that is hereby given shall be published and posted everywhere necessary, so that no one can ignore it. Registered by the clerk delivered at Grenoble 18 October 1755 signed Grenier l'Aîné [Grenier the Elder], substitute in the absence [of the town clerk].

1.47 A Frisian midwife

Catharina Schrader, *Memoryboeck van de vrouwens. Het notitieboek van een Friese vroedvrouw 1693–1745*, ed. M. J. van Lieburg (Amsterdam: Rodopi, 1984).

The year 1701: Holy God, give me Your blessing now this new year has started. That I can do my work with honour and praise Your holy Name, to be good to my fellow-man. . . . Please be always with me, when I have to do difficult things. I give You all my worries and problems. Lord, thou shall make it well. Bless me Lord, so I will be blessed. I will always place my hope in You and I am yearning for You in my prayers. For Jesus Christ sake, Amen. Catharina Gertruyt Schraders, widow Crammers.

1702 on 12 October delivered two sons to the knitter, Swaantie. The first came properly, the second with his stomach [first]. Had difficulty with turning. Still all was well for mother and children. The Lord be praised and thanked. . .

1710 the 5th February was with Jan Gorrtzacke's Hinke, whose husband, Wattse, was a corn merchant. A son. Lived but half an hour. Was a wonder of nature. Found that between the stomach and the gut there was an opening as big as a gold guilder, all round it grew a horny border. Out of this hung the intestines with the bowels. Had grown outside the body. One saw there the heart, liver, lungs, clear and sharp, without decay. . . . I enquired if she had also had a fright or mishap. She declared that she was unaware of anything, but that [when] it had been the killing time they had slaughtered a pig. They had hung it on the meat hook, and the butcher had cut out the intestines and bowels.

1711 on 10 February I was taken to Nijkerk to Wattse Jennema, whose wife was called Alltie Jouwkes. She wanted me to attend her, but didn't call for me. And fetched a midwife from Morra, who tortured her for three days. She turned it over to the man-midwife, doctor Van den Berrg. He said, he must cut off the child's arms and legs. He took her for dead. Then I was fetched in secret. When I came her husband and friends were weeping a great deal. I examined the case, suspected that I had a chance to deliver [her]. The woman was very worn out. I laid her in a warm bed, gave her a cup of caudle, also gave her something in it; sent the neighbours home, so that they would let her rest a bit. An hour later her strength returned somewhat. I had the neighbours fetched again. After I had positioned the woman in labour, [I] heard that the doctor came to sit by my side. I pulled the child into the birth canal and in half of a quarter of an hour I received a living daughter. And I said to the doctor, here is your dead child, to his shame. He expected to earn a hundred guilders there. The friends and neighbours were very surprised. The mother and child were in a very good state. . .

In 1721 the 26th September, Mrs Pousma of Ostermeer, the wife of the cavalry captain. A daughter. After 6 weeks she delivered another a stillborn son. It was a wonder.

1722 the 2nd of April, Thursday Jan Volkers. A son and a daughter delivered. He came with his back first. Turned it round. Came bottom first. The girl came out with her shoulder, in a hurry. I turned her also. Then she came with her feet first. The placenta was very firmly attached. It was a lot of work. But very happy for mother and children. Jan Volkers merchant, and his wife Janke.

1723, the 18th of April at Sunday evening at half past eleven my daughter delivered a son. It was hard work. The child was behind the pubic bone. That was a lot of work. I had to do everything with my hands. Nature could not help her.

Note

1 Old Swedish measures: A lod is 13.28 g; an aln is 60 cm, a lispund is 8,5 kg, a skålpund is 0.425 kg and a kanna is 2,62 litres.

3　Wider worlds

Gendering the Enlightenment

Rulers

Women have always been involved in politics, but with the modern emphasis on democracy and voting, their activities have often been ignored or seen as only 'pillow-talk'. One of the more important groups has been rulers, who, by virtue of their position, had the potential for great power. The eighteenth century saw several female rulers. Empress Maria Theresa came to the throne after her father's unexpected death in 1740 as an ill-prepared 23-year-old. Because many would not accept a woman, especially the Prussian Emperor, Frederick II, she had to act decisively and swiftly to keep her hold on the Austro-Hungarian Empire. Her *Political Testament* reveals some of her concerns and personal political guidelines as she navigated uncharted territory. Similarly, on a smaller stage, Anna Amalia unexpectedly became ruling Duchess of Saxe-Weimar-Eisenach, responsible for an infant male heir. She saw her mission as holding the Duchy intact and preparing her son for rule. She established a court of intellectual distinction, being herself a composer, as well as governing. In extracts from her *Gedanken* [Thoughts] and correspondence, she shared Maria Theresa's concerns about rule, and demonstrated to Frederick II her passionate regard for her Duchy. Catherine II of Russia was another 'enlightened' monarch. Her accession was bloody, however, and she was implicated in her husband's assassination. Her *Grand Instructions* demonstrate some of the contradictions of eighteenth-century monarchy. She draws on enlightened thought, while retaining absolute rule. The subtleties of her thinking recognise the limits of the possible in a country so relatively undeveloped, uneducated and enormous as Russia.

1.48 Political testament

Kaiserin Maria Theresias Politisches Testament, 1749–50, Josef Kallbrunner, ed. (Vienna: R. Oldenburg, 1952), 25–6.

Instructions drawn up out of motherly solicitude for the especial benefit of my posterity. . . .

When the unexpected and lamentable death of my father of blessed memory occurred, this being especially painful for me because I not only loved and honoured him as a father, but . . . was at the time the more devoid of the experience and knowledge needful to rule dominions so extensive and so various because my father had never been pleased to initiate or inform me in the conduct of either internal or foreign affairs, I found myself suddenly without either money, troops, or counsel.

I had no experience in seeking such counsel, and my natural great timidity and diffidence, born of this inexperience, itself made the choice of this most necessary advice and information particularly difficult; . . . I therefore resolved not to conceal my ignorance, but to listen to each [Minister] in his own department and thus to inform myself properly. . . .

From the outset I decided and made it my principle, for my own inner guidance, to apply myself, with a pure mind and instant prayer to God, to put aside all secondary considerations, arrogance, ambition, or other passions, having on many occasions examined myself in respect of these things, and to undertake the business of government incumbent on me quietly and resolutely – a principle that has, indeed, been the one guidance which saved me, with God's help, in my great need, and made me follow the resolutions taken by me, making it ever my chief maxim in all I did and left undone to trust only in God, Whose almighty hand singled me out for this position . . . and Who would therefore also make me worthy through my conduct, principles, and intentions to fulfil properly the tasks laid on me, . . . which truth I had held daily before my eyes and maturely considered that my duty was not to myself personally but only to the public.

After I had each time well tested my intentions by this principle, I afterwards undertook each enterprise with great determination and strong resolution, and was consequently tranquil in my spirit in the greatest extremity as though the issue did not affect me personally at all; and with the same tranquillity and pleasure, had Divine Providence so disposed, I would instantly have laid down the whole government and left it to the enemies who so beset me, had I believed that in so doing I should be doing my duty or promoting the best welfare of my lands, which two points have always been my chief maxims. And dearly as I love my family and children, so that I spare no effort, trouble, care, or labour for their sakes, yet I would always have put the general welfare of my dominions above them had I been convinced in my conscience that I should do this or that their welfare demanded it, seeing that I am the general and first mother of the said dominions.

1.49 Regent for a son

Frances Gerard, *A Grand Duchess, The Life of Anna Amalia, Duchess of Saxe-Weimar-Eisenach and the Classical Circle of Weimar* (London: E.P. Dutton, 1902), 39–41, 57–8.

Gedanken (c.1758)

Never did I pray with such devotion as I did in this my hour of need. I believe I might have become a saint. The situation was indeed peculiar. So young to be regent, to command, to rule, I, who all my life had been humiliated, depressed. I am afraid that after a little time I began to look upon my position with a certain amount of vanity. But a secret voice whispered: 'Beware!' I heard it, and my better reason came to my help. Truth and self-love struggled for the mastery, and truth prevailed.

. . . every ruler owes to the country which he governs the duty of raising it to a higher position; . . . [she studied to become mistress of her new duties]. I longed for success – for praise. I also felt the absolute need I had of a friend, in whom I could place entire confidence. There were several who sought to be my confidants or my advisers. Some tried flattery, others commended themselves by a show of sincerity, but in none could I detect the ring of true affection which is above all temptations. If a prince and the individual he selects as an intimate or confidant are both noble-minded, the sincerest affection may exist between them; and this is the only way to answer the question, 'Can kings have true friends?'

To the Prussian king, Frederick the Great, her uncle, February 1759
SIRE,

A requisition has been made to me by Monsieur d'Anhalt to furnish him with 150 recruits for your army. Your Majesty knows too well my feelings of respect and affection to doubt my submission to any order of Your Majesty's, but Your Royal Highness is too merciful to command me to do what would cause the ruin of the country over which I have to govern.

Your Majesty will call to mind the violence with which the Imperial Court has forced us to supply contingents to the army of the so-called Empire. Nevertheless we have managed to evade this order as much as possible and have only sent as few men as we could spare. If I am obliged to furnish the 150 recruits asked for by d'Anhalt, I must take them from the plough and from the workshops, which will infallibly cause the total ruin of a country as near annihilation as it can be. This terrible situation has induced me to oppose the demands made by Vienna, . . . I do not deny, Sire, that it was my reliance on your goodness that gave me strength boldly to refuse the demands of Austria; and now I implore you to grant your protection to this my unfortunate and ruined country. I beseech Your Majesty to cancel the order for the levy of the before-named 150 recruits and to believe that I shall return this great favour by the most grateful affection. These sentiments have, in fact, filled my heart since my early childhood when I was first made aware that I had the honour of belonging to you, and these feelings will remain in my heart as long as I continue to live. [He did not release her.]

1.50 Grand Instructions

The Grand Instructions to the Commissioners Appointed to Frame a New Code of Laws for the Russian Empire: Composed by Her Imperial Majesty Catherine II (London: T. Jeffreys, 1768), 69–195.

1   The Christian Law teaches us to do mutual Good to one another, as much as possibly we can.

2   Laying this down as a fundamental Rule prescribed by that Religion, which has taken, or ought to take Root in the Hearts of the whole People; we cannot but suppose that every honest Man in the Community is, or will be, desirous of seeing his native Country at the very Summit of Happiness, Glory, Safety, and Tranquillity.

3   And that every Individual Citizen in particular must wish to see himself protected by Laws, which should not distress him in his Circumstances, but, on the Contrary, should defend him from all Attempts of others that are repugnant to this fundamental Rule.

9   The Sovereign is absolute; for there is no other authority but that which centres in his single Person that can act with a Vigour proportionate to the Extent of such a vast Dominion.

10   The Extent of the Dominion requires an absolute Power to be vested in that Person who rules over it. It is expedient so to be that the quick Dispatch of Affairs, sent from distant Parts, might make ample Amends for the Delay occasioned by the great Distance of the Places.

12   Another Reason is; That it is better to be subject to the Laws under one Master, than to be subservient to many.

13   What is the true End of Monarchy? Not to deprive People of their natural Liberty; but to correct their Actions, in order to attain the *supreme Good*.

14   The Form of Government, therefore, which best attains this End, and at the same Time sets less Bounds than others to natural Liberty, is that which coincides with the Views and Purposes of rational Creatures, and answers the End, upon which we ought to fix a steadfast Eye in the Regulations of civil Polity.

15   The Intention and the End of Monarchy is the Glory of the Citizens, of the State, and of the Sovereign.

16   But, from this Glory, a Sense of Liberty arises in a People governed by a Monarch; which may produce in these States as much Energy in transacting the most important Affairs, and may contribute as much to the Happiness of the Subjects, as even Liberty itself.

19   *I* have said, that the intermediate Powers, subordinate and depending, proceed from the supreme Power, as in the very Nature of the Thing the Sovereign is the Source of all imperial and civil Power.

20   The Laws, which form the Foundation of the State, send out certain Courts of judicature, through which, as through smaller Streams, the Power of the Government is poured out, and diffused. . . .

33 The Laws ought to be so framed, as to secure the Safety of every Citizen as much as possible.

34 The Equality of the Citizens consists in this; that they should all be subject to the same Laws.

41 Nothing ought to be forbidden by the Laws, but what may be prejudicial, either to every Individual in particular, or to the whole Community in general.

63 In a word, every punishment which is not inflicted through necessity is tyrannical. The Law has its source not merely from Power [but also from] Nature.

67 Civil liberty flourishes when the laws deduce every punishment from the peculiar nature of every crime. The Application of Punishment ought not to proceed from the arbitrary Will, or mere Caprice of the Legislator, but from the Nature of the Crime. . . .

123 The Usage of Torture is contrary to all the Dictates of Nature and Reason; even Mankind itself cries out against it, and demands loudly the total Abolition of it. We see, at this very Time, a People greatly renowned for the Excellence of their civil Polity, who reject it without any sensible Inconveniencies. It is, therefore, by no Means necessary by its Nature. . . .

158 The Laws ought to be written in the *common* vernacular Tongue; and the Code, which contains all the Laws, ought to be esteemed as a Book of the utmost Use, which should be purchased at as *small* a Price as the Catechism. . . . Crimes will be less frequent in *proportion* as the Code of Laws is more *universally* read, and *comprehended* by the People. And, for this Reason, it must be ordained, That, in all the Schools, Children should be taught to read *alternately* out of the Church Books and out of those which contain the *Laws*.

210 Proofs from fact demonstrate to us that the frequent Use of capital Punishment never mended the Morals of a People. . . . the Death of a Citizen can *only* be useful and necessary in *one* case: which is, when, though he be *deprived* of Liberty, yet he has *such Power* by his *Connections* as may *enable* him to raise Disturbances dangerous to the publick Peace. . . . But in a Reign of Peace and Tranquillity, under a Government established with the united Wishes of a whole People . . . and where the whole Power is lodged in the Hands of a Monarch; in such a state there can be *no* necessity for *taking away the Life* of a Citizen. . . .

247 There is yet another Expedient to *prevent* Crimes, which is by *rewarding* Virtue.

248 Finally, the *most sure* but, at the same Time, the *most difficult* Expedient to mend the Morals of the People, is a perfect System of Education.

513 The supreme art of governing a State consists in the *precise* Knowledge of that Degree of power, whether *great* or *small*, which ought to be exerted according to the *different* Exigencies of Affairs. For, in a Monarchy, the Prosperity of the State depends, in Part, on a mild and condescending government.

Political culture

Women shaped political culture from within the system, resident in European courts, through their correspondence, and in the streets, influencing elections with patronage and support. Charlotte Schimmelmann was a Danish *salonnière* and the wife of finance minister Ernst Schimmelmann, and their household was a centre of conversation and politics. In 1784, Denmark was ruled by mentally-ill Christian VII, but his mother, Dowager Queen Juliane Marie, his half-brother, Prince Frederik and the Queen's private secretary, Ove Høegh-Guldberg, conducted state affairs. The Crown Prince, the future Frederik VI, came of age on 14 April 1784, and a group of young noblemen supported his palace coup: brothers Counts Johan Ludvig and Christian Ditlev Frederik Reventlow, Ernst Schimmelmann and Andreas Peter Bernstorff, nephew of the deposed foreign minister. Charlotte's letters to Louise Stolberg, sister of the Reventlows and her childhood friend and confidante, describe the events and feelings of the days of the coup.

In the same year, the Westminster Election was fought, involving several elite women in the campaign, including Georgiana, Duchess of Devonshire. The sexualised language is apparent in the extract while the 'lovers of truth and justice' also manage a double-edged critique of those who engage in the 'un-British' practice of slandering the 'ladies'.

1.51 Palace coup

Louis Bobé, ed. *Efterladte Papirer fra den Reventlowske Familiekreds i Tidsrummet 1770–1824* (Copenhagen: Lehmann og Stages Forlag, 1910), IV, 85–90.

Copenhagen 19th April 1784

Judge for yourself, dear Louise, with what impatience we are waiting for Bernstorff . . . I can assure You, that if one leaves out all other interests, this moment has been incredibly interesting to those, who witnessed it. The public noise was pleasant, the applause would not stop. The excited consciences – and of those there were many! – started the rumour and sowed the bacteria of fear everywhere.

After such an immense effort, one would expect great harshness; one was dizzy, one did not know where one was; but as we see that it will not be a question of the citadel, or of going to Munkholm [prisons for high treason], one starts to breathe and some heads that were lowered raise themselves again.

Guldberg can say like Augustus: 'Have I not fulfilled my role to the last moment?' He has taken his part as a great captain, and we find that he conducts himself well. He has told someone, that he remembers a couple of sentences that my husband said to him last summer, which he now better understands and he also told Numsen, I think: 'You have all conducted yourselves as gentle people'; after all, Guldberg finds many who feel sorry for him among his numerous enemies. . . .

The Queen asked me to play on her team last night, an honour that would not have been given me this past winter. The Hereditary Prince was there; he is bored like a dog. He is no longer the master. The Queen said to me: 'Now, Madame Schimmelmann, You must definitely be feeling better, you already look much better tonight' – I was overheated because there were so many people present. I answered her, that it was too hot for one's cheeks not to take on some colour, but that no doubt, the spring would put me back on my feet; She said some terrible things to Lady Løvenskiold at her meeting with the Queen, and compared to that and to the other things that she has said to people, I was treated well and there are those who assure me, that it has been said at court: 'At least the Schimmelmann's have not deceived anyone'; I must admit that I am not insensible to that kind of account.

27th April 1784

On the 14th of April, if I may return to this day, Sybille [her sister], Ludvig, Numsen and Münter lunched at our place. Your eldest brother arrived and found us at the table, at 4 o'clock all the gentlemen left us. Münter thought that they had all been stung by a tarantula; we had not included her in what was coming, you see.

We spoke of other things, and at last we surrendered to the illusion: At 5, I dressed myself and around 6 o'clock we went to the carriages to have tea with Mrs. Sperling, who knew nothing about the significance of this day. As we drove through the gates of my house, we met Mrs. Christian Reventlow, who knew nothing either, she wanted to pay a visit; we were relieved to avoid this and she went to Mrs. Conrad Reventlow's, innocently ignorant.

When Sybille and I arrived at the palace, who did we meet? Godsche Moltke. We assumed the worst from this, it was far too early, we could not think that everything had already taken place. As I put my foot inside the palace walls, everything there seemed much darker than usual, and I felt caught, the further I proceeded.

We spent an hour at Mrs. Sperling's in this condition on the verge of tears. Sybille had the hiccups and I thought I would have a fever; we comforted ourselves by explaining it all to Mrs. Sperling. At least then we could talk about it. Finally, at around 8 o'clock, the door of Mrs. Sperling's apartment opened, and the giant was there, all pale, but joyous, and a moment after, Ernst arrived, roughly in the same condition and I threw myself around his neck, in his arms; I do not know how. Some feelings cannot be accounted for.

When it comes to Madame Guldberg, the loyal von der Luhe, barely catching her breath, came to her at the critical moment and advised her to take care of her papers. It is said that at first she declared in a clear voice, that all the papers should stay there, for everyone to see, but it is also said, that she threw a few of them in the flames a mere moment after.

1.52 The Westminster election

Lovers of Truth and Justice (James Hartley and Thomas Rowlandson), *History of the Westminster Election* (London, 1774), 231, 232, 242, 248, 252, 310, 312.

When the D—ss of D—e [Duchess of Devonshire] alighted, on Friday, at a tradesman's in T— street to solicit his vote for Mr. Fox, the man told her Grace, that her person was charming, her eyes bewitching, her *mouth inviting*; but all these made no alteration in the principles or conduct of Mr. Fox, he should adhere to his former declaration in the address, by giving his vote to Sir Cecil Wray. . . .

We can assure the public, that the beautiful and accomplished Duchess of Rutland does not drive about the streets and alleys, or otherwise act in a manner unbecoming a lady of rank and delicacy.

The three *seducing* Duchesses have been *indefatigable* in their canvass, which they have managed in a *different way*. The old Dowager Duchess of Portland has attacked with *chit chat* and voluble persuasion. The Duchess her daughter with *mildness* and sensible moderation; while the *lively captivator* has ensnared with a glance, and carried her point by the majestic sweetness of her graces. . . .

Who would not purchase the *kiss of a favourite one* at any price? Does not the *Duchess* who gives a *kiss* for a *vote*, pay for it a *valuable consideration*? Have a care, fair D—n; bribery is by common law either imprisonment or the pillory. . . .

A person who sells oranges within a mile of Mount-street, Grosvenor-square, was honoured a few days ago with a visit from the lovely Duchess. The Duchess examined his fruit; she pronounced them fine; they were truly excellent; they were incomparable! then ordering the servant to take a certain quantity into the carriage, she coolly placed five pieces in the palm of the orange merchant's hand, significantly observing at the same time she did it, that the oranges were fine, and she had *paid* for them. And now, says her Grace, I am sure you will oblige me, in giving Mr. Fox a plumper. The man paused – stared – examined the cash – and then putting it quietly into his pocket, protested he was infinitely sorry he could not oblige her Grace, as he had polled for Lord Hood and Sir Cecil Wray about half an hour before. . . .

If, in the present contest, her Grace of *Devonshire* exposes her *person*, she must *give pleasure* to every man, consequently the *indecent* animadversions of a correspondent are below notice. . . .

The *Duchess of Devonshire* transacts business in a very *expeditious* manner, and therefore deserves much praise from her *favourite member*, canvassing for voters, she avoids being loquacious – but *kisses* and comes at once to the *point*. . . .

There are three different motives assigned for the alacrity a certain Duchess shares in her present canvass of the Electors of Westminster. The first is, to secure the yielding affections of a certain great Personage, which she fears are now *sinking* under *the weight* of her *encreasing charms*. The second is, a love for her husband's family, part of which, it is apprehended, must soon starve, unless Mr. Fox is again Secretary of State; . . . The third, last, and weakest motive is, her personal regard for Mr. Fox himself . . . and to do justice to her Grace's taste, we must pronounce the latter motive to be least probable. . . .

It is universally observed, that, in every *ministerial publication* of the present period, there is a regular and systematic attack against the ladies. This remark is strictly true; examine any ministerial publication, and if it does not contain gross and unmanly reflections on the *loveliest* and most *amiable* of the sex, then the point in question shall be given up; but, on the contrary, if there appears an invariable practice in all ministerial writings, to sneer at *women*, then let us feel like Englishmen, and detest a *habit* so foreign to the native gallantry of British hearts, so unworthy the natural feelings of virtue and honour. . . .

What have the ladies done to call down the whole weight of pensioned pens, and ministerial mercenaries? . . .

While the Duchess of Devonshire and her suite are rattling through the alleys on the one side, and the Duchess of Rutland on the other, the first is treated in a profligate morning print with all the *dirty* and *obscene cant* of a common *brothel*, and the second is treated in all the *other* newspapers, with the *gallantry* and *respect* due to *female beauty*. *Voila la différence!*

Intellectual rights

Women operated in the worlds of mind and intellect, sometimes for sheer interest, joining current debates, especially the vociferous discussions of gender, and sometimes to earn a living. Charlotte Smith engages directly with perceptions of appropriate subjects for women, making a spirited claim to be allowed to discuss whatever shaped women's worlds. Fanny Burney echoes the doubts of many female authors. At the same time, she claims the right to produce literature, and despite her 'backhanded' modesty shows pride in her creation. Both Smith and Burney managed to live from their publications, sometimes succeeding quite handsomely. Charlotte Biehl, on the other hand, positions her success against her struggle to gain appropriate remuneration. Journalism was also an important forum. In October 1761, Madame de Beaumer became the first of three female editors of the *Journal des Dames*. In her vigorous 'Avant-Propos' [Introduction] she defends the existence of a 'woman's' magazine, positioning women foremost in her concerns, acknowledging the role of amusement and information in her journal.

Swiss Madame De Staël was one of the most respected writers and thinkers of her day and, like others, took up the debate over woman's nature and social expectations, pointing to the tensions around serious study. Rousseau's ideas were an important challenge to many intelligent women and, like Wollstonecraft and Macaulay, Swede Charlotte Nordenflycht directs her defence of women specifically at him. As with the German writer Amelia Holst, the underlying issue was whether women's 'domestic' nature could be balanced with a useful and responsible education and whether women's intellectual activities could or should be accepted by society. Catherine Macaulay may have said that 'the mind has no sex', and these extracts prove her right.

1.53 Charlotte Smith

'Preface', *Desmond: A Novel* (London: GGJ and J Robinson, 1792).

In sending into the world a work so unlike those of my former writings, which have been honoured by its approbation, I feel some degree of apprehension which an Author is sensible of on a first publication. . . .

As to the political passages dispersed through the work, they are for the most part, drawn from conversations to which I have been a witness . . .

But women it is said have no business with politics – Why not? – Have they no interest in the scenes that are acting around them, in which they have fathers, brothers, husbands, sons, or friends engaged? – Even in the commonest course of female education, they are expected to acquire some knowledge of history; and yet, if they are to have no opinion of what *is* passing, it avails little that they should be informed of what *has passed*, in a world where they are subject to such mental degradation; where they are censured as affecting masculine knowledge if they happen to have any understanding; or despised as insignificant triflers if they have none.

Knowledge, which qualifies women to speak or to write on any other than the most common and trivial subjects, is supposed to be of so difficult attainment, that it cannot be acquired but by the sacrifice of domestic virtues or the neglect of domestic duties. – I however may safely say, that it was in the *observance,* not in the *breach* of duty, *I* became an Author; and it has happened, that the circumstances which have compelled me to write, have introduced me to those scenes of life, and those varieties of character which I should otherwise have never seen; . . .

For that asperity of remark, which will arise on the part of those whose political tenets I may offend, I am prepared; those who object to the matter . . . and exclaim against the impropriety of making a book of entertainment the vehicle of political discussion. I am however conscious that in making these slight sketches, of manners and opinions, as they fluctuated around me; I have not sacrificed truth to any party . . . I can only say, that against the phalanx of prejudice kept in constant pay, and under strict discipline by interest, the slight skirmishing of a novel writer can have no effect: we see it remains hitherto unbroken against the powerful efforts of learning and genius – though united in that cause which *must* finally triumph – the cause of truth, reason, and humanity.

1.54 Fanny Burney

Evelina; or, The History of a Young Lady's Introduction to the World (London: W. Lowndes, 1808), xi–xiv.

The following letters are presented to the Public – for such by novel writers, novel readers will be called, – with a very singular mixture of timidity and confidence, resulting from the peculiar situation of the editor; who, though trembling for their success from a consciousness of their imperfections, yet fears not being involved in their disgrace, while happily wrapped up in a mantle of impenetrable obscurity. . . .

Perhaps, were it possible to effect the total extirpation of novels, our young ladies in general, and boarding-school damsels in particular, might profit from their annihilation; but since the distemper they have spread seems incurable, since their contagion bids defiance to the medicine of advice or reprehension, and since they are found to baffle all the mental art of physic, save what is prescribed by the slow regimen of Time, and bitter diet of Experience; surely all attempts to contribute to the number of those which may be read, if not with advantage, at least without injury, ought rather to be encouraged than contemned.

Let me, therefore, prepare for disappointment those who in the perusal of these sheets entertain the gentle expectation of being transported to the fantastic regions of Romance, where Fiction is coloured by all the gay tints of luxurious imagination, where Reason is an outcast, and where the sublimity of the Marvellous rejects all aid from sober Probability.

To avoid what is common, without adopting what is unnatural, must limit the ambition of the vulgar herd of authors: . . . however I may feel myself enlightened by the knowledge of Johnson, charmed with the eloquence of Rousseau, softened by the pathetic powers of Richardson, and exhilarated by the wit of Fielding and humour of Smollett, I yet presume not to attempt pursuing the same ground which they have tracked; whence, though they may have cleared the weeds, they have also culled the flowers; and, though they have rendered the path plain, they have left it barren.

The candour of my readers I have not the impertinence to doubt, and to their indulgence I am sensible I have no claim; I have, therefore, only to entreat, that my own words may not pronounce my condemnation; and that what I have here ventured to say in regard to imitation, may be understood as it is meant, in a general sense, and not to be imputed to an opinion of my own originality, which I have not the vanity, the folly, or the blindness, to entertain.

Whatever may be the fate of these letters, the editor is satisfied they will meet with justice; and commits them to the press, though hopeless of fame, yet not regardless of censure.

1.55 A writing career

Charlotte Biehl, *Mit Ubetydelige Levenets*, 114–16, 118–19, 122–3, 126.

When my Works were immediately translated to foreign languages, my name quickly appeared in foreign journals and it brought me a horde of visitors, strangers as well as countrymen. . . . My view for the future was bleak, according to nature I was to expect to outlive my father, and . . . I knew it would be futile to hope my father would provide for me. . . . I was to send the application to the King for funding for my work, which he granted, and so I was given the 200 Rigsdaler for my pension . . . kindly granted for me to continue my Works which had drawn the attention of foreign nations to me. . . . I had given eight original comedies and many translations to the Danish Theatre without receiving one penny for them, so far I had not reaped any good from my work except honour, insults, critique and many enemies. . . .

It is my misfortune to be born to the female sex in which I cannot be of value to the State nor to myself. . . . I am the only one who has worked for the Danish Theatre for nothing; for nine years they have reaped the fruits of my work without the least remuneration, and so I believe it cannot be counted as presumption since all others have been paid for their work, that I should be entitled to enjoy the worth of my work, the 1500 Rigsdaler the King has promised yearly to those who write for the Theatre. This advantage was promised me . . . but not adhered to. . . . Even when the government was seen as harsh and gruesome, Count Struensee allowed the art director Morels' widow a three-quarter year to organise her husband's books, yet I, a fatherless child, the mild and merciful government would make homeless a mere few weeks after the severe blow had fallen.

Late in 1779 the most vexing letter was sent to me, returning a play for which I was expecting payment, with the words that the Theatre could no longer accept my contributions . . . I had nothing to live off and instead of receiving money I deserved, the hope of earning money in the future was taken from me.

1.56 On female literature

Germaine de Staël, *The Influence of Literature on Society*, 1800 (Boston: W. Wells and T.B. Wait, 1813), II, 151–5.

I shall begin by considering what is the fate of literary women in a monarchy, and also what awaits them in a republic. . . .

In a monarchy they have ridicule to fear, and in a republic, hatred. It is to be expected from the nature of things, that in a monarchy where a strict conformity to fashion and prejudice prevails, every extraordinary action, every attempt to move out of the sphere in which you are placed, must at first appear ridiculous. . . .

Indeed, men may always disguise their self-love, and their desire of applause, under the mask or the reality of the most energetic and noble passions: but when women take up the pen; as their first motive is generally supposed to be a wish to display their abilities, the public is not easily persuaded to grant them its approbation, and, knowing this approbation to be essential to them, feels still more inclined to withhold it. In every situation of life it may be observed, that no sooner does a man perceive himself to be eminently necessary to you, than his conduct is changed into a cold reserve. Thus it is when a woman publishes any work; she puts herself so entirely in the power of opinion, that the dispensers of that opinion fail not to make her painfully sensible of her dependence. . . . An honourable delicacy may occasion even men to feel some repugnance to submit to all those criticisms which public notice must draw upon them: how much greater reason, therefore, have they to be displeased at seeing those beings whom it is their duty to protect, their wives, their sisters, or their daughters, expose themselves to the public judgment, and boldly render themselves the general topic of conversation? Great talents, undoubtedly, would triumph over all these objections; but, nevertheless, a woman must find it extremely difficult to carry off with credit to herself the reputation of an authoress; to unite it with the independence of elevated rank, and to lose nothing, in consequence of such reputation, of that dignity, that grace, that ease, and those unaffected manners, which ought to characterize her habitual manner and conduct.

Women are readily allowed to sacrifice their domestic pursuits to fashion and dissipation, but every serious study is treated in them as pedantry; and if they do not from the first rise superior to the pleasantries levelled at them from all sides, those very pleasantries will in the end discourage genius, and check the course of well-grounded confidence and elevation of mind.

1.57 *Journal des Dames*

Madame de Beaumer, *Journal des Dames* (October 1761, vol. 3), iii–vi; (March 1762, vol. 1), 223–6.

'Avant-Propos', October 1761

Stop, gentlemen critics, you should know that this is a woman who speaks, that she is responsible for the care of the *Journal*, and that she does not scruple to speak highly of her sex, who perhaps has the sole right to soften you; the French people being the most gallant of the Universe, you agree that they should protect work to which we are devoted? I have no other merit than that of knowing everything that applies to my sex, and wanting to contribute to its glory and its amusement. That I would be happy to be able to avenge this offensive idea where a few barbarians among our fellow citizens have barely granted us the ability to think & write! . . .

All that marks the talents of women, will, without doubt, have the place of honour in this *Journal*; the works of men will have the second rank, yet it is necessary that their writings are not foreign to my sex. We will take a quick glance at the books of the day, we will focus on those that suit us, because I always come back to my first judges, and my true protectresses.

We will speak with impartiality of the dramatic pieces printed. We will applaud without insipidity, criticize without bitterness, and we will attempt to banish the same disposition [in our readers]. Here, it will be said, is a terrible commitment to woman. One flatters herself to submit & give gentlemen lessons in moderation & fairness towards our wits.

Reason will enter into our *Journal*, provided it appears with a smile of the Graces. One will not fear to associate with the most frivolous of the arts of fashion. If you should find a well-composed toilette, *Montesquieu* & *Racine* next to tassels & ribbons, it is necessary that the library of a woman must also admit the lightest tracts.

One must not forget to mention the productions of artists, especially those relating to the ladies; there will be no Sciences, until stripped of their pedantic humbug, which will appear in my journal. . . .

In a word, we seek to please both at the virtue, the mind & the Graces. We crave the approval of my sex, and assure myself of that of men.

'Avant-Propos', March 1762

The success of the *Journal des Dames* allows us to triumph over those frivolous persons who have regarded this periodical as a petty work that includes only a few bagatelles suitable to help them kill time. In truth, you do well to honour us gentlemen, to believe that we could not provide things that unite the useful with the agreeable. To set your error straight, we have made our *Journal* historical, with a view to putting before the eyes of the youth striking images that will incline them toward virtue; it is for virtue that we are formed, and only by aspiring to virtue can we be esteemed. A historical *Journal des Dames*! these Gentlemen rationalists reply: how ridiculous! It is not in the nature of this work, which calls only for little pieces to create amusement during the toilette. Well! It is precisely this that I wish to avoid. A female philosopher seeks to instruct; she makes too little of the toilette, in order to contribute to its pleasures. For pity's sake, Gentlemen wits, mind your own business and let us write in a manner worthy of our sex; I love this sex, I am jealous to uphold its honour and its rights. If we have not been raised up in the sciences as you have, it is you who are the guilty ones; for have you not always abused, if I may say so, the physical strength that nature has given you? Have you not used it to crush our capacities, and to bury the particular prerogatives that this same nature has lavished on women . . .

We would be well avenged, Gentlemen, if today, like our ancient Amazons, we could make you spin or make braids; especially you, Frivolous Gentlemen, so enamoured of yourselves, just like Narcissus, you pass part of your time trying on the newest fashions, artistically powdering and rouging yourselves, and artistically placing beauty spots; you chatter continually while you pick at your plates; in one word, you are even more effeminate than the Coquettes you are seeking to please. Since heaven has given you strength, do not debase it; use it in the service of the King and for the fatherland; become good Compatriots; go to the battlefields, defy and confound our enemies; throw yourselves at the feet of the French Monarch; he deserves to be king of the entire universe, and leave to us the duty of cultivating *belles lettres* & we will prove to you that they are in good keeping in our hands.

1.58 Woman's defence against Rousseau

Hedvig Charlotta Nordenflycht, 'Fruentimrets Försvar emot JJ Rousseau', in *Utralde Arbeten* (Stockholm: 1781), 162–74.

Sometimes the habits and prejudices that rule the world, earned like licences to trade . . . can weaken the judgement, particularly the perception that generally is ascribed to the female sex, the limited way it has been brought up and the narrow limits within which its gifts and duties became confined. . . .

It is not common people's reputation and manner of thinking that I intend to deny. That would be an equally vain and foolish attempt. But the enlightened and objective minds, which are discrete in their findings, who could examine truths, see them in their breadth and strength . . . are skilled in the world's history, know the customs of earlier times, all the dispositions of nations and are well versed in law, government method and habit . . . can separate the reasonable and safe laws from those like unquenchable desire, violence, stupidity and art . . . these that despite their enlightenment, yet could be mistaken on this topic [women], which they could happen to pass over, those are the ones I wish to win over with my reasons. It is not a half-learned but a true philosopher's thought that provokes my eagerness . . . but Rousseau's opinion that provoked my pen this time.

In his letter to Mr. D. Alembert . . . he seems above all to want to blame the female sex for the wrongs that make our time spoiled and ridiculous, [although] . . . he secretly seems to admit our strength and discern our rights, because why else should the strong and enlightened sex accept the taste of the weaker one? If woman is cause for the follies that rule our times, why then do men value [their taste] and by their approval like it? . . . Mr Rousseau continues, furthermore, to make the female sex criminal and despicable. . . .

He proposes that justice and truth are the primary obligations of an individual, love of mankind and her mother country the primary connections. I venture to confess that I too know of these undertakings: respect for truth, love for justice, affection for the value and rights of my sex, which has been trampled so long by the tyranny of habit, and inflamed my eagerness. Mr Rousseau has the interest of his mother country and I have one half of mankind to speak for.

If you separately take up his words and examine each comment, it would be easy to be convinced of a rushed judgment and the obvious obstinacy of his sentences. When for example he says that the female can succeed in small clever works that require no more than speed, light judgement, taste and pleasantness, he ends the same sentence [saying] that she can even have success in philosophy, comprehend reason, etc. And therefore science and learning; even though at the beginning he deprived them of all talents and in the end deprived them of their soul, flame and vivacity. . . .

But I think, however loudly he tries to deny the female sex's strength and passion, and so its fire, that it would be revealed from their pens, that if

Cleopatra, Fulvia, Julia, Agripina, Fredegonde, Brunehaut, Theodora, Jeanne de Neaple, Marguerite d'Anjou, Chioya, Catherine de Medici, Mary Queen of Scots and many of the kind had written their biographies and shown their hearts, Mr Rousseau would have seen the strongest paintings, the liveliest picture of all human facilities; a Sappho and the others, whom he, . . . was pleased to accept, were not the only ones who had feeling and flame, . . . as soon as he allows one of the female sex to have these qualities, then at least it ought to become a possibility for the others.

1.59 Intellectual education

Amelia Holst, *Über die Bestimmung des Weibes zur höhern Geistesbildung* (Berlin: Heinrich Frölich, 1802), viii–xiv, 1–4, 6.

Does the higher education of the soul and the immediate occupation of women as wives, mothers and housewives come into conflict?

Recently much has been written about female destiny. Men have dared to draw a line on our minds and what fields of knowledge it should not cross into; they imagine this higher education of our understanding to be in conflict with our individual duties. . . .

This I do not believe. So many wonderful products from all subjects of knowledge disprove this statement. Or they have never felt how embarrassing it is, to have to only stand behind men to have their position demonstrated. . . .

In the name of the entire sex, I urge men to prove to us the right they claim to hold the entire half of the human race back, denying us access to the source of sciences and at most allowing us to skim the surface of it. And will we grant this presumption, will they justify it and have they been able to so far?

Two reasons are given by these authors against the higher education of women. Our physical and mental capacities make us unable to become equal with men in the regions of knowledge, and secondly this high degree of mental cultivation goes against our personal duties. If both assertions had a foundation, then it would be foolish to go against it. In the first case we could not and in the second we should not pursue such high flights of thought. It would be forbidden fruit that we would not be allowed to taste. If we have to acknowledge that women are physically weaker than men, then does this necessarily also mean that the mind is weaker? Furthermore, does the one follow the other? are our brains then organised differently from those of men? . . .

Since it cannot be proven that physical powers and mental powers are the same; . . . then I cannot understand why all these writers who have written about the destiny of women, still so happily employ this unproven claim and draw the conclusion of our subordinate intellectual powers. . . .

If I could only let my sex know that the duty of humanity is to improve all its strengths, that we cannot claim the honour of humanity without this higher education; we would take this fair business further than men. Because in our case so many selfish ambitions, which men have more of in their education than we do, fall away, apart from the duty of humanity nothing would encourage the education of our minds more than the wretched attempt to shine and how pathetic this ambition would be. Men however have these selfish ambitions far more than we do; they make the sciences their livelihoods, and through this rise to honour and dignity; for us such drives are denied, we can therefore be much more human in the finest sense of the word. We wish and require nothing more, the honour of humanity is enough for us.

Science and intellect

Despite the rhetoric against women's intellectual faculties, the eighteenth century was blessed with a number of women who took sciences seriously. While they were often described as 'interpreters' or 'translators', like Émelie du Châtelet, the work of many women was original, and actively shaped the scientific world. Catherine II appointed Elisabeth Dashkova as Director of the Russian Academy of Arts and Sciences. Here she describes her reluctance to take up the appointment – but also her serious and sensitive approach to the post. Introducing *Analytical Institutions*, Maria Agnesi lays claim to her right to publish on mathematics and openly acknowledges women's right to intellectual achievement. Anglo-German Caroline Herschel is more circumspect, and indeed spent her life in her brother's shadow – a position she willingly claimed, belittling her achievements. And yet, methodical, thorough, she managed to juggle the needs of the household with regular and detailed observation of the heavens.

1.60 Academic director

Memoirs of the Princess Daschkaw, 1804, Mrs. W. Bradford, ed. (London: H. Colburn, 1840), I, 291–305.

[c.1782] there was a ball given at court, on some occasion or other, which I forget, when her majesty, after her usual round, and addressing herself to the several ladies of honour and foreign ministers, returning to me, said, 'I have something particular to say to you, princess', . . . and if I had really just dropped from the clouds, I could not have felt more amazement than I did at that instant, when her majesty proposed to appoint me Director of the Academy of Arts and Sciences! . . .

'No, madam,' I at length had power to reply, 'it is not for me to accept an office which I am far from having the capacity to fill; and did I not think your majesty were in jest, I should say that if I could willingly stoop to render myself ridiculous, I could never consent to compromise your majesty's dignity and discernment by accepting an appointment for which I am every way unfit.' . . . Her majesty persevered. . . . The eyes of all the court were now directed towards us. 'Well, well,' replied her majesty, 'let matters rest as they are for the present; though, as to your refusal, it only confirms my opinion that I cannot possibly make a better choice.'. . .

[Despite continued protests] I received . . . a copy of an ukase which had already been transmitted to the senate, appointing me director of the Academy of Sciences, and at the same time annulling the power of a commission, under which its affairs had been lately administered, in compliance with a requisition of all the professors and other persons concerned, setting forth the misconduct of the late director, M. Domashneff. . . .

The first thing, however, which I took upon myself to do was, in sending a copy of the ukase to the academy, to desire that the commission should continue in force for two days longer, and that I should be furnished immediately with some account of the several branches of the establishment . . . that the heads of each department should next day make me a report of the duties they had to perform, and of everything committed to their respective charge. I begged at the same time of the commissioners, that they would be pleased to communicate every particular they could collect concerning the office and duties of a director, in order that I might form a general idea of what I had to do, before I attempted to act even in the merest trifle; and in conclusion, I begged these gentlemen themselves to believe, and to assure the rest of the academy, that I already had prescribed it to myself, as a first and most imperious duty, to preserve for every member of that learned body all the consideration and esteem which their several merits demanded. I flattered myself that I should thus from the beginning avoid every occasion in this respect of exciting jealousy and discontent. . . .

The third day after my nomination, which was a Sunday, I received a visit from the professors, the inspectors, and other officers of the academy. I told them it was my intention to go next day to the academy; and I begged them to understand that on all occasions, whenever they might wish to confer with me on matters of business, they had full permission to enter my house without ceremony. The whole of that evening I was occupied in reading the several reports which had been presented, earnestly intent on gaining some clue to the intricacies of that labyrinth in which I was involved, under a full persuasion that every step I took would be a subject of criticism . . . and the next morning, before I went thither, I paid a visit to the celebrated [Swiss mathematician Leonhard] Euler, who had known me for many years, and had always treated me with kindness and consideration.

This learned person was, without question, one of the first mathematicians of the age. He was, besides, well versed in every branch of science . . . I begged of him to accompany me that morning, that on my first appearance at the head of a scientific body I might have the advantage and sanction of his attendance . . . He appeared flattered at my request. . . . Addressing the professors and members there assembled, I lamented my own deficiency in scientific attainments, but spoke of the high respect I entertained for science, of which M. Euler's presence at the academy, would, I hoped, be received as the most solemn pledge I could offer. After having delivered these few words

I took my seat, and remarked that M. Schteline, professor of Allegory, as he was called, had taken his place next to the director's chair . . . as he thought, a claim to the highest distinction amongst the members of the academy. Turning, therefore, to M. Euler, 'Sit down, Sir,' I said, 'wherever you please, and whatever seat you may happen to take, that seat must consequently be deemed the highest.'. . . I observed, that a general idea had gone abroad of the great neglect and malversation which had been suffered under the late director, . . .

'Henceforward,' I said, 'it must be our common duty to redress these abuses; . . . I am resolved neither to enrich myself at its expense, nor to allow the smallest peculation in any of the subordinate offices; and could I but persuade every one to regulate his conduct strictly by this principle, I should very soon be in a situation to recompense the zealous and deserving, by promotion or some addition to their salaries.'

1.61 On calculus

Maria Gaetana Agnesi, *Analytical Institutions*, 1748 (London: Taylor & Wilks, 1801), xviii–xxiv.

THERE are few so unacquainted with Mathematical Learning, but are sensible the Study of Analyticks is very necessary, especially in our days; . . . But, notwithstanding the necessity of this science appears so evident as to excite our youth to the earnest study of it; yet great are the difficulties to be overcome in the attainment of it. For it is very well known, that persons able and willing to teach it are not to be found in every city, at least not in our Italy; . . . This I know by my own experience, as I must ingenuously confess; for, notwithstanding the strong inclination I had to this science, and the great application I made use of to acquire it; I might still have been lost in a maze of inextricable difficulties, had I not been assisted by the secure guidance and sage direction of the very learned Father *Don Ramiro Rampinelli*, . . . now Professor of the Mathematicks in the Royal University of Pavia; to whom I acknowledge myself indebted for what little progress I may possibly have made in this kind of study; . . . True it is, the aforesaid inconvenience may, in some measure, be removed, by having recourse to good books, written with perspicuity, and (what is above all) in a proper method. . . . I am very sensible, that these Institutions of mine may seem, at first sight, to be needless, so many learned Men having thus amply provided for the occasions of the Public. But, as to this point, I desire the candid reader to consider, that, as the Sciences are daily improving . . . many important and useful discoveries have been made by many ingenious writers; . . . Therefore, to save students the trouble of seeking for these improvements, and newly-invented methods, in their several authors, I was persuaded that a new Digest of Analytical Principles might be useful and acceptable. The late discoveries have obliged me to follow a new arrangement of the several parts; and whoever has attempted any thing of this kind must be convinced, how difficult it is to hit upon such a method as shall have a sufficient degree of perspicuity, and simplicity, omitting every thing superfluous, and yet retaining all that is useful and necessary; such, in Short, as shall proceed in that natural order, in which consists the closet connexion, the strongest conviction, and the easiest instruction. This natural order I have always had in view; but whether I have always been so happy as to attain it, must be left to the judgment of others.

In the management of various methods, I think I may venture to say, that I have made some improvements in several of them, which I believe will not be quite devoid of novelty and invention. . . . It was never my design to court applause, being satisfied with having indulged myself in a real and innocent pleasure; and, at the same time, with having endeavoured to be useful to the Public. . . .

To conclude; As it was not my intention, at first, that the following Work should ever appear in public; a work begun and continued in the *Italian* tongue, purely for my own private amusement, or, at most, for the instruction of one of my younger Brothers, who might have a taste for mathematical studies; . . . then I thought I might be excused the trouble of translating it into Latin. . . . Far am I therefore from laying the least claim to any merit arising from that purity and elegance of style, which in subjects of a different nature may be laudably attempted; being fully satisfied if I have always expressed myself, as I sincerely endeavoured, in a plain, but clear and intelligible manner.

1.62 Sweeping the heavens

Memoir and Correspondence of Caroline Herschel, Mary Herschel, ed. (London: J. Murray, 1876), 60–7.

[1786] July 3. – My brothers William and Alex left Slough to begin their journey to Germany. Mrs [Alex.] Herschel was left with me at Slough. By way of not suffering too much by sadness, I began with bustling work. I cleaned all the brass-work for seven and ten-foot telescopes, and put curtains before the shelves to hinder the dust from settling upon them again.

4th. – I cleaned and put the polishing-room in order, and made the gardener clear the work-yard, put everything in safety, and mend the fences.

5th. – I spent the morning in needle-work. In the afternoon went with Mrs. Herschel to Windsor. We chose the hours from two to six for shopping and other business, to be from home at the time most unlikely for any persons to call, but there had been four foreign gentlemen looking at the instruments in the garden, they had not left their names. . . .

12th. – I put paper in press for a register, and calculated for Flamsteed's Catalogue. . . . By July 23rd the whole Catalogue was completed all but writing it in the clear, which at that time was a very necessary provision, . . . Many sweeps nearer the Pole than the register of sweeps, which only began at 45°, being made, it became necessary to provide a register for marking those sweeps and the nebula, discovered in them. . . .

18th. – I spent the whole day in ruling paper for the register; except that at breakfast I cut out ruffles for shirts. Mr. and Mrs. Kelly and Mrs. Ramsden (Dollond's sister) called this evening. I tried to sweep, but it is cloudy, and the moon rises at half-past ten.

19th. – In the evening we swept from eleven till one.

20th. – Prince Charles (Queen's brother) Duke of Saxe-Gotha and the Duke of Montague were here this morning. I had a message from the King to show them the instruments.

I had intended to go on with my Diary till my brother's return, but it would be tedious, . . .

But I had rather copy a few days more, as they contain the discovery of my first comet, and will serve also to show that I attempted to register all discovered nebula, after a precept my brother had left me, as this was necessary for revising the MS. of the catalogue of the first thousand nebulae, which he expected at his return to find ready for correction from the printers.

24th. – I registered some sweeps in present time and Pole distance. Prince Resonico came with Dr. Shepherd to see the instruments. I swept from ten till one. . . .

29th. – I paid the smith. He received to-day the plates for the forty-foot tube. Above half of them are bad, but he thinks there will be as many good among them as will be wanted, . . . I registered sweeps to-day. . . . The rest of the day I wrote in Flamsteed's Catalogue. The storm continued all the day, but now, 8 o'clock, it turns to a gentle rain.

30th. – I wound up the sidereal timepiece, Field's and Alexander's clocks, and made covers for the new and old registers. . . . Mem. – I find I cannot go on fast enough with the registering of sweeps to be serviceable to the Catalogue of Nebula. Therefore I will begin immediately to recalculate them, and hope to finish them before [William's] return.

August, 1. – I have counted one hundred nebulas to-day, and this evening I saw an object which I believe will prove to-morrow night to be a comet.

2nd. – To-day I calculated 150 nebulae. I fear it will not be clear to-night. It has been raining throughout the whole day, but seems now to clear up a little.

1 o'clock. – The object of last night *is a comet.*

3rd. – I did not go to rest till I had wrote to Dr. Blagden and Mr. Aubert to announce the comet. After a few hours' sleep, I went in the afternoon to Dr. Bind, who, with Mr. Cavallo, accompanied me to Slough, with the intention of seeing the comet, but it was cloudy, . . .

August 2, 1786.
Sir [Dr. Blagden], –

In consequence of the friendship which I know to exist between you and my brother, I venture to trouble you, in his absence, with the following imperfect account of a comet: – The employment of writing down the observations when my brother uses the twenty-foot reflector does not often allow me time to look at the heavens, but as he is now on a visit to Germany,

I have taken the opportunity to sweep in the neighbourhood of the sun in search of comets; and last night, the 1st of August, about 10 o'clock, I found an object very much resembling in colour and brightness the 27 nebula of the *Connoissance des Temps*, with the difference, however, of being round. I suspected it to be a comet; but a haziness coming on, it was not possible to satisfy myself as to its motion till this evening. I made several drawings of the stars in the field of view with it, and have enclosed a copy of them, with my observations annexed, that you may compare them together. . . . By the naked eye the comet is between the 54 and 53 Ursæ Majoris and the 14, 15, and 16 Comæ Berenices, and makes an obtuse triangle with them, the vertex of which is turned towards the south. . . . These observations were made with a Newtonian sweeper of 27-inch focal length, and a power of about 20. The field of view is 2° 12′. I cannot find the stars *a* or *c* in any catalogue, but suppose they may easily be traced in the heavens, whence the situation of the comet, as it was last night at 10 h 33′, may be pretty nearly ascertained.

You will do me the favour of communicating these observations to my brother's astronomical friends.

Travelling women

Contrary to the perception that women stayed at home and men travelled, women like Grisell Baillie were experienced and knowledgeable tourists. Not only did she live in exile for a time, she but travelled widely. Writing in hindsight, but obviously relying on detailed notes and diaries, she gives insightful practical and cultural information to her grandsons, Earl Hadinton and Mr Baillie, embarking on the Grand Tour.

1.63 Memorandums on travelling

Household Book of Lady Grisell Baillie, 397–400.

Oxford, March 10th, 1740

Going in to Italy over the Alps

At Francolino we took water to Venice. We hierd two piotte (having 3 chaises in company), for which we payd at the rate of a hunger to each man that rowed. You may go by land but it is excessive bad road and dear. You will be two days going and must take provisions in the boat with you. We coud neither get beds nor any thing to eat the night stopt by the way.

At Venice

Lodge at Monsieur D'Henrys on the great Canall where we were well used and cheap. See the Church and Procuratories of St. Mark. The smal church dedicated to St. Geminiano, which stands at one end of the Place of St. Marks, was built by Sansovino. Mr. Law . . . your countryman is buried there. If

LADY GRISELL BAILLIE
From the Engraving by G. J. Stodart of the Original Painting at Mellerstain.

Figure 1.10 Lady Grisell Baillie, age 69

Mr. Consul Broun be alive who is a worthy honest Scots man send to him and he will do every thing for you when he knows who you are. Your hierd servant will cary you to all the churches worth seeing. In the Church and Convent of St. Giorgio Maggiore are fine paintings by Titian, Tintoret and other masters of the Venetian school, in the refectory is the famous Marriage of Cana by Paul Veronese. There is good paintings in the schools of St. Rocco and St. Marco. The Palaces best worth seeing are Grinani – Maniani – Grassi – Delphino – Pisani – Barberigo. The Doge's Palace and the Courts of Justice are adornd with fine paintings of Titian, Tintoret, Paul Veronese, Bassan, etc. Observe in going into the Palace the statues of Adam and Eve much esteemd. The Arsenal is well worth seeing and the Treasury and Tower of St. Mark. The

Library of St. Mark contains several fine busts, statues and other remains of antiquaty, the roof is finely painted. The Realto, a bridge over the great Canal, is very fine and many fine buildings by Paladio. Eat Serbetti at a house near St. Marks famous for making every thing in Ice the best of any place, it is like a Coffie house.

Venice to Padua

We went by water doun the Brent, hierd a Bercello which is a large boat, for which we payd 48 pauls; it conveniently holds a great many with chaises and baggage, and is a most agreeable way of going, great numbers of fine houses being all along that river.

At Padua

Lodge at the post house, see the Church of St. Guistina, it is one of the finest in the world, was built after a plan of Palladio's, the Convent behind the Church is very pritty, the Libary and Cellers are commonly seen by straingers. The Church of St. Antonio di Padua. The Chappel del Santo. The Bas relief that adorns it is the history of his life and miracls, very fine; the Scuola di St. Antonio is well painted by Titian. See the toun house in which is the Monument of Titus Livius the Roman Historian; see the Garden of Simples and Papafava. It is a large toun once well inhabited and fine Colleges for studying and many students but now quite ruinous and no body there.

Padua to Vicenza

Posts: Padua to Slesega 1; To Vicenza 1. Here you pay 16½ pauls per chaise each post.

   Vicenza, lodge at the post house. The tounhouse is a noble pice of Archetecture. Many of the Palaces within the toun were built by Palladio or Sansovano and are esteemd the best in Italy. The Olimpick Theatre is a noble work of Palladio's. The Triumphal Arch as you go out of toun, the house of Marquis Capra a little way out of toun is well worth seeing, it is cald the Rotunda.

Vicenza to Verona

. . . From Padua quite through the Venetian State there can be no regulation for the price of post horses, they will have what they please, there being no limited order. We some times payd 18½, 16½ and 15 pauls per chaise, and in proportion for a single horse. It being thought dear makes most people go by Voiturino's, but it is a mistake. We endeavourd to agree with those people from Venice to Trent, but found afterwards their demands was realy more then it cost us post: they woud have taken double time with all the inconveniences of rising, etc., that atend traveling that way.

Intermezzo
The Revolutionary era

Rights of women

The Revolutionary era saw a flowering of arguments for rights for women. This volume opened with two, Olympe de Gouges and Mary Wollstonecraft, while others also sprang to defend women – and to challenge them. Condorcet went further than most in claiming women's right to be voters and representatives. Dutchwoman Etta Palm D'Ælders was just one of the outspoken women who claimed rights not only as women but also as citizens to take part in government and in the defence of the Revolution by taking up arms. The third extract represents only one of the many *cahiers,* or grievances, lodged with the new Republican government. Although the author begins by asking for suffrage, other claims are drawn out in her brief but pointed missive. The final two extracts reflect on the reception of Wollstonecraft's work, in Italy, where Elisabeth Camina Turra found common ground with her, and in her obituary by the conservative *Gentleman's Magazine*, which grudgingly gave credit to her abilities, if not her ideas.

1.64 Admitting women to citizenship

Marie-Jean-Antoine-Nicolas Caritat, Marquis de Condorcet, *Sur l'admission des femmes aux droits de Cité*, 1790, trans. Alice Drysdale Vickery (Letchworth: Garden City Press, 1912), 5–7.

. . . have they not all violated the principle of the equality of rights in tranquilly depriving one-half of the human race of the right of taking part in the formation of laws by the exclusion of women from the rights of citizenship? Could there be a stronger proof of the power of habit, even among enlightened men, than to hear invoked the principle of equal rights in favour of perhaps some 300 or 400 men, who had been deprived of it by an absurd prejudice, and forget it when it concerns some 12,000,000 women?

To show that this exclusion is not an act of tyranny, it must be proved either that the natural rights of women are not absolutely the same as those of men, or that women are not capable of exercising these rights.

But the rights of men result simply from the fact that they are rational, sentient beings, susceptible of acquiring ideas of morality, and of reasoning concerning those ideas. Women having, then, the same qualities, have necessarily the same rights. Either no individual of the human species has any true rights, or all have the same; and he or she who votes against the rights of another, whatever may be his or her religion, colour, or sex, has by that fact abjured his own.

It would be difficult to prove that women are incapable of exercising the rights of citizenship. Although liable to become mothers of families, and exposed to other passing indispositions, why may they not exercise rights of which it has never been proposed to deprive those persons who periodically suffer from gout, bronchitis, etc.? . . . It is said that no woman has made any important discovery in science, or has given any proofs of the possession of genius in arts, literature, etc.; but, on the other hand, it is not pretended that the rights of citizenship should be accorded only to men of genius. It is added that no woman has the same extent of knowledge, the same power of reasoning, as certain men; but what results from that? Only this, that with the exception of a limited number of exceptionally enlightened men, equality is absolute between women and the remainder of the men; that this small class apart, inferiority and superiority are equally divided between the two sexes. But since it would be completely absurd to restrict to this superior class the rights of citizenship and the power of being entrusted with public functions, why should women be excluded any more than those men who are inferior to a great number of women? . . .

Women are not governed, it is true, by the reason (and experience) of men; they are governed by their own reason (and experience). . . . Excluded from public affairs, from all those things which are judged of according to rigorous ideas of justice, or according to positive laws, the things with which they are occupied and which are affected by them are precisely those which are regulated by natural feelings of honesty (or, rather, propriety) and of sentiment. It is, then, unjust to allege as an excuse for continuing to refuse to women the enjoyment of all their natural rights motives which have only a kind of reality because women lack the experience which comes from the exercise of these rights.

If reasons such as these are to be admitted against women, it will become necessary to deprive of the rights of citizenship that portion of the people who, devoted to constant labour, can neither acquire knowledge nor exercise their reason; and thus, little by little, only those persons would be permitted to be citizens who had completed a course of legal study. If such principles are admitted, we must, as a natural consequence, renounce the idea of a liberal constitution. . . .

But, it will be said, this change will be contrary to general expediency, because it will take women away from those duties which nature has reserved for them. This objection scarcely appears to me well founded. . . .

They would only be the better fitted to educate their children and to rear men. It is natural that a woman should suckle her infant; that she should watch over its early childhood. Detained in her home by these cares, and less muscular than the man, it is also natural that she should lead a more retired, a more domestic life. . . . This may be a motive for not giving her the preference in an election, but it cannot be a reason for legal exclusion. . . .

I now demand that opponents should condescend to refute these propositions by other methods than by pleasantries and declamations; above all, that they should show me any natural difference between men and women which may legitimately serve as foundation for the deprivation of a right.

1.65 The necessity for women's influence in government

Etta Palm d'Aelders, *Appel aux Françoises sur la régénération des moeurs et nécessité de l'influence des femmes dans un gouvernement libre* (Paris: Cercle Social, 1790), 1–9.

Gentlemen, since you allow me to defend my sex, I begin by seeking indulgence, if my enlightenment and my means do not satisfy the task I have undertaken, and that it does not do justice to the cause, and to you, gentlemen, I ask you to consider that I am a woman, born and raised in a foreign country. If the construction of my sentences is not 'according to the rules' of the French Academy, it is because I have consulted my heart more than the Dictionary of the Academy.

Gentlemen, you have admitted my sex to this patriotic club The Friends of Truth; this is a first step towards justice; the august representatives of this happy nation have just applauded the intrepid courage of the Amazons in one of your departments and have permitted them to raise a corps for the defence of the nation. This is a first shock to the prejudices, which have enveloped our existence; it is a violent blow to the despotism which has been all the more difficult to uproot.

Do not be just by halves, Gentlemen; . . . soon the walls of these proud fortresses which shaped the humiliation and degradation of the French, will collapse with a crash; destroy these same walls of prejudice, perhaps more dangerous, because they are harmful to the general happiness. Justice must be the premier virtue of free men, and justice demands that the laws are common to all beings, like the air and the sun, and yet everywhere, the laws favour men, at the expense of women, because all the power is in your hands. What! Will free men, an enlightened people living in an age of light and philosophy, will they consecrate what has been the abuse of power in an age of ignorance?

Be fair to us, gentlemen, . . . you have given us the difficult challenge of sharing in virtue, and the training of our delicate nature has more deeply engraved your injustice, since instead of supplementing it through education and by laws in our favour, it seems that 'we are formed only for your delight', while it would be so sweet, so easy to associate us with your glory!

The prejudices which surrounded our sex relied on unjust laws which only accord us a secondary existence in society and often force us into the humiliating necessity of winning over the ferocious or cantankerous character of a man, who, by the greed of those close to us has become our master, [those prejudices] have changed for us the sweetest and the most sacred duties as wife and mother, into a painful and horrible slavery. . . .

Oh! What could be more unjust! Our life, our freedom, our wealth are not ours; leaving childhood, delivered to a despot whom often the heart rejects, the most beautiful days of our lives pass in groans and tears, while our fortune falls prey to fraud and debauchery.

Oh! do we not daily see abiding citizens, family men, trained in the stinking sewers. . ., drunk with wine and debauchery, who forget that they are husbands and fathers, and who sacrifice burnt offerings on the altar infamy, the tears of a virtuous wife, property and the lives of those who need them . . . insensible, but delicate and virtuous.

Oh! Gentlemen, if you wish us to be enthusiastic about the happy constitution that renders men their rights, begin therefore by being just toward us; now that we are your voluntary companions and not your slaves? Let us merit your attachment! Do you think that the success we desire is less appropriate to us, that our reputation is less dear to us than to you? And if devotion to study, if patriotic zeal, if virtue itself, which rests so often on love of glory, is as natural to us as to you, why do you not give us the same education and the same means to acquire them?

Yes, gentlemen, nature has created us to be the companion of your work and your glory. . . . she made us your equal in moral strength, and possibly your superiors by the vivacity of our imagination, delicacy of sentiment, by our resignation in reverses, our strength in pain, patience in suffering, finally generosity of spirit and patriotic zeal, and if these natural qualities were strengthened by a careful education, by encouraging your approval, by public rewards, I am not afraid to say our sex often would surpass yours. . .

The French citizenesses, your wives, your sisters and your mothers, gentlemen, have they not given the world a sublime example of patriotism, courage and civic virtues? Were they not eager to sacrifice their jewellery for the need of the country? And this heroic ardour with which their delicate hands have shared your heavy work in the field of the confederation, you have used them in your efforts to form the altar of the nation, which received the oath that consolidates this freedom, this equality, happiness, no longer only a band of brothers.

Yes, gentlemen, it is [women] that drive your daily courage to persevere and relentlessly fight the enemies of your freedom. It is they who endow the soul of your dear children, and who gathered these words on the lips of the dying victim of the nation: Live free or die.

1.66 Cahiers, grievances and complaints of women by Mme. B. B.

Charles-Louis Chassin, ed., *Le génie de la révolution. Les cahiers de 1789* (Paris: Pagnerre, 1863), 477–8.

In the lower classes, one believes that good women spin, sew and take care of the household. In the upper classes, we imagine they are good at singing, dancing, making music, playing and smiling. However it is work for them, as men work in the fields, in commerce, etc.; and we have seen several take the reins of government as well as and better than men. – The people are recovering their rights, we speak of enfranchising negroes, why not also enfranchise women? – In some provinces, like Normandy, sisters are partly excluded from inheritance, which benefits only their brothers: they come together to recover their equality in the family that they possess from nature! . . . Restore peace and mutual trust between the two sexes! – But it is especially important to change the rules of girls' education: 'we are raised more as if we were destined for the pleasures of the seraglio. . . . Do not deprive us of the knowledge that can put us in a position to help you either by our advice, or by our work, . . . and if you are removed by a natural or premature death, you leave us in charge of the support and education of your children.' –The author, who began by asking for the admission of women to the Estates-General, insists only on the reform of education, the abolition of prejudice that enslaves us and the injustice which remains for the most part with paternal inheritance.

1.67 The view from Italy

Elisabetta Caminer Turra, *Selected Writings of an Eighteenth-Century Venetian Woman of Letters*, Catherine Sama, ed. (Chicago: University of Chicago Press, 2003), 188–9.

Nuovo giornale enciclopedico d'Italia, October 1792, 125–6.
    On the Vindication of the Rights of Woman
    This woman is the champion of her sex. But what will she gain? Revolutions are not so easy or frequent in all genres.
    In his national education project the bishop of Autun focused almost entirely on men, and, in accordance with the gentility that is typical of such men, he almost completely neglected that which pertains to women. Chastising him for this, the author of the work we are announcing is attempting to make up for his omission by extensively addressing everything that concerns her sex, which she is trying to bring up out of the void in which some would leave it. It is true that in Europe educated women are praised and adored, and they have a tremendous and perhaps the principal influence in the most serious of matters: but at what price? All their power depends upon youth and beauty, rather than stemming from that distributive justice which should base their

power on a better education, on the development of their intellectual abilities, on the cultivation of their reason, and on the knowledge of their own purpose and their own duties. This is the source from which Madame Wollstonecraft would like female power to spring, and this is the system on which her book turns. Her book proves for the millionth time that women might deserve the honour of being considered part of the human race.

1.68 Wollstonecraft's obituary

'Obituary of Remarkable Persons; with Biographical Anecdotes', *Gentleman's Magazine* (October, 1797), 894.

In childbed, Mrs. Godwin, wife of Mr. Wm. G. of Somers-town; a woman of uncommon talents and considerable knowledge, and well known throughout Europe by her literary works, under her original name of Wollstoncroft [*sic*], and particularly by her 'Vindication of the Rights of Women, 1792' . . . Her first publication was 'Thoughts on the Education of Daughters, with Reflections on Female Conduct in the more important Duties of Life, 1787,' . . . 'The Rights of Man, 1791,' . . . against Mr Burke on the French Revolution, of the rise and progress of which she gave an 'Historical and Moral View' in 1794, . . . 'Elements of Morality for the Use of Children, . . . 1791,' . . . 'A Vindication of the Rights of Woman, with Strictures on moral and political Subjects, 1792,' . . . 'Letters written during a short Residence in Sweden, Norway, and Denmark, 1796,' . . . Her manners were gentle, easy, and elegant; her conversation intelligent and amusing, without the least trait of literary pride, or the apparent consciousness of powers above the level of her sex; and, for soundness of understanding, and sensibility of heart, she was, perhaps, never equalled. Her practical skill in education was even superior to her speculations upon that subject; nor is it possible to express the misfortune sustained, in that respect, by her children. This tribute we readily pay to her character, however adverse we may be to the system she supported in politicks and morals, both by her writings and practice.

Reflections on revolution

Women were active revolutionaries and took to the stage in great numbers. They also were victims. In this section, women reflect on how revolutions and violence had a local and personal impact. Mary Leadbeater describes the impact of the Irish rebellion of 1798 on her rural community, capturing the confusion and fear this engendered. The final three are testaments by women who lost their heads – literally – in the French Revolution, dying between 16 October and 8 November 1793. The section begins with the last to die, Manon Roland, who wrote her memoirs in prison. A supporter of the Revolution and an influential member of the Girondist faction, as the Revolution turned to Terror she and her husband lost favour, and were purged as part of Robespierre's attack on the moderates. Marie Antoinette was tried for being Queen, but the charges focused on her Austrian connections and amounted to an attempt to make her appear depraved and scheming. Treated far less deferentially than her husband, she was conveyed to her death like a common criminal. In her last letter, to her sister-in-law, she shows the dignity with which she met her attackers in court. Olympe de Gouges, like Roland a supporter of the Revolution, also fell foul of the Terror. In this letter to her son, she describes the court and treatment of her case. Like Roland's, her dismay about the direction the Revolution took is palpable.

1.69 Rebellion in Ireland, 1798

Mary Shackleton Leadbeater, *The Leadbeater Papers*, 2nd ed. (London: 1862), 252–7.

THAT pretty cottage built by poor Dr. Johnson, to which he had brought his bride, was now a blackened ruin. Many families sheltered themselves under hedges, or wherever they could thrust their heads; and some poor women brought forth their babes under these sorrowful circumstances. Yet the houseless wretches expressed thankfulness that their lives were spared, . . . Great was the terror in which the army were held. A soldier was an unwelcome sight, unconscious that the time was not far distant when they should be most welcome. And this dread was not without cause; we frequently saw the blaze of burning houses on the surrounding hills, and several men were shot by the military when going about their lawful business, so that people were afraid to cut their turf, save their hay and corn, or even to sleep in their own abodes.

When the corn had shot into ear, three months after her poor husband's death, Dolly Finn went to her little farm to look at her crop. She was alone; she entered among the black walls of her ruined cottage; her heart was oppressed with horror and grief, and she vented her anguish in tears and groans of despair, lamenting her deplorable condition. A soldier was passing at the time; he heard the sound of sorrow, and through the aperture which had once been a window he saw a lovely woman, whose appearance inspired his depraved heart with sentiments very different from compassion. He alighted from his horse . . . and then attempted to seize her. She ran out of the walls, shrieking, believing his intent was to render her still more wretched; he followed, and compelled her to walk beside him. The trembling widow looked around and cried aloud for succour, in vain; the highroad was now solitary, war and terror had depopulated it. Some persons who had taken shelter in a deserted stable at length came out, when her enemy immediately assuming the character of a friend advised her not to frequent those ruins again, and departed. Her alarm was such that for a long time she feared to walk anywhere alone, and her fancy pictured every furzebush to be a soldier! . . .

When we went to the monthly meeting of Carlow we saw marks of dismay on all sides, especially in the pale and immoveable countenances of two women sitting before an open window. . . . The state of the times engrossed all conversation, till we longed to shut our ears from hearing of blood; and we scarcely dared to utter humane sentiments, the tide ran so strongly against those who had put the inhabitants in such jeopardy. All our friends rejoiced over us, as beings delivered from the jaws of danger and of death. We hastened back to Ballitore, where, once more, all wore the appearance of peace and security; . . . But all sensations of cheerfulness had fled, and our spirits wore a covering of sadness which forbade our enjoyment of the beauties of Nature. . . .

John Jeffers of Narraghmore, returning from Kilcullen to Athy, was waylaid near the ruins of his own house, which had been burned by the insurgents, and shot dead. His mother-in-law was within hearing of the shot; she got assistance to take away the body, and although most probably in the midst of enemies, was treated with kindness and compassion. . . . Most of our neighbours who had been prisoners at Naas, now returned and came joyfully to see us. They had been acquitted after a confinement of nine weeks. One, however, still remained behind. I was requested to write to Captain Chenery on his behalf; I did so, and the captain sent my note into the court, where it was to be decided whether Pat Lyons should remain a prisoner or return home a free man. When it was perceived that the note came from a female, it was treated with contempt; 'Women did not care what they said, and it was from a woman.' On further inspection they observed the date; 'Quakers tell truth, and it was from a Quaker' – and accordingly Pat was liberated. . . .

Mourning was the language – mourning was the dress of the country.

1.70 Manon Roland reflects

Manon Roland, *The Private Memoirs of Madame Roland*, 1793, Edward Gilpin Johnson, ed. (Chicago: AC McClurg, 1901), 35–9, 105–7, 208–9.

Prison of Sainte Pelagie,
Aug. 9, 1793

THE daughter of an artist, the wife of a man of letters (who, become a minister, remained an honest man), now a prisoner, destined perhaps to a violent and unexpected death, I have known both happiness and adversity, I have seen glory at hand, and I have experienced injustice. . . . My station has created me enemies; personally I have had none; by those who have spoken the most ill of me I have never been seen. . . .

August 28

I FEEL my resolution to pursue these Memoirs deserting me. The miseries of my country torment me; the loss of my friends unnerves me; an involuntary gloom penetrates my soul and chills my imagination. France is become a vast Golgotha of carnage, an arena of horrors, where her children tear and destroy each other.

The enemy, favoured by civil strife, advances in every quarter; the cities of the North fall into their power; . . . the rebels of la Vendee continue to lay waste a large extent of territory; the Lyonnese, wantonly provoked, have burst into open resistance; Marseilles flies to their Succour; the disorder spreads to the neighbouring Departments; . . . Our government is a species of monster, whose form is as odious as its appetites are depraved; it destroys whatever it touches, and devours even itself. . . .

The armies, ill conducted, and worse provided, alternately fly like cowards, and fight with the courage of despair. The ablest commanders are accused of treason, because certain Representatives, ignorant of war, blame what they do not comprehend, and brand as aristocrats all who are more enlightened than themselves. A legislative body, characterized by debility from the moment of its existence, presented us at first with lively debates, as long as it possessed sufficient penetration to foresee the national dangers, and courage to announce them. The just and generous spirits, who aspired to the welfare of their country and dared attempt to establish it, denounced audaciously under the most odious colours and in forms the most contradictory, have been at last sacrificed by ignorance and fear to intrigue and peculation. Chased from a body of which they were formed to be the soul, they left behind them an inane and corrupt minority, who have united the oppression of despotism with the license of anarchy, and whose follies and crimes dig their own tomb, while they are consummating the public ruin.

. . . but, at least the revolutions of fortune shall not find me unprepared. Such were my reflections in October, 1792, when Danton sought by magnifying me to belittle my husband, and was silently preparing the calumnies by which he meant to assail us both. I was ignorant of his proceedings, but I had observed the course of things in revolutions. I was ambitious only to preserve my soul pure, and to see the glory of my husband equally unsullied. I well knew that this kind of ambition rarely leads to other species of success. My wish is accomplished: Roland, persecuted and proscribed, will not wholly die to posterity. I am a captive, and shall probably fall a victim; but my conscience requites me for all. . . . I wished but for the peace of the righteous, and I also shall have some existence in future generations.

1.71 Widow Capet, her last letter

'Dernière Lettre de Marie Antoinette à Madame Elisabeth', 1793, in M Émile Campardon, ed., *Marie Antoinette à la Conciergerie* (Paris: Chez Jules Gay, 1863), 125–8.

It is to you, my sister [in-law], that I write for the last time. I have just been condemned – not to a shameful death, for that is only for the criminal – but to rejoin your brother; innocent, like him. I hope to show the same firmness as he did in his last moments. I am calm, as one is when the conscience reproaches nothing. I feel a profound regret at abandoning my poor children: you know that I existed only for them and you, my good and tender sister. You who have in your friendship sacrificed everything to be with us, in what a position I leave you! I learnt in the course of the trial that my daughter was separated from you. Alas! the poor child: I dare not write to her – she would not receive my letter. I do not know whether even this will reach you. . . .

Let my son never forget the last words of his father, which I expressly repeat, – that he is never to seek to avenge our death. . . .

I die in the catholic, apostolic and Roman religion, of my fathers, in which I was brought up and which I have always professed. I have no spiritual guide in attendance, not even knowing whether there still exists in Paris any priest of that religion. I ask pardon of God for all the faults that I might have committed while I lived. . . . I ask pardon of all those I know, and of you, my sister, in particular, for all the sorrow, which, without intending it, I may have caused them. I pardon all my enemies the evil they have done me. In conclusion, think ever of me. I embrace you with all my heart, as well as those poor and dear children. My God! how heartrending it is to leave them for ever!

Adieu! adieu!

1.72 Olympe de Gouges to her son

1793, *Archives Nationales*, Dossier 21.

To Citizen Degouges, Officer General in the armies of the Rhine
I die, my dear son, a victim of my idolatry for the country and for the people. Their enemies, under the specious mask of republicanism, led me certainly to the scaffold. . . .

Could I believe that the tigers would become mad judges themselves against the law, against the same public that soon joined their blame by my death? From the moment of this act, the law gave me the right to see my supporters and all the people I know. . . . The law also gave me the right to choose my jury: I signified the list at midnight and the next day at seven o'clock I was sent down to the court sick and weak and without the art of speaking in public. I asked for the advocate that I had chosen. I was told that . . . he would not be responsible for my cause. I asked for another in his absence, I was told that since I have enough pride to defend my friends, I had probably had enough left over to defend my innocence. . .

You know the benefits of services I have rendered to the people. Twenty times I made my tormentors turn pale, not knowing what to reply to each sentence that marked my innocence against [their] bad faith.

I die my son, my dear son, I am dying helplessly. It violated all the laws for the most virtuous woman of the century. . . . Remember my teaching. . . .

Olympe Degouges

Farewell, my son, I will not be alive when you receive this letter. Repair injustice that has been done to your mother.

Part II

Domesticity and industrialism

Prelude
Legacy of the Enlightenment

Enlightenment ideas led to an ambivalent view of women, contributing to a vision of the ideal wife and mother, while also validating the idea of female education and improvement. If many women's lives remained largely unchanged because of the need to work for a living, for the middle classes and increasingly the educated working classes, a greater ideal of legal equality became fundamental to the debate on the 'woman question'. The women's movement spoke to a number of interrelated causes, building a case for legal rights, for education and ultimately for political rights.

The voices that open this this part addressed two of these key areas. Caroline Norton's carefully argued case for the right of mothers to have access to their children was a *cause célèbre* and one of the first direct challenges to male authority. Though Norton believed in male superiority, she also thought it was unnatural that mothers could be denied access to their children or that the law had no power to take into consideration the circumstances. Her attack is usually credited with the success of the Custody of Infants Act, 1839, which permitted a mother to petition for custody of her children up to the age of seven, and for access in respect of older children.

Fredrika Bremer's novel, *Hertha*, explicitly tackled the rights of single women who remained under fathers' 'protection' long after they had reached the age of 'maturity'. Addressing legal minority in Sweden, her arguments had resonance across most of Europe. The novel sharply demonstrated the restrictions on education and choice of lifestyle faced by many young women. Her main characters had inherited from their mother, but, under their father's guardianship, despite being aged 27 and 29, they had no access to this money and to the choices it might offer them. This semi-autobiographical novel has been credited with influencing Swedish legal changes in women's rights, and the largest Swedish women's organisation adopted the eponymous title.

2.1 Custody of infants

Caroline Norton, *The Separation of Mother and Child by the Law of 'Custody of infants' Considered* (London: Roake and Varty, 1838), 1–3, 6–9.

The law which regulates the Custody of Infant Children, being now under the consideration of the legislature, it is very desirable that the attention of the public and of Members of Parliament in particular, should be drawn towards a subject, upon which so much misconception and ignorance prevails.

It is a common error to suppose that every mother has a *right* to the custody of her child till it attain the age of seven years. By a curious anomaly in law, the mother of a *bastard child* HAS *this right*, while the mothers of legitimate children are excluded from it. . . .

The custody of legitimate children is held to be the right of the Father *from the hour of their birth*: to the utter exclusion of the Mother, whose separate claim has no legal existence, and is not recognised by the Courts. No circumstance can modify or alter this admitted right of the father: though he should be living in open adultery, and his wife be legally separated from him on that account. He is responsible to no one for his motives, should he desire entirely to exclude his wife from all access to her children; nor is he accountable for the disposal of the child; that is, the law supposing the *nominal* custody to be with him, does not oblige him to make it a *bona fide* custody by a residence of the child under his roof and protection, but holds 'the custody of the father' to mean, in an extended sense, the custody of whatever stranger the father may think fit to appoint in lieu of the mother; and those strangers can exert his delegated authority to exclude the mother from access to her children; without any legal remedy being possible on her part, by appeal to the Courts or otherwise; the construction of the law being, that they have *no power to interfere* with the exercise of the father's right.

Should it so happen that at the time of separation, or afterwards, the children being in the mother's possession, she should refuse to deliver them up, the father's right extends to forcibly seizing them; *even should they be infants at the breast*. Or he may obtain, on application, a writ of habeas corpus, ordering the mother to produce the child in Court, to be delivered over to him; and should this order be disobeyed, he can cause a writ of attachment to issue against her; or, in other words, cause her to be imprisoned for contempt of court. The fact of the wife being innocent and the husband guilty, or of the separation being an unwilling one on her part, does not alter his claim: the law has no power to order that a woman shall even have occasional access to her children, though she could prove that she was driven by violence from her husband's house, and that he had deserted her for a mistress. The Father's right is absolute and paramount, and can no more be affected by the mother's claim, than if she had no existence.

The result of this tacit admission by law, of an individual right so entirely despotic . . . is exactly what might have been expected. Instances have arisen from time to time in which the power has been grossly and savagely abused. It has been made the means of persecution, and the instrument of vengeance: it has been exerted to compel a disposition of property in favour of the husband, where the wife has possessed an independent fortune: it has been put into force by an adulterous husband to terrify his wife from proceeding in the Ecclesiastical Courts against him: in short, there is scarcely any degree of cruelty which has not been practised under colour of its protection. . . .

We are told that the difficulty is to meet every individual instance of alleged hardship, and to enter into private complaints and family disputes, as must necessarily be the case if the Court is called upon to decide the right of access of the mother, against the inclination of the father. But it is notorious that both the Court of King's Bench and the Court of Chancery do ALREADY assume to themselves the power of meeting and deciding on individual cases. They will interfere, as aforesaid, for the security of property, and on account of religious, or even political opinions; and have established a rule that *at a specified age*, namely, 14 years, a child cannot be forced back to the custody of its father, *if the child himself be unwilling to return.* . . .

It can neither be said that a new principle of litigation is sought to be established; nor a new principle of interference with the common law right of the father. The only new principle sought to be established is, that *whereas hitherto the Courts have refused to consider the suffering and wrong done in very many instances to the mother,* . . . some recognition and acknowledgment may *now* be made of the mother's separate existence, and right to protection.

On what principle of *natural* justice the law is founded, which in cases of separation between husband and wife, throws the whole power of limiting the access of a woman to her children into the hands of her husband, it is difficult to say. A man should hardly be allowed to be accuser and judge in his own case, and yet such is the anomalous position created by the law. Whatever be the *cause* of separation, whether incompatibility of temper, or imputation of graver offence, the feelings on both sides must be very bitter, bitter almost to desperation, before the parties can consent to publish their quarrel to the world, and break through ties voluntarily formed, and cemented by holy vows. The husband who contemplates such a separation, is certainly angry, probably mortified, and in nine cases out of ten, *eager to avenge* his real or fancied injuries. To this angry man, to this mortified man, the law awards that which can rarely be entrusted to any human being, even in the calmest hours of life, namely, DESPOTIC POWER! Surely it requires no eloquence to move, no argument to convince, in a case like this. There stands the one man in the world who is least likely to be *able* to judge his wife with the smallest particle of fairness or temperate feeling, and HE is the man to whom the *real* judges of the land yield their right of protection, their intelligence of decision, – their merciful consideration of individual wrong, – and their consistency in securing, under all circumstances, PUBLIC JUSTICE. To *him* it is permitted to make the power of their Courts a MOCKERY, and (in homely but expressive terms) to 'take the law into his own hands.'

2.2 Legal minority

Fredrika Bremer, *Hertha, eller en själs historia,* trans. Mary Howitt (London: Arthur Hall, Virtue & Co., 1856), 65–73.

'Alma, my Alma! Sister, dear sister!' And burning tears wetted the hand which she, with inexpressible love, laid upon her face. . . . 'I am afraid that you are going away – away from me, my Alma! . . . when you are gone – you, my good angel! I shall become stern and full of hatred, because both God and man are alike unjust and severe.' . . .

'My sweet Hertha, do not talk so! There is so very much which we are not able to understand.'

'There is, however, a great deal which we do understand, Alma! – a great deal which our conscience tells us, and which stands written there in ineffaceable characters, . . . I have held my peace so long, I have left unspoken so much that stirs my whole being, Alma! . . . when I think that it is our father's fault that you are lying here heart-broken; that you might have been the happy wife of the man who loved you if our father's obstinacy and covetousness had not separated you! . . . oh, Alma, sweet Alma! I feel that I shall hate him!'

'Do not hate him. Pity him rather. Believe me, he is not happy. He has not always been as he is now . . .'

'But he is also unjust and severe! Had he given us our right, then you would not have been as you now are. Why does he withhold from us our mother's property? Why does he render us no account of what we possess, or of what we ought to have?'

'We have, in fact, no right to desire it. We are, according to the laws of our country, still minors, and he is our lawful guardian.'

'And we shall always continue to be minors, if we do not go to law with our father, because it is his will that we should ever be dependant [*sic*] upon him, and the laws of our country forbid us to act as if we were rational, independent beings! Look Alma, it is this injustice towards us, as women, which provokes me, not merely with my father, but with the men who make these my country's unjust laws, and with all who contrary to reason and justice maintain them, and in so doing continue to keep us in our fettered condition. We have property which we inherit from our mother; yet can we not dispose of one single farthing of it. We are old enough to know what we desire, and to be able to take care of ourselves and others, yet at the same time we are kept as children under our father and guardian, because he chooses to consider us as such, and to treat us as such. We are prohibited every action, every thought which would tend to independent activity or the opening of a future for ourselves, because our father and guardian says that we are minors, that we are children, and the law says 'it is his right; you have nothing to say!''

'Yes,' said Alma, 'It is unjust, and harder than people think. But, nevertheless, our father means well by us; and manages our property justly and prudently with regard to our best interests.'

'And who will be the better for it? We? When we are old and stupid, and no more good for anything! See, I shall soon be twenty-seven, you are twenty-nine already, and for what have we lived?'

Alma made no reply, and Hertha continued: 'If we had even been able to learn anything thoroughly, and had had the liberty to put forth our powers, as young men have, I would not complain. Is it not extraordinary, Alma, that people always ask boys what they would like to be, what they have a fancy or taste for, and then give them the opportunity to learn, and to develop themselves according to the best of their minds, but they never do so with girls! They cannot even think or choose for themselves a profession or way of life. Ah, I would so gladly have lived upon bread and water, and been superlatively happy, if I might but have studied as young men study at the universities, have had freedom, and by my own efforts have made my own way. The arts, the sciences, – oh, how happy are men who are able to study them; . . . How glorious to live and labour day by day, for that which makes the world better, more beautiful, lighter. How happy should one feel, how good, how mild; how different that life must be to what it is, where there seems to be no other question in the world but, 'What shall we eat and drink, and what shall we put on?' and where all life's solicitude seems to resolve itself into this. Oh, Alma, are we not born into this world for something else? How wretched!' and as if overwhelmed by the thought, Hertha buried her face in her hands. Presently she became calmer, and continued,

'. . . [Men] are allowed each one to grow according to his bent and his nature, and to become that which the Creator has called them to be; but woman, precisely they who should improve every power to the utmost, they must become unnatural, thoughtless, submissive tools of that lot to which men have destined them. They must all be cast in one mould and follow one line, which is chalked out for them as if they had no souls of their own to show them the way, and to give them an individual bent. And yet how different are the gifts and the dispositions of woman; what a difference there is, for instance, among us sisters, all children of the same parents. . . . – ah, I do not know, I cannot tell what I was created to become. I yet seek for myself; but if I had been able to develop myself in freedom, if the hunger and the thirst which I felt within me had been satisfied, then I might perhaps have become something more than ordinarily good and beneficial to my fellow-creatures. Because, though it may be bold to say or to think it, I know that I might have been able to acquire the good gifts of life in order to impart them to the many; I would liberate the captive and make the oppressed soul happy; I would work, and live, and die for humanity. Other objects are for me too trivial. There was a time when I believed what people and books said about home and domestic life, as woman's only object and world; when I thought that it was a duty to crush all desires after a larger horizon, or any other sphere of action; weak, stupid thoughts those, which I have long since cast behind me! My inward eye has become clearer, my own feelings and thoughts have become too powerful for me, and I can no longer, as formerly, judge myself by others. . . . Marriage is to me a secondary thing, nay, a wretched thing, if it do not tend to a higher human development in the service of light and freedom. That which I seek for and which I desire is a life, a sphere of labour, which makes me feel that I live fully, not merely for myself, but for the whole community, for my country, my people, for humanity, for God, yes, for God! if he be the God of justice and goodness – . . . never will I submit, never will I cease to maintain that [woman] has been created for something better, something more; yes, if she were able fairly and fully to develop all the noble powers which the Creator has given her, then she would make the world happier. Oh! that I could live and labour for the emancipation of these captive, struggling souls, these souls which are yearning after life and light; with what joy should I live, with what gladness should I then die, yes, even if to die were to cease for ever! I should then, nevertheless, have lived immortally!'

4   Intimate worlds
Self, sex and family

Educating women

By the early nineteenth century the tone of the debate about girls' upbringing had shifted. Enlightenment ideas that valorised the domestic female featured, but a strong critique of 'useless' education reflected a growing sense that females should have access to useful education. Karoline Milde claims the right of women to act rather than be passive, to employ their wits and abilities in an intelligent manner. The critique of accomplishments was alive and well, as Finn Minna Canth attests, couching her disapproval in the context of women's responsibilities as wives and mothers. Emily Faithful's comments on public education for French girls show that education was more widely accepted, if only through voluntary efforts. The tension with church-provided education is apparent. Céléstine Hippeau takes this further, arguing, through her idealised comparison with the United States, that funding should be provided through taxes and thus quality education for girls be safeguarded. The other tension, made explicit by Swede Laura Fitinghoff, was with home education. She was wary of practical subjects being taught at school, arguing that homes could do it better. Spaniard Emilia Pardo Bazán draws a comparison with men's education, arguing that the principles underlying education for the two sexes was fundamentally different, so that an intensive education was seen as making women unfit for their natural role while for men that same education was a badge of honour. Emily Davies, champion of higher education in Britain, challenges the idea that she and others wished to make women's education identical to men's while arguing their right to be tested in an academic world.

2.3 Think, judge and act

Karoline Milde, *Der deutschen Jungfrau, Wesen und Wirken* (Leipzig, 1890), 11–15.

From clear thinking comes useful action, and both must relieve each other in life like breathing in and out, one without the other is impossible. The woman is in her sphere, just like the man, answerable to her words, as well as her actions. Both must be able to give account of this, they should think logically and consequently act.

In general the man is more guided by his intellect and his judgment, the woman follows her heart, her feelings more.

. . . And indeed there are also females with a capacity to make quick decisions that are immediately executed. Shy and withdrawn as they may be on quiet days, they come across with a wonderful strength of spirit in difficult times, and a certain security of opinion when it comes to finding the true solution. Not losing her head or behaving in despair, but calmly and bravely facing the emergency, these are properties that are not actually unfeminine.

Presence of mind is indeed an invaluable virtue in women, which may be of utmost importance and of highest blessing! How often you have the opportunity to observe the strength of such women who have been dealt the most devastating blows of fate!

Accidents, such as loss of assets, that break the spirit of men, just seem to awake the willpower of the weak sex and boost their character, sometimes bordering on magnificence and greatness. Nothing is more touching than to see a delicate feminine being, who at first appears quite weak and dependent, suddenly rise to full fortitude and to comfort her family by making any sacrifice to overcome misfortune.

The noble Duchess Louise of Saxe-Weimar stepped in after the battle of Jena in front of the proud, arrogant conqueror Napoleon with so much female dignity and honour, that she managed to calm his anger against her husband Karl August and to rescue the independence of the country. . . .

Through desperation, reckless courage awoke in a Scottish mother, whose child . . . was snatched by a golden eagle while it was sleeping in a basket and lifted into the air to a nest on a rough cliff. Male bystanders were paralysed with fear and even the mad cries of the woman could not make them move. Thus the despair of the weak woman lent her wings, and with these she flew up dizzying heights and with almost supernatural strength managed to snatch the prey of the predator back, and carry down the still-alive child in her arms.

2.4 Educating women

Minna Canth, 'Education of Our Daughters', *Keski-Suomi* (1874), 18.

Where can we find institutions of education, which will provide our growing daughters sufficient knowledge to guide their lives, so that in the future they can meet their duties with the strength of noble spirit, understanding and skill? After searching in vain, we must acknowledge: there are none in the whole Grand Duchy of Finland. If you have means, send her to Switzerland, if not, you must with sorrow leave her to the mercies of the world with a very shallow education. Before our times, a wife's understanding was even less developed. If she learned to read her catechism by heart and used a little bit of writing – that was enough education for her! . . . an active mistress, great cook and skilful with handicrafts . . . she was perfectly suitable. . . . In modern times even the wife's mind longs for more knowledge. She wants to shake off her chains and demands mental development. . . . Unfortunately this happened at a time when a grand and hypocritical Parisian education ruled the world. Our schools for girls were formed after this manner and even in homes, education was organized this way. In schools, foreign languages were the main subject. Subjects like religion, natural sciences, physical sciences, history, etc. are taught with unbelievable negligence and superficiality. Anatomy and pedagogy that would be essential for a wife are totally forgotten. . . . In short: in our times the education of daughters both at home and at school means basically brilliant wisdom for the parlour and frivolous social life. . . . What good harvest this superficiality produced for the people of France I will not go into, but we know that for the poor daughter of Finland it won't do. She must be prepared to become an active mistress, who with great skill and intelligence takes care of the household and organises it properly. She leads her servants with patience and treats them kindly. She must prepare herself to become a wife, who can raise herself to the level of her husband and she will be respected for her purity of heart and nobleness of her mind. She must prepare herself to become a mother, who not only takes care of her children with patience and skill but also looks after their education.

2.5 Public education

Emily Faithful, 'Female Education in France', *Victoria Magazine*, 11 (May–October 1868), 80–81.

On the 30th of October, 1867, M. Duruy, the Minister of Public Instruction, issued a circular letter, in which he pointed out that the utter inadequacy of the provision made for the secondary instruction of girls left a gap much to be regretted in the French system of education; whilst for boys, when they quitted the primary schools, colleges, lyceums, schools of technical instruction, free schools of every description were all provided, for girls nothing whatever had been done. M. Duruy appears to have arrived at a lively apprehension of the truth, which has already dawned upon the minds of not a few intelligent Englishmen, that the women of any nation constitute a good half of that nation, and that to leave them stationary in the midst of so much progress, dark in the midst of so much light, is a course as much opposed to the enlightened self-interest of men, as it is to all generosity and right feeling. M. Duruy did not satisfy himself with pointing out the necessity of a better education for girls, but showed to some extent the way in which it might be secured, and by inducing the municipal administrations to furnish suitable accommodation for students, and the university establishments to supply the teaching staff, has at least provided for the working-out of a valuable experiment, to the results of which we shall look with the greatest interest. If the experiment is thought to succeed, it is understood that the Government may draw up an official programme. The associations are voluntary bodies – just as much so as our own associations for a somewhat similar purpose here in the North of England, and will display probably the energy and elasticity, perhaps also the fitfulness and want of method, characteristic of voluntaryism. . . . If unsuccessful, the experiment can be abandoned without shame or loss to anyone – if successful, the way is prepared for schemes of a yet larger scope.

2.6 Drawing on the United States

Célestin Hippeau, 'L'éducation des femmes et des affranchis en Amérique', *Revue des deux mondes*, 93 (1869), 450–3.

What gives the organisation of public schools in the United States a special character is the necessity, highly recognised and proclaimed from the outset, to ensure the broadest and most liberal education for a people called to settle its own destiny without making any difference between the sexes.

On this point, no doubt has ever arisen, the question of whether it is right to raise the intellectual level of the class which fate has placed at the lower levels of society has never been seriously raised; . . . It was the people themselves who provided the funds needed to build these schools, for the purchase of furniture for classes, and for teachers' salaries. Taxes have never obtained a more unanimous consent. . . . It is a maxim generally adopted, that every citizen should serve [the] country and the country must in turn provide its children with the means to acquire the greatest amount of skill. . . .

Freely open to all boys and girls from five to eighteen years, these public schools (common schools, free schools) embrace our primary education at all levels . . . and much of the teaching of our colleges and our schools. . . . One who has travelled the full circle of these studies is thus in possession of a large and comprehensive professional education, and is sufficiently prepared, if he aspires to professional and scholarly teaching at colleges and universities. . . .

In America, the impolitic distribution of knowledge is unknown that for so long has been regarded in France and in other countries as a kind of social need, giving the poor and rural residents often very limited basic education, and reserving secondary and higher education for those favoured by fortune.

. . . The very liberal spirit in which the system for public education was designed intended that studies should be intelligent and informative, since the most basic levels to the highest were common to young men and girls, most often taught in the same establishments, and finally after the years just passed [the Civil War], to establish schools for negroes; nobody thought to restrict the teaching and circumscribe it within narrow limits. The participation of girls in higher education, the generous impulse that brought the people of the United States to improvise in a few years a vast system of education for freed Negroes . . . we thought was worthy of being treated at some length.

While in England, France and in several states of Europe, we call into question the right of women to higher education, we are going to deny them sufficient intelligence for Scientific Studies, . . . The United States, has used experience to provide the basis for all theories, and did not begin by asking what could be the consequences for family and society of an extension of the education of women; they have opened all schools; they wanted that they should not remain foreign to any of the branches of education. The wonderful results they have obtained are the best answer that can conquer the objections that arise wherever the issue of intellectual emancipation of women is not yet out of the field of discussion.

2.7 Tension with home education

Laura Fitinghoff, 'About the home and the school', *IDUN; praktisk Veckotidning för Kvinnan och Hemmet,* 2 (178), 15 May 1891.

Nowadays families often ask: What will she, the daughter, become – as what will he, the son, become?

More and more the wise opinion is that even girls should be able to follow their vocation and *'become something'* making their voice heard – and how would one succeed in this if not by seeking education 'from outside'.

From their more or less good homes, in the cities or in the countryside, young girls flow into the educational institutes, which are going to make them competent to follow the inclinations they have shown. And there are schools for every such talent. We are now not talking about those schools . . ., there are others, . . . from the magnificent practical schools with hundreds of pupils, to the schools of home economics, weaving or needlework and soon schools of darning and patching.

The simplest works are going to be taught at schools – in the perfect negligence of the fact that a large part of what the latter schools are teaching, the young girl or daughter could and should be taught in her own home.

Freedom is the motto of the time. – freedom of religion, freedom of thought, self-determination. – There is no *compulsion* of any kind except – the compulsion of going to school. This compulsion still exists – and therein lies the reason that such despised jobs as the darning of stockings, etc. *can* be taught at school.

But why in the name of all the good home gods the simple practical jobs cannot now, as before, be learned at home!

. . . It is the morals, which are looser. The respect, the *obedience* to elders' opinions, wishes or orders is lacking among the most of them. . . .

A kind, excellent girl, and the young girls *are* kind for the most part if one understands them, is willingly making herself useful at home. And what a saving it is to have you at home! What a harmony, what tidiness you can create.

2.8 Male and female education compared

Emilia Pardo Bazán, 'La educación del hombre y la de la mujer', *Nuevo Teatro Crítico,* 2, No 22 (October 1892), 18–21.

Considering the similarities and differences that exist between the education of the man and that of the woman, immediately [we see] that the latter are much more serious and numerous than the former, which, these days, explicitly confirms that the relations of female and masculine education are no more than superficial, and that the differences, or better said the oppositions, are situated in the intimate and fundamental. . . .

While masculine education is inspired by the optimistic assumption; that is the faith in the perfectibility of the human naturalism, which ascends in a smooth and harmonious development until realising the fullness of his rational essence, female education derives from the pessimistic assumption; that is the assumption that a conflict of authority or evident contradiction exists between the moral law and the intellectual law of the woman, lessening the pain and prejudice of morality when it is of benefit to the intellectual; and that – to talk in simple language – the woman is all the more fit for her providential destiny the more ignorant and stationary she is; and the intensity of education, which for the male constitutes honour and glory, for the female dishonour and almost a monstrosity.

This dark and terrible pessimism, which encloses half of the human race in an iron circle of immobility, which prohibits them from associating with the progressive movement that roughly the other half slowly complies with; this pessimism . . . the error of confirming that the role of the woman corresponds to the reproductive functions of the species, determines and limits the remaining functions of her human activity, removing the whole individual significance from her destiny and not only giving it up but having her tied to male destiny. That is to say that the axis of the female life . . . is not her dignity and own happiness, but that of another, that of the husband and children, and if there is neither children nor husband, that of the father or brother, and when these are missing, that of the abstract entity of the abstract masculine race.

2.9 Special treatment?

Emily Davies, 'Special Systems of Education for Women', *Victoria Magazine*, 11 (May–October 1868), 356–66.

Is the improved education which, it is hoped, is about to be brought within reach of women, to be identical with that of men, or is it to be as good as possible, but in some way or other specifically feminine? . . . – Which is best, to extend methods of education admitted to be imperfect, or to invent new ones presumably better? . . .

[Special treatment] is urged on the ground that there are differences between men and women which educational systems ought to recognise; or supposing this to be disputed, that at any rate the conditions of women's lives are special, and ought to be specially prepared for; or there is a latent feeling of repugnance to what may appear like an ungraceful, perhaps childish, attempt to grasp at masculine privileges – an idea which jars upon a refined taste. Considerations of this sort, resting mainly upon sentiment or prejudice, can scarcely be met by argument. It is usually admitted that we are as yet in the dark as to the specific differences between men and women – . . .

Cannot we use the light of experience, and, avoiding exploded errors, march straight on to perfection by the nearest road? To a great extent, Yes. There is no reason, for example, to imitate boys' schools in their excessive devotion to physical sports; or in the exclusion of music from the ordinary school routine; or to take up methods of teaching of which the defects have been discovered. Again, looking to the higher stage, no one would wish to reproduce among women either the luxurious idleness of the lower average of university men, or the excessive strain of the competition for honours which is said to act so injuriously on the studious class. . . . There is at present not much fear that girls will take too much out-of-door exercise, that they will give too little time to music, or that governesses will blindly model their teaching on the plans in vogue in boys' schools. Fashionable young ladies are not in danger of idling their time away at college and the studious are not tempted by valuable rewards attached to academical distinction. It is not in its weak points that male education is likely to be imitated by women. . . .

Probably only women who have laboured under it can understand the weight of discouragement produced by being perpetually told that, as women, nothing much is ever to be expected of them, and it is not worth their while to exert themselves – that they can write lively letters, full of graphic description and homely touches, but that anything like original research or profound learning is not for them to think of – that whatever they do they must not interest themselves, except in a second-hand and shallow way, in the pursuits of men, for in such pursuits they must always expect to fail. Women who have lived in the atmosphere produced by such teaching know how it stifles and chills, how hard it is to work courageously through it. Every effort to improve the education of women which assumes that they may, without reprehensible ambition, study the same subjects as their brothers and be measured by the same standards, does something towards lifting them out of the state of listless despair of themselves into which so many fall. Supposing that the percentage of success attained by women should be considerably less than that of men, the sense of discouragement thus engendered would be as nothing compared with the general self-distrust produced by having it taken for granted that they are by nature disqualified to stand the ordinary tests.

Bridging two worlds

The transition from girl to adult woman embraced a number of potential rites of passage. Confirmation was an important turning-point in many European girls' lives, marking the transition to 'adolescence' and ultimately adulthood. Austrian Adelheid Popp worked from a young age but felt keenly the importance of this rite of passage, only feeling 'grown-up' after the ceremony. Young women did not often discuss their adolescent dreams and longings, but Marie Lafarge describes how she 'spoke' to her 'beau ideal', but was wise enough to keep this to herself. Trousseaus were important for young women across society and, like the dowry, matched personal circumstances. The Swedish magazine *IDUN* gives an excellent description of an ideal trousseau for middle-class women. Its emphasis on quantity and quality is significant – but so is the importance of practical utility.

Courtship took many forms, and the extracts here show some of the contrasts. Fanny Lewald describes the problems facing a middle-class Jewish couple in Prussia, with settlement restrictions and family dissension that delayed their marriage. In contrast, Josefa Náprstková narrates her experience as the daughter of a brewery worker and a servant, courted by the proprietor's son and brewery manager. A major obstacle was the suitor's mother's determination to remain in charge of the house during her lifetime.

Of course, not all courtships went well, and neither did all marriages. Suzanne Voilquin seems to have been unlucky in both. She describes her first love and its distressing outcome. She later agreed to marry another, but without love, and was to be disappointed by a husband whose venereal disease prevented her bearing children. Later, influenced by Saint-Simonian views, they separated.

2.10 Confirmation

Adelheid Popp, *Autobiography of a Working Woman* (London: Fisher Unwin, 1912), 74.

Only one thing was wanting to make me perfectly contented – all my comrades had been confirmed. They would talk of how splendidly it had gone off, and what presents they had received from their godmothers. But I had not been confirmed, as my mother was too proud to beg any one to be my godmother, and she herself could not afford the white dress and the other things which went with it, however much she would have wished to do so; and I had always been obliged to abandon all thought of it. . . . When I was sixteen, and a man first spoke to me of marriage, I answered in all seriousness: 'Why I am not yet confirmed.' According to my view, a true Catholic must first receive this sacrament before she could think of marriage. I was now seventeen, and did not want to wait any longer. A fellow-worker who was engaged to a young man in better circumstances wished to be my godmother. At a shop where I could pay by instalments I bought a pretty, light dress, elegant shoes, a silk sunshade, pretty gloves, and, crowning all, a hat trimmed with flowers. Those were splendid things! In addition came the drive in an open carriage, the ceremony in the church with the bishop's laying on of hands, then an excursion, a prayer-book, and some useful presents. Now, for the first time, I seemed to myself quite grown up.

2.11 Dreaming of husbands

Marie Lafarge, *Memoirs of Madame LaFarge*, 2 vols (London: Henry Colbourn, 1841), I, 152–3.

My aunt approved my love of study, telling me that cultivated talents and accomplishments were very proper in a marriageable young lady; while, for my own part, I only saw in the development of my mental faculties a means of making myself beloved, and adorned my mind for the sake of the being as yet undreamed of, but whom I vaguely hoped time would bring to complete my existence. Whenever I wrote a noble sentiment, I repeated it aloud to him; on conquering a musical difficulty, to him I sang my triumph; I was proud in dedicating to him a good action, but to him my thoughts never dared revert when I was dissatisfied with myself; in a word, the object of my dreams was not a man, but an angel, a being formed to love me. I carefully abstained from speaking to my aunt of my beau ideal; I sounded her once or twice, and had been told that nothing was further removed from my dream than the reality of a husband; that to indulge such ideas was fatal to young ladies, who should only aspire to a position in society, fortune, pleasure, rich bride's-clothes, and brilliant jewels, and that all other wishes, if unfortunately formed, should be stifled even in thought.

2.12 Practical trousseaus

IDUN, 20/178 (15 May 1891), 158.

The trousseau is so important for the newly formed household that it should be every mother's absolute duty to arrange it as well and as practically as possible.

Nothing is more annoying for the young housewife than an impractical trousseau; this applies especially to the linen supplies where new acquisitions are expensive and during the first years viewed sceptically by the master of the house. It is therefore especially essential to choose this part of the trousseau to be practical, that it to say hardwearing, beautiful and meeting all reasonable requirements. . . .

As far as [tablecloths and serviettes] are concerned it may be necessary to mention that one should have at least the finer linen with the same pattern, so that in case of a bigger service the linen doesn't have to be 'stitched up'. For the same reason the principle of similarity should be followed when purchasing coloured linen. Embroidery and laces on coffee serviettes, large and elegant monograms are beautiful and modern, but in more modest circumstances it is best to give these up so that one can buy half a dozen more serviettes.

Figure 2.1 IDUN: Practical Weekly Newspaper for Women and Home

For sheets and pillowcases one prefers linen, because shirting, etc. soon yellows and cannot be compared to linen in durability. . . . crocheted and easily broken laces should be avoided on beddings meant for everyday use. . . .

White piqué and even light coloured tricot blankets are much used abroad and should not be missing in the trousseau. Because they are not just light and comfortable during the warm season but if necessary they can be used as covers for beds and sickbeds. . . .

Regarding that part of the trousseau, which the young wife is meant to wear herself, it is of course in the owner's own interest to choose the best materials. But decorations, which need much time and effort when ironing, should be avoided, and for daily use hand-sewn flaps with or without decorative stitches are the most beautiful and most durable decoration. . . . It often takes only a few years for a slender girl to become a plump wife and so many linens become unused when they are not even close to being worn–out.

Regarding kitchen cloths there is greatest liberalism; a young wife can never have too many towels and dust cloths. In contrast to tablecloths and serviettes here it is desirable to choose individual sorts as different as possible. All the cloths that go through the servants' hands should be as distinctly recognisable as possible. Because it is not pleasant if glass towels are used for drying cooking vessels or if a servant girl uses a dust cloth in the kitchen. An eye catching difference in patterns and colours is therefore often more useful than marking. . . .

In the servants' linen one includes sheets and towels which are marked for them and naturally made very simply, . . . White clean aprons always give the maid the characteristic of style. The maid who opens the door in an untidy dress gives a bad impression to the guest, while the maid in a clean and proper dress necessarily gives grounds for conclusions about the care of the whole household, which cannot be anything but a delight for the mistress of the house.

2.13 Jewish courtship

Fanny Lewald, *Meine Lebengeschichte* (Berlin: Otto Zante, 1861), I, 20–5.

Of course, my parents knew each other by sight from childhood, since the Jewish community was very small at the time. My mother told us that as a twelve-year-old girl, she sat with her father, as my father, who was three years older than she, passed by their house. She had always heard good things about him; whenever the never-ending misfortunes of the Markus family were discussed, people always praised the wonderful children, and especially the diligence and loyalty of little David Markus, who was active from dawn to dusk for his parents. That had touched my mother and the great beauty of my father had made such an impression on her that . . . in childish enthusiasm, she exclaimed, 'Oh, Papa! I want to marry that David Markus!' – which naturally caused great laughter from her siblings. But there was no real social contact between the two families; my parents only got to know each other personally when my mother was seventeen and my father twenty. . . .

But it was not easy for Prussian Jews to get married then; each Jewish family was allowed legal residence in Prussia for one child, and without this home and work were impossible. In my mother's family, this permit had been used for the benefit of the eldest and very unattractive daughter, so that she could find a husband; my father's eldest sister had married a Jew with a permit . . . my uncle Beer Markus had the permit for the Markus family, that he was disinclined to cede to my father, since he himself was . . . in fact, courting my mother. . . .

From her family's point of view, it was most convenient for the youngest sister to marry in Königsberg without special petitions to the government; furthermore, my uncle Beer was a clever and cultivated man, but he was very sickly, . . . my much-courted mother initially accepted and encouraged Beer's courtship, but she soon turned her affections toward the younger and more attractive brother. . . .

My mother's relatives resented my father making their sister's comfortable marriage difficult, and my father's sisters took it very ill that they were causing such heartbreak for the older and ailing brother. The two poor young people found themselves in an isolated and hostile position in the family. . . . had they been of age, the young couple would probably have chosen to convert to Christianity as the way out. My mother was strongly attracted to the idea, and my father saw all religious dogma as equally valid, but all my mother's family . . . would not hear of such a step. The usual threats of cursing and expulsion were not spared. My mother could not handle such discord, and the betrothed couple were left with no choice but to go to the authorities with petitions, bribes and personal pleas to procure permission to settle in Prussia, . . . It lasted years, and this struggle produced in my mother, who was of a very mild and gentle nature, a lively distaste for Judaism and everything connected with it. She saw it as a misfortune to be a Jew. As for my father, whose strong intellect clearly saw the irrationality of the contemporary Prussian laws concerning the

Jews, the greater obstacles under which he had to suffer personally only increased his abhorrence of irrationality and tyranny.

2.14 Social difference

Josefa Náprstková, 'Autobiography', in Wilma Abeles Iggers, ed., *Women of Prague* (Oxford: Berghahn, 1995), 102–107.

In October 1855 I was . . . not quite seventeen. Old Mrs. Náprstková said to father who was a distiller in the brewery house: 'Adolf, I would like to try out your daughter, have your wife bring her'. . . . I tried to get along with everybody. I enjoyed my work. . . I was so happy. . .

On 25 February 1858, Mr. Vojtěch, as everybody called him, came to Prague after a ten-year stay in America. . . . as soon as the carriage. . . stopped, a figure jumped out and with one jump he was upstairs in panímaminka's room. . . . The next morning I was in the back storeroom, when around 10 o'clock panímaminka brought Mr. Vojtěch, and showed him how everything was arranged. From then on, instead of panímaminka, Mr. Vojtěch started coming to the storeroom and wrote the bills which formerly Mr. Kraemer used to write. . . .

In 1860 the Prague typographers had their first ball. My brother Emil was a typesetter in the Haase printshop. He purchased a ticket and persuaded me to go with him. Panímaminka did not like it, but still she gave me permission. . . . When we went into the hall . . . the music brought tears to my eyes, I don't know why. When Emil saw it he took me to dance. . . . Then the organizers of the ball came and told me that Mr. Náprstek was there also. I replied 'So?'. . . I looked at the gallery and saw Mr. Vojtěch Náprstek, who looked at me with a smile; I am writing this after thirty-three years, and my heart begins to pound. I think of that moment reverently and with gratitude. Before you could count to five, Mr. Vojtěch stood next to me and said to my brother Emil: 'May I?' My brother stepped back and Mr. Vojtěch said to me 'Pepičko, are you here alone?' I said I was with my mother and father and Uška and two brothers. Then Mr. Vojtěch said: 'I don't mean it that way, I mean does anybody have a claim to you?' I blushed and said 'nobody.' From that moment on I danced only with Mr. Vojtěch, and not at all with my brother. I was so blissful and happy that to this day I feel what I felt in my soul.

You can imagine what stir this caused. . . . the young master 'u Halánků' who was so distinguished chose a very ordinary common girl. There were more attractive girls present, but only I was treated with such distinction. It seems to me that it was all a dream. . . . When I first came home after that ball, my dear mother took me aside and said: 'My girl, yesterday all envied us the honor Mr. Vojtěch paid us when he danced with you the whole time. You looked nice together. But what's the use? Don't think of a gentleman's love. As they say, it jumps after rabbits. Therefore, dear child, think of your honor and of what you owe yourself and your family. I am not afraid because I know you, but it is my duty as your mother to tell you.' She kissed me and never mentioned it again. . . .

One day in 1867 on a Sunday evening at the time when Mr. Vojtěch used to always read to her and I used to come and ask if panímaminka had any wish I could fulfill, Mr. Vojtěch jumped up toward me, took me by my hand, put his arm under mine and . . . said: 'Panímaminka, how would Pepička and I look together?' Panímaminka said 'nice', and Mr. Vojtěch said 'So, you wouldn't have anything against my marrying Pepička?' Panímaminka replied: 'I have nothing against it, but as long as I live, I want to be the only lady of the house.' Then Vojtěch: 'Is this your last word?' and she replied: 'You know me.' . . . We continued to live as before, and I did my work as before, only I was convinced that Mr. Vojtěch and I were fond of each other.

So the years passed for us, sometimes in contentment and sometimes not, as is common in human life. . . . [Then] my dear mother died; before that she said calmly: 'I am dying peacefully because I have your promise [to come home to look after father].' . . .

After the funeral I asked my father to tell panímaminka that he was taking me home. . . . He said: 'I know panímaminka, she will not say anything; she will let you go, and after a while she will let me go, and then we are both going to be at home, and then the question will be what we are going to live on . . . I am old and won't find a job so easily.' What was I to do? I went to the cemetery to my mother's grave and asked her to forgive me for not living up to my promise . . .

Our wedding on 25 February 1875 was simple. The ceremony took place at the Old Town Hall at ten o'clock in the morning. When we returned home, we immediately went to the store. The employees had what they call a double dinner, and we had dinner as usual. Our people each received gifts of money and books.

2.15 Disillusionment

Suzanne Voilquin, *Souvenirs d'une fille du people* (Paris: Sauze, 1866), 41–7.

In the course of this blessed summer, everything helped to strengthen my confidence in the loyal intentions of my beloved. . . . For five months, happiness was unmixed with tears of concern; some more ardent caresses, but chaste, were not always refused, . . .

But even these innocent testimonies of my affection were not enough for him anymore. Already he complained of my indifference. This was my fault, he said, the mark of a cold heart incapable of much love; and his sulks, his reproaches made me cry; I knew then that this was the usual tactic of men to get their goal. I loved, and if I could resist my own emotions during these long and frequent confrontations, it was only the memory of my mother who was my strength; . . . I thought this was stronger than the fear of God himself. . . .

Stanislas, the strength of this approach known and approved of my family, wanted to treat me as his wife; he became even more pressing; were we not united by our love and by the consent of our parents? He had no doubt of their consent. Moreover, he said, I would imitate the example of his mother, who, before her marriage, had loved his father enough to refuse him nothing. This confidence struck me; and I could see it as evidence of the strength and truth of his love; without that excuse would he have the audacity to accuse his mother who he seemed to love tenderly?

However I still had the strength to refuse; I cried; I suffered from his rudeness, and our interviews became increasingly stormy.

. . . We resolved all four, my brother Philippe, Stanislas, my sister and I, to walk outside the gates; . . . Well! this man, who had that morning, pressed the hand of a father too confidently, chose this very day to renew his attacks. Towards evening, being alone in my room, he became violent, and passionate, he made such a brutal assault on me that terror seized me. . . . I closed my eyes, I was shaking, my body was in turmoil, as it seemed to me that this huge volume would crush me. . . . I had no awareness of what was happening.

This state lasted all night to dawn; thanks to painkillers given to me, the hallucinations stopped, I slept more calmly; when I woke up I was broken, but the ghosts were gone and had carried away the memory of what had happened the night before. My brother seeing me better went back to work, . . . I was exhausted, I was not thinking, so, with fresh attempts this man obtained all the success he wanted. From that moment I was with him! . . . The following days, he dried my tears with kisses and calmed my conscience with the oath to marry me as soon as possible; only then he told me that his parents' answer had been received a long time ago; it contained no denial of his dearest wishes, but his father insisted on the necessity that his son waited his majority before marriage, . . .

Towards the beginning of March 1823, Stanislas' visits became less regular. . . ., after a few days absence, he suddenly came into my room; he found my face discomposed by tears; he became furious, threw his hat angrily at the other end of the room and cried in an imperious tone: 'always, always crying! . . .' I lay shattered by the violence and bitter words . . .

After some painful moments, Stanislas seemed to make a resolution and said without any preparation, 'Listen, friend, come to me, my studies disturb me, my thesis is not finished yet, come share my life, it will force me to work; are we not united? You will bear my name if you like; *nothing* should hold you back.'

. . . No, a hundred times no, that is impossible! I feel guilty enough without adding scandal to my fault . . . He retired, cold and dismissive, saying that I did not know love . . .

Obviously this man was looking for an excuse to break ties that had become too heavy. He still came to see me sometimes, but he was no longer the same. Finally, . . . regardless of oaths before God once lavished with so much love, he walked away. From that moment on I never saw him again! ever! . . .

From the moment that I was convinced of his cowardly desertion, my faith and love was killed; in my heart only contempt for him and his sex remained.

Marriage

Marriage remained the most important goal for most women, and many manuals existed to help guide wives through what was (and is) a complicated relationship. Joachim Friedrich Campe's *Väterliche Rath*, published in 1789, continued to be popular across the German-speaking world into the nine-teenth century. Noted for practical advice, it follows the trend for sensible 'womanly' advice and the aversion to accomplishments. Gustave Droz' *Monsieur, Madame et Bébé* was even more popular, with 266 editions in French and multiple editions in English between 1866 and 1924. Based on the idea that love was the foundation for marriage, Droz argues for affection, both physical and spiritual, in relationships. Fredrika Bremer's extract on the 'Improvised Dinner' plays into the expectations of many women whose job was to please their husbands and who suffered for inconsequential failings.

2.16 Marital duty

Joachim Friedrich Campe, *Väterliche Rath für meine Tochter* (Braunschweig, 1809), 14–17.

You are not really meant to be just big children, shallow dolls, fools or even Furies; you should achieve much more − . . . become gratified wives, fine mothers and exemplary mistresses of the internal affairs of the house; Wives, who as half of the human race, should sweeten the greater pains, sorrows and hardships of men with tenderness, love, care and concern. The mother, should not just give birth to children, but also instil the first seeds of virtue of every beautiful person, to wisely develop the first buds of the aptitudes of their souls. . . .

Mistresses of the household shall through attention, order, cleanliness, diligence, thrift, economic knowledge and skills, ensure the wealth, honour, domestic peace and happiness of the acquiring spouse, in meeting food needs, and making his house a place of peace, joy and bliss. Aim quite firmly for this high and dignified purpose of your sex, my child, and see how the wellbeing of the entire society ultimately depends on how well or how badly you have been prepared for it. Then not only domestic bliss, but also − what might at first sound incredible − the public good of the state lies to a great extent in your hands, and hangs in large part if not entirely, on the way in which the female sex fulfil their natural and civil purpose. *Like the source, so the stream*; so like the woman, so the citizen, who is born of a woman, who from her receives the first impressions of good and bad, . . .

Like the source, so the stream; as the domestic lives of men, so the public; as the domestic family bliss, so the wellbeing of the public state. . . .

As the spring at the heart of the body politic, [if women] do their duty, so the public members will do the same, the manly sex; so everything goes as it should; then the happiness of the family and the state will blossom; if this is not done, then what has happened before will happen again; then the members wither, family happiness sickens, then the entire body will never be completely strong or permanently healthy.

2.17 Women from angels

Gustave Droz, *Monsieur, Madame et Bébé* (Paris: 1886), 44–51.

MY DEAR SISTERS:

Marriage, as it is now understood, is not exactly conducive to love. In this I do not think that I am stating an anomaly. Love in marriage is, as a rule, too much at his ease; he stretches himself with too great listlessness in armchairs too well cushioned. . . . in the too-relaxing warmth of a nest, made for him, he yawns over his newspaper, goes to sleep, snores, and pines away. . . .

'Alas!' you say, 'is it then all over? One summer's day, then thirty years of autumn, to me, who am so fond of sunshine.'. . . Lacking self-confidence and ignorant of yourself, you have made it a virtue to keep silent and not wake your husband while he sleeps; . . . then he has gone out to his club, where he has been received like the prodigal son, . . . This state of things I regard as absolutely detestable. I look upon you, my dear sisters, as poor victims, . . .

Figure 2.2 'I sup with my wife', cover image for a story from *Monsieur, Madame et Bébé*

Esteem and friendship between husband and wife are like our daily bread, very pleasant and respectable; but a little jam would not spoil that, you will admit! . . . It is all very well that you should be treated like saints, but do not let it be forgotten that you are women, and, listen to me, do not forget it yourselves.

A husband, majestic and slightly bald, is a good thing; a young husband who loves you and eats off the same plate is better. If he rumples your dress a little, and imprints a kiss, in passing, on the back of your neck, let him. When, on coming home from a ball, he tears out the pins, tangles the strings, and laughs like a madman, trying to see whether you are ticklish, let him. Do not cry 'Murder!' if his moustache pricks you, but think that it is all because at heart he loves you well. He worships your virtues; is it surprising hence that he should cherish their outward coverings? No doubt you have a noble soul; but your body is not therefore to be despised; and when one loves fervently, one loves everything at the same time. Do not be alarmed if in the evening, when the fire is burning brightly and you are chatting gaily beside it, he should take off one of your shoes and stockings, put your foot on his lap, and in a moment of forgetfulness carry irreverence so far as to kiss it; if he likes to pass your large tortoise-shell comb through your hair, if he selects your perfumes, arranges your plaits, and suddenly exclaims, striking his forehead: 'Sit down there, darling; I have an idea how to arrange a new coiffure.'

If he turns up his sleeves and by chance tangles your curls, where really is the harm? Thank Heaven if in the marriage which you have hit upon you find a laughing, joyous side; if in your husband you find the loved reader of the pretty romance you have in your pocket; if, while wearing cashmere shawls and costly jewels in your ears, you find the joys of a real intimacy – that is delicious! In short, reckon yourself happy if in your husband you find a lover. . . .

A marriageable young lady is a product of maternal industry, which takes ten years to fructify, and needs from five to six more years of study on the part of the husband to purify, strip, and restore to its real shape. In other words, it takes ten years to make a bride and six years at least to turn this bride into a woman again. . . .

The sole guaranty of fidelity between husband and wife is love. One remains side by side with a fellow-traveller only so long as one experiences pleasure and happiness in his company. Laws, decrees, oaths, may prevent faithlessness, or at least punish it, but they can neither hinder nor punish intention. But as regards love, intention and deed are the same. . . .

Yes, I favour marriage – I do not conceal it – the happy marriage in which we cast into the common lot our ideas and our sorrows, as well as our good-humour and our affections. . . . Seek to please your husband. Be amiable. Consider that your husband is an audience, whose sympathy you must conquer. . . .

My sisters, my sisters, strive to be real; that is the blessing I wish you.

2.18 The improvised dinner

Fredrika Bremer, *Hemmet eller familje-sorger och fröjder*, trans. Mary Howitt (London: Henry G. Bohn, 1853), 49–52.

'To-morrow!' exclaimed Elise, half terrified. 'Yes, to-morrow,' answered her husband, peremptorily. 'I told her that to-morrow morning you would pay her a visit, but she insists on first coming to you. You need not trouble yourself much about the dinner to-morrow . . . Emelie will not expect much from an improvised dinner. . . .'

Elise went to rest that night with a depressed heart, and with an indefinite but most unpleasant feeling, thought of the next day's dinner, and then dreamed that her husband's 'old flame' had set the house on fire, and robbed the whole family of its shelter.

You housewives who know the meaning of a roast, who know the difficulties which sometimes overwhelm you, especially when you must improvise a dinner; you know that not withstanding all inspiration, – and inspiration is necessary to all improvisation – one cannot inspire either chickens or heath-cocks to come flying into the important dish, when the crust is ready to put on it; you housewives who have spent many a long morning in thoughts of cookery and in anguish, . . . can sympathize in Elise's troubles, as she, on the morning of this important dinner, as the finger of the clock was approaching twelve had not been able to improvise a roast.

. . . and as if to make the difficulty still greater, Elise, on this very day, was remarkably in want of assistants. . . . The cook, too, was confused to-day in a remarkable manner; the children were in a fermentation; Eva and Lenore quarrelled; Petra tore a hole in her new frock; Henrik broke a water bottle and six glasses; the baby cried and screamed for nothing; the clock was on the stroke of twelve and no roast would come!

Elise was just on the point of falling into despair over roasts, cooks, the dinner, the child, nay, over the whole world, when the door opened, and the words, 'your most devoted servant,' were spoken out shrilly and joyously, and the widow of the Court Chamberlain – to Elise she seemed an angel of light from heaven – stood in the room, with her beaming friendly countenance, took out of her most monstrous reticule one chicken after another, and laid them upon the table, . . .

'Adieu, dear Elise; I wish you the happiness of getting the dinner and the young folks in order.' Gunilla went, dinner-time came, and with it the guests and the Judge, . . .

Emelie, the Colonel's widow, was elegant in the highest degree; looked handsome, and distinguished, and almost outdid herself in politeness; but still Elise, inspite of herself, felt stiff and stupid by the side of her husband's 'old flame'. Beyond this, she had now a great distraction. 'Oh, that the chickens may be nicely done!' was the incessant master-thought of Elise's soul; and it prevailed over . . . every subject on which they talked.

The hour of dinner was come, and yet the dinner kept the company waiting. . . .

Elise began to esteem the Colonel's widow very highly, because she kept up such a lively conversation, and she hoped this would divert attention from any dishes which were not particularly successful. The Judge was a polite and agreeable host, and he was particularly fond of dinner-time, when he would willingly make all men partakers of his good appetite, good humor and even his good eating – if this really was good – but if the contrary happened to be the case, his temper could not well sustain it.

During dinner Elise saw now and then little clouds come over her husband's brow, but he himself seemed anxious to disperse them, and all went on tolerably till the chickens came. As the Judge, who adhered to the old customs, was cutting them up, he evidently found them tough, whereupon a glance was sent across the table to his wife which went to her heart like the stab of a knife; but no sooner was the first pang over than this reproachful glance aroused a degree of indignation in her which determined her to steel herself against a misfortune which in no case was her fault; she, therefore grew quite lively and talkative, and never once turned her eyes to her husband, who, angry and silent, sat there with a very hot brow, and the knife sticking in the fowls.

But, after all, she felt as if she could again breathe freely when the dinner was over, and on that very account longed just to speak just one word of reconciliation with her husband; but he now seemed to only have eyes and ears for Emelie . . . as she perceived something cold and depreciating in the manners of her husband towards her.

Singletons

Numerous women remained single until late in life or never married. For some it was a choice, for others it was circumstances. Fredrika Bremer, staunch feminist and author, determined not to marry so as to have the freedom to pursue her craft, and her life. Frequently, enterprising women also remained single, to continue working or perhaps run businesses. However, the thread of lesbianism runs through the lives of singletons. Marianne Woods and Janet Pirie ran a prestigious girls' school in Edinburgh, and were accused in 1810 of sexual misconduct and lewd behaviour in the same bed where a sixteen-year-old girl was sleeping. To protect their reputations and business, the teachers brought a counter case against Dame Helen Cumming Gordon, whose part-Indian granddaughter had brought the original allegations. The extract is distinctive for Lord Meadowbank's belief that the crime could not exist.

2.19 On not marrying

Fredrika Bremer, *Life, Letters and Posthumous Works*, 115–6, 140–1.

Letters arrived about this time; one for my mother and one for me. The young gentleman, who therein offered me his hand and heart, spoke with such warm sincerity, goodness and real excellence of soul, and with so much candour and openness of himself, that I was deeply touched by it. I felt no aversion for him; but I did not wish to marry. By the refusal which I gave, I considered that I had forever placed a barrier between myself and marriage. I did not fear that the fulfilment of my duties as a wife and a mother would not be my chief aim if I entered into the married state; but it became clear to me that my mission as an authoress would then become totally neglected, because I knew and I felt that one cannot unite these two vocations without failing in both; while by devoting myself exclusively to the latter, – that of an authoress, – I believed that I could make myself as useful as my power admitted.

The third volume of my 'Sketches', which I wrote in the winter of 1831, in a hurry-skurry, appeared in print in the following spring, and the success which it met with, together with the advice of several highly estimable persons, determined me to devote myself seriously to the life of an authoress, and to develop my talent as much as possible.

2.20 Lord Meadowbank's argument

Miss Marianne Woods and Miss Janet Pirie against Helen Cumming Gordon, Transcripts of the trial, 25 June 1811, 1–8.

No cause was ever more extraordinary, or required a more grave and mature consideration. The pursuers are two women of fair and irreproachable character, whose ruin has been accomplished by communications relative to their conduct, which, however confidentially conceived, could not fail to produce that effect. The defender is an honourable and very respectable Scottish Matron, who thought herself called upon, by the strongest moral duties, to save from contamination her own grandchildren, that she had placed at the pursuers' school; and to apprise the friends and relatives of others, that had been placed there, as she might suppose, in consequence of her recommendation or example, . . . There are also the young persons, or at least one young person, from whom the information of the fatal imputation proceeded, – one, unfortunately wanting in the advantages of legitimacy, and of a European complexion, – and of consequence the more dependent on the favour of her connections and protectors. These persons have been brought forward as witnesses, to establish the truth of the imputation; . . . And in my mind, there is a fourth party whose interest is deeply at stake, I mean the public; for the virtues, the comforts and the freedom of domestic intercourse, mainly depend on the purity of female manners, and that, again, on their habits of intercourse remaining as they have hitherto been, – free from suspicion. . . .

The extraordinary nature of the case must unavoidably bestow on it the character of a *cause célèbre*. The ruin of the pursuers is justified, by charging them with the guilt of committing with one another a species of the *venus nefanda* [monstrous lusts] hitherto unknown in this country, even as a calumny against any of the sex. Where the facts alleged are of so extraordinary a character, that the evidence of them comes to be addressed, rather to the imagination than to actual observation, a species of intoxication is apt to appear among all concerned, . . .

I must acknowledge, that with respect to the nature of the crime charged, I labour under a very high degree of incredulity. . . . There is no sort of doubt, that women of a peculiar conformation, from an elongation of the clitoris, are capable both of giving and receiving venereal pleasure, in intercourse with women, by imitating the functions of a male in copulation; and that in some countries this conformation is so common, that circumcision of the clitoris is practised as a religious rite. . . . I dare say, it is also true enough, that . . . women have been employed to kindle each others' lewd appetites. Nor is it to be disputed, that by means of tools, women may artificially accomplish the venereal gratification. But, in this case, the use of tools is excluded by the defender's evidence, . . . [Miss Pirie] is represented as always performing the male functions, which surely could afford no gratification to herself if performed only by means of tools. . . . nothing short of the gratification of mutual and furious lust, could have induced the pursuers to resort to each others' beds for the gratification, where girls of sixteen years of age were sleeping with them. . . .

But if tools and tribadism are out of the question, then I state as the ground of my incredulity . . . the important fact that the imputed vice has been hitherto unknown in Britain. Neither the pruriency of corrupt imaginations has brought it forward in works of professed obscenity, nor has the wantonness of satire ever ventured to suggest it as a ground of obloquy. . . . Your Lordships, then, will judge as to the probabilities of two Scotch women, of admitted intelligence, educated, as it is established the pursuers were educated, and undertaking such a profession as they did undertake, discovering a venereal gratification which Lucian [Greek rhetorician] was not able to describe, and rushing into a vice which, hitherto, even the most corrupt imaginations in this country had not so much as fancied; and what is perhaps equally extraordinary, that they should have dared to disclose to each other the secret of such depraved inclinations, and that, too, while it is still problematical, whether a venereal gratification can in this manner be accomplished or not.

. . . sure I am, that I decide soundly when I hold, that nothing short of the clearest and most decisive evidence can authorise a Judge to find the pursuers guilty of a crime, while, if I may so express myself, the *corpus delicti* of a crime is still a question, and even if there were such a crime in possibility, while it has hitherto remained unknown, and even unthought of, in this part of the world.

Mothers and children

The newer attitudes toward children and emphasis on motherhood created a decisive shift in the nineteenth century. A mother's affection is obvious in Victoria's, Empress Frederick of Prussia, letter to her mother, Queen Victoria, on the birth of her son. In contrast, Fanny Lewald's resistance and obstinacy are readily recognised by women living 150 years later, while her mother's insistence on housewifely duties over reading are understandable in the context of valorisation of the housewife and mother.

The Spanish magazine *Correo de las Damas* overtly utilises Enlightenment language to claim women's responsibilities for young children, and criticises mothers who think that nursing their babes is adequate 'motherhood'. Situated in the shifting value of motherhood, the Child Custody Act of 1839 was a hallmark, and thus Caroline Norton's campaign on behalf of mothers opened this section (2.1). Harriet Martineau describes the passage of the Bill and comments on its significance. This had wider effect than in England alone; as the 'first blow', it was an example across Europe.

2.21 Daughter and mother

Letters of the Empress Frederick, Frederick Ponsonby, ed. (London: Macmillan & Co., 1948), 24–5.

February 28 [1859], to Queen Victoria
   Your grandson is exceedingly lively and when awake will not be satisfied unless kept dancing about continually. He scratches his face and tears his caps and makes every sort of extraordinary little noise. I am so thankful, so happy, he is a boy. I longed for one more than I can describe, my whole heart was set upon a boy and therefore I did not expect one. I cannot say I think him like anyone at present, although now and then he reminds me of Bertie and of Leopold, which I fear you won't like. I feel very proud of him and very proud of being a Mama.

2.22 Childcare advice

P.P.d.l.H., 'Educación', *Correo de las Damas*, 13 (1805): 290–2.

If the root is poisoned, it is certain that the tree will be bad and the fruits worse; it is true that today there are only a few ladies and well-off people . . . who have the proper appreciation of the title of Mothers; . . . they do not like to share this honour with another, wishing to be paid respect, not only for the love that naturalism inspires but also for gratitude; and the satisfaction of depriving those who trust wet nurses with the upbringing of their children. This is commendable, but it is not that these affectionate mothers are caring; by feeding their own children they distance themselves from what corresponds to education. Guided by this enormous error, that they are incapable of ideas, children at the tender age are abandoned to the care and treatment of a maid without principles. In the most precious age, when everything in us operates by imitation and use; where one is marked like soft wax, and it lasts forever like bronze; how much one hears, one sees, one touches, we should consider how difficult it will be to uproot the defects acquired by custom.

2.23 Mother–daughter tensions

Fanny Lewald, *Lebengeschichte*, 218–22.

I had become a true reading wolf [before I was 11], and whatever device my mother used to cure me of the overwhelming inclination to learn and of the distaste for any housework, of any kind of work that was not intellectual, failed. My mother was very distressed about this; she felt personally offended. Anything my mother wanted me to do with her, I had to be forced; anything my father undertook with me in his few free hours, I was ready and happy to do. I felt it myself; I was very unhappy with myself when mother constantly complained about me. I struggled with good intentions, but still I resisted; . . . Just as mother had formerly encouraged my inclination for learning, father now forced me to do certain tasks around the house, which I did only with inward resentment, because I saw that the housekeeper could perform these just as well and that I was only forced to do them because I did them reluctantly and poorly. Few days passed without my mother commenting that there was nothing more offensive or useless than an educated impractical young woman, and that I had every prospect of becoming one. Few weeks went by without my father reminding me that we had little money and would have to do without the housekeeper soon; then I would have to help my mother, who was in poor health. I could do nothing but reassure them, weeping, that I also wanted to do things gladly, if they would leave me alone, but to run after me, to supervise me constantly, was unbearable. I had other and better things to do.

Basically, I was completely right. Children quickly learn when the chores required of them are useful and necessary, and perform them quite cheerfully if they provide a feeling of importance. They have a definite instinct to help. But if these chores are imposed on them only as an exercise, they have equally a pronounced dislike that my parents could not recognise. Had I been asked, for example, to dress my younger siblings or otherwise take care of them, it would have given me pleasure. But to go through the rooms to see if any items were left lying there, to put away the sugar after afternoon coffee, while the housekeeper cleared everything else made me angry, and because my mother always complained about my behaviour in front of my father, it made me very resentful of her from which I – without any reason – finally believed that she loved my oldest brother and my sister, who remained the youngest for a long time, because of the deaths of my two little brothers, much more than me.

2.24 Child custody

Harriet Martineau, *History of the Thirty Years Peace* (London: Chambers, 1878) V, 574–6.

The session of 1839 was a memorable one to at least half the nation, for yielding the first act of what must become a course of legislation on behalf of the rights of women, who are in so many ways oppressed by the laws of England that Lord Brougham's objection to the measure was based on his fear to touch a mass of laws so cruel and indefensible as that all must come down if any part were brought into question. The object now was to obtain for mothers of irreproachable conduct who should be separated from their husbands, access to their young children by petition to the judges, in whose power it was to regulate the terms of that access. When this was clearly stated in the House in 1838 . . . that by the law of England a husband of the most profligate character had the power of preventing his virtuous wife from ever seeing her children that it was on behalf only of mothers irreproachable in the eye of the law that access to their children was asked for and that this access was to be obtained only by permission of the equity judges – the object sought appeared so mere a fraction of what was due to domestic claims, so small a restitution of natural rights profusely stolen by a barbarous law, that the Bill called the Custody of Infants' Bill was passed by the Commons rapidly, and by large majorities. In the Lords, however, there was opposition; and Lord Brougham recorded his views in a speech which ought to be preserved as a specimen of the morality professed in high places in the 19th century. . . .

He was ready to admit that the law was harsh and cruel in its operation on those cases which had been stated; and also that their small number was no guarantee that many more did not exist which had never seen the light. His noble friend had stated the evils of the present state of the law; he had shown how unjust the law was with regard to the treatment and the custody of the offspring of the wife by her husband; he had shown how it had operated harshly on the wife; and he had pointed out instances in which that law might have entailed evil on the children; and then he contended that his bill must be accepted as a remedy, because it would be a less evil than the evils pointed out. But there were many evils which the bill did not profess to remedy. Could anything be more harsh or cruel than that the wife's goods and chattels should be at the mercy of the husband, and that she might work and labour, and toil for an unkind father to support his family and children, while the husband repaid her with harshness and brutality, he all the time rioting and revelling in extravagance and dissipation, and squandering in the company of guilty paramours the produce of her industry? The law was silent to the complaints of such a woman . . . He knew that there were anomalies and a thousand contradictions in the marriage-law; but the existence of those anomalies and contradictions should operate as so many warnings against the introduction of new anomalies and changes in that marriage law . . .

Lord Brougham's conclusion was adverse to the Bill: but that was of little moment in view of the service he rendered to the oppressed by his exposure of the position of married women in England. As he said, 'they were not properly represented in the legislature.' They were not represented at all. . . . In the case before us, it was, as was openly declared at the time, precisely the men who despised and distrusted women, and had no conception of such an ideal as the virtuous matronage of England, who exerted themselves to prevent the passage of the law which should permit a blameless mother occasionally to see her children, by an order from the equity judges. . . . The result was, . . . Bill thrown out. . . .

There were circumstances connected with the final effort which can never be forgotten . . . for all the women of Great Britain were insulted by the methods pursued to defeat the bill. . . . In the course of the argument or exposition, several of the most eminent ladies in Great Britain were insulted by name, and every woman in the world by implication. . . . Lord Wynford, the chief agitator against the Bill . . . observed: 'His noble and learned friend had truly said that the custody of the children belonged by law to the father. That was a wise law, for the father was responsible for the rearing up of the children; but when unhappy differences separated the father and mother, to give the custody of the child to the father, and to allow access to it by the mother, was to injure the child; for it was natural to expect that the mother would not instil into the child any respect for the husband whom she might hate or despise. The effects of such a system would be most mischievous to the child, and would prevent its being properly brought up.' Lord Wynford did not go on to say whether he thought it would be good for the child, in the custody of a profligate father, to hear that father's way of speaking of the irreproachable mother. . .

The Bill was read a third time on the 2d, and received the royal assent on the 17th, of August. If the Queen understood the full significance of this Bill, as the first blow struck at the oppression of English legislation in relation to women, it must have been with singular pleasure that she made the bill law.

5   Community spaces

Keeping a good house

One of the most famous housekeeping manuals from the period is Isabella Beeton's *Book of Household Management*, a collection of articles written for her husband's magazine, and published when she was only twenty-five, in 1861. Household books, however, were a thriving industry and one of the arenas to which many women turned their hands. Henriette Davidis published *Hausfrau*, when Beeton was only eight years old, and with seventy-six editions to 1963 it was a definitive guide to cooking and household management which left a decisive mark on German cuisine. Dane Anne Mangor was also highly popular, with forty editions of her *Cookbook for Small Households* between 1837 and 1910, and a successor volume of twenty-nine editions. Although the extract is somewhat whimsical, it captures the ambience that housewives were to achieve. Frenchwoman Cora Millet-Robinet was herself a countrywoman with a mission to better educate rural French women and her *Maison rustique* is a classic. The range covered by these books, which went beyond simple housekeeping and cleaning, is exemplified by her concern to understand and be able to deal with household medical matters – and to know when not to.

The final extract advises middle-class women on how to deal with 'at home' or reception days, normally associated with the elite. The Swedish author is concerned to help them not to appear foolish, or to spend money wastefully, while finding an appropriate and discreet way to create reception days. Of course, many aspiring bourgeois homes relied on servants, and indeed domestic service was the single most popular job for young women, despite conditions that were trying and often very difficult. Doris Viersbeck, from Hamburg, describes how they were at the beck and call of their employers, often with little appreciation of them as people.

2.25 Defining the housewife

Henriette Davidis, *Die Hausfrau, Praktische anleitung zur selbständigen und sparsamen führung ein Stadt und Landhaushaltung* (1845), 5th ed. (Leipzig: 1870), vii, ix–xi.

One of the most glorious descriptions that belong to a woman is when the Man says of her: 'I have a housewife'.

The duties of the housewife are numerous, the house is her realm; her desire – to act sensibly and with enjoyment to work and to create, to respect and supervise both small and large tasks, not to shy away from labour, but rather look after every member of the household with her best efforts, through cleanliness and order, through diligence and thrift to ease the sorrows of the man, to increase prosperity and set a good example. We may therefore rightfully call a housewife the soul of the house, whose activities are widely perceived, in the living room, as in the nursery, in the kitchen as in the basement, in the pantry as in the cupboards, in her own bedroom as in the servants' chambers; Nothing that is sheltered under her roof, is too low for her attention. . . .

If the young housewife also lives under circumstances, where she does not have to do any of the work on her own, then she shall not be superfluous; she should at least learn the main branches of the household, in case she has to give the servants orders, not to learn from them at the cost of her authority. . . . In the present work, the content is not based on theory, but every single item is from the realm of experience, . . . [which] with a thankful heart I have based on the example and word of my long-deceased, revered mother. What . . . seemed so completely foreign to her and the many difficulties, which she had to fight against as a young woman, gave me the idea.

My beloved mother was raised as a city dweller; in the household she was completely ignorant; rural work she did not even know the name of, from which her position as a country pastor's wife led to the most embarrassing moments of all kinds. Piety, wisdom, care, a lively spirit and the desire to bless her family, she gradually learned to become one of the ablest and most experienced housewives. With her children it would be different. So she sought to awaken them early to the sense of domesticity and, as far as it was possible in her restless household, to guide them well. It is possible to learn much through the example of an understanding mother, who knows to treat life practically, especially in a hospitable parsonage, where many children and guests require a decent and thrifty facility. . . .

May this work then through the spread of my mission, be a friend and reliable counsellor to young women.

2.26 Three domestic spices

Anne Marie Mangor, *Kogebog for smaa huusholdninger* (1837), 12th ed. (Copenhagen, 1860), iii–iv.

Three Domestic Spices

which are recommended to young housewives because they cost little, never lose their strength and have that quality that the simpler the food the more they will improve its taste.

T he first spice consists of *a fixed and firm eating time*, because husbands and others who eat together are commonly never more impatient than during the period between the fixed eating time and the time when the food is actually on the table.

T he second spice is *a snow white tablecloth, a clean table setting*. Even the simplest food has added good taste when the eye rests pleasingly on white linen, shining porcelain, and clear glass – thoughts of a capable housewife are instinctively connected to this.

T he third spice is *the housewife's mild and friendly face*, which like the sun shines over everything and chases away the small bits of dissatisfaction or downheartedness, which might otherwise hover in the house's sky and eventually collect themselves into a raincloud.

2.27 Domestic medicine

Cora-Elisabeth Millet-Robinet, *La Maison rustique des dames* (1845), 4th ed. (Paris: 1859), II, 5–7.

In the art of healing, the main difficulty is not only to apply the remedy once the trouble is known, but also to recognize with certainty the nature of the illness. Symptoms are very variable and often misleading, the practice of medicine is very difficult, always speculative, and requires constant study, informed by long experience. Allow me to present here an opinion that will appear unusual: that it is difficult for a doctor to write a good treatise on domestic medicine. . . .

When one possesses any subject well, it seems to us clear, simple, easy to grasp and to apply. We believe that everyone should see it and understand it as we do. A doctor who writes a domestic medical treatise, probably without realising it, . . . would present many gaps, and science, which he believed would place [it] within the reach of all readers, would then involve them in a multitude of errors from their ignorance or their imperfect knowledge needed to understand. . . .

A treatise of domestic medicine should instead be used to awaken attention to cases where it is necessary to resort to a doctor. . .

A good treatise should simply teach some very clear rules of hygiene and easy remedies for cases where medical intervention is not strictly necessary.

It is important to find therapeutic methods to use first in case of accidents and early disease, in treatment of minor ailments manifested by symptoms so clear, it is almost impossible to ignore. Finally the medical textbook must understand the need to monitor and manage accurately the treatments prescribed by a doctor.

All readers will readily understand these instructions, which can be given, without presumption, to a woman accustomed to observe and care for her family and the poor of her neighbourhood. The simplicity of these instructions, clear from any claim to science, places limits on the ambitions of people who might be tempted to give too much latitude in domestic medicine. . . . if I am not afraid to approach a work so difficult, it is that for many years I found myself, by necessity and by choice, in a position to acquire this limited but often useful knowledge. . . . I rely on popular indulgence for the rectitude of my intentions and my strong desire to be useful.

2.28 Reception days

'Mottagningsdagar', *IDUN*, 15 May 1891, 159.

To have reception days, as we all know, is a habit which here in Sweden is mainly adopted by the rich and noble. Only they dare to declare to their acquaintances that they have reserved a certain day of the week or the month for receiving guests . . . in order to be able to spend time undisturbed however they want.

But what will happen when some more or less unimportant little Mrs in town or country informs her acquaintances that there are certain specific days when she will receive her friends who wish to visit her? I am afraid that the majority would receive her kind announcement with a mocking laughter and she would be accused of . . . being pretentious and maybe also of being inhospitable.

What does the rule of social behaviour then demand from such little unimportant Mrs who cannot adopt such noble habits? Yes, quite simply it demands that her house will always be open for strangers. . . .

In addition to the declaration that it is impolite not to be on one's toes for strangers there is also another rule which says: in a proper house there should always be food which is appropriate for receiving strangers. . . . These are quite useless and stupid expenses. And it is intolerable tyranny that one has to be hospitable, as it is so nicely put, in order not to fall out with people.

But could one not sort this hospitality somewhat and bring a little reason to it so that it would not be so exhausting? It should definitely be pleasant both for the guests and the hosts.

Let us think how a young newly-wed couple should manage reasonable arrangements for this. First they should, instead of restlessly flying around on feasts and visits, spend time in peace and enjoy their young happiness. In due course they can take their time to discuss how large a society they can afford and which persons they think it is really a pleasure to associate with. Those will then be sent a visiting card that says which days the young couple is at home for their friends. . . .

These receptions should be so delightful. The masters of the house have amused themselves for the day . . . The guests are also in a good spirit. All have wanted to come just that day, . . . It is also very simple. The masters of the house have not offered anything, they have just promised to be at home for their friends.

2.29 Beck and call

Doris Viersbeck, *Erlebnisse eines Hamburger Dienstmädchens* (Munich: Ernst Reinhardt Verlag, 1910), 34–8.

[1889–90] If the bell rang once, it was for me; when twice for the maid; and three short rings in succession meant the manservant. When they rang for me, I was allowed to ask at the speaking tube what they wanted; the maid and the manservant had to rush right upstairs; often just for a trifle. At the speaking tube I had to say, 'What do you wish?' That's what the ladies wished. If no answer came, I had to run upstairs. Now, very frequently, I had something on the stove that couldn't be left long. At the very least I had to take it off to make sure that it wouldn't boil over or burn, because the conferences upstairs could drag on. But for the ladies this was a long time, so they rang again, loudly and persistently, and when possible a third time, before I got upstairs. I was received crossly with mean looks. My God, where have you been? – that was usually the beginning. My apologies were not accepted. 'Empty excuses' they called them. It often happened that they made me come up many times a day for no reason. Then they'd say scornfully as I left, 'See how fast you can get away!' And so they drove us pointlessly to exhaustion. . . .

The [invalid] master didn't give us any peace downstairs either. There was a hand bell over his bed that rang downstairs . . . to use when he woke up at noon to call the manservant if he happened to be downstairs at the time. Sometimes he'd ring the bell constantly during the night. I complained to Frau Sparr about it and asked her to disconnect the bell for the night because we needed to have some sleep. It was late enough anyway before we could get to bed, never before twelve and often not till twelve-thirty or one o'clock. But what was her answer to me? 'What do you mean? The bell is there to be rung, not to be silent. If the master rings he has some wishes, and they must be respected at all times.' I replied that's why he had the manservant sleeping in his room, and he had a bell on his nightstand to wake him. 'Well, he can't find it sometimes,' she retorted, 'don't make such a fuss'.

The mistress was always very crude in her speech . . . exasperating with her sarcastic talk and false suspicions. Shortly after this she ordered me to make a fresh cup of coffee for the master every night at two o'clock; he didn't like cold coffee, and reheated coffee not at all. I looked at her in astonishment and told her that I really couldn't guarantee that I'd always wake up. 'Oh,' she said in her usual scornful tone, 'just let me take care of that, I'll see that you wake up.'. . .

For fourteen days I did it, then I went on strike. When I complained that in the long run I just couldn't hold up if I got so little sleep, she gave me her answer: 'You're big and fat, you'll hold up. I wish it and the master prefers to have fresh coffee'. . . .

On this evening, I asked if [the manservant] would be so good as to take the little spirit stove upstairs with him so he could heat up the master's coffee; . . . He thought I was right in finally revolting against this abuse, as he called it. . . .

On this night . . . she appeared suddenly like a ghost in our room, in a long, flowing white nightgown, with her hair down. She shook me on the shoulder, and not very gently either. Get up! Get up! Make coffee for the master! she called several times; I considered what would be best: to jump up in her face, also like a ghost, or continue to sleep. I chose the latter. But it didn't help. I had to wake up after all, but I did not intend to get up. I had resolved. So I asked her what she wanted from me. 'The girl still has to ask,' she yelled. 'You're supposed to get up and make coffee for the master.'

'No, Frau Sparr,' I said, 'I told you yesterday that I couldn't do it anymore. I'm not getting up because I just have to sleep, and I have to get up tomorrow at six o'clock to begin work. Anyway, there is coffee up there and Heinrich will heat it up for the master.'

As I said this I sat upright because I was really afraid that she would 'give me a couple of slaps' as the Hamburgers say, and I wanted to be in on the fight. Well, nothing happened; she dropped her fists. . . . rushed out of the room, snorting that she'd never known such abominable impudence.

'Impudent again', I thought. . . . I often wondered after such scenes whether I'd really behaved impudently without provocation. I could always say no with a clear conscience. I just wanted to be treated as a human being, and this right is all too often denied to servants.

Rural worlds

Many women moved between jobs during a lifetime of work. In interviews with a British Parliamentary commission, women describe agriculture, factory work, apprenticeship and domestic service. All are mothers, some are widows, and all relate lives of hard work and hardship. However, they also have distinct views on their roles as mothers and workers and their life stories reveal many of the variances of working life shared across rural regions.

Mary Haynes, an English widow, describes her life and work in much the same terms as married women did. However, in Ireland the Commissioners found that widows were almost destitute. They place some of the blame on absentee landlords, which certainly had an impact on Irish conditions, but they also observe that widows were unfamiliar with agricultural work and had few other skills to turn to. While this may be an issue of perception, it also strongly suggests the significance of different landowning patterns, inheritance practices and agricultural circumstances which shaped the worlds of rural women across Europe.

2.30 Rural women

Great Britain Parliamentary Papers, *Reports of Special Assistant Poor Law Commissioners on the Employment of Women and Children in Agriculture*, 1843, XII, 66–9, 109.

Mrs Britton, Wife of —— Britton, of Calne, Wiltshire, Farm-labourer.

I am 41 years old; I have lived at Calne all my life. I went to school till I was eight years old, when I went out to look after children. At ten years old I went to work at a factory in Calne, where I was till I was 26. I have been married 15 years. My husband is an agricultural labourer. I have seven children, all boys. . . .

I have worked in the fields, and when I went out I left the children in the care of the eldest boy, and frequently carried the baby with me, as I could not go home to nurse it. I have worked at hay-making and at harvest, and at other times in weeding and keeping the ground clean. I generally work from half-past seven till five, or half-past. When at work in the spring I have received 10d a-day, but that is higher than the wages of women in general; 8d or 9d is more common. . . . I never felt that my health was hurt by the work. Hay-making is hard work, very fatiguing, but it never hurt me. Working in the fields is not such hard work as working in the factory. I am always better when I can get out to work in the fields. I intend to do so next year if I can. Last year I could not go out, owing to the birth of the baby. . . . We grow potatoes and a few cabbages, but not enough for our family; . . . We have to buy potatoes. One of the children is a cripple, and the guardians allow us two gallons of bread a-week for him. We buy two gallons more, according as the money is. . . . We could eat much more bread if we could get it; sometimes we can afford only one gallon a-week. We very rarely buy butcher's fresh meat, certainly not oftener than once a-week, and not more than sixpenny worth. I like my husband to have a bit of meat, now he has left off drinking. I buy ½lb. butter a-week, 1 oz. tea, ½lb. sugar. The rest of our food is potatoes, with a little fat. The rent of our cottage is 1s 6d a-week; there are two rooms in it. We all sleep in one room, under the tiles. Sometimes we receive private assistance, especially in clothing. Formerly my husband was in the habit of drinking, and everything went bad. He used to beat me. I have often gone to bed, I and my children, without supper, and have had no breakfast the next morning, and frequently no firing. My husband attended a lecture on teetotalism one evening about two years ago, and I have reason to bless that evening. My husband has never touched a drop of drink since. He has been better in health, getting stouter, and has behaved like a good husband to me ever since. . . . I send my eldest boy to Sunday school; them that are younger go to the day school. My eldest boy never complains of work hurting him. My husband now goes regularly to church: formerly he could hardly be got there.

Mary Haynes, Widow, Calne, Wiltshire.

I have been accustomed to work in the fields for the last 16 years, all the year through, except just the winter months. I am employed in stone-picking, weeding, hay-making, reaping, turnip-hoeing, heating manure, &c. I have always been employed by the same master, who is particular in his labourers, and whom he pays well. I have always received 5s in summer, and 4s 6d in the other months, a-week; those are the regular wages. I am a good reaper, as good as many men; and in harvest, when I have worked by the job, I have earned 2s sometimes 2s 6d a-day, but only for a short time. The hours in harvest depend on the work, at other times from half-past seven in the morning, till five and half-past five in the evening. I think reaping the hardest of all the work I have ever done; it makes me very stiff at first, but that goes off in a few days. I always work in my stays, which get wet through, and they are still wet when I put them on again in the morning. My other clothes are also often wet when I take them off, and are not dry when I put them on again in the morning. I have not a change of clothes; but I have never had my health affected by the hardness of the work or damp things. In general, the women don't mix much with the men whilst working in the fields, except at hay-making. I never heard of anything improper happening from their mixing together. My master was always particular in choosing respectable people to do his work. . . .

My father had a little property when I was young, and I was sent to school. I was at school just two years. I was afterwards maid-of-all-work with the master for whom I have always since worked, and afterwards in the dairy. I have always found that being maid-of-all-work was of great use to me after I was married. The work was hard in the dairy, but it never hurt me.

Mary Puddicombe, Wife of Samuel Puddicombe, of Exeter, Labourer.

My father was a farm-labourer at Bridford. I am 41. I cannot read or write. I was apprenticed to Matthew Coleridge, of Bridford, when I was nine years old. My master died when I was 14; I was not apprenticed afterwards. When I first went, there were two boys and a girl apprentices; when my master died, there were three girls and four boys apprentices. The girls slept in our master's daughter's room, the boys in another room. We had to go through the boys' room to our room. Three of us slept in one bed: the four boys slept in one bed.

The family got their dinner all together, and supper too. There was no difference in the meat, and we always had wheaten pudding. There was wheaten bread ready, if anybody came in. I lived much better there than I should have done at home. We might go to the bread and cheese whenever we liked, any of us. We were not clothed very well. I didn't go to church for a long time, not for three years, and then because the clergyman interfered: then we got better clothes for Sunday. We were never taught to read prayers, and we never said our catechism: people were not so strict in those days as now. It is a good thing for children now that they are brought up to education. It is a good thing for children to read and write; it keeps them out of mischief. Most all my children go to school.

I used to be employed when I was apprenticed in driving bullocks to field, and fetching them in again; cleaning out their houses, and bedding them up; washing potatoes and boiling them for pigs; milking; in the fields leading horses or bullocks to plough: maidens would not like that work now. Then I was employed in mixing lime and earth to spread, digging potatoes, digging and pulling turnips, and anything that came to hand, like a boy. I reaped a little, not much; loaded pack-horses; went out with horses for furze. I got up at five or six, except on market mornings twice a-week, and then at three. I went to bed at half-past nine. . . .

When my master died, I went as servant at Blackiston for two years. I was treated very bad there: the people beat their servants. I used to be beat black and blue. The servants beat me; my master used to bang me. I never was much hurt. I never complained to a magistrate. I told my father and mother, and they told me to be a better maiden next time. . . . One maiden had her arm cut to the bone with a stick the young master cut out of the hedge at the time, for not harrowing right, . . . That went to a justice: master was fined 5£, and had to pay the doctor's bill. . . . The parish did not bind any apprentices after that.

I worked in the fields many years after I married; lately I have done washing. I think washing is harder than working in the fields.

2.31 Irish widows

Great Britain Parliamentary Papers, *The condition of the agricultural classes of Great Britain and Ireland* (London: John Murray, 1842), I, 160–1.

Province of Munster, county of Clare.
   The Commissioners are convinced that it is impossible for the women to earn their subsistence; nearly all the lands of the parish belong to absentee proprietors, and when the question was put whether these ever contributed to the relief of those who paid them rent, it was answered with a laugh that expressed astonishment at such a thought being entertained. A tithe-valuator, who knew the circumstances of every holding in the parish, declared that he never knew an instance where a widow was spared either in tithe or rent; that no one of them ever obtained ground or a cabin rent-free; and, on the contrary, that in many cases, in proportion to their misery, they paid a higher rent. A widow, who does not beg, seeks her only means of support in the acquisition of a small piece of conacre, because the neighbours will dig it for her gratuitously. A collection is made at the Protestant church, and among thirteen persons who participate in this money, there are about six widows, all Roman Catholics, and no attempt has ever been made to withdraw them from their faith. This relief, however, does not exceed 2s a year. One witness stated that there was also a collection made at the Catholic chapel.

County of Cork
   The number of widows is twenty-eight. Their misery is very great, . . .
   Widows, burdened with children, have added a new complication in the free state which Christianity has introduced into society. In the state of slavery, a woman losing her husband did not lose the means of subsistence for herself and her children, the master was always obliged to feed, clothe and lodge them. But in the free state, a widow becomes the head of a family, to sustain which

she has none of the resources afforded by the profession of arms, of navigation, of administration or the law. The widow is almost equally a stranger to the labours of agriculture, to the handicraft of the artisan, to manufactures and to commerce; she can neither work in the mine nor at the anvil. In all ages the only resource of women has been to spin, and modern inventions now deprive them of their sole means of earning a livelihood.

Let it be attentively remarked, that this number of families, the heads of which are incapable of supporting them, amount to more than a tenth of the whole. Who then is there to provide for so much want, if not the Catholic clergy, a class of men living in celibacy, who by their position constitute the intermediate link between the rich and the poor, the strong and the weak? How much greater too was the security of society, when the religious orders, the great owners of the land, accumulated by their skill and industry in agriculture immense stores of the means of subsistence, for which their only use was to aid the poor, as they were themselves subjected to sumptuary laws, a fixed residence and a regular employment of their time!

Urban workers

Manufacturing work took place in small workshops, in increasingly large factories and at home. Much of it remained unmechanised handwork, but machinery was progressively introduced into processes. Austrian Adelheid Popp began work as a very young girl, helping to support her large family, forced to leave school, working in workshops and ultimately in factories. Her account illustrates the character of the work, the risks young women faced and the near-disasters she encountered. Ottilie Baader explains the impact of the sewing machine on shirtmaking at the end of the century, and how factory work migrated into sweated homework. Amalie Seidl provides a vivid account of the working conditions in a large finishing plant and the progress of the first women's strike in Austria.

2.32 A working woman

Adelheid Popp, *Autobiography of a Working Woman*, 32–5, 46–9, 59–61, 66–71.

[c. 1879] I was taken into a workshop where I learned to crochet shawls. I earned from five pence to sixpence a-day, working diligently for twelve hours. . . . I used to run to my work at six o'clock in the morning, when other children of my age were still sleeping. And they were going to bed, well fed and cared for, when I was hastening home at eight in the evening. Whilst I sat bent over my work, making one row of stitches after another, they played, or went for a walk or to school. I took my lot then as a matter of course; only one eager desire came to me again and again − . . . I wanted to sleep till I woke of my accord – that seemed to me to be a most splendid and beautiful thing . . . [at home, she worked] after my mother had wakened me she gave me a chair in bed, so that I might keep my feet warm, and I crocheted on from where I had left off the previous evening. . . . I knew nothing, really nothing, of childish joys and youthful happiness . . . The proceeds of the sweating of so many young girls formed everywhere the foundation of the living of whole families. I frequently worked for the wives of officials or the employees of commercial businesses who could only keep up an appearance suitable to their station by the exploitation of our labour. . . . I was in my twelfth year when my mother decided to apprentice me. . . . For twelve hours a-day I was obliged to make ornaments out of pearls and silk lace for ladies' ready-made clothes. I received no fixed wage. . . . We had to work continuously without being allowed a moment's rest. . . . With what longing I looked at the clock when my pricked fingers pained me and when my whole body felt tired out! . . .

I came in my search for work to the office of a manufacturer of bronze goods. . . . I received a place among twelve young girls, and was once more in a warm, heated room. I was shown how to string chain links, and soon acquired some dexterity. The chief was kind to me. . . . I worked ten months uninterruptedly in the bronze factory. I received, according to my ideas at that time, nice clothes, ventured to buy pretty shoes, and also many things which please young girls. . . . After some months another kind of work was assigned to me which was better paid, but it was harder. I had to solder with a pair of bellows driven by gas, which did not appear to do me any good. My cheeks grew paler and paler, a great unconquerable feeling of tiredness overcame me, and I had giddy attacks, and often had to sit down. . . . They found me undernourished and bloodless to the last degree, and advised exercise in the open air and good nourishment. How was I to follow their orders? . . .

I had not been allowed to remain in the bronze factory because the work was undermining my health; but now I was working in a metal factory, where I had to tend a press, and where I, as the latest comer, had to carry up the burning material from the underground room, always tormented by the fear of fainting in climbing or descending the bad stairs. [A few weeks later] I had to be supported by passers-by, as I began to totter, and I again became unconscious. . . . As they were not clear what was the matter with me, I was taken to the mental hospital. Half a child still, I was not aware of the fearful significance of being obliged to live with the mentally afflicted. It was, paradoxical as it may sound, the best time I had ever had. . . . The search for work began again. I left home early in the morning to be the first at the gates, but it was always a vain quest.

My mother had been exceedingly kind to me from the time of my illness, . . . But now she became cross again because I was so long earning nothing. . . . I tried for [work] in a cardboard box factory, in a shoe factory, at a fringe-maker's, in a workshop where fresh colours were worked on Turkish shawls, and in many other trades. . . . Three weeks had passed in this way when the giddy attacks began again, and these were followed by a severe fainting fit. . . .

One day I was told that there was no prospect of my becoming healthy and capable of continuous work, and, therefore . . . in a few minutes I found myself in the receiving room of the workhouse. I was exactly fourteen years and four months old. . . . I did not know my native parish. I had never lived there, and did not understand the language spoken in it. I was quite desperate, and the desire just to be able to die again overwhelmed me. I stammered that I had a mother who worked, and that I myself had worked since I was ten years old [her mother fetched her] . . . I began also to consider the criminality of bureaucratic routine, which placed me, a child, deprived through labour and hunger of all childish pleasures, in a home for old and infirm women, . . . A wave of bitterness came over me as I realised all this, . . .

[At a glass–paper factory] Up till now I had not been acquainted with the life and drive of a factory; and I had never felt so uncomfortable. Everything displeased me. The dirty, sticky work, the unpleasant glass dust, the many employees, the common tone, and the whole manner in which the girls and married women talked and behaved. . . . They often talked of Mr Berger, the traveller for the firm, who was expected back now. All the women idolised him, so that I was very curious to see the man. I had been there a fortnight when he arrived. . . . Mr Berger sent me for something, and made a stupid remark at the same time about my 'beautiful hands.' When I came back it was dark, and I had to pass an empty anteroom, which was not lighted, . . . Mr Berger was in the room as I came through. He took me by the hand and enquired sympathetically into my circumstances. I answered him truthfully, and told him of our poverty. He spoke very kindly, praised me, and promised to use his influence to get my wages raised. Naturally I was much pleased at the prospect held out to me, . . . I stammered a few words of gratitude, . . . Before I rightly knew what had happened, Mr Berger had kissed me. He sought to soothe my horror with the words: 'It is only a fatherly kiss.' He was twenty-six and I nearly fifteen, so that there could not be much question of fatherliness. . . . I did not know what to think of what had happened; I considered the kiss as something disgraceful, . . .

On the next day a fellow-worker . . . whom I had liked best of all of them – overwhelmed me with reproaches. She complained that I had taken her place with the traveller . . . The other girls joined in; . . . When I spoke of it at home I was severely scolded; it was curious. My mother, . . . who had always given me warnings and instructions not to talk to men was in this instance against me. I was called over excited. A kiss was nothing bad, and if I received higher wages from it, it would be stupid to give up my work. . . . On Monday my mother woke me as usual, and impressed on me, as she went to work, not to be stupid, but to think that in a few days it would be Christmas. . . . I wanted to conquer myself and go into the factory; I came to the door, then I turned back. . . . all that had happened . . . seemed to me disgrace. . . . So I did not go in. . . .

But at last things became better. I was recommended to a great factory which stood in the best repute. Three hundred girls and about fifty men were

employed. I was put in a big room where sixty women and girls were at work.
. . . We had to sort the goods which had been manufactured, others had to
count them, and a third set had to brand on them the mark of the firm. We
worked from 7am to 7pm. We had an hour's rest at noon, half-an-hour in the
afternoon. Although there was a holiday in the week in which I began to
work, I received the full wages paid to beginners. . . . Besides that, the
prospect was held out to me after a few months' steady application of receiving an increase . . . in six months I was earning ten shillings; later I received
twelve shillings. I seemed to myself to be almost rich. . . . As I had been
accustomed to extraordinary privations, I should have considered it
extravagant to spend more now on my food. . . . I only wanted to be well
dressed, so that if I went to church on Sunday no one should guess I was a
factory worker. For I was ashamed of my work. . . . When I was an apprentice
I had always heard it said that factory girls were bad, disorderly, and depraved.
. . . I had also adopted this false notion. . . . The girls were kind; they
instructed me in my work in the friendliest manner, and introduced me to
the customs of the factory. . . . From the women of this factory one can judge
how sad and full of deprivation is the lot of a factory worker. Here were the
best-recognised conditions of work. In none of the neighbouring factories
were the wages so high; we were envied everywhere. . . . Every one strove to
give perfect satisfaction to avoid being dismissed. . . . And even here, in this
paradise, all were badly nourished. . . .

I saw amongst my colleagues, the despised factory workers, instances of
extraordinary self-sacrifice. If any special poverty was found in a family, they
put their farthings together to help. When they had worked twelve hours in a
factory, and when many had walked for an hour to get home, they would
mend their clothes, . . . Even the intervals for meals were not devoted to rest.
The eating of the scanty meal was quickly accomplished, and then stockings
were knitted, crocheted or embroidered. And in spite of all the diligence and
economy, every one was poor, and trembled at the thought of losing her work.
All humbled themselves, and suffered the worst injustice from the foremen,
not to risk losing this good work, not to be without food.

2.33 The sewing machine

Ottilie Baader, *Ein steiniger Weg. Lebenserinnerungen einer Sozialistin* (Berlin: JW
Dietz, 1921), 17–21.

[c.1860s] I had tried all kinds of work. But now I learned to sew on a machine
and worked in one of these factories on Spandauerstrasse [Berlin]. There were
about fifty women working at sewing machines and about an equal number
engaged in preparing the pieces for the sewers. Every sewer was teamed with
a preparer and the pay was split between them.

The workday lasted from eight in the morning until seven at night without
any significant breaks. At noon you ate the bread you'd brought with you, or

else you ran to the canteen next door to get something hot for a few groschen. Together, the preparers and the sewers got seven, at most ten, talers a week. Since the machine sewing was more strenuous than preparing, it was customary for the sewer to get 17½ and the preparer 12½ groschen of every taler. But before the division was made, they deducted the cost of wasted thread and broken needles, which usually came to about 2½ groschen per taler.

The first stimulus to change these conditions came with the Franco-Prussian War [1870]. Immediately after its outbreak, business in the clothing industry came to a standstill. Women were let go and stood around penniless because they hadn't been able to save anything on their low wages. Our company wanted to take the 'risk' of keeping up full employment during the slack time if we wanted to work for half pay. We . . . were in a crisis situation since most of the women depended on themselves for support; they lived, so to speak, from hand to mouth. So we agreed to try it for a week.

So we started the drudgery. But the result was pitiful. The full cost of thread and needles was still deducted from our half wages. The owner's brutal actions made us start thinking. We decided unanimously that it was better to quit than to work for such wretched pay, which you couldn't even exist on. We selected three women, among them me, to tell this to the boss. When our delegation announced our common decision, he tried to calm us by telling us that as soon as there was news of victory in the war, business would go back up and wages would climb. He carefully avoided saying that they would 'reach their former levels.' Luckily we had the presence of mind to say that the wages would never rise as fast as they had been cut and, moreover, that there was a full warehouse of articles produced at the lower wages. When the boss realised that he couldn't fool us so easily, he got so angry his face turned red and he screamed at us, 'OK, then I'll pay you the full wages again! Are you going to work now?' We told him curtly, 'Yes, we'll work again.'

We were surprised by our success. And it was just as much a novelty to the owner that working women would get together and make common demands. He had been taken by surprise, but it was also true that collar makers were very much in demand at that time. Shortly thereafter the boss called me into his office and told me that I didn't have to fear that my participation in this matter would hurt me at work. . . . That sounded very good, but it really wasn't true. He began to find fault with my work, and it wasn't long before I got tired of this and left voluntarily. The unity of the women, which had brought us success, did not last long. . . . But the owners had learned. They didn't act as brutally as before but rather proceeded more carefully. They negotiated individual wage cuts with women who were in particularly dire straits. Of course this generated mistrust instead of unity among the women, and it took many years before they understood what was happening and confronted management with closed ranks. For many women it was a long and hard path.

I now bought my own machine and worked at home. I got to know all too well the fate of women working at home. I pedalled at a stretch from six o'clock in the morning until midnight, with a one-hour lunch break. At four o'clock I got up and did the housework and prepared meals. There was a little clock in front of me as I worked, and I watched carefully that each dozen collars took no longer than the previous dozen. Nothing made me happier than being able to save a few minutes.

This went on for five years, years that went by without my noticing that I was young, years in which life gave me nothing. . . . my fate was the same as many single daughters who don't make their own happy life at the right time: they have to hold everything together, . . . I supported my father for over twenty years, and I was always able to work hard enough to have an apartment with a living room and a kitchen. . . .

I can't say that I was always very happy. I'd hoped for something else out of life. Sometimes I was just sick of life: Sitting year after year at the sewing machine, always the collars and cuffs before me, one dozen after another; there was no value to life, I was just a work machine with no hope for the future. I saw and heard nothing of all the beautiful things in the world; I was simply excluded from all that.

2.34 Women strike

Amalie Seidl, *Gedenkbuch 20 Jahre österreichische Arbeiterinnenbewegung,* Adelheid Popp, ed. (Wien, 1912), 66–9.

In 1893 [Vienna], I worked in a factory that employed about 300 men and women workers of whom a majority did not earn more than 7Kr a week. . . . As a packer in the warehouse, however, I was paid the splendid wage of 10Kr and was among the best-paid female workers. . . . I succeeded in making my colleagues understand the importance of a May Day celebration, and we succeeded in getting the May Day off. Naturally, the next day, the only topic of conversation in the factory was the events of May Day, and during the rest period in the large factory hall I tried to prove that with the right organisation, we could improve our working conditions. During my speech, which was intently listened to, no one noticed that the head of the factory had also listened . . . Needless to say, punishment followed immediately, specifically, my dismissal. . . . when I reached the narrow street where my parents lived, I was more than a little astonished to see police stationed at the front door to the building . . . The rather large courtyard was crowded with female workers from the factory waiting for me and shouting that they would not take my dismissal quietly. I addressed them, standing on the chopping block, telling them that this was all very nice, but if they did want to strike, they should demand more than just my reinstatement. None of us knew what to demand, but we did want to strike! We agreed in the end that I should show up at the factory the next day (May 3); by then they would agree on their demands and perhaps also on the colleagues who would present the demands . . . demands for a reduction of working hours from 12 to 10 and my reinstatement were rejected by the firm. Because of the great heat in the workrooms, the women stood about half dressed and went barefoot, but at a moment's notice, they left the factory, their clothes on their arms and carrying baskets with their meagre midday meal or coffee thermos. . . . I rushed to comrade Dworschak [Popp] to deliver the news of the strike. . . . The women in three other factories joined us, so that after a few days about 700 women were on strike. Naturally, this being the first women's strike, it caused a sensation, and the bourgeois press took notice of it, complaining that now female workers were also being 'incited'. There were also exceptions. The correspondent of an English bourgeois daily wrote that 'the strikers who used the fourteen days mainly for recuperation in the fresh air, looked considerably better at the end of the strike than before.' No wonder! They could hardly be expected to look good with a work day of twelve and thirteen hours in rooms where the temperature sometimes rose to 54°C or in the bleaching plant with its stench of chlorine, or in the dye shop where 'lovely' aromas made breathing a torture. Thanks to the solidarity of the labour movement, we were so well supported that we received only a little less money than what we normally earned in the factory. There was no question that the strikers would not give in; they were going to stand firm. After holding out for fourteen days, . . . the demands were met: a ten-hour work day, a weekly minimum wage of 8Kr, May 1 to be a holiday, and also my reinstatement . . . A great number of women joined the organisation but only to turn their backs on it soon after I left the factory. . . .

I naturally had to do a lot of speaking during the strike (as well as I then could) and thus was drawn into the workers' movement. I had . . . attended a women's meeting where I heard comrade Anna Boschek speak. The fact that such a young woman dared to speak in public made a great impression on me . . . I lacked the courage. But on May Day 1893, I gave it a try nevertheless at a large gathering of the dyers in the Mariensaal hall in Rudolfsheim. Then came the strike and I had to speak. At some meetings in the summer and fall of 1893, a few of my speeches got me indicted for several violations of the penal code and sentenced to three weeks' imprisonment, . . . I still remember how pleasantly surprised I was when I entered 'the cell'. It was a large, well-lighted, friendly room, which I had to share with twelve to seventeen convicts. . . . Surely I was better off than when I had been a maid with a monthly wage of 6Kr.

But a 'subversive person' I must have been! . . . After my discharge I had to sign an affidavit at police headquarters, which gave the police the right to remove me from Vienna, should I be convicted again.

Business and professions

Increasingly, middle-class women went to work, drawing on motives ranging from a straightforward need to earn, to a desire to 'not be a burden', to a genuine wish to be independent and useful. Many continued in business as widows had done for centuries, as Finn Marie Hackman announced in a circular letter to her customers. Singletons were prominent in the push to obtain work, and so widow Louise Kaufmann followed a well-travelled route for educated and entrepreneurial women, running a school. Starting from a more unusual position, nine-year-old Leonilda Sjöström began teaching mathematics in her father's navigation school, supporting him and her brother until their deaths and then carrying on herself. The tone in *IDUN*, a Swedish women's magazine, expresses the sense of wonder that women could do such things.

Medicine, a time-honoured female domestic occupation, became one of the areas that women targeted in the fight for education and careers. Nursing training and the profession grew alongside the vigorous struggles to gain access to medical work. Extracts by Russian Maria Pokrovskaya, Pole Varvara Kashevarova-Rudneva and in the *Victoria Magazine* expose some of the difficulties of training, qualification, access and validation as doctors that women faced.

2.35 Sole manager

Central Archives for Finnish Business Records: Hackman & Co, B30 I.

Wyburg, the 31st December 1812

The Contract for the Firm of Ignatius & Hackman erected the 1st February 1798 expiring today, I take leave to inform You, that from the beginning of the Year 1813, I will continue the trade, existing hitherto under the above mentioned Firm, under my own name.

I, having been the only managing partner of the house since the death of my husband, and remaining in possession of all Stocks, active and passive debts, assure You, that no other change takes place in this trade, and that all engagements will be accomplished fore & aft with the Known punctuality.

Be pleased to take notice of my signature, and to continuate [*sic*] Your esteemed confidence and friendship.

I remain respectfully
    J.Fr. Hackman's Widow

2.36 Applying for a teaching licence

Louise Kauffman to DABSV, 30 June 1815, Journal sager nr. 151, 1815–14, Christianshavns Døttreskole, København Stadsarkiv.

Respectfully Promemoria

Since, up to now, I have not had a ——— licence to run my ——— Institute, currently located at Gothersgade no. 334, I hereby take the liberty of humbly asking the honoured Board if such a licence could not be issued to me.

In the Institute, writing and arithmetic are taught by Lt. Kauffmann; religion, German and Danish grammar, as well as composition in both languages are taught by Mr. Lund, M.A. in Theology; French is taught by Mr. Marville; drawing by Mr. LeMaire; geography, natural history, regular history, German and French reading, as well as translation to Danish from both languages are taught by the Headmistress, Mrs. Kauffmann; embroidery by Miss Damsgaard, and sewing, knitting and Danish reading are taught by Miss Kauffmann. During the 6 winter months, dance is taught by Mr. ——— Pio.

Copenhagen, June 30, 1815

Very sincerely yours

Louise Kauffmann, nee Kaas

widow of deceased Major Hans Kristian Kauffmann

2.37 Mathematics teacher

'Leonilda Sjöström', *IDUN*, 20, 178 (15 May1891), 1.

The last of May in 1886 we, the inhabitants of Stockholm, were surprised by a festive scene: in all our harbours the ships had a gala appearance with multi-coloured waving flags and pennants up in the masts! That day Leonilda Sjöström turned fifty. . .

Figure 2.3 Leonilda Sjöström

Leonilda Sjöström was born in Stockholm 31 May in 1836 into a family of seamen; her father, a flagship captain in the royal navy, P. Sjöström founded a private school for navigation pupils. . . The old seaman's schooling methods were not among the most modern and when in 1842 mathematics was introduced as an obligatory subject in the navigation exam he failed completely: he had no understanding at all for this modern subject.

His young daughter, still only a child, became his 'saving angel'. She had early shown great talent and interest in her father's schooling; now the small child surprisingly quickly learned geometry as well as arithmetic and algebra and – as miraculous as it may sound – she was not yet ten years old when she, the small girl, sat in the middle of her first pupils in her father's school, three bearded old sea captains.

In 1855 the school was taken on by Leonilda's brother, engineer Edvin Sjöström; since those days the sister stood by her brother's side as a loyal co-teacher until his death last October and she now takes care of the school alone. It is not only mathematics this exceptionally capable woman masters, but also she is widely familiar with all the subjects, which fall into the art of seafaring such as shipbuilding, navigation, astronomy, etc. . . .

It is unusually an intensive and comprehensive teaching activity what we have here before us –. . . A burning enthusiasm for her work, care for her pupils' best interests, . . . these have always characterised Leonilda Sjöström's work. . . .

And besides all this work that may be regarded as not especially 'womanly' according to old-fashioned views, she still has time to do ordinary ladies' work. Her hands never rest; they are in constant movement with crochet, sewing, knitting, all kind of needlework, during the lessons when the brain thinks, the mouth teaches. This is truly a sign of the most unusual kind of enthusiasm for work.

2.38 Community medicine

Maria Pokrovskaya, *Kak ya byla gorodskim vrachom dlya bednykh* [How I worked as a town physician] (St. Petersburg: B.i., 1903), 3, 27–30.

Soon after completing the medical course for women at Nicholas military hospital, I applied for a position as the head of the outpatient clinic at X. The answer did not take long to come. The head of the local municipality, Pyotr Ivanovich Nazarov, sent me a very nice letter inviting me to come. He wrote that until now the municipality had not had any female physicians, but there was one in Zemstvo, they were happy with her. He did not have any doubts that if I wanted to I would find understanding in the local community and would be useful to the poor. . . .

In the hospital, I met the head of the other outpatient clinic in the town. Shubin had one patient with a rare disease and Frenkel (another physician) came to have a look at him. Shubin was not there; . . . but the nurse told him

. . . the female physician was here and she could show the patient to him, and brought him to me. . . .

'Pleased to meet a colleague', he said and bowed . . .

I showed the patient to Frenkel. After the examination he asked if I agreed with Shubin about the diagnosis. I pointed out some signs that contradict it. Frenkel agreed that Shubin was perhaps not quite right. He asked me to show him some more interesting patients. I readily agreed.

'This one was brought in today. Shubin has not seen him yet, and I am not sure about the disease. Have a look', I said.

Frenkel complied with my request. He examined the patient and said that my assumption was probably correct.

'Do you come here often?' he asked me.

'Every day. I value the hospital very much. It helps me improve my knowledge,' I replied.

'Don't you have enough work to do?'

'There is enough work in the outpatient clinic. In addition, I visit the sick at their homes. But I still find the time to come to the hospital.'

'It is not mandatory for you visit the sick at their homes', Frenkel noted.

'It is my own wish. It is interesting for me to check the diagnosis and to watch the patients. Moreover, some of the sick cannot come to the clinic, and they do not have money to pay the doctor. That is when I go.'

'So you visit them for free?' Frenkel asked with disappointment.

'Yes.'

'For goodness sake, you will spoil the population and the municipality. We all will be forced to visit the poor for free'; he was annoyed. I did not expect such an argumentation and got confused.

'So you are not visiting the poor?' I asked.

'I do, but they pay me, as much as they can. You should also charge them, at least 30–50 kopecks for a visit', Frenkel said.

'But what should I do if they cannot pay at all?'

'Let them be brought to the clinic. If you go on visiting them for free, it would be against comradely spirit. We already have to work a lot for our small salary', Frenkel added when saying good-bye.

Several days afterwards I had a conversation with Shubin on the same topic. . . .

'We work a lot for the town anyway, and they pay us so little. And you invent extra work for yourself. It is good that you do not have a family and can be satisfied with a small salary. But I have a family. The municipal salary is not enough for me. You should act in a comradely manner and support us. You have your outpatient clinic and this is enough. You can work in a hospital. If you want, you can spend a whole day here. But do not spoil the population with free visits', Shubin said.

I was a newcomer to community medicine and was not yet filled with the corporative spirit, therefore the reproaches of Frenkel and Shubin puzzled me. I thought that I was doing good when I visited the poor for free and that I brought benefit to society. But they say that does harm to physicians, because they will be required to do more. How to reconcile the interests of society and the interests of corporation? It seems that I need to sacrifice the first for the latter; this is what the physicians say. But Nazarov, defending the interests of the town, claims that the municipal doctor should devote all his time to the poor people, because he was invited to serve them. In his opinion, the ideal municipal doctor should refuse any private practice among the wealthy people.

2.39 Midwifery training

Varvara Kashevarova-Rudneva, *An Autobiography*, in Toby W. Clyman and Judith Vowles, eds, *Russia Through Women's Eyes* (New Haven: Yale University Press, 1996), 162–5.

While I was studying midwifery at the Grand Duchess Elena's maternity clinic, . . . I travelled with the same people, mostly elderly officials whose families were living in the dachas in Pargolovo. . . . One of my fellow passengers . . . was curious to learn why I had to get up so early to go into the city. I told him I was training to be a midwife and had to attend classes almost every day. My revelation startled my travelling companions. They could not imagine why someone as young as me had decided to pursue such an occupation. Midwives were not particularly well respected in those days. My companion then asked me what I intended to do when I got my diploma. I said I would like to get a government position, but, unfortunately, that was unlikely since the men who made those assignments only gave them to their friends or to people with the right connections. I could see by his face that my companon was taken aback by my statement. The others, who were all listening, were obviously embarrassed about something. They kept making signs at me, but I did not understand and continued to hold forth on a subject that interested me.

My companion tried to argue with me. He said that the midwives themselves were to blame because they did not want to accept positions in remote areas, and they all wanted to practice in St. Petersburg. I replied that I was ready to go to the ends of the earth as long as I could earn an honest crust of bread and be of some use to society. [He] remarked that a position was now vacant in the Orenburg region because the woman who had been trained at government expense did not want to work in such a remote area. But if I wanted that position I would first have to train at the Kalinkinsky Hospital [military hospital specializing in venereal disease]. I declared that I was prepared to do whatever was required as long as I could find a position. [He] told me to go and see Dr. V. M. Tarnovsky, the house surgeon at the Kalinkinsky Hospital. . . . Imagine my horror when I learned that the man I was talking to was the very man I had been slandering . . . I had to go to the medical department to request a letter of introduction from the man I had unwittingly insulted. . . . I went to see Tarnovsky, my letter of introduction in hand, but nothing was said about a position. I was only given permission to study at the Kalinkinsky Hospital with the other women students.

I had earned my midwifery diploma, but I still had no means of support until I found a position. I was advised to see Professor Krasovsky [at a venereal clinic] and to ask him to help me find work. The professor had attended the final midwifery examination for my class and had been pleased with my answers (I graduated with honours although I had trained for less than a year). He greeted me warmly and promised to do what he could, but he warned me that my youth was against me. . . .

I returned to my studies at the Kalinkinsky Hospital and there learned of a position soon to be vacant. . . . The position required a year's training, but only four months of the course were left. . . . I filled out all the forms and signed all the papers that obliged me to serve six or eight years in return for a stipend of twenty-eight rubles a month for four months. At least now I knew I was no longer in danger of dying of hunger, and I began studying hard. . . . In less than a month I went to the top of the class and made them forget my

Figure 2.4
Danish nurse, 1909

predecessor, but I was difficult to get along with because I would not allow them to treat me as casually as they treated the other women students. Because of this they called me a proud Pole. When I was on duty I hounded the supervisors and the inspector to carry out Dr. Tarnovsky's instructions to give the most nourishing food to the weaker patients, who were sometimes forgotten altogether. To retaliate, they hounded me with rules and regulations and insisted that I keep bobbing up and down and curtseying to the head supervisor and inspector. Instead, I stopped curtseying altogether and told them that I took orders from only one man, Dr. Tarnovsky. They complained to him about me more than once, but although he reprimanded me in the presence of his superiors, he could hardly keep from laughing.

2.40 Society of Apothecaries

Victoria Magazine, 11 (May–October), 1868, 73–4.

– We cannot refrain from referring to the action which has been taken by the Society of Apothecaries with regard to opening its examinations to women. It is one of the things not very generally known, that this society numbers among its examinations one in Arts, the passing of which is a preliminary step to the examinations which would qualify a candidate to become a licentiate of the society, . . . and to practice as a duly qualified medical practitioner. . . . Of course there did enter into the minds of women who were anxious to advance the cause of the medical education of their sex, the recollection that the Society of Apothecaries was the one which had been the means of giving Miss Garrett her recognised place in the medical profession; and there was, therefore, more than ordinary interest taken in the Arts' examination, for the sake of what might follow.

But the Society of Apothecaries had reconsidered matters. Miss Garrett's success in the profession which she has chosen, has caused the rulers of that body to feel that, in admitting women to the position of licentiates, they may have been acting very unwisely for their own interests and those of future male licentiates; and so they have discovered that to admit female candidates to their professional examinations is not strictly in accordance with their charter. Therefore to all future applicants the answer in effect is to be, Sorry for you; wish we could help you; but, really, you know, we cannot consent to aid such illegal proceedings.

We wonder whether the illegality of the matter would have exhibited itself in so striking a light had Miss Garrett's attempt turned out a failure, or had there been no candidates willing to follow in her footsteps. . . . No doubt that the Society of Apothecaries considers that it has done the right thing; but there may exist a consciousness in the breasts of some of its leading members, that the world has shown a tendency to impute the exclusion of women from its higher examinations to no more exalted motive than professional jealousy.

6   Shaping wider worlds

Political women

Women's political activity ranged from the top, with queens, to women working in their own communities, for their own class and for others as benefactors. From the middle classes, Minna Canth, one of the foremost Finnish social activists, wrote on a range of social issues. Her writing also serves as an important reminder that writing, literature and political activism merged in many women's lives. Viennese activist Adelheid Popp describes her political education as she moved from working in sweated and factory jobs to understanding the political context of her life and the women around her. Ultimately she also realised the gendered character of working women's issues.

In countries as far apart as Finland, Spain, Austria, and France, women's issues increasingly made it to the table for discussion and action. Emilia Bazán describes the position of women in Spain, making points that had resonance across Europe, especially her focus on the doll-like middle-class ideal. Showing increasing concern for working women, Flora Tristan spoke directly to working men, claiming women's place at the centre of their household. This was not a plea to let women leave the workplace, however; she and Popp wanted a significant shift in attitude as well as action to address the physical realities of their working and domestic worlds. Political action was also important to women, and, like Amalie Seidl, Popp and others in the union movement, Maud Gonne became an activist in the Irish struggle for justice against absentee landlords, and in the political drive for Irish independence.

Women long had been active in philanthropy, and for many this led to formal political activities. The Irish Ladies Charitable Clothing Society, described by the Mayor of Cork, undertook its endeavours in the wake of the distress caused by the failure of the potato crop in the 1840s. This extract illustrates a number of features that were typical of philanthropic ventures, including the gendered characteristics of the organisation.

2.41 Discovering injustice

Minna Canth, 'Autobiography', *Päivälehti* [The Daily], 1891, 147.

I was born in 1844 in the city of Tampere where my father Gustaf Wilhelm Johnson served as foreman in one of the biggest cotton factories in our country. . . . Although my father was not well off, he made sure that I would get as good an education as it would be possible for a girl in our country. . . . My mother on the other hand was not at all pleased with her daughter who was constantly with a book and who spoiled her eyes with reading and handled the needle and the knitting needle very clumsily and showed no inclination for domestic matters. . . .

In 1863 the first seminary for elementary school teachers and mistresses was founded in the city of Jyväskylä. Suddenly it became clear to me that there I could find a satisfactory profession. I was one of the first students of the seminary. Excited about the idea of national elementary schools, I wanted to commit myself to its service and the year I carried out my intention was the happiest of my life. But after only a year, [she married] . . . I now had to give up all my desires in order to do handicrafts, prepare dinners and arrange my home and family, all those things that my character was not fit for. But I bravely started to work and stopped reading anything but newspapers and tried to suppress my longing if this was possible. One thing was clear: I had to be submissive to my husband. I took this thought so seriously that during the first years of our marriage I never spoke an inventive thought. . . . For eight years I suffered from the lack of mental nourishment, but then my husband started to edit a newspaper: 'The Wife is created to be her husband's helpmate'. My stupid conscience no longer created objections. I could once again give up myself to intellectual activities and I did it with joy and thrill. . . .

[She started writing plays.] When half the piece was finished, my husband died of a brain infection. After being married for thirteen years, I became a widow with seven children. The youngest was born almost seven months after my husband's passing away. . . . I had nobody to turn to and besides I was ill. The future looked very grim to me and I didn't know how to support my large family. My father had filed bankruptcy, but I decided to move to Kuopio to start the same kind of trade he had done. I finished 'Murtovarkaus' [Burglary] and sent it to the Finnish Theatre. I now thought that I was forced to give up all my literary work forever. During that time Suomalainen Kirjallisuuden Seura [Finnish Literature Society] had given me an award for 'Murtovarkaus'. . . . They encouraged me to carry on. . . .

I wrote 'Työmiehen vaimo' [Worker's wife] where I severely criticised injustices of legislation against women, unnatural religious concepts, drunkenness and the obscenities of men, the stupidity of women, superficiality and prejudice, in short everything that was warped and bad that I knew existed in the world. At that time I didn't even notice anything good in it. . . . People didn't spare me. Accusations poured in. They represented me as an atheist.

Parents forbade their children to come to visit me. A great number of friends gave me up and those who stayed had to possess great moral courage in order to recognise me as their friend. Not only was 'Työmiehen vaimo' to blame for all this. I had written similar pieces for newspapers, naturalistic short stories . . . Apparently there was no worse person in our country than I. . . . But I still had my mission. I wanted to fight to the last for the oppressed and those suffering from injustices.

2.42 Political education and the woman question

Adelheid Popp, *Autobiograpy,* 82–3, 85–91, 93–6, 105–6.

I also began to take an interest in public events. I was barely fifteen when a state of martial law was proclaimed at Vienna [1884]. One of the procla-mations, which began, 'My dear Count Taffe,' was nailed up in the street in which I worked. As far as I remember, it forbade the assembling of several persons. I read this proclamation with the greatest interest, . . . I cannot now say what kind of mood overcame me; but I know very well that I mounted on our work-table and made a speech to my 'brothers and sisters,' in which I made known the proclamation of martial law. I did not really understand anything of the matter; I had no one to talk with about it, and I was, moreover, not democratically inclined. . . . But everything political interested me vividly. . . . Even whilst I was an apprentice, I often went without food to be able to buy a newspaper. It was not the news that interested me, but the political leading articles. Now that I had a fixed wage, I bought myself a paper that came out three times a week. . . .

Everything that I read of them seemed so high and lofty that it would have appeared absurd to me to think that I, an ignorant, unknown, and poor creature might also one day take a part in their struggles. There was unrest among the workers: unemployment had much increased, whole industries were at a standstill, and the police . . . broke up trade unions and confiscated their funds. . . . In the evenings I rushed in the greatest excitement from the factory to the scene of the disturbance. The military did not frighten me; I only left the place when it was 'cleared'. Later on we lived with one of my brothers . . . Friends came to him, among them some intelligent workmen. . . . One of these workmen was particularly intelligent, and I liked talking with him best of all. He had taken several journeys, and could talk on many subjects. He was the first Social Democrat whom I learnt to know. He brought me many books, and explained to me the difference between Anarchism and Socialism. I heard from him, also, for the first time, what a republic was, and in spite of my former enthusiasm for royal dynasties, I also declared myself in favour of a republican form of government. I saw everything so near and so clearly, that I actually counted the weeks which must still elapse before the revolution of state and society could take place. From this workman I received the first Social Democratic party organ. . . . The theoretical parts I could not at first understand, but I understood, and took hold of, all that was written of the sufferings of the working classes, and I first learnt from it to understand and judge of my own lot. I learnt to see that all that I had suffered was the result not of a divine ordinance, but of an unjust organisation of society. The descriptions of the arbitrary application of the laws against the workers filled me with boundless indignation.

I had not been at any meetings; I did not even know that women could attend their meetings. Besides, it was quite against my ideas to go alone to an inn. . . . Now that I had an object before me and was thoroughly saturated with the thought that every one ought to know what had been made known to me, I gave up my reticence, and told my [factory] comrades all that I had read of the workers' movement. Formerly I had often told stories when they had begged me for them. . . . I now held forth on oppression and exploitation. I told of accumulated wealth in the hands of a few, and introduced as a contrast the shoemakers who had no shoes and the tailors who had no clothes. I read aloud in the intervals the articles in the Social Democratic paper, and explained what Socialism was as far as I understood it. . . . When I entered the sales-room of the Social Democratic party for the first time, I felt as though I were entering a sanctuary. And when I gave my first 2½d towards the election fund of the German Social Democracy under the name of 'Firm Will,' I felt myself already a member of the great army of combatants, although I did not yet belong to any union, and, with the exception of my brother's friend, had not yet spoken to any Social Democrat. As I constantly read in my paper, 'Get new subscribers,' 'Increase the circulation of your paper,' I struggled to work in this direction. When I was able to fetch every week not only one paper, but two, then three, and finally ten copies, my feeling of joy was beyond all comparison. . . .

I had no notion yet of the 'Woman Question.' There was nothing about it in my newspaper, and now I only read Social Democratic publications. . . .

Then I read one day the following article in the Social Democratic newspaper.

> . . . If the whole spectacle had not been a hypocritical lie, a diabolical self-deception, had a single ray of the naked truth penetrated into the glittering hall, then, indeed, the picture of 'Woman in the Nineteenth Century' would have sufficed to rouse the management from their infatuation, to frighten them away in shame and horror. But they are blind, and where they are not blind, they hug their self-deception. How could they live without this self-created blindness?'

I read that in the Social Democratic paper, . . . and its effect on me was indescribable. I did not sleep – it was as though scales had fallen from my eyes, and I pondered over what I had read. My state of excitement continued, and everything in me spurred me on to action. I could not possibly keep what I had read to myself – the words came to my lips in due form when I wanted to speak. I mounted a chair at home, and held forth as I would have done if I had to speak at a meeting. . . . 'If I were only a man,' I kept repeating. . . . I never heard nor read of women in meetings, and besides, all the exhortations in 'my paper' were directed towards workmen and men. . . .

Shortly afterwards I made my first public speech. It was on a Sunday morning at a branch meeting. . . .

The meeting was attended by three hundred men and nine women, as I learnt later from the branch paper. As women's work was beginning to play an important part in this branch, and the men were already feeling the effect of the supply of cheaper women workers, at this meeting the meaning of trade organisation was to be discussed. There had been a special endeavour to make the meeting known to working women and although hundreds worked in a single factory only nine women had come. When the convenor of the meeting announced this and the speaker referred to it, I felt great shame at the indifference of my companions of my own sex. . . . The speaker described the conditions of women's labour and showed that the holding back, the absence of wants, and the contentedness of women workers were crimes which drew all other evils after them in their train. . . . When the speaker had finished the chairman announced that those present should express their opinions on this important question. I had the feeling that I must speak. I fancied that all eyes were directed towards me, that all were wanting to hear what I could say in defence of my sex. I lifted my hand and requested permission to speak. They cried 'Bravo' before I opened my mouth; merely from the fact that a working woman wanted to speak. As I mounted my steps to the platform my eyes swam and my throat was parched – I felt as though I were choking. But I conquered my excitement and made my first speech. I spoke of the sufferings, the sweating, and the mental poverty of working women. . . . I spoke of all that I had experienced and had observed among my fellow workers. I demanded enlightenment, culture and knowledge for my sex, and I begged the men to help us to them. The applause in the meeting was boundless; . . . and [they] requested me to write an article addressed to working women for the Union paper on the lines of my speech.

2.43 Women of Spain

Emilia Bazán, *The Living Age*, 182, no. 2351 (20 July 1889), 153–68.

. . . the social distance between the two sexes is today greater than it was in the old Spain. Men have gained rights and privileges in which women have no share. Each new conquest made by the stronger sex in the field of political liberty deepens the moral abyss that separates it from the weaker, and makes the rôle of the latter more passive and ill-defined. Educational freedom, religious freedom, right of public meeting, the suffrage and the whole parliamentary system only serve to transfer to the one-half of society, the masculine, the strength which the other half is gradually losing. Nowadays no woman in

Spain, from the occupant of the throne downward, enjoys the slightest political influence, and the female intelligence is but a pale reflection of the ideas suggested by men. . . .

I have already stated that in my native land, so far from desiring that his womankind should think and feel like himself, the man's aim is that they should live a moral and intellectual life not only inferior to but entirely different from his own. . . . I remember that some time ago in my native town, Coruña, a meeting of freethinkers was got up. The promoter and president was a professor of very republican opinions, and he gave notice in the newspapers that ladies might be present. When after the meeting he was asked why he had not brought his own wife, he answered, horror-struck, 'My wife? My wife is no freethinker, thank God!'

From this dualism in the male judgement spring extremely curious contrasts between the public and private life of Spanish statesmen. Whilst abroad they pose as innovators, and even as destructives, in the family circle they worship tradition and take part in the religious duties of the household. . . . Whilst the women are hearing mass their husbands await them, leaning against the pillars of the porch. . . .

It cannot be denied that some [of the elite] live very superficial lives, their only thoughts being of dress, amusement and trifles. But in addition to the fact that this is rather the result of want of brains than of wickedness, we must, before passing condemnation, look and see if the man, from whom the woman receives the moral impulse, gives her any better example. I do not hesitate to

Figure 2.5 Emilia Pardo Bazán

affirm that such is not the fact, and that the stronger sex is equally guilty of frivolity as the weaker. In the man the fault is less excusable. The woman in being frivolous, in passing her life between the hairdresser and the dressmaker, is only confining herself to the region to which she has been relegated, and playing the part imposed upon her, that of ornament. It is a common saying in Spain that only two professions are open to women, that of tobacconist, or that of queen. To these have been added lately those of . . . telegraph clerk. To men, on the other hand, every path lies open.

2.44 Why I mention women

Flora Tristan, 'POURQUOI Je mentionne les Femmes', *Union Ouvriére*, 3rd ed. (Paris: 1844), 43–71.

In the lives of workers, the woman is everything. She is their sole providence. If she fails them, they lack everything. As they say: 'It is the woman who makes or breaks the household,' and this is the exact truth; that is why it is a proverb. But what education, what teaching, what direction, what moral or physical development does the woman of the people receive? None. As a child she is left at the mercy of a mother and grandmother who, themselves, have had no education. . .

Instead of sending her to school,[1] we keep her at home in preference to her brothers, because she has more use in the household, to rock the children, run errands, watch the soup, etc. At twelve years of age she is apprenticed; there she continues to be exploited by her mistress and often also to be abused as she was with her parents.

. . . First injustice hurts us, we grieve, we despair, then when it is prolonged, it irritates, exasperates us, and no longer dreaming of anything but our revenge, we end up becoming hard, unjust, and mean. This will be the normal state of the poor girl at age twenty. Then she will marry without love, because you only get married if you want to escape the tyranny of parents. . . . in her turn, she will be totally incapable of raising her sons and daughters suitably; she will be as brutal to them as her mother and her grandmother were to her.

Women of the working class, observe well, I beseech you, that in pointing out what currently exists concerning your ignorance and your inability to raise your children, I do not intend to accuse you and your character. No, it is society that I accuse . . .

Poor working women! They have so many irritations! First the husband. (one must admit that there are few workers' households that are happy.) He has a bit more education: he is master by law, and also by virtue of the money he brings into the household. He believes himself (and it is the fact) very much superior to the woman, who brings only her small daily wage and is only a humble servant in the house.

It follows from this that the husband at the very least treats his wife with great disdain. The poor woman, who feels humiliated at each word and each look that her husband addresses to her, revolts openly or secretly, according to her character; which gives rise to violent, painful scenes that lead to a constant state of irritation between master and servant. . . . The situation becomes so painful that the husband, instead of staying home talking with his wife, hastens to flee, and as he has no other place to go to, he goes to the tavern to drink absinthe with other husbands as unhappy as he, in the hope of drowning his sorrow. . . .

This means of distraction aggravates the evil. The wife who waits for Sunday's wages in order to feed her family during the week is in despair seeing her husband spend most of it in the tavern. Then her irritation reaches its peak, and her brutality and ill-nature are doubled. . . . From reproaches and insults they go to blows, then tears, discouragement, and despair. . . .

I repeat, the woman is everything in the life of the worker. As mother, she influences him during his infancy; . . . As sweetheart, she affects his entire youth, and what a powerful influence a young, beautiful, loved girl could have! As wife, she influences him for three-fourths of his life. Finally, as daughter she influences him in his old age. . . . It follows from this situation that it is of the greatest importance from the point of view of the intellectual, moral, and material betterment of the working class for the women of the people to receive from their infancy a rational, solid education, suitable for developing all their good, natural bents, in order that they might become skilful workers in their trade, good mothers of families, capable of raising and guiding their children . . . and in order, too, that they might serve as moralising agents for the men over whom they have influence from birth to death.

2.45 My first speech

Maud Gonne, *A Servant of the Queen*, Norman Jeffares and Anna McBride White, eds (University of Chicago Press, 1994), 119–23.

Tim Harrington called on me one evening in Dublin: 'You said you wanted to work for Ireland; I have some work for you.'

'But you don't want women's work. None of the parties in Ireland want women. . .

'Well, I have some work for you now. There is a by-election at Barrow-in-Furness in Lancashire. It is such a Conservative stronghold that the Liberal Party have refused to fight it. The Irish will fight it on the evictions and Home Rule issue.'

I shook my head: 'That's not the work I want. I know nothing and care less about English elections. It is in Ireland the work must be done. I am going back to Donegal to help Father MacFadden and Pat O'Brien build houses.'

'. . . It will only mean one week's hard work and you can go back then to Donegal. You have just come from those evictions; you would be a great help.' . . . Harrington said I would be good at canvassing and that that was far more essential in winning elections than public speeches. Next morning Harrington and I were on the boat for Liverpool and little Pat O'Brien waved us good-bye and shook his fist at Harrington for carrying off his 'master builder'.

Some of the election committee met us at the station and said a meeting was in progress and Harrington was to speak at it. Harrington insisted I should come to the meeting as it would make canvassing easier if I were seen on the platform. I was soon seated on the right hand of the elderly chairman, facing an audience of 1,500 English people. The chairman asked if I would speak next. 'I am not a speaker, I have only come to help canvass.' I did not know it, but he was stonedeaf, and to my horror I heard him announce in a loud voice: 'Miss Gonne, a young Irish lady, will now address you.'. . .

I got up: 'Ladies and Gentlemen,' my voice, owing to my stage training, rang out alarmingly clear, then I stopped. 'Tell them about the evictions you have seen,' prompted Harrington, and I began. It was easy telling a straightforward story of the scenes which I had witnessed and which were so terribly in my mind. . . . I forgot where I was and then suddenly I remembered and I became aware of a dead silence, of thousands of eyes looking at me and my mind a complete blank. I stopped in the middle of a sentence, my knees began to shake and I sat down and began to cry; I would have given worlds to hide, to disappear. I was too confused for a long time to know what was happening and vaguely thought the meeting was breaking up because I had made a fool of myself. I did not realise that, after the intense silence which had startled me, the audience had risen to its feet and was applauding me. . . . next morning Harrington read me the local papers full of my speech, all interpreting my stage-fright as evidence of the sincerity of my emotions. 'You made a great impression; I have rarely seen an English audience so thrilled,' Harrington said.

2.46 Ladies' Charitable Clothing Society

John Francis Maguire, *The Industrial Movement in Ireland* (Cork: John O'Brien, 1853), 168–71.

At a General Meeting of the Society, . . . 31st of January, 1848; . . . it was proposed and unanimously resolved – That a report of the proceedings of the Society, during the past year, should be published.

The want of clothing for the sick poor has at all times been a source of anxiety to the clergymen and other benevolent professional and private individuals, who were in the habit of visiting them, particularly wherever, as in Cork, their wretched and overcrowded abodes, rendered cleanliness an indispensable aid to their recovery as well as a safeguard against infection. To meet, in some degree, this pressing necessity, a Society was formed in March, 1845, by the Rev. William O'Sullivan, for the benefit of the poor in the North Parish; . . .

A meeting, at which, notwithstanding the inclemency of the weather, many ladies assembled, was held on the 20th January, 1847, in the vestry room of St.

Patrick's church, and it was unanimously resolved that every endeavour should be made to alleviate a form of distress, which was peculiarly accessible to female benevolence. So great was the amount of clothing required, and so small the means to provide it, . . . the ladies were compelled to limit their orders to the manufacture of Gingham, and of that even in small quantities. Fully aware, however, that the only effectual mode of relieving public distress, is the giving of employment, they resolved that, should their undertaking prosper, and their funds increase, they would carry out the suggestion to the fullest extent possible.

A second meeting was held on the 3rd of February. – The funds arising from donations and subscriptions amounted on this day to £48 15s. 4d. With this sum, the ladies, trusting that the acknowledged utility of their under-taking would soon create a greater interest and bring them further support, immediately purchased materials for clothing. A committee of management was appointed, whose duties consist in preparing the various articles to be made, in distributing and receiving the work, and in the sale of the clothing.

One point which received great consideration, was the fitness of employing poor women to make up the clothing. . . . the arrangements adopted by the society have been attended with good results. Had the Society directly employed paid work-women, it would have been unable, in a short time, from the want of funds, to carry out its principal object, – the providing of clothing. – To prevent so disappointing a result, it was made a primary rule of the society, that the members should themselves take the work when prepared and return it completed to the repository; one good effect of this arrangement is, that a large number of the members employ poor women free of any expense to the Society, and this in addition to their donations or subscriptions. Another result (and its value cannot be overrated) is, that the junior members have now a really useful occupation for their many spare hours. A very general excuse for not supporting Clothing Societies is the statement, that the poor do not keep the clothing given them; it is, however, found, that when it is judiciously disposed of, the proper use is made of it. To secure this desirable object, the rule of the Clothing Society, in place of gratuitous distribution, obliges the members to purchase the clothing, at a very reduced price it is true, but sufficient to make each inquire as to the merits of the person she wishes to relieve, that her bounty may not be unavailing. . . .

From the 3rd of February, 1847, on which day the Clothing Society commenced its operations, the gradual but steady progress in public opinion, and the increase of funds, were such, as to encourage the ladies to carry into effect their resolution of purchasing none but Cork manufactured goods, when procurable. The fact that no body of tradesmen in the city were suffering such privations as the poor weavers, though willing to work and capable of doing so, induced the Society to give large orders for Gingham and immediately after for flannel, which were promptly and satisfactorily executed. Orders for checks followed, and with the same results. . . . The improvement in each of the above manufactures is evident, and it is with great satisfaction the ladies are enabled to state, that, owing to the impulse given by their necessarily slight, but united efforts, whereas on the 3rd of February, 1847, but twenty weavers had employment, and that of a very slight nature, there are at present – February, 1848 – one hundred and twenty at full work.

Worlds of talent

In the nineteenth century, the novel became heavily associated with women as readers, while women more frequently turned to it for income and creativity. Yet, as Charlotte Brontë, George Sand and George Eliot show, making a career and forging a place within literature, as opposed to writing as entertainment, was a difficult prospect. The compulsion to create is implicit in these texts. Sarah Bernhardt's reflections on her art and George Sand on hers represent the depth of vocation and self-belief that was necessary. The canon privileged male writers, actors and painters, and carving out a niche could be painful and exceedingly difficult.

The world of science and intellect was even more forcefully seen as a male world, but as in the previous century, outstanding individuals, often quietly, made their way. Mary Somerville explains the struggle she had to find time and resources to learn, doing so largely for her own pleasure. Yet, both she and Ada Lovelace were prevailed upon to publish, and were firm in their intention to do it on their own terms. Their scientific curiosity and the values of male and female networks are apparent in their memoirs and correspondence, as Lovelace's letters to Andrew Crosse, experimenter with electricity, show. At the same time as women were fighting to be allowed to enter universities, academics had their own struggle to gain university posts, and ultimately positions worthy of their abilities. Sofia Kovalevskaya became the first full professor of mathematics in the world, when she ultimately gained her academic post through the commitment and support of Gösta Mittag-Leffler, Swedish mathematician, professor of mathematics at Stockholm and member of the Swedish Academy of Sciences. He also intervened to give Marie Curie the Nobel Prize with husband, Pierre, in 1903. Her letter to her friend, statesman Georg Vollmar, describes some of the difficulties contingent upon this appointment.

2.47 Pseudonyms

Currer Bell [Charlotte Brontë], 'A Biographical Notice of Ellis and Acton Bell', Ellis and Acton Bell, *Wuthering Heights and Agnes Grey* (London: Smith, Elder and Company, 1850), 5–14.

IT has been thought that all the works published under the names of Currer, Ellis, and Acton Bell, were, in reality, the production of one person. . . . now, on the occasion of a reprint of Wuthering Heights and Agnes Grey, I am advised distinctly to state how the case really stands. . . .

About five years ago, my two sisters and myself, after a somewhat pro-longed period of separation, found ourselves reunited, and at home. Resident in a remote district where education had made little progress, and where, consequently, there was no inducement to seek social intercourse beyond our own domestic circle, we were wholly dependent on ourselves and each other, . . . The highest stimulus, as well as the liveliest pleasure we had known from childhood upwards, lay in attempts at literary composition; formerly we used to show each other what we wrote, but of late years this habit of communication and consultation had been discontinued; hence it ensued, that we were mutually ignorant of the progress we might respectively have made. . . .

We had very early cherished the dream of one day becoming authors. This dream, never relinquished even when distance divided and absorbing tasks occupied us, now suddenly acquired strength and consistency: it took the character of a resolve. We agreed to arrange a small selection of our poems, and, if possible, get them printed. Averse to personal publicity, we veiled our own names under those of Currer, Ellis, and Acton Bell; the ambiguous choice being dictated by a sort of conscientious scruple at assuming Christian names positively masculine, while we did not like to declare ourselves women, because – without at that time suspecting that our mode of writing and thinking was not what is called 'feminine' – we had a vague impression that authoresses are liable to be looked on with prejudice; we had noticed how critics sometimes use for their chastisement the weapon of personality, and for their reward, a flattery, which is not true praise.

The bringing out of our little book was hard work. As was to be expected, neither we nor our poems were at all wanted; but for this we had been prepared at the outset; . . . The great puzzle lay in the difficulty of getting answers of any kind from the publishers to whom we applied. . . . I ventured to apply to the Messrs. Chambers, of Edinburgh, for a word of advice; they may have forgotten the circumstance, but I have not, for from them I received a brief and business-like but, civil and sensible reply, on which we acted, and at last made a way. . . .

Ill-success failed to crush us: the mere effort to succeed had given a wonder-ful zest to existence; it must be pursued. We each set to work on a prose tale. . . . These MSS. were perseveringly obtruded upon various publishers for the space of a year and a half; usually, their fate was an ignominious and abrupt dismissal.

At last *Wuthering Heights* and *Agnes Grey* were accepted on terms somewhat impoverishing to the two authors; Currer Bell's book found acceptance nowhere, nor any acknowledgment of merit, so that something like the chill of despair began to invade his heart. As a forlorn hope, he tried one publishing house more – Messrs. Smith and Elder. Ere long, in a much shorter space than that on which experience had taught him to calculate – there came a letter, which he opened in the dreary expectation of finding two hard hopeless lines, . . . instead, he took out of the envelope a letter of two pages. He read it trembling. It declined, indeed, to publish that tale, for business reasons, but it discussed its merits and demerits so courteously, so considerately, in a spirit so rational, with a discrimination so enlightened, that this very refusal cheered the author better than a vulgarly expressed acceptance would have done. . . .

I was then just completing *Jane Eyre*, . . . This was in the commencement of September 1847; it came out before the close of October following, while *Wuthering Heights* and *Agnes Grey*, my sisters' works, which had already been in the press for months, still lingered under a different management.

They appeared at last. Critics failed to do them justice. The immature but very real powers revealed in *Wuthering Heights* were scarcely recognised; its import and nature were misunderstood; the identity of its author was misrepresented; it was said that this was an earlier and ruder attempt of the same pen which had produced *Jane Eyre*. Unjust and grievous error! We laughed at it at first, but I deeply lament it now. . . .

Neither Ellis nor Acton allowed herself for one moment to sink under want of encouragement; energy nerved the one, and endurance upheld the other. They were both prepared to try again; . . . [But] In the very heat and burden of the day, the labourers failed over their work [both dying of consumption in rapid succession]. . . .

I may sum up all by saying, that for strangers they were nothing, for superficial observers less than nothing; but for those who had known them all their lives in the intimacy of close relationship, they were genuinely good and truly great.

This notice has been written, because I felt it a sacred duty to wipe the dust off their gravestones, and leave their dear names free from soil.

CURRER BELL. 1 September 19, 1850

2.48 On critics

George Sand, *Indiana*, trans. G. Burnham Ives (Philadelphia: George Barrie & Son, 1900), 2–10.

INTRODUCTION

I wrote *Indiana* during the autumn of 1831. It was my first novel; I wrote it without any fixed plan, having no theory of art or philosophy in my mind. I was at the age when one writes with one's instincts, and when reflection serves only to confirm our natural tendencies. Some people chose to see in the book a deliberate argument against marriage. I was not so ambitious, and I was surprised to the last degree at all the fine things that the critics found to say concerning my subversive purposes. Criticism is far too acute; that is what will cause its death. It never passes judgment ingenuously. . . .

At the time that I wrote *Indiana*, the cry of Saint Simonism was raised on every pretext. Later they shouted all sorts of other things. Even now certain writers are forbidden to open their mouths, under pain of seeing the police agents of certain newspapers pounce upon their work and hale them before the police of the constituted powers. If a writer puts noble sentiments in the mouth of a mechanic, it is an attack on the bourgeoisie; if a girl who has gone astray is rehabilitated after expiating her sin, it is an attack on virtuous women; if an impostor assumes titles of nobility, it is an attack on the patrician caste; if a bully plays the swashbuckling soldier, it is an insult to the army; if a woman is maltreated by her husband, it is an argument in favor of promiscuous love. And so with everything. Kindly brethren, devout and generous critics! What a pity that no one thinks of creating a petty court of literary inquisition in which you should be the torturers! Would you be satisfied to tear the books to pieces and burn them at a slow fire, and could you not, by your urgent representations, obtain permission to give a little taste of the rack to those writers who presume to have other gods than yours? . . .

I did not expect so much honor, and I consider that I owe to those critics the thanks which the hare proffered the frogs, imagining from their alarm that he was entitled to deem himself a very thunderbolt of war.

[1842] When I wrote *Indiana*, I was young; I acted in obedience to feelings of great strength and sincerity which overflowed thereafter in a series of novels, almost all of which were based on the same idea: the ill-defined relations between the sexes, attributable to the constitution of our society. These novels were all more or less inveighed against by the critics, as making unwise assaults upon the institution of marriage. *Indiana*, notwithstanding the narrowness of its scope and the ingenuous uncertainty of its grasp, did not escape the indignation of several self-styled serious minds, whom I was strongly disposed at that time to believe upon their simple statement and to listen to with docility. But, although my reasoning powers were developed hardly enough to write upon so grave a subject, I was not so much of a child that I could not pass judgment in my turn on the thoughts of those persons who passed judgment on mine. . . .

Certain journalists of our day who set themselves up as representatives and guardians of public morals – I know not by virtue of what mission they act, since I know not by what faith they are commissioned – pronounced judgment pitilessly against my poor tale, and, by representing it as an argument against social order, gave it an importance and a sort of echo which it would not otherwise have obtained. They thereby imposed a very serious and weighty rôle upon a young author hardly initiated in the most elementary social ideas, whose whole literary and philosophical baggage consisted of a little imagination, courage and love of the truth. Sensitive to the reproofs and almost grateful for the lessons which they were pleased to administer, he examined the arguments which arraigned the moral character of his thoughts before the bar of public opinion, and, by virtue of that examination, which he conducted entirely without pride, he gradually acquired convictions which were mere feelings at the outset of his career and which to-day are fundamental principles. . . .

To-day therefore, having re-read the first novel of my youth with as much severity and impartiality as if it were the work of another person, . . . I find myself so entirely in accord with myself with respect to the sentiment which dictated *Indiana* . . . that I have not chosen to change anything in it save a few ungrammatical sentences and some inappropriate words. . . .

I repeat then, I wrote *Indiana*, and I was justified in writing it.

2.49 Silly novelists

George Eliot, 'Silly Novels by Lady Novelists', *Westminster Review*, 66 (1856), 442–61.

Silly Novels by Lady Novelists are a genus with many species, determined by the particular quality of silliness that predominates in them – the frothy, the prosy, the pious, or the pedantic. But it is a mixture of all these – a composite order of feminine fatuity – that produces the largest class of such novels, which we shall distinguish as the mind-and-millinery species. The heroine is usually an heiress, probably a peeress in her own right, with perhaps a vicious baronet, an amiable duke, and an irresistible younger son of a marquis as lovers in the foreground, a clergyman and a poet sighing for her in the middle distance, and a crowd of undefined adorers dimly indicated beyond. Her eyes and her wit are both dazzling; her nose and her morals are alike free from any tendency to irregularity; she has a superb contralto and a superb intellect; she is perfectly well dressed and perfectly religious; she dances like a sylph, and reads the Bible in the original tongues. Or it may be that the heroine is not an heiress – that rank and wealth are the only things in which she is deficient; but she infallibly gets into high society, she has the triumph of refusing many matches and securing the best, and she wears some family jewels or other as a sort of crown of righteousness at the end. . . . In her recorded conversations she is amazingly eloquent, and in her unrecorded conversations amazingly witty. She is understood to have a depth of insight that looks through and through the shallow theories of philosophers, and her superior instincts are a sort of dial by which men have only to set their clocks and watches, and all will go well. The men play a very subordinate part by her side. You are consoled now and then by a hint that they have affairs, which keeps you in mind that the working-day business of the world is somehow being carried on, but ostensibly the final cause of their existence is that they may accompany the heroine on her 'starring' expedition through life. . . . For all this she as often as not marries the wrong person to begin with, and she suffers terribly from the plots and intrigues of the vicious baronet; but even death has a soft place in his heart for such a paragon, and remedies all mistakes for her just at the right moment. . . . Before matters arrive at this desirable issue our feelings are tried by seeing the noble, lovely, and gifted heroine pass through many *mauvais* moments, but we have the satisfaction of knowing that her sorrows are wept into embroidered pocket handkerchiefs, that her fainting form reclines on the very best upholstery, and that whatever vicissitudes she may undergo, from being dashed out of her carriage to having her head shaved in a fever, she comes out of them all with a complexion more blooming and locks more redundant than ever. . . .

We had imagined that destitute women turned novelists, as they turned governesses, because they had no other 'ladylike' means of getting their bread. . . . we were glad to think that the money went to relieve the necessitous, and we pictured to ourselves lonely women struggling for a maintenance, or wives and daughters devoting themselves to the production of 'copy' out of pure heroism – perhaps to pay their husbands [*sic*] debts or to purchase luxuries for a sick father. . . . But no! This theory of ours, like many other pretty theories, has had to give way before observation. Women's silly novels, we are now convinced, are written under totally different circumstances. The fair writers have evidently never talked to a tradesman except from a carriage window; they have no notion of the working-classes except as 'dependents'; they think five hundred a year a miserable pittance; . . . It is true that we are constantly struck with the want of verisimilitude in their representations of the high society in which they seem to live; but then they betray no closer acquaintance with any other form of life. If their peers and peeresses are improbable, their literary men, tradespeople, and cottagers are impossible. . . . The epithet 'silly' may seem impertinent, [but] . . . If, as the world has long agreed, a very great amount of instruction will not make a wise man, still less will a very mediocre amount of instruction make a wise woman. . . .

No sooner does a woman show that she has genius or effective talent, than she receives the tribute of being moderately praised and severely criticised. By a peculiar thermometric adjustment, when a woman's talent is at zero, journalistic approbation is at the boiling pitch; when she attains mediocrity, it is already at no more than summer heat; and if ever she reaches excellence, critical enthusiasm drops to the freezing point. Harriet Martineau, Currer Bell, and Mrs. Gaskell have been treated as cavalierly as if they had been men. . . . For it must be plain to every one who looks impartially and extensively into feminine literature that its greatest deficiencies are due hardly more to the want of intellectual power than to the want of those moral qualities that contribute to literary excellence – patient diligence, a sense of the responsibility involved in publication, and an appreciation of the sacredness of the writer's art. . . . The foolish vanity of wishing to appear in print, instead of being counter-balanced by any consciousness of the intellectual or moral derogation implied in futile authorship, seems to be encouraged by the extremely false impression that to write at all is a proof of superiority in a woman. . . . And so we have again and again the old story of La Fontaine's ass, who puts his nose to the flute, and, finding that he elicits some sound, exclaims, 'Moi, aussie, je joue de la flute' [me, too, I play the flute] – a fable which we commend, at parting, to the consideration of any feminine reader who is in danger of adding to the number of 'silly novels by lady novelists.'

2.50 Creating a role

Sarah Bernhardt, *My Double Life* (London: W. Heinemann, 1907), 83–6,

I made up my mind that I would have the first prize for comedy, and with the exaggeration that I have always put into everything I began to get excited, and I said to myself that if I did not get the first prize I must give up the idea of the stage as a career. My mystic love and weakness for the convent came back to me more strongly than ever. . . . I felt a genuine vocation for the convent when distressed about losing the prize, and a genuine vocation for the theatre when I was hopeful about winning the prize. . . .

It was under these special conditions and in this frame of mind that I went on to the stage when my turn came. The choice of my role for this competition was a very stupid one. I had to represent a married woman who was 'reasonable' and very much inclined to argue, and I was a mere child, and looked much younger than my years. In spite of this I was very brilliant; I argued well, was very gay, and made an immense success. I was transfigured with joy and wildly excited, so sure of a first prize. . . .

I was in the doorway, ready to rush up to the stage. . . . 'First prize for comedy awarded unanimously to Mademoiselle Marie Lloyd.' The tall girl I had pushed aside now went forward, slender and radiant, towards the stage. . . .

We were great friends, and I liked her very much, but I considered her a nullity as a pupil. . . . I was simply petrified with amazement.

'Second prize for comedy: Mademoiselle Bernhardt.' I had not heard, and was pushed forward by my companions. On reaching the stage I bowed, and all the time I could see hundreds of Marie Lloyds dancing before me. Some of them were making grimaces at me, others were throwing me kisses; some were fanning themselves, and others bowing . . . My face, it seems, was whiter than my dress.

. . . and this first lesson, which was so painful at the time, was of great service to me in my career. I never forgot Marie Lloyd's prize, and every time that I have had a *rôle* to create, the personage always appears before me dressed from head to foot, walking, bowing, sitting down, getting up.

. . . my mind has been thinking of the soul that is to govern this personage. When listening to an author reading his work, I try to define the intention of his idea, in my desire to identify myself with that intention. I have never played an author false with regard to his idea. And I have always tried to represent the personage according to history, whenever it is a historical personage, and as the novelist describes it if an invented personage.

I have sometimes tried to compel the public to return to the truth and to destroy the legendary side of certain personages whom history, with all its documents, now represents to us as they were in reality, but the public never followed me. I soon realised that legend remains victorious in spite of history. . . . We cast aside all the failings of humanity in order to leave them, clothed in the ideal, seated on a throne of love. We do not like Joan of Arc to be the rustic, bold peasant girl, repulsing violently the hardy soldier who wants to joke with her, the girl sitting astride her big Percheron horse like a man, laughing readily at the coarse jokes of the soldiers, . . . having on that account all the more merit in remaining the heroic virgin. . . . In her childish eyes there is something from another world, and it is from this that all the warriors drew strength and courage. It is thus that we wish it to be, and so the legend remains triumphant.

2.51 Bride of science

'Correspondence between Ada Lovelace and Mr. Andrew Crosse', *The Lady's Friend*, VII (Jan.–Dec. 1870), 80–1.

Dear Mr. Crosse:
   I think I may as well send you the enclosed documents at once. . . . I am anxious that *we should try the experiments* mentioned; and you may require a little preparation, possibly, for the purpose. [on sound produced in a bar of iron by electro-magnetism]. . . The letter in the large handwriting is an account of an experiment with the muscles of frogs, which I hope we may manage; but I should think it required delicate manipulation. . . . I am anxious to consult you about the most convenient, and manageable, and portable forms for obtaining constantly acting batteries; not great intensity, but continual and uninterrupted action. Some of my own views make it necessary for me to use electricity as my prime-minister, in order to test certain points experimentally as to the nature and *putting together* of the molecules of matter. . . . By eventually bringing high *analysis* to bear upon my experimental studies, I hope one day to do much.
      Ever yours, Augusta Ada Lovelace

Dear Mr. Crosse:
   On Monday, the 18th, then, we expect you, . . . Perhaps you have felt already, from the tone of my letter, that I am more than ever now the bride of science. Religion to me is science, and science is religion. In that deeply felt truth lies the secret of my intense devotion to the reading of God's natural works. . . . The intellectual, the moral, the religious, to me all naturally bound up and interlinked together in one great and harmonious whole. . . . there is too much tendency to making *separate* and *independent bundles* of both the physical and the moral facts of the universe. Whereas, all and everything is naturally rotated and interconnected. A volume could I write you on this subject. . . . With all my wiry tower and strength, I am prone at times to bodily sufferings, connected chiefly with the digestive organs of no common degree or kind. . . . I do not regret the sufferings and peculiarities of my physical constitution. They have taught me, and continue to teach me, that which I think nothing else could have developed. It is a force and control put upon me by Providence, which I *must* obey. . . . They *tame* in the best sense of that

word, and they *fan* into existence a pure, bright, holy, unselfish fame within that sheds cheerfulness and light on many. Ever yours truly,

A. A. Lovelace

2.52 Mécanique celeste

Personal Recollections of Mary Somerville, Martha Somerville, ed. (London: J. Murray, 1873), 77–82, 154, 161–164, 172–73.

[1807] I was much out of health after my [first] husband's death, and chiefly occupied with my children, especially with the one I was nursing; but as I did not go into society, I rose early, and, having plenty of time, I resumed my mathematical studies. By this time I had studied plane and spherical trigonometry, conic sections, and Fergusson's 'Astronomy.' I think it was immediately after my return to Scotland that I attempted to read Newton's 'Principia.' I found it extremely difficult, and certainly did not understand it till I returned to it some time after, when I studied that wonderful work with great assiduity, and wrote numerous notes and observations on it. . . . I became acquainted with Mr. Wallace, who was, if I am not mistaken, mathematical teacher of the Military College at Marlow, and editor of a mathematical journal published there. I had solved some of the problems contained in it and sent them to him, which led to a correspondence, as Mr. Wallace sent me his own solutions in return. Mine were sometimes right and sometimes wrong, and it occasionally happened that we solved the same problem by different methods. At last I succeeded in solving a prize problem! . . . and I was awarded a silver medal cast on purpose with my name, which pleased me exceedingly. . . . When I told him that I earnestly desired to go through a regular course of mathematical and astronomical science, even including the highest branches, he gave me a list of the requisite books, which were in French, . . . I was thirty-three years of age when I bought this excellent little library. I could hardly believe that I possessed such a treasure when I looked back on the day that I first saw the mysterious word 'Algebra', and the long course of years in which I had persevered almost without hope. It taught me never to despair. I had now the means, and pursued my studies with increased assiduity; concealment was no longer possible, nor was it attempted. I was considered eccentric and foolish, and my conduct was highly disapproved of by many, especially by some members of my own family. . . .

I had now read a good deal on the higher branches of mathematics and physical astronomy, but as I never had been taught, I was afraid that I might imagine that I understood the subjects when I really did not; so by Professor Wallace's advice I engaged his brother to read with me, and the book I chose to study with him was the 'Mécanique Celeste'. Mr. John Wallace was a good mathematician, but I soon found that I understood the subject as well as he did. I was glad, however, to have taken this resolution, as it gave me confidence in myself and consequently courage to persevere. We had advanced but little in this work when my marriage with my cousin, William Somerville (1812), put an end to scientific pursuits for a time. . . .

[Fifteen years, taken up with children, travels, living abroad and mixing with scientific circles at the highest level.]

All the time we lived at Chelsea we had constant intercourse with Lady Noel Byron and Ada [Lovelace], who lived at Esher, and when I came abroad I kept up a correspondence with both as long as they lived. Ada was much attached to me, and often came to stay with me. It was by my advice that she studied mathematics. She always wrote to me for an explanation when she met with any difficulty. . . .

March 27th, 1827

From Lord Brougham to Dr. Somerville.

MY DEAR SIR,

I fear you will think me very daring for the design I have formed against Mrs. Somerville, and still more for making you my advocate with her; through whom I have every hope of prevailing. There will be sent to you a prospectus, rules, and a preliminary treatise of our Society for Diffusing Useful Knowledge, and I assure you I speak without any flattery when I say that of the two subjects which I find it most difficult to see the chance of executing, there is one, which – unless Mrs. Somerville will undertake – none else can, and it must be left undone, though about the most interesting of the whole, I mean an account of the *Mecanique Celeste*;. . . In England there are now not twenty people who know this great work, except by name; and not a hundred who know it even by name. My firm belief is that Mrs. Somerville could add two cyphers to each of those figures. Will you be my counsel in this suit? . . .

This letter surprised me beyond expression. I thought Lord Brougham must have been mistaken with regard to my acquirements, and naturally concluded that my self-acquired knowledge was so far inferior to that of the men who had been educated in our universities that it would be the height of presumption to attempt to write on such a subject or indeed on any other. A few days after this Lord Brougham came to Chelsea himself. . . . I said, 'Lord Brougham, you must be aware that the work in question never can be popularized, since the student must at least know something of the differential and integral calculi, and as a preliminary step I should have to prove various problems in physical mechanics and astronomy. Besides, La Place never gives diagrams or figures, because they are not necessary to persons versed in the calculus, but they would be indispensable in a work such as you wish me to write. I am afraid I am incapable of such a task: but as you both wish it so much, I shall do my very best upon condition of secrecy, and that if I fail the manuscript shall be put into the fire.' Thus suddenly and unexpectedly the whole character and course of my future life was changed. I rose early and made such arrangements with regard to my children and family affairs that I had time to write afterwards; not, however, without many interruptions. A man can always command his time under the plea of business, a woman is not allowed any such excuse. At Chelsea I was always supposed to be at home, . . . However, I learnt by habit to leave a subject and resume it again at once, like putting a mark into a book I might be reading. . . . Frequently I hid my papers as soon as the bell announced a visitor, lest anyone should discover my secret. . . .

I received letters of congratulation from many men of science. I was elected an honorary member of the Royal Astronomical Society at the same time as Miss Caroline Herschel. To be associated with so distinguished an astronomer was in itself an honour.

2.53 Mathematics professor

Sofia Kovalevskaya, 'Letter to [Georg] Vollmar', in Michele Audin, *Remembering Sofia Kovalevskaya* (London: Springer-Verlag Limited, 2011), 153–5.

My dear friend!
12.6.82
Mittag-Leffler left Paris yesterday. We spoke a good bit about Stockholm and my future position. He is not just an important and talented scholar, but he's also a very sympathetic person and very well educated in all areas, and if I were to judge all Swedes by him, then I would think that I will be really very happy in Stockholm. Everything he tells me about things in Stockholm has increased my desire to be recruited. For my part, I spoke to him quite frankly and brought his attention to the particulars of my personal situation, which could make a position in a rather bourgeois society disagreeable. For example, I am Russian and as such already suspected of nihilism (which in my case is not far from the truth), secondly, I do not live with my husband, and that, a woman separated from her husband, for whatever reason, is something dangerous and suspect in the eyes of every right-thinking matron. And educated women are judged more harshly than the others.

That I do not exaggerate on these matters, I see perfectly in the behavior of the local mathematicians whose acquaintance I have made recently. They visit me and pay me compliments, but none of them has presented me to his wife, . . .

You can imagine that these absurdities bother me little in Paris. In Stockholm this could be completely different. I have also said all that to Mittag-Leffler. He thinks that in Stockholm I will be considered differently. But a fear remains for me: he himself is a great idealist and has so much friendship for me that he thinks everything I do is good and cannot conceive that others could judge me differently.

In any case, after having thought much, I have taken the following decision and ML has also ended up admitting that this is the most practical and most reasonable. Since in Stockholm presently, outside of the university authorities concerned, no one yet knows anything of our plans, I will go at the beginning of November to Stockholm under the pretext of paying a visit to ML. I will give a communication to the mathematical society there and a talk in the mathematical seminar. If this is successful and if I like Stockholm, I can begin teaching at the beginning of the new year. Otherwise I will simply return and everything will be as before, without any damage.

Note

1   I have learned through a person who passed the exams for keeping an infant school that, from orders received from above, teachers of this kind of school must concern themselves with developing the ability of the boys more than of the girls. . . .

Intermezzo
La Belle Époque

Female health

During the Belle Époque, female health and sexuality became heated political issues, situated in discourses about race and eugenics as well as women's rights. Contraception had become more available and slowly gained acceptance, but as Aletta Jacobs shows, feelings were impassioned, and contraception was not well received even among medical personnel. Large families continued to exist, and in Figure 2.6, note the arrangement of the picture, and that the wife is again pregnant. Josephine Butler's campaign against the English Contagious Diseases Acts was one of the most important manifestations of the reaction to discourses that perceived women's bodies as needing policing, a campaign she took to international audiences. At the fourth congress of Russian physicians, Dr Ekunina-Fiveskaya, a pioneer female doctor like Jacobs, described in meticulous detail the operation of a compulsory clinic for prostitutes in Moscow. Depicted as a well-run and efficient operation, it implies that inspections were in the prostitutes' best interest. Both passages also are reminders of the kinds of work many early female doctors either chose or were allocated.

2.54 'Arbitrary maternity'

Aletta Jacobs, *Herinneringen van Dr. Aletta Jacobs* (Amsterdam: Holkema & Warendorf, 1924), 81–5, 88.

The free medical consultations I held for poor women and which put me in contact with the so-called working class were the reason I took up this serious problem again. Almost daily I had to diagnose sicknesses that were the direct results of unwanted pregnancies; moreover the children were burdens to their parents and society, in a material and moral sense.

Still searching for means to deal effectively with this problem, in early 1882, in a German medical journal, I found an article by Dr. Mensinga of Flensburg in which he recommended the use of the *pessarium occlusivum* [vaginal suppository]. . . . Although Dr. M. assured me that the method was effective and completely harmless to the woman's health, I wanted to convince myself first before I dared recommend it.

Figure 2.6 Middle-class Icelandic family, before 1920

Regularly, women of various social classes had consulted me about a means to avoid conception; all of them had social, moral and medical reasons for this and always I had to let them leave without advice. Some of these women who would benefit most, I sent letters, and told them that possibly I had a means that could help them but if they wanted to use it they had to come for several months for medical examination. A few women were willing. The results were such that after a few months I quietly declared that I had a harmless, effective means of contraception. . . .

Not for a moment had I thought that this part of my medical work would be welcomed by my colleagues. I knew too well how encrusted they were in traditional concepts and concerned about their place in society. I did not expect cooperation. On the other hand, I had not expected that my actions would arouse such a storm of indignation. Throughout the medical world their wrath came crashing down on me, and the few who agreed with me stayed silent for fear that the outrage would hit them. Tough times I have gone through. . . I had good friends but because of their lack of medical and sociological knowledge they did not fully understand the great importance to humanity that this part of my work was. They mostly advised that I should publicly declare I was mistaken and should renounce offering my help in future. I never contemplated taking this advice. Too much had I seen, and the blessings of my work, in my opinion, society and humanity awaited.

Certainly it was difficult and painful, as the only female doctor in the country, having to row against the stream of lies and slander widely spread by my male colleagues. The conviction however that this was worth my full attention and that my work was of great social importance gave me the strength to stand up and continue. Still I was not spared hours of doubt. . . . I further reasoned, knowledge of birth prevention would reduce the number of unwanted pregnancies, and should this not be welcomed, both from a social and an individual standpoint? If fewer undesirable people came into this world, this was only to be welcomed as a contribution to the improvement of race, social welfare and human happiness. . . .

However, the experience of those days of struggle caused my belief and good faith in people to be shaken. I knew in advance that people with narrow understanding could not share my views. I was also convinced those whose religious and social beliefs conflicted with mine would oppose me. This did not bother me. I even cherished the hope, in speeches and writing, to convince a few of them. That my colleagues, and among them especially midwives and gynaecologists who thought my work threatened their livelihood, did not refrain from the meanest libel to make my work impossible, I had not expected. . . .

Now, at the end of my life, I taste the satisfaction to see that senior men and women in scientific fields acknowledge the necessity of controlling births, not only from an economic but also from a social, medical and eugenic point of view.

2.55 Examining prostitutes

Maria Ekunina-Fiveskaya, 'Medical examination of prostitutes in the Moscow free municipal hospital', *Fourth congress of Russian physicians, 1891* (Moscow, 1892), 178–184.

Many years will pass before it becomes possible to find a solution to the question of how to eliminate prostitution and together with it the harm that it brings to society. Before that we have to limit ourselves to attempts to more or less successfully tackle the problem of maximum possible neutralisation of prostitution. . . .

Since there is no chance to implement more practically important measures, such as complete removal of all the sick from the rows of prostitutes and protection of prostitutes from contamination through the preliminary examination of men visiting them, we have to willy–nilly focus our attention and efforts on the improvement of those methods of the neutralisation of prostitution that we have at our disposal. No doubt that if periodical medical examinations of prostitutes do not fully remove the chance of them carrying syphilis, they reduce the risk of contamination to a minimum. . . .

When the control over prostitution was put under the municipal authority, the Moscow Municipal Board on March, 1, 1889 opened free sanitary clinics for the examination of prostitutes in relation to venereal diseases; the city also created the Central Sanitary Bureau for medical and financial reporting about the Myasnitskaya hospital clinics. . . .

The municipal sanitary clinic premises are located on the first floor and have a separate access from the street. The premises consist of the anteroom, hall, three rooms for patients' examination, a room for a doorman and two toilets. To prevent prostitutes from hiding the signs of suppuration there are no devices for washing. The anteroom with two windows, 51 square *arshin* [c.36m²] has enough hangers for outerwear. The waiting hall with seven windows, 130 square *arshin* [c.92m²] is furnished with wooden couches. Each examination room, 65 square arshins [c.46m²], is well illuminated with three windows. Each cabinet has two examination chairs, two desks, a cabinet for instruments and linen, a washstand with a pedal and wooden couches for undressing. The floor is covered with grey woollen carpet. The examination chair is made from ash [wood]. . . .

The clinic medical personnel include seven male doctors, two female doctors and six nurses. Three of the doctors are also resident doctors at the Myasnitskaya hospital; others have been external students there. Six male doctors examine brothel prostitutes, two female doctors examine apartment prostitutes, and one doctor acts as replacement if anybody is absent. He is also responsible for examination of women brought by the police. All the nurses completed the course at Dolgorukovskaya nursing school under the Myasnitskaya hospital. Apart from the medical personnel, the clinic has six female medical aides and one doorman who is also a courier.

The clinic works daily from 10am till 3pm apart from Sundays, Easter Sunday and Monday, Christmas and New Year. To avoid crowding, the Central Bureau has divided the brothels into groups, so each brothel comes at its time, always to the same doctor: thus, women from one brothel come at 11:00, from the other at 11:30, from the third at noon, etc. Single prostitutes come for examination from 1 till 3pm. Women brought by the police are usually examined from 10am till noon.

Brothel prostitutes should come for examination twice a week, single prostitutes only once. A photo of each prostitute is made at municipal expense, one copy is put into the sanitary album which a prostitute brings to the examination, the other – on a special card . . . the so-called 'sanitary card' where a doctor marks the results of examination; three photographs are held at the sanitary bureau. Each of the photos, both on the sanitary card and in the sanitary album, has a prostitute number under which she is registered in the Central Bureau.

The examination itself happens in the following manner: on the doctor's instructions, the aide invites all the brothel women into the room, or only some of them, if the brothel is very big. Simultaneously the room can comfortably accommodate about twenty women. The brothel owner or the housekeeper accompanying the prostitutes gives the sanitary albums to the doctor who checks them against the sanitary cards. . . .

If the examination shows that the prostitute is clear of venereal disease, the doctor marks her sanitary album with the stamp *No signs of venereal diseases*, puts the date and his signature. This visa is valid for brothel prostitutes for three and a half days, for single prostitutes for seven days. . . . If the prostitute is sick, he adds the word *sick* to the sanitary card, and the card together with the detained album are sent to the Central Bureau, while the prostitute gets a ticket for free treatment at the Myasnitskaya hospital. When the prostitute is discharged from hospital, she is given back her album with the doctor's agreement, while her card returns to the clinic. . . .

Each doctor has to examine between 40 and 50 women daily. Initially after opening the municipal clinic the doctor spent 4–5 minutes examining one woman, but now, when both doctor and patient are accustomed to the technique of examination, it takes about 2 and a half minutes.

Votes for women

After the omission of women from the 1867 British legislation to extend male suffrage, the female suffrage movement gathered steam. Most campaigners agreed that the vote was a tool to improve women's rights, but many also saw it as a right in itself. However, a key difference emerged in the approaches represented by Millicent Garrett Fawcett and Emmeline Pankhurst. The extracts capture the measured legislative approach of Fawcett, which has echoes of Condorcet (1.63), and the militant stance of Pankhurst, which reached a crescendo in the years prior to the First World War. The movement was international, and Frenchwoman Hubertine Auclert entreats working men to embrace women's rights, invoking the spirit of 1789 – the French Revolution, liberty, equality and fraternity, and echoing arguments of Flora Tristan (2.44). Despite the fact that women often worked alongside men, working men were very reluctant supporters of women's movements, often because they feared competition for work and wages, but also for a myriad of other reasons. We hear the voice of Scandinavia in Frida Stéenhoff's plea, 'Why should women wait?' Like Auclert and Pankhurst, she draws on the liberation ideas of the French Revolution, but her pamphlet is situated in the Scandinavian context and follows on the heels of the 1905 revolution in Russia, which appeared to herald a new world for men and women. This is echoed in the speech of Maria

Vakhtina, a 'non-partisan' Russian woman who argues that the cause is greater than partisan politics. Notably, the naiveté and excitement of the era are palpable in her text. Most Scandinavian women gained the vote by 1915 (not Sweden), and to mark the occasion when women gained the vote as apart of an overhaul of the 1849 constitution in Denmark, on 5 June 1915 more than 12,000 women marched in procession to the square in front of the Amalienborg royal palaces (Figure 2.7).

2.56 Electoral disabilities of women

Millicent Garrett Fawcett, *The Fortnightly Review*, VII (Jan.–June, 1870), 622–32.

It can hardly be too often repeated that the removal of the electoral disabilities of women is not exclusively a woman's question; above all it is not one in which the interests of men and women are opposed. If the extension of political power to women is in accordance with reason and justice, both sexes are equally bound to support the claims of women to the suffrage. If it is in opposition to these, both sexes are equally interested in the withholding of electoral power from women.

It is frequently said that women are sufficiently represented under the present system, and that their interests have always been jealously protected by the legislature. This argument must be very familiar to all who took part in, or remember the great reform agitation which preceded the Reform Bill of 1867. Those who were opposed to an extension of the suffrage were never weary of repeating that working men were quite well represented; . . . Surely working men, and all who took their part in the great reform agitation, will not cast aside and repudiate the very arguments which they found so useful during that struggle. . . . Are women sufficiently represented? Are there no laws which press unjustly on them? Is that state of the law equitable which renders a married woman incapable of owning or of acquiring property, and which allows her husband to deprive her even of her earnings? Is that law just which gives a married woman no legal right to the guardianship of her own children? If women were virtually represented, would they be excluded from participation in the great educational endowments of the country? Would the door of nearly all lucrative, and, at the same time, honourable employments be shut against them? Finally, using the very same argument which has been so often applied to the working classes, is it right or just that any one should be forced to contribute to the revenue of the country, and, at the same time, debarred from controlling the national expenditure? Either this argument is good for nothing, or it applies to women as forcibly as it does to men.

Another argument sometimes urged against women's suffrage is, that a woman is so easily influenced. . . . This is a very curious argument; it would be a serious thing for men as well as for women if originality were a necessary qualification for the franchise. . . .

Let us now consider the validity of the fourth objection. . . . 'The ideal of domestic life is a miniature despotism, in which there is one supreme head, to whom all other members of the family are subject. This ideal would be destroyed if the equality of women with men were recognised by extending the suffrage to women.' . . . Why has the name 'liberty' always had such a magic spell over men? . . . Is it not because it has been felt, more or less strongly at all times, that man's liberty is essential to the observance of man's duty? . . . he has a *right* to it. . . . The only limitation to perfect liberty of action is the equal liberty of all. . . . How then can the ideal of family life be despotism, when despotism is proved to be antagonistic to the divine will? . . .

We will now pass to the consideration of another objection . . . – that the family is woman's proper sphere, and if she entered into politics she would be withdrawn from domestic duties. It may be mentioned in passing . . . that there are some million or so women in this country without families and without domestic affairs to superintend. . . . But let us look at the case of women who are married, . . . what does this objection, . . . really come to? Why soon it will be objected that women should not go to church or out for a walk, because so doing withdraws them from their domestic duties. It may, however, be urged that it is not merely the exercise of the franchise, but all that an interest in political questions involves – the reading of newspapers, the attending of meetings, and the like – that would have a mischievous influence in withdrawing women from their domestic duties. But surely the wife and mother of a family ought to be something more than a housekeeper or a nurse . . . It is, however, quite erroneous to suppose that an attention to domestic duties and to intellectual pursuits cannot be combined. . . .

We now pass to another objection – That the line must be drawn somewhere, and if women had votes they would soon be wanting to enter the House of Commons. . . . The would-be witty caricatures of sickly women fainting in the House of Commons . . . would lose their brilliancy and point in the cold light of stern reality. No constituency would deliberately choose a representative who would be quite incapable of serving it faithfully and well. . . .

Another objection sometimes urged against women's suffrage is that most women are Conservatives, and that their enfranchisement would consequently have a reactionary influence on politics. But this is an objection, not so much to women's suffrage, as to representative government. Do those who object to the enfranchisement of women, on the ground that they are usually Conservatives, think that all Conservatives ought to be disfranchised? . . . A representative system which excludes half the community from representation surely is a farce.

2.57 Freedom or death

Emmeline Pankhurst, Speech, Hartford, Connecticut, 13 November 1913.

I do not come here as an advocate, because . . . [female suffrage] has entered into the sphere of practical politics. It has become the subject of revolution and civil war. . . .

I am here as a soldier who has temporarily left the field of battle in order to explain – it seems strange it should have to be explained – what civil war is like when civil war is waged by women. . . . I am here – and that, I think, is the strangest part of my coming – I am here as a person who, according to the law courts of my country, it has been decided, is of no value to the community at all: and I am adjudged because of my life to be a dangerous person, under sentence of penal servitude in a convict prison. . . . I dare say, in the minds of many of you . . . that I do not look either very like a soldier or very like a convict, and yet I am both. . . .

It would not be necessary for me to enter into explanations at all – the desirability of revolution if I were a man, . . . If an Irish revolutionary had addressed this meeting, . . . it would not be necessary for that revolutionary to explain the need of revolution beyond saying that the people of his country were denied – and by people, meaning men – were denied the right of self-government. That would explain the whole situation. . . . But since I am a woman it is necessary in the twentieth century to explain why women have adopted revolutionary methods in order to win the rights of citizenship. . . .

It is clear to the meanest intelligence that if you have not got the vote, you must either submit to laws just or unjust, administration just or unjust, or the time inevitably comes when you will revolt against that injustice and use violent means to put an end to it. . . . I want to first of all make you understand that this civil war carried on by women is not the hysterical manifestation which you thought it was, but was carefully and logically thought out, and . . . that we could not do anything else, that there was no other way, that we had either to submit to intolerable injustice . . . or we had to go on with these methods until victory was secured; . . .

When women asked questions in political meetings and failed to get answers, they were not doing anything militant. To ask questions at political meetings is an acknowledged right of all people who attend public meetings; . . . men have always done it, . . . The first people who were put out of a political meeting for asking questions, were women; they were brutally ill-used; they found themselves in jail before twenty-four hours had expired. . . .

We found that all the fine phrases about freedom and liberty were entirely for male consumption, and that they did not in any way apply to women. When it was said taxation without representation is tyranny, . . . everybody quite calmly accepted the fact that women had to pay taxes and even were sent to prison if they failed to pay them – quite right. . . .

You have two babies very hungry and wanting to be fed. One baby is a patient baby, and waits indefinitely until its mother is ready to feed it. The other baby is an impatient baby and cries lustily, screams and kicks and makes everybody unpleasant until it is fed. . . . That is the whole history of politics. . . . You have to make more noise than anybody else, you have to make yourself more obtrusive than anybody else, you have to fill all the papers more than anybody else, in fact you have to be there all the time and see that they do not snow you under, if you are really going to get your reform realized. . . .

We wear no mark; we belong to every class; . . . and so you see in the woman's civil war the dear men of my country are discovering it is absolutely impossible to deal with it: you cannot locate it, and you cannot stop it.

'Put them in prison,' they said, 'that will stop it.' But it didn't stop it. They put women in prison for long terms of imprisonment, for making a nuisance of themselves – . . . instead of the women giving it up, more women did it, . . . until there were three hundred women at a time, who had not broken a single law, only 'made a nuisance of themselves' as the politicians say. . . . the British government, . . . has passed more stringent laws to deal with this agitation than it ever found it necessary during all the history of political agitation . . .

Well, they little know what women are. Women are very slow to rouse, but once they are aroused, once they are determined, nothing on earth and nothing in heaven will make women give way; it is impossible. And so this 'Cat and Mouse Act' . . . has failed. . . . At the present time there are women lying at death's door, . . . There are women who are being carried from their sick beds on stretchers into meetings. They are too weak to speak, but they go amongst their fellow workers just to show that their spirits are unquenched, and that their spirit is alive, and they mean to go on as long as life lasts. . . . we have brought the government of England to this position, that it has to face this alternative: either women are to be killed or women are to have the vote. . . .

Human life for us is sacred, but we say if any life is to be sacrificed it shall be ours; we won't do it ourselves, but we will put the enemy in the position where they will have to choose between giving us freedom or giving us death.

2.58 Workers and women

'Discours d'Hubertine Auclert au Congrès ouvrier socialiste de Marseille' (1879).

Fellow Citizens . . .

Admit women to your midst, on the same basis as proletarians, to form an offensive and defensive alliance against our common oppressors. . . . Like you, we have been victims of abuse of power. In our modern society, like you, we are still under the tyrannical force of those who hold power, to which is added the tyrannical force of those who have rights. . . . Ah! we live in a Republic, proving that the most sublime words become empty labels. . .

In this massive assembly, if I asked this question: 'Are you supporters of human equality?' All answer me 'Yes', because the vast majority hear human equality,

equality between men. But if I changed the theme, so combining the two terms
– man and woman – . . . I say: 'Are you supporters of equality of men and
women?' Many would reply: 'No'. While you talk about equality, you who are
yourselves under the yoke, want to keep your loved ones beneath you. . . .

But we have never thought about putting the woman in a situation identical
to that of man, so that she can compete with him and prove the equivalence
of her faculties. . . . No one has ever tried to take a certain number of children
of both sexes, subjecting them to the same method of education under the
same conditions of existence: 'Let's reverse conditions, says an author, so that
we put boys, 12 to 16 years old, cooking, sewing and allowed girls into
industrial schools, so they come into the possession of all the rights which have
hitherto been the exclusive lot of men; surround young men with the labels
and prejudices with which we gagged women, and soon the relationship
between the valuation of both sexes will be completely reversed.'

You do not want this experience? . . . Continuing to leave us in an atrophied
state, you imitate, you civilized men, the barbarians, slave owners, who exploit
with great profit the alleged inferiority of their fellows. . . .

Know this, citizens, it is only on the equality of all beings that you can press
your claim to be entitled to freedom.

If you do not base your claims on justice and natural law, if, proletarians,
you also want to keep your privileges, the privileges of sex, I ask you, what
authority do you have to protest against class privileges? . . . Proclaim equality
between human beings that accident of birth made male or female. . . . Finish
with issues of pride and selfishness. The rights of women do not take away
your rights. So, quite bluntly, put natural rights in place of authority, because
if under this authority, the man oppresses women, by the very fact of this
authority, man oppresses man.

2.59 Why should women wait?

Frida Stéenhoff, *Hvarför, skola kvinnorna vänta?* (Stockholm: Börck & Börjesson,
1905), 3–6,12–15.

The women's movement and through that women's right to vote are, like all
other phenomena, still on the rise. They have become the same sore wound to
the entire nation: that the powerful exploit and take advantage of the weak. . . .

The woman has been politically ignored even after the [French] Revolution.
In recent years, however, motions about women's right to vote have emerged.
Those motions have gained considerable support. Brochures and articles have
come out in the press, associations are founded and meetings are held. In those
places people publicly discuss women's right to vote and express their wish
that those in power should never again just forget and forget again. . . .

Here in Sweden, women desire to have a right to vote more than is usually
seen or heard. In fact the Swedish woman does not want to make a fuss about
herself.

Her existence is so dependent on how she pleases men. That is why she usually does not want to talk about subjects that men think are unpleasant or uninteresting. Those subjects may also insult her present or future provider. . . . I don't understand those people who say that because women have not fought for their rights, they should not have them at all. . . . It is clear enough that women need the same protection, rights and guarantees as other citizens. For her, autonomy and liberty to act have as precious mental value as for men. But these valuable things can be taken away from women if they cannot have influence on legislation through suffrage. . . .

If the government and parliament are unanimous about public suffrage, why should women wait? The answer to this question often is: Women are not ready. Is it even necessary to demonstrate how false this answer is? The principle of public suffrage has nothing to do with readiness or maturity. . . . Who can promise that all men who have the right to vote are politically mature? . . .

Women have never opposed existing society – they never could because of their physique – that is why, and only that reason, men talk to them about immaturity. But women should never accept this kind of old-fashioned rhetoric. . . . It is necessary to fight against oppression and slavery. It is necessary that we protect minorities from injustices. It is necessary that the laws are not against one. For women, just like any other creatures with no rights or protection, legislation is against them. . . .

Unfortunately in this country there has long been a tendency to encourage women's interests in petty bourgeois matters. A man has kept her aside so that she would not get involved in public matters. A man has scolded her, laughed at her and plagued her for her high mind, for deep thoughts, . . . To keep her locked up at home was the goal of antifeminist men. . . . Women just like men take responsibility for society. They work and pay taxes. It is only fair that she is recognized as a citizen, when she actually is that. In order to deny her citizenship, a man places her in a situation of utter inferiority and maybe the day will come that there is in the parliament a question that only concerns women. But she cannot vote. . . .

Among the reforms that were discussed last summer at the zemstwo-meeting in Moscow there was a proposal that the right to vote should include women. During the negotiations, like many times before, women were forgotten. But then a male council member stood up and reminded the meeting of what kind of role women have played in recent events. 'They were our mothers, wives and sisters' he shouted, 'who pushed us to claim our rights, to shed off the burden of autocracy; they were our women that made revolution happen in Russia.' The proposal about female suffrage was unanimously accepted. . . .

For us women of Sweden there is no revolutionary time or heroic actions to refer to. The only thing we can refer to is women's daily work for the common good. . . . It is a very meaningful time we live for in Sweden. We have a left-wing government with a great mission to have a radical suffrage reform act. Are women included? Or do women still have to wait?

2.60 A 'non-partisan' view

M. Vakhtina, 'Vzglyad bespartiynoi na zhenskoe osvoboditel'noe dvizhenie', in *Referaty po zhenskomy voprosu, chitannye v klube zhenskoi progressivnoi partii* (St. Petersburg: Tipografiya Stasyulevicha, 1908), 3–7.

As a strict nonpartisan, I generally attach little importance to political platforms, while for this society I even consider it harmful; . . . I think of our current liberation movement, including, of course, the women's movement, in a much broader and deeper way.

The current liberation movement depends, like everything else in the world, on universal laws and is completely subordinated to them. . . . the contemporary movement is caused not only by the course of history but also by the great course of universal evolution, . . .

Mankind is already doomed for degeneration and death, it should give way to the emerging and spiritually stronger type, the type that Nietzsche called a superman and Dostoevsky called a man-God!

But in order for that strong type to develop and multiply it is necessary that his woman-mother becomes free. She should be liberated from the slavery weighing upon her and from the outrageous discrimination, which is the deepest disgrace to our society. When a woman is an intimidated slave, she gives birth to weak-willed and powerless offspring resembling her; when liberated, she will bear free and independent citizens without any prejudices. . . .

Once a woman is liberated, humanity will liberate itself! . . .

When striving for her liberation, a woman is governed not by political platforms but by the same immutable law, to which everything is subordinated. . . . We are greeting the emerging freedom of women with which comes the freedom of mankind.

It is obvious from everything I have said that we, narrow feminists, as Miss Kollontai wishes to call us, are fighting not for class interests and not for the bourgeoisie, as Miss Kollontai says, and not even particularly for women; no, we, members of the Women's Progressive Party, are fighting for the whole of mankind.

A country, where prostitution is legally allowed, where half of the population has no rights, has no reason to call itself civilized or, even less, free. This country is immersed in slavery, in the slavery of obsolete

Figure 2.7 Danish suffragettes celebrate gaining the vote, 1915 (The Women's History Archives, State Library, Århus, Denmark)

customs and inveterate prejudices, and this slavery is even more horrible when people stay in it voluntarily and do not want to abandon it.

That is why I am repeating again: once a woman is liberated, the whole humanity will be liberated!

Travel and empire

This period saw a flowering of opportunities for women to explore wider worlds through travel and the zeal of Empire. Gertrude Bell, who made a name for herself as a Middle-Eastern expert, shares the joy and freedom that travel to unfamiliar places brought. Many women followed husbands, occasionally brothers, to far-flung places; others, like Bell, travelled on their own. Still others took advantage of assistance schemes 'to go to Empire'. The purpose of people like Maria Rye was two-fold, to assist so-called 'surplus women', but also to supply servants and wives in colonial regions like Canada and Australia. Other women went with a mission, often to provide education – on a European model – to 'natives'. The Dutch Missionary Society's report demonstrates the double edge of such work. While admonishing members to be sensitive to local needs and customs, their undisguised criticism of non-Christian attitudes to women is apparent.

2.61 Persian pictures

Gertrude Bell, *Safar Nameh, Persian Pictures* (London: R. Bentley and Son, 1894), 18–9, 38–9.

With the silence of an extinct world still heavy upon us, we made our way to the Upper end of the valley, but at the gates of the plain Life came surging to meet us. A wild hollyhock stood sentinel among the stones; it had spread some of its yellow petals for banner, and on its uplifted spears the buds were fat and creamy with coming bloom. Rain had fallen in the night, and had called the wilderness itself to life, clothing its thorns with a purple garment of tiny flowers; the delicious sun struck upon our shoulders; a joyful little wind blew the damp, sweet smell of the reviving earth in gusts towards us; our horses sniffed the air and, catching the infection of the moment, tugged at the bit and set off at racing speed across the rain-softened ground. And we, too, passed out of the silence and remembered that we lived. Life seized us and inspired us with a mad sense of revelry. The humming wind and the teeming earth shouted 'Life! life!' as we rode. Life! life! the bountiful, the magnificent! Age was far from us – death far; we had left him enthroned in his barren mountains, with ghostly cities and out-worn faiths to bear him company. For us the wide plain and the limitless world, for us the beauty and the freshness of the morning, for us youth and the joy of living! . . .

Every man, says a philosopher, is a wanderer at heart. Alas! I fear the axiom would be truer if he had confined himself to stating that every man loves to fancy himself a wanderer, for when it comes to the point there is not one in a thousand who can throw off the ties of civilized existence – the ties and the comforts of habits which have become easy to him by long use, of the life whose security is ample compensation for its monotony. Yet there are moments when the cabined spirit longs for liberty. A man stands a-tiptoe on the verge of the unknown world which lures him with its vague promises; the peaceful years behind lose all their value in his dazzled eyes; . . . he pines to stand in the great free sunlight, the great wide world which is all too narrow for his adventurous energy. For one brief moment he shakes off the traditions of a lifetime, swept away by the mighty current which silently, darkly, goes watering the roots of his race. He, too, is a wanderer like his remote fore-fathers; his heart beats time with the hearts long stilled that dwelt in their bosoms, who came sweeping out of the mysterious East, pressing ever resistlessly onward till the grim waste of Atlantic waters bade them stay. He remembers the look of the boundless plain stretching before him, the nights.

2.62 Assisted passages

'Female Emigration to Canada', *Victoria Magazine*, 11 (May–October 1868), 73.

– Miss Maria S. Rye, whose labours in connection with female emigration to our colonies are so well known, has been in communication with the Government of Canada, and has been informed that many respectable young women can be placed most comfortably there. Miss Rye intends going out to Canada in May, and taking 100 women with her. They will go by steamer, and start from Liverpool on May 28. There are good openings at Canada for general servants, nursemaids, housemaids, washerwomen, dressmakers, and needlewomen. Wages are not excessively high (they vary from £10 to £20 a year) but young women are sure of being kindly treated in a new country like Canada, and certain of getting employment at all times. The cost will be £6, which will include bedding and all the messing utensils wanted for the voyage. Emigrants will land at Quebec, and be passed on west at the expense of the Government, and Miss Rye will not leave them until they are respectably placed.

2.63 The place of Javanese women

A. Kruyt, *De plaats die de Javaansche vrouw inneemt in de samenleving en in de Christengemeente*. Referaat gehouden in de Jaarvergadering-van het Nederlandsche Zendelinggenootschap, Rotterdam, 8 Juli 1908, 318–22, 326–7.

When we live in a nation, which has habits and norms that are very different from ours, we have to be very careful with our judgement of the situations we find. By prolonged observation and comparing the phenomenon, . . . we learn to understand that situations which appear to be strange at first, will be clearer and more reasonable: we learn that the circumstances the nation has to live with made it this way, and any effort at improvement, will lead to absolutely nothing, because it does not fit the situation they are accustomed to. . . . We will not deny, there have been mission people who did not always keep this in mind. . . . But we have to be careful, that we do not identify with Western ideas and opinions. With preaching from the evangelical spirit we cannot allow our mentality to intrude on Eastern nations, which does not fit there. . . .

The woman-question that occupies us now is certainly one of the most important issues. For the Javanese it is not as important as it is with us, but we certainly have to give our attention to it, to decide which kinds of persuasion to use in the Mission.

First we have to find out what place the Java-woman has in her society, and after that, the position she occupies in the congregation of Christ. What do we see when we arrive in Batavia? That in the streets and squares there is a large number of women. . . . We see women with things to buy, balanced on their hats or carried in a towel at the left hip. It is not just at the main towns, it happens in the countryside as well. . . . At the market stalls women are restlessly busy making food and drinks, serving customers. Very early in the morning they get up busy with everything and when night falls, they are still busy! When we walk in the country, we hear the sound of stomping the rice. Again it is women, . . . Somewhere else an odd 'klik-klak-klik-klak' alternating with another dull one, a woman weaving. Here and there when you enter a house, you find women and girls busy with batik. . . . Everywhere the Java-woman is working. Add to this all the care of her family, making food for them every day, making clothes, sweeping the floor of the house and yard, bathing the children . . . For her it is mostly toil and slavery, as long as her health can take it. . . .

Just like Malayan-Polynesian communities, everything in Java is about marriage. No Javanese girl . . . stays unmarried. It would be shameful for her. So, her place in the family is also her place in the community. We believe what Javanese Mohammedan morality says: her place is to be humble. The woman exists for the wishes of the man. That is so, as Allah wanted, as he only created the woman for the man. She will honour him, as her master and serve him! And real life teaches us that the man can cast off his wife for no reason and marry another right away. He can, if he wants, have more than one wife; in short, he can treat a woman or women however he wants. [Women] have been married 5, 10, 15, yes 20 times, and again and again cast-off. . . . The ease of divorce is leading to the destruction of all proper feeling between the man, the woman, the parents, the community. . . . Also the way the woman has been treated is very often wicked. Typical is a story a colleague at Java told me. He had a Mohammedan neighbour, who abused his wife daily. The screaming exhausted him; he went to his neighbour and asked about it. He got a completely controlled answer: 'If you cannot beat your own wife anymore, who can you beat?' It is clear that generally speaking the life of Javanese women is not a 'bed of roses'. . . .

Mohammadism with its severe patriarchal mentality suppresses the woman's position. . . . We do not at least have trouble getting girls from our Christian congregation to our mixed school. With the Christian–Battaks to date we have not succeeded. Now you should expect, that in a Mohammedan country like Java, to attract girls would be difficult. And it is true, the number of Mohammedan girls at our schools is distressingly small! But – and that is the point we have to pay attention to, as soon as the population is free from the spell of Mohammadism, and feels free, there is no objection to sending the girls. Islam restricts all development for the woman, is harmful for the woman and dangerous for the man.

Part III
Modern times

Prelude
Carrying Linda's stones

The title of this prelude comes from Suzanne Stiver Lie, Lynda Malik, Ilvi Jõe-Cannon and Ruth Hinrikus, eds, *Carrying Linda's Stones: An Anthology of Estonian Women's Life Stories* (Tallinn: Tallinn University Press, 2006). The narratives in that collection demonstrate the significance of war and similar disruptions that punctuated the twentieth century. War wove through much of the century; while women's voices were employed to encourage their men and promote the interests of nation, other voices argued for peace, from Austrian Bertha von Suttner, with whom the section opens, to women at Britain's Greenham Common. Briefly employed by Alfred Nobel, Suttner has been credited with encouraging him to establish the Peace Prize, so it was fitting that she became the first woman to be honoured with it for her long-standing work for peace, highlighted by her successful novel, *Die Waffen nieder!* [Lay Down Your Arms!] (1889). Her acceptance speech captures her pacifist commitment.

During this century, women's voices became louder and in many ways also more diverse, representing the kaleidoscope of female views and experience. Another significant thread was continued pressure for equal rights: political, economic, educational, cultural and social. Feminism gave a voice to many women, and its myriad resonances changed the context of experience. Simone de Beauvoir's, *Le Deuxième Sexe*, written in 1949, underpinned feminism in modern Europe, though more accessible voices and direct action probably changed women's lives more. De Beauvoir's book was epoch making and its publication shocked people for its explicit language and range of topics; friends thought her courageous and she faced many verbally violent responses. Beginning with trying to understand women 'in general' and to understand the relations between the sexes, and their apparent incoherence, she unpeeled myth after myth about women. In the extract below, from the introduction, she postulates woman as 'other', one of the best-known concepts from the book.

3.1 Evolution of the peace movement

Bertha von Suttner, 'Die Entwicklung der Friedensbewegung', Nobel Lecture, April 18, 1906, in Per Theodor Cleve, *Le Prix Nobel*, ed. (Paris: Imprimerie Royale, 1907).

The stars of eternal truth and right have always lit up the firmament of human knowledge, but only slowly were they brought down to earth, poured into practical forms, filled with life, and put into action.

One of those truths is that peace is the foundation and the ultimate goal of happiness, and one of those rights is the individual's right to his own life: The most powerful of all instincts is self-preservation, as a legitimisation of this right, affirmed and sanctified by the ancient commandment, 'Thou shalt not kill.' It is unnecessary for me to say how little this right and this commandment are respected in the present state of civilisation. To date, the military organisation of our society has been founded upon a denial of the possibility of peace, a contempt for the value of human life, and an acceptance of the urge to kill. And because it is so, and because it was so as long as our – oh so short, what are a few thousand years? – so-called history goes, so some believe, most believe that it must always remain so. That the world is ever changing and developing is still not widely recognised, since knowledge of the laws of evolution, which control all life – the geological or the social – belongs to a recent period of scientific development.

No, the belief in the eternal nature of the past and present is an erroneous belief. . . . That the future, the goals will always be one degree better than what is past and discarded is the conviction of those who understand the laws of evolution and try to assist their action. Only through knowledge, conscious use of natural laws and forces of nature, both physical and moral, will the technical inventions and the social institutions be created that will make our lives easier, richer, and more noble. One calls these ideals, as long as they remain floating in the realm of ideas; they stand as achievements of progress as soon as they are transformed into visible, living, and effective forms. . . .

Alfred Nobel himself testified that he had gradually become convinced that the movement had emerged from the cloud of pious theories to that of practically attainable and realistic goals, which he proved by his Will. In addition to other things that he recognised as serving the demands of culture, namely science and idealistic literature, he added the aims of the peace conferences, namely attainment of international justice and consequent diminution of armies. Alfred Nobel was of the view that social changes take place slowly, and sometimes by indirect means. . . .

The belief in the possibility, the need, and that it would be a blessing to have an assured judicial peace between nations is already deeply embedded in all social strata, even in those that wield the power. The task is already so clearly outlined, and so many are already working on it, that it must sooner or later be accomplished. . . .

Let us look round us in the world of today and see whether we are really justified in claiming for pacifism progressive development and positive results. . . . Even the printed programme of the second Hague Conference [1907] proclaims it as virtually a council of war. Now in the face of all this, can people still maintain that the peace movement is making progress?

Well, we must not be blinded by the obvious; we must also look for the new growth pushing up from the ground below. We must understand that two philosophies, two eras of civilisation, are struggling with each other and amidst the thrashing of the Old, a vigorous New spirit is pushing up, no longer weak and formless, but already widely established and vigorously alive. Quite apart from the peace movement, which is a symptom rather than a cause of change, a process of internationalisation and unification is taking place in the world. Together technical inventions, improved communications, economic interdependence, and closer international relations penetrate society and half-unconsciously – how the shoots grow – prevail, because self-preservation drives human society, and rebels against the constantly refined methods of annihilation and against the destruction of humanity.

In addition to these unconscious factors that are striving toward an era free of war are people who are working deliberately toward this goal, who visualise the main essentials of a plan of action, who are seeking methods that will accomplish our aim as soon as possible. . . .

So clearly envisaged, so apparently near and easy to reach the goal may be, the road to it must be traversed a step at a time, and countless obstacles have to be overcome. . . . Powerful vested interests are involved, trying to maintain the old order and to prevent the goals being reached. The adherents of the old, the existing, order have a mighty ally in the natural law of inertia inherent in humanity, which is, as it were, a natural defence against change. So it is not an easy battle that lies before pacifism. This question of whether violence or law shall prevail between states is arguably the most important and momentous. For just as unimaginable are the benefits of a secure world peace, just as unimaginably terrible are the consequences of the looming world war which many misguided people are prepared to precipitate. The advocates of pacifism are well aware of the insignificance of their personal influence and power. They know how weak they are in number and authority, but when they modestly think of themselves and the ideal they serve, they do not think modestly. They see it as the biggest cause of all. Their solution will determine whether our Europe will become the scene of ruin and collapse, or whether we can prevent this danger and so enter sooner the coming era of secure peace and law in which a civilisation of unimagined glory will develop.

3.2 Woman as 'other'

Simone de Beauvoir, *Le Deuxième Sexe* (Paris: Galimard, 1949), 11–19.

For a long time I have hesitated to write a book on woman. The subject is irritating, especially for women; and it is not new. The quarrel over feminism has caused enough spilt ink, and perhaps we should say no more about it. We still talk about it though. And it does not seem that the voluminous nonsense charged to it during the last century has done much to illuminate the problem. Indeed, is there a problem? And what is it? Are there even women? . . . But first: what is a woman? . . . Everyone is agreed in recognising that there are females in the human species, today as formerly they comprise almost one half of humanity, and yet we are told that 'femininity is in danger'; we are exhorted, 'Be women, remain women, become women'. So, every human female is not necessarily a woman; she must share in that mysterious and threatened reality known as femininity. Is it something secreted by the ovaries? Or enshrined in a Platonic heaven? Is a frilly petticoat enough to bring it down to earth? Although some women zealously endeavour to embody it, the model has never been patented. . . . But conceptualism has lost ground: biological and social sciences no longer believe there are immutably determined entities that define given characteristics like those of the woman, the Jew, or the Black; . . . If femininity no longer exists today, then it never did. . . . The antifeminists have had no trouble in showing that women simply are not men. Assuredly woman is, like man, a human being; but such a declaration is abstract. The fact is that every concrete human being is always a singular separate individual. To refuse such notions as the eternal feminine, the Black soul, the Jewish character, is not to deny that Jews, Blacks, women exist today – this denial does not represent a liberation for those concerned, but rather a flight from reality. It is clear that no woman can claim without bad faith to be situated beyond her sex. Some years ago a well-known woman writer refused to permit her portrait to appear in a series of photographs specifically devoted to women writers; she wished to be counted among the men; but to obtain this privilege she utilised her husband's influence. Women who affirm that they are men claim no less masculine consideration and respect. . . . In truth, to proceed with one's eyes open is enough to find that humanity is divided into two classes of individuals whose clothes, faces, bodies, smiles, gaits, interests, and occupations are manifestly different. Perhaps these differences are superficial, perhaps they are destined to disappear. What is certain is that at this moment they do most strikingly exist.

If the female function is not enough to define woman, if we decline also to explain by the 'eternal feminine' and yet if we admit that, even temporarily, there are women on earth, we have to ask what is a woman?

The statement of the problem suggests to me at once an initial response. It is significant that I ask it. A man never would have the idea to write a book on the peculiar situation occupied by the human male. If I wish to define myself,

I have first to declare: 'I am a woman'; this truth constitutes the basis for all further discussion. A man never begins by positioning himself as an individual of a certain sex; he is a man, it goes without saying. . . . The relation of the two sexes is not like that of two electrical poles, man represents both the positive and the neuter, as is indicated by the common use of 'man' to designate human beings. . . . Woman appears as the negative, so that any determination is imputed as a limitation, without reciprocity. I'm annoyed sometimes in abstract discussions to hear men say to me 'You think such a thing because you're a woman,' but I knew that my only defence was to say 'I think so because it is true,' thereby eliminating my own subjectivity; there was no question of replying 'And you think the contrary because you are a man'; because it is understood that being a man is no peculiarity; a man is right in being a man; it is the woman who is in the wrong. . . . Woman has ovaries, a uterus: these are unique conditions that enclose her in her subjectivity: It is often said that she thinks with her glands. Man superbly forgets the fact that his anatomy also includes hormones, testicles. He grasps his body as a direct and natural connection with the world, which he believes he apprehends objectively, while considering the woman's body as burdened by all that specifies an obstacle, a prison. 'The female is a female by virtue of a certain lack of qualities,' said Aristotle; 'we should regard the character of women as afflicted with a natural defectiveness.' And St Thomas for his part pronounced woman to be an 'imperfect man', an 'incidental' being. . . .

Humanity is male and man defines woman not in herself but in relation to him; she is not regarded as an autonomous being. . . . And she is nothing other than what man decides; thus she is called 'the sex', meaning that she appears essentially to the male as a sexed being. . . . She is defined and differentiated with reference to man and not he with reference to her; she is the inessential, in opposition to the essential. He is the Subject, he is the Absolute – she is the Other.'. . .

Why do women not contest male sovereignty? No subject will spontaneously position themselves as the inessential; it is not the Other who, in defining himself as the Other, creates the One. The Other is posited as such by the One in positing himself as the One. But for the Other not to become the One, the Other has to submit to this alien point of view. Whence comes this submission in the case of woman?

7 Intimacy and independence

Finding their way

By the twentieth century, psychology and feminist reformers played a larger part in conceptualising ideas about the female. Marthe Francillon, a doctor, treats menstruation as largely normal, advising exercise and a more active life for young women. Dutchwoman Nellie van Kol similarly conveys sex education in a sensitive but nevertheless factual manner. Presented as a dialogue to help mothers teach their daughters about sex, it is part of a series begun in 1904 by *Les Cahiers du feminism* on sex education, illustrating the growing importance of sexual knowledge as preparation for marriage.

Two women who went on to become famous themselves describe growing up: Karen Horney, psychologist, and Simone de Beauvoir, philosopher and author, whose *Second Sex* is extracted earlier. Karen Danielsen, later Horney, describes her struggle to get a good education against the wishes of her obdurate father. The support of others in her family is notable, whereas de Beauvoir depicts her family, and especially her father, as essentially traditional, lacking understanding of this clearly outspoken non-conformist daughter and of the shifting values in society. In contrast, two working-class English women, Joyce Storey and May Hobbs, describe their less sheltered upbringing, detailing a world of hardship with fewer options and expectations. Norwegian Cora Sandel's story is a gentle reflection on the process of becoming a woman.

3.3 Puberty

Marthe Francillon, *Essaie sur la puberté chez la femme* (Paris: Felix Alcan, 1906), 197–8.

Influence of menstruation on the female psyche – Menstruation is considered by certain authors as the cause of inevitable trouble for women's physical health. Stolz [Joseph-Alexis, Professor of Obstetrics, Strasbourg] has taught women that the time of menstruation is a state bordering on disease, while others have even assigned a pathological origin to the function. These opinions appear exaggerated to me. We cannot accept that a physiological state is normally accompanied by disorders that can interfere, at least temporarily, with the activity of women.

The published statistics that show the number of female patients at the time of menstruation is greater than the number of healthy women, [we believe] is seriously in error. This [view] creates a sick clientele. Rigorously exact statistics are difficult to establish because of the fact that the number of healthy women is beyond our control, and it is difficult, indeed to ask a healthy person how she is. . . . However we know how organic menstrual effects in general can impact on the reproductive system and cause troubles in its functioning. . . .

Hygiene in puberty. . . . at this moment more than any other time in their life, it is necessary to monitor their physical hygiene.

During menstrual function, ensure that the periods are neither too heavy nor too frequent, they appear at regular intervals, without causing problems for overall health.

Fatigue, intellectual overwork, should be avoided at this time of organic overload.

Food should be carefully monitored; stimulating dishes can promote the digestive disorders observed at puberty.

Try to ensure the girl has adequate ventilation, with plentiful air and light to help withstand the crisis of puberty and often prevent tuberculosis, so dreadful at this age.

We insist on the advantages of her doing gymnastics. It is not complicated or strenuous exercise, but the movements are destined to develop the muscles, relax the joints, assure ventilation of the lungs and nasal breathing. Easy exercises, that demand no special equipment and which take a minimum of time and effort, are within the reach of all.

3.4 Sex education

Nellie Van Kol, 'L'education sexuelle', *Cahier Feministes*, December 15, 1904, 7–8.

'Mama, what happens to the baby while it is in the mother's body? What does it do? Does it sleep and wake up? Does it eat? Does it drink?' This was what Marie, a nice little girl, asked some time after having learned all that she had to know about the union of man and woman.

Like many children, she had been satisfied to learn that a baby grows in its mother's body and for some time she had not questioned beyond that. But since her mother had given her a frank and satisfactory answer to her question 'How do babies come into the mother?' she had a lot to think about. For children, who are blessed with a healthy and active understanding, do not rest until they have grasped the problem in its entirety. . . . Her mother was intelligent enough to guess what was going on in her daughter's mind; thus, she was eager to answer her queries in an affectionate manner.

'All right,' she said, 'I'll explain it all to you. . . . In the lower part of a woman's belly there is a special organ, a kind of sack, having the shape and size of an average pear but which can expand a great deal. This organ is called the womb. [The physiology of impregnation and birth follows]. . .

'It will probably be your turn for [menstruation to begin] in a few months, but it will not frighten you because it is a natural occurrence. Just be sure to let me know so that I can show you a few useful precautions to take for two or three days each month.

'Let us return to our lesson. You have learned that fluid which comes from the man fertilizes the egg in the woman. From this egg a human being, male or female, will be born. . . . The growing baby does not have an independent life. It neither eats nor drinks. It is completely dependent on its mother. If she has all she needs, the infant lacks for nothing; if she is without what she needs, it suffers. . . .

'But for hours, mothers suffer beyond words to bring their babies into the world.

'Fortunately, all of them, almost without exception, love their babies even before their birth and eagerly and joyfully await them.

'A great consolation for the mother is to be aware of the father standing near the bed, to hear him speak tenderly and to be the object of his anxious care. A sensitive husband who loves his wife himself suffers at this time. He is aware that he experienced only pleasure in the act that brought the baby to life, while his mate has borne a burden that has grown heavier and heavier during pregnancy, and undergoes a great deal of pain in order to bring it into the world.

'There is nothing that can resist nature, that is certain. But a good man like your father, Marie, is aware of more exacting obligations to his mate. In his wife, he respects his child's mother, the mother of all human kind. Thus he strives to assure his wife a place of respect in the family and in society.

'He takes care to provide his daughter with a healthy, natural upbringing so that she in her turn will experience successful childbirth. He grants the wife and mother rights and freedoms which allow her to be a responsible person, bound by ties of love to her husband, her children and her home. . . .

'A last word, my child, and very important! Before long you will be old enough to hear talk of love. Know how to look after yourself. Don't give yourself to someone who will flatter you and make pretty promises. The union of the sexes is not for pleasure; it can cause the arrival of a child. The child has a right to its father's care, not only for his material well-being, but for his moral upbringing as well. Therefore, do not let passion cloud your judgment. Give your body only to the man you judge worthy to be the father of your child. And always have confidence in your mother!'

3.5 Craving education

Karen Horney, *The Adolescent Diaries of Karen Horney* (New York: Basic Books, Inc., 1980), 8–13, 19, 24–27.

1 August 1899

Today Berndt went back to school for the first time. If only I could take his place. Yesterday we climbed the 'Tyrolese Mountains' [amusement park]. Now people are even building mountains. It is magnificent. It is supposed to remain 5 years, . . . And how far along will I be in 5 years? In the Gymnasium?

10 August 1899

Lots of fine things have happened. For one, Mother has written to Hannover to ask for a prospectus for the Gymnasium there, where I could take a teacher's examination. That would already be a certain step toward my plans for the future. . . . Only 4 more days and school begins again. . . .

25 December 1900

Life is really pretty boring without school. I've been going to church in the mornings. Unfortunately this winter I will have to go whenever Pastor von Ruckteschell preaches, because I am to be confirmed at Easter. My religion is in a desperately sad state at the moment. I am stirred by questions and doubts that probably no one can solve for me. . . . Confirmation lessons don't make it any clearer for me. . .

26 December 1900

Mother is ill and unhappy. Alas, if only I could help my 'dearest in the whole world.' – How miserable you feel when you see your loved ones suffer. If only she is spared for Berndt and me, so that later on she can lead a friendly life with the two of us – when Berndt is a lawyer and I am a teacher. It is probably just as well that one cannot lift the veil of the future, and so can go on hoping. Yet I am always thinking of the future. How wishes and plans for later keep changing! Earlier, when I was still in private school, I did not think about the future at all. Then, when I went to the Convent School, I wanted to become a teacher. Then I went beyond that, and wanted to study. I wanted to go right away to the Gymnasium for girls, in my thoughts I was there already, but I had not taken Father into account. My 'precious Father' forbade me any such plans once and for all. Of course, he can forbid me the Gymnasium, but the wish to study he cannot. My plan for the future is this:

Stay with Mother till Michaelmas, (29 September) and then take my 1st exam.
From Michaelmas 1901 to Easter 1902 to Paris.
From Easter 1902 to 1905 to Wolfenbüttel. [teacher training]
A couple of years as a teacher or tutor and preparing myself for final exams and medicine, on my own hook.
And ultimately: doctor.

You see, dear diary, Fate will have an easy time with me, for I prescribe everything for him.

But for the time being, I am still a student at the Convent School and am frightfully fond of going to school. . . .

10 January 1901

I'm furious at myself. No sooner am I happy about [moving to] Reinbeck when another wish comes up in me, a burning desire. For in Hamburg a Gymnasium course is beginning at Easter, 4 or 5 years leading to the Arbitur [final Gymnasium examination]. I'd like to get there at Easter. Oh, wouldn't that be wonderful!! But Father. . . .

11 January 1901

Yesterday brought so much that was exciting and new that I couldn't sleep at all last night. . . . Three of Mother's friends came one after the other yesterday, to work on Mother to send me to the Gymnasium. Mother spoke with Father afterward. He doesn't seem opposed to the matter itself, for him it's a question of money. So my chances have improved enormously. Beside that Berndt heard a lecture on 'the woman question' by a gentleman who greatly praised the Gymnasium for girls. Berndt had to tell Father the whole lecture. When he goes to Tante Clara she will work on him too. Today Berndt is going to a lady who can inform us about admissions, age, courses, etc. I believe more and more that I 'must' get there.

12 January 1901

My chances for the Gymnasium are getting better. . . . Once Father has digested the monstrous idea of sending his daughter to the Gymnasium, Mother will talk with him further. He is approachable now. . . .

18 January 1901

This uncertainty makes me sick. Why can't Father make up his mind a little faster? He, who has flung out thousands for my stepbrother Enoch, who is both stupid and bad, first turns every additional penny he is to spend for me 10 times in his fingers. And we did make it clear to him that he has to feed me only as long as I attend school. Once I have my diploma I most certainly don't want another penny from him. He would like me to stay at home now, so we could dismiss our maid and I could do her work. . . .

19 January 1901

It's really true, at Easter I'm going to the Gymnasium. Father has just decided, when Mother handed him a document drawn up in verse, in which Mother and I promise that after I graduate he need do nothing for me. Oh, how happy I am!! And thankful!! First to the good Lord, for the fine gifts, then to Mother for her warm intercession and the way she handled it, then to Father for this permission!! Hurray!!

3.6 Disappointing daughter

Simone de Beauvoir, *Memoirs of a Dutiful Daughter* (New York: HarperCollins, 1974), 175–9, 270–2.

In those days, people of my parents' class thought it unseemly for a young lady to go in for higher education; to train for a profession was a sign of defeat. It goes without saying that my father was a vigorous anti-feminist . . . he considered that a woman's place was in the home, that she should be an ornament to polite society. . . . Before the war, his future had looked rosy; he was expecting to have a brilliant career, to make lucrative investments, and to marry off my sister and myself into high society. He was of the opinion that in order to shine in those exalted spheres a woman should not only be beautiful and elegant but should also be well-read and a good conversationalist; so he was pleased by my early scholastic successes. Physically, I was not without promise; if in addition I could be intelligent and cultured, I would be able to hold my own with ease in the very best society. . . . When he announced: 'My dears, you'll never marry; you'll have to work for your livings,' there was bitterness in his voice. . . . The war had ruined him, sweeping away all his dreams, destroying his myths, his self-justifications, and his hopes. . . . he would complain particularly about the sacrifices his daughters imposed upon him. . . . I was not just another burden to be borne: I was growing up to be the living incarnation of his own failure. The daughters of his friends, his brother, and his sister would be 'ladies': but not me. Of course, when I passed my school-leaving examinations he rejoiced in my success; it flattered him and lifted a load off his mind: I should have no difficulty in making a living. . . .

Soon I would be a traitor to my class; I had already renounced the privileges of my sex, and that was something else my father could not be reconciled to; he was obsessed by the 'well-bred young lady' idea: it was a fixation. My cousin Jeanne was the incarnation of this ideal: she still believed that babies were found under cabbages. My father had attempted to keep me in a state of blissful ignorance; . . . he now accepted the fact that I read whatever I liked . . . If I had only kept up the outward appearances, at least! . . . My friends, including Zaza, played their worldly roles with ease; they put in an appearance on their mothers' at-home days, served tea, smiled and smiled, and talked amiably about nothing; I found smiling difficult, I couldn't turn on the charm, make cute remarks, or any kind of concession to polite chit-chat. . . .

On the whole, apart from when the news came that I had passed my exams, I was not an honour to my father; so he attached extreme importance to my diplomas and encouraged me to accumulate them. His insistence on this point convinced me that he was proud to have a brainy woman for a daughter; but the contrary was true: only the most extraordinary successes could have countered his dissatisfaction with me. . . .

My cousin Madeleine came to spend a few days in Paris: I jumped at the opportunity. She was twenty-three, and my mother gave permission for us to go alone to the theatre every evening: in fact, we had made up our minds to visit a few dens of vice. Our plans nearly fell through because, just before we left home, Madeleine put a little rouge on my cheeks as a joke: I thought it looked very pretty, and when my mother ordered me to wash it off, I protested. She probably thought it was Satan's cloven hoof-mark she saw on my cheeks; she exorcized me by boxing my ears. I gave in, with very bad grace. However, she let me go out and my cousin and I wended our way towards Montmartre. For a long while we wandered under the light of the neon signs; we couldn't make up our minds. We slunk into a couple of bars, both of them dead as dairies, and . . . in a frightful little hole where young women of easy virtue awaited their customers. . . . We stayed there for some time, both of us bored to death: the place made me feel sick.

3.7 Housewifery and ignorance

Joyce Storey, *Our Joyce* (Bristol: Bristol Broadsides, 1987), 79–81.

[1931] In our last year at school, we had what used to be called Housewifery Classes. About six of us would walk across the playground to Mr. Webley, the Caretaker, and he used to escort us in a file to a flat next door to his own. . . . Inside the flat was a sitting room, kitchen, bedroom and toilet. There was a doll in a pram and there was a tin bath. We had a rota of cleaning jobs we had to complete to learn how to keep house, and we had to dust and sweep and polish. The baby had to be changed and bathed and rocked to sleep.

Usually though, as soon as the door closed upon us, we would bounce on the bed and shriek with laughter, tell each other jokes or play hide-and-seek in all the rooms. Over endless cups of tea we'd bring out our penny dreadfuls and read the spicy bits to one another. As for the baby – it fared dreadfully, often being upended and its head stuck in the potty, whilst Gladys did the 'splits' with her dress tucked into her knickers for decency.

One of us always stayed on guard for the surprise visit of a teacher so that we were never caught out. And by the time she swept in, we were models of good behaviour, industriously polishing the already gleaming furniture or washing the always spotless floor. . . .

As for us, we enjoyed these excursions to the flat enormously. It was a change from the severe discipline of the classroom and none of us took the domestic side of it seriously. It was a welcome break; and if its real purpose was to prepare us for the hard and often drab reality of the real world outside the school gates, we were simply not ready for it.

Looking back, it seems amazing to me how ignorant we were. . . . woefully ignorant of sexual matters. Nobody told us anything. Grown-ups suffered from crippling shyness in discussing anything 'in front of the children'. There were half-embarrassed, half-giggling references to the Stork or being found under a gooseberry bush. But people were not only very Victorian in their attitudes, but as I realise now, incredibly ignorant about the workings of their own bodies. Small wonder then, that in answer to my anxious question, my Mother would often shake her head and sniff, 'You'll find out soon enough, my girl.'

So, I knew nothing of the great secret of how babies happened. . . . and nothing that I heard persuaded me in favour of marriage or being a wife and mother. Rather the reverse. And what I did know, what I had already found out appalled me. All my uncles were often the worse for drink and sexually and physically abused their wives. The women in our family often wore the cowed and care-worn look of the constantly afraid – except that is, for my own Mother. My Dad never hit any us, but then he was seen as being 'weak'!

If it got to the point where a woman couldn't stand it any more, there was nowhere for her to go. The woman who left her husband and went back to her Mother was sharply told, 'You made your bed, now you must lie on it.'

And Father would say, 'No man must interfere between man and wife,' and pack his errant daughter off home again.

And if an unmarried girl got into trouble, she was a bad girl. She got a thrashing from her father and if the man would not marry her, she was often sent away to a Home. Most women would feel a kind of sympathy for her and you would often hear the comment, 'Poor little bitch.'. . .

So I think it was a kind of act of rebellion that we put the doll's head in the pee-pot. We all knew that there was some sort of inevitability about our lives that we couldn't avoid, so that hanging on to this innocence was a memory we would cherish forever.

3.8 Evacuated and fostered

May Hobbs, *Born to Struggle* (London: Quartet, 1975), 14–17, 19, 28–31.

Being so young at the time I was evacuated, I remember very little about the years I was away – except the misery. . . .

Down in Somerset the kids from the East End were like foreigners in a strange land. . . . the one thing you knew for certain was that the people you were evacuated to did not want you. . . . As you were a burden to them, and they could not refuse to take you in, they took an instant dislike to you. What I remember most is this attitude towards us and all the wallopings. . . .

I suppose I was about five or six by the time I came back from evacuation to sample the better world we had all been promised. That is one day I remember as if it happened last week. They told me at the home that my dad would be coming to collect me. Well, by that stage I had completely forgotten what my mother or father looked like, or that I had one or the other. Neither one of them had been down to visit me in all that time, . . .

Anyway, this man did arrive to collect me one day later. I first saw him through the iron gates. He was very tall – about six foot two inches – and to me, still being so little, he looked like a giant, He was wearing his RAF uniform, of which he seemed very proud, and I have to admit that at that age I was impressed myself. . . .

During the journey back to London, however, he told me that I would not be going home to Hoxton at all. Instead, I was going to stay with this very nice couple, he said, who had a house in Slough as he and my mother could not have me back – could not have me or did not want me. . . .

My foster parents in Slough, Sheila and Tim, were nice enough. They clothed me and fed me and taught me to call them mum and dad. I am sure they convinced themselves they loved me and were doing their best for me. At the same time, a child always knows whether love is really there or not. . . .

Shortly after I left school, Lil, my real mother, decided she wanted me back. I had to go because, as the law said, she was my natural mother, . . . I ask what sort of law is it that supports the 'natural' mother coming along after years of silence and saying, 'Ta very much, I'll have it back now,' as if the child was a parcel that had been minded? That doesn't sound like a 'natural' mother to me – though a biological mother she may be. . . .

As for me, I went back to live in my real parents' flat and hated every minute of it. . . . In their home I was treated as an unpaid servant, a real skivvy. . . . The day started with me being pulled out of bed at six o'clock to light the fire, make the tea, get the breakfast and clean up before any of the others got out of bed at seven thirty, God help me if I did not finish it all. In she would come, raving, shouting and using her hands. After all that was over, I had to get their two smallest ones ready for school and then get off to work myself. . . .

I had to hand over all my pay packet to my mother each week, and out of it she allowed me 6d a day. . . . During the dinner hour I used to have to get back home to run the errands. Before she left for work herself, my mother made out a list of the things we needed. [Ben] would sometimes get the errands for me so that at least I could have my lunch break. But when he did he never dared to tell Lil. . . .

3.9 The child who loved roads

Cora Sandel, in Katherine Hanson Ia Dübois, ed., *Echo, Scandinavian Stories About Girls*, trans. Barbara Wilson (Seattle: Women in Translation, 2000), 46–55.

Most of all she loved roads with the solitary track of a horse down the middle and with grass between the wheel ruts. Narrow old roads with lots of bends and nobody else around and here and there perhaps a piece of straw, fallen from a load of hay. On these roads the child became springy, light as air. She was filled with happiness at breaking free, at existing. Behind every bend waited unknown possibilities, however many times you'd gone down the road. You could make them up yourself if nothing else. . . .

There's a lot grownups don't understand. You have to give up on explaining anything to them and take them as they are, an inconvenience, for the most part. No one should grow up. No, children should stay children and rule the whole world. Everything would be more fun and better then.

Early on the child learned that it was best to be alone on the road. A good ways in front of the others anyway. Only then did you come to know the road as it really was, with its marks of wheels and horses' hooves, its small, stubborn stones sticking up, its shifting lights and shadows. Only then did you come to know the fringes of the road, warm from sun and greenness, plump and furry with chervil and lady's mantle – altogether a strange and wonderful world unto itself, where you could wander free as you pleased, and everything was good, safe, and just the way you wanted it. . . .

'You're so contrary;' said the grownups. 'Can't you be nice and sweet like the others, just a little? You should be thankful anyone wants to be with you,' they said.

'It won't be easy for you when you're older;' they also said.

The child forgot it as soon as it was said. She ran off to the road or paths and remembered nothing of anything so unreasonable, so completely ridiculous. . . .

Grownup, well, you probably had to turn into one. Everyone did; you couldn't avoid it. . . .

The grown-ups didn't have much that was worthwhile. It was true they got everything they wanted, could buy themselves things they wanted and go to bed when they felt like it, eat things at the table that children didn't get all the best things, in short. They could command and destroy, give canings and presents. But they got long skirts or trousers to wear and then they *walked*. *Just* walked. You had to wonder if it had something to do with what was called Confirmation, if there wasn't something about it that injured their legs. There probably was, since they hid them and walked. They *couldn't run* any longer. . . .

Maybe it was their minds something was wrong with? Everything truly fun disappeared from their lives, and they let it happen. None of them rebelled. On the contrary, they grew conceited about their sad transformation. Was there anything so conceited as the big girls when they got long skirts and put up their hair!

They walked, they sat and embroidered, sat and wrote, sat and chatted, knitted, crocheted. Walked and sat, sat and walked. Stupid, they were so stupid! . . .

One day a boy of that sort came after the child, grabbed her arm squeezed it hard and said, 'You know what you are? Do you?'

No answer.

'You're just a girl. Go home where you belong.'

Hard as a whip the words struck the child. Just a girl – *just* . . . .

From that moment she had a heavy burden to bear, one of the heaviest, the feeling of being something inferior, of being born that way, beyond help.

With such a burden on your back the world becomes a different place for you. Your sense of yourself begins to change.

But the roads remained an even bigger consolation than before.

On them even 'just a girl' felt easy, free and secure. . . . On the summertime roads you forgot your troubles. . . .

Time passed. The child ran, long braid flapping, on the roads.

If she was overtaken by the grown-ups, she heard, 'You're too old now to be running like that. Soon you'll be wearing long skirts, remember. A young lady walks, she holds herself nicely, thinks about how she places her feet. Then she can't rush away like you do.'

The child ran even faster than before. . . . The child thought – one day I won't turn around when they call, I won't wait for anyone. . . .

But one of the big boys, the kind that were practically uncles, suddenly popped up out of nowhere. . . . a university student. . . .

He had a strange effect on the child; he upset her from the first moment in a way that was both painful and good. It was impossible to think of him when he was nearby and could turn up; you can't think when you're blushing in confusion. But out on the roads he crept into her thoughts to the extent that she couldn't get him out again; . . .

The child grew fiery red with embarrassment if he so much as made an appearance. . . .

The child was beginning to walk on the roads. Slowly even. She stood still for long moments at a time. For nothing, to fuss with the tie on her braid, to curl the end of the braid around her fingers, to scrape her toe in the gravel, stare out in space. . . .

'Well now, finally you're acting like a big girl,' said one of the aunts, pleased. 'Not a minute too soon. Good thing we don't have to nag you anymore. Good thing there's still a little hem to let out in your dress. . . .'

Hardly was it said than the child set off at full speed, in defiance, in panic.

Without her having noticed or understood it, she had allowed something to happen, something frightening, something detestable. Something that made them happy. But nothing should make them happy. For then they'd be getting you where they wanted you, a prisoner, some kind of invalid. . . .

Follow the road, never become what they call grown-up, never what they call old, two degrading conditions that made people stupid, ugly, boring. Stay how you are now, light as a feather, never tired, never out of breath. . . .

And then she ran on, over the farmyard, right up the path to the hill where the fresh breeze blew.

Changing values

A feature of the twentieth century was the extent to which the ideal of marriage and family underwent a profound transition, as family became a pivotal element in discourses about the nation. Swede Ellen Key was a central figure in the debate about sex and marriage and here she criticises the view that the individual should be sacrificed for the state in contracting marriage to suit political purposes. She also illustrates the importance that eugenics and the nature of the species held in shaping ideas about love and procreation. Alexandra Kollontai takes this further in the communist view of family that the state will improve women's position, through services that help workers to gain what thus far only the bourgeoisie have been able to enjoy. Inge Marie Holten–Nielsen's Danish handbook explicitly evokes a domestic world where men ask for a woman's hand and women accept knowing that their 'job' will be to maintain house and home. At the same time, she realistically refers to the underlying tensions that modern marriage and housekeeping presented. Alva Myrdal's study *Family and Nation* describes the sociological changes that took place in Swedish marriage patterns in the first half of the century. Emilie Müller–Zadow, speaking for Nazi Germany, evokes again the image of family and nation, which Kollontai addressed, albeit directing the emphasis toward motherhood and the production of a domestic, homely foundation on which to build the state. The Charter issued by the Catholic Church in 1983 illustrates how tensions in family values sparked a vigorous response from the Church as a representative of those trying to sustain a 'traditional' view of marriage and familial relations, recasting these in a late twentieth-century framework.

3.10 Love and ethics

Ellen Key, *Love and Ethics* (New York, B. W. Huebsch, 1911), 7–21

IN love, in which the happiness of the individual and the well-being of society so frequently conflict, the present conception of duty demands the unconditional sacrifice of the individual to society. All the state needs, we are told, is healthy fathers and mothers, the certainty of the permanent union of the parents to secure the education of their progeny. Whenever the happiness of the individual interferes with this requirement, the individual must be sacrificed. That this entails suffering upon him is no reason for loosening the marriage bond, and certainly not so long as the majority of parents are agreed that children are best cared for in the family. Therefore, it is said, the state is not interested in any change in marriage forms. To facilitate divorce would not remove the causes of the discords that arise whenever human beings live in close union. . . . At the present time easy divorce would only slacken the marriage tie by making for disintegration. The destruction of the family, hence of the nation, would be the result. Accordingly, for love to demand happiness is downright rebellion against the welfare of the state. History, ethnography, and nature do not bear out the theory that happiness is to be achieved by individualism in love. The lesson they teach is that of quiet self-denial and courageous fulfilment of duty. As soon as children come, it is said, the parents' demands for their own happiness must cease. . . .

   The great error in this theory of duty, not only as it affects love but even all other human relations, is the notion that society is *necessarily* benefited by the sacrifice of the individual. And the evidence adduced to prove this theory is equally false. . . . As a matter of fact, the horrors of the present system are such that what we should do is compare them with the possible dangers of a new system and see which are to be dreaded the more. Even if the social conditions to-day were not the cause of much impurity and unhappiness, the question is not, 'Are modern marriages good enough for the needs of society?' The question is, 'How can we find a more efficient ethical code than the present one for improving the species?'

If all social problems, customs, usages, and pleasures were to be measured by their effect upon the human race, we should perhaps arrive at that *absolute* ethical standard which is now lacking. But all this must first be investigated. . . . the modern sex problem consists in finding the proper equilibrium between, on the one hand, the requirements for the improvement of the species and, on the other hand, the increased demands of the individual to be happy in love; . . . The sex ethics that proceeds from this new equilibrium will be the only true ethics. It will effect an upliftment of life in both the species and the individual.

3.11 Communist utopia

Alexandra Kollontai, 'Communism and the Family', *The Worker*, 1920, *Selected Writings of Alexandra Kollontai*, trans. Alix Holt (London: Allison & Busby, 1977), 250–8.

Will the family continue to exist under communism? Will the family remain in the same form? These questions are troubling many women of the working class and worrying their menfolk as well. Life is changing before our very eyes; old habits and customs are dying out, and the whole life of the proletarian family is developing in a way that is new and unfamiliar and, in the eyes of some, 'bizarre'. No wonder that working women are beginning to think these questions over. Another fact that invites attention is that divorce has been made easier in Soviet Russia. . . . divorce is no longer a luxury that only the rich can afford; henceforth, a working woman will not have to petition for months or even for years to secure the right to live separately from a husband who beats her and makes her life a misery with his drunkenness and uncouth behaviour. . . . But others, particularly those who are used to looking upon their husband as 'breadwinners', are frightened. They have not yet understood that a woman must accustom herself to seek and find support in the collective and in society, and not from the individual man. . . .

There is . . . no reason to be frightened of the fact that the family is in the process of change, and that outdated and unnecessary things are being discarded and new relations between men and women developing. . . .

The wages of the 'breadwinner' being insufficient for the needs of the family, the woman found herself obliged to look for a wage and to knock at the factory door. . . . What kind of 'family life' can there be if the wife and mother is out at work for at least eight hours and, counting the travelling, is away from home for ten hours a day? . . . Capitalism has placed a crushing burden on woman's shoulders: it has made her a wage-worker without having reduced her cares as housekeeper or mother. Woman staggers beneath the weight of this triple load. . . .

Instead of the working woman cleaning her flat, the communist society can arrange for men and women whose job it is to go round in the morning cleaning rooms. . . . In Soviet Russia the working woman should be surrounded by the same ease and light, hygiene and beauty that previously only the very rich could afford. . . .

Communism liberates woman from her domestic slavery and makes her life richer and happier. . . .

But even if housework disappears, you may argue, there are still the children to look after. But here too, the workers' state will come to replace the family, society will gradually take upon itself all the tasks that before the revolution fell to the individual parents. . . . The family is supposed to bring up the children, but in reality proletarian children grow up on the streets. . . . Communist society will come to the aid of the parents. . . . We already have homes for very small babies, crèches, kindergartens, children's colonies and homes, hospitals and health resorts for sick children, restaurants, free lunches at school and free distribution of text books, warm clothing and shoes to schoolchildren. All this goes to show that the responsibility for the child is passing from the family to the collective. . . .

The playgrounds, gardens, homes and other amenities where the child will spend the greater part of the day under the supervision of qualified educators will, on the other hand, offer an environment in which the child can grow up a conscious communist who recognises the need for solidarity, comradeship, mutual help and loyalty to the collective. . . .

Working mothers have no need to be alarmed; communists are not intending to take children away from their parents or to tear the baby from the breast of its mother, . . . No such thing! . . . 'Everyone has the right to happiness. Therefore live your life. Do not flee happiness. Do not fear marriage. . . . Do not be afraid of having children. Society needs more workers and rejoices at the birth of every child. You do not have to worry about the future of your child; your child will know neither hunger nor cold.'. . .

In place of the individual and egoistic family, a great universal family of workers will develop, in which all the workers, men and women, will above all be comrades. . . . These new relations will ensure for humanity all the joys of a love unknown in the commercial society of a love that is free and based on the true social equality of the partners.

3.12 Proposing marriage

Inge Marie Holten-Nielsen, *Hjemmets verden. Haandbog og Rådgiver for ethvert Hjem* (Copenhagen: 1923), 5–8.

Figure 3.1
The world of the home

INTRODUCTION

It is definitely not easy to propose marriage.

One can draw this conclusion when one considers that there are, to date, no examples of a young man saying precisely that which should be said at that time. . . .

It does not follow that it is always *worse* than one had thought. Life has its own inconsiderate way of creating consequences which largely, but also cruelly, may surpass the human imagination. It will certainly be *different*. . . .

The words which he said to her might then have sounded like this:

'Do you have the courage to follow me into the unknown, which is called the future. Will you agree to take responsibility for our common home and to work there for the rest of your life; it might often be a tiring and boring job, but also, in its way, precious and uplifting. Are you willing to do this without help, if conditions should prove that we cannot afford help?

Will you also support me, so that you stand by my side and assist me when I need it?

Will you give up your personal independence, your acquaintances and interests so that they, in any case, come far behind our home and that which belongs with it?

Will you be economically dependent on me, so that I have the right to censor every one of your expenses, and will you, with sacrifice, take care of any children we may have?

In exchange, I offer you my love, trust and confidence, such that you will always be the first one I discuss my plans with and seek advice from. Additionally, you will have a part in our home and of my eventual earnings so that you may call it yours, as much as I call it mine. And finally, you will have the possibility to have children whom you not alone can *call* yours, but who *are* yours, and who will allow you to use the richness of mother love which lies hidden in your soul. But you dare not forget that precisely the most terrible sorrows can strike you – and me – through these children. There is only that hope that it will be something of a comfort that we stand together.'

If he had been able to speak so, she would not later have felt so disoriented as has often been the case. There probably would not be as many divorces, because she, in many cases having thought it through more carefully, would not have agreed to the bargain. Those who *did* agree to this, probably did so in almost 100 per cent of the cases, in order to have an opportunity to have children. Nature has made longing for the joys of motherhood that intense. That the sorrows of motherhood can follow with this, she only knows in theory. No one believes in advance that she will be the victim of sorrow and disappointment. So cleverly has nature organized life. If a woman knew, if she had any inkling of what it meant, no woman would have the courage to get married.

Whenever you enter into an agreement, it is advisable to check the contract carefully before you close the deal. But in the case of marriage, it is doubly advisable, because it is absolutely preferable that it last for life. If it fails, more threads are broken than one can ever expect to make whole again.

3.13 Nazi vision

Emilie Müller–Zadow, 'Mothers who give us the future', in Roderick Stackelberg and Sally A. Winkle, eds, *The Nazi Germany Sourcebook* (London: Routledge, 2002), 184–6.

There is a growing recognition that mothers carry the destiny of their people in their hands and that the success or ruin of the nation depends on their attitude toward the vocation of motherhood. Nation and race are facts of creation, which we, too, are called upon to share in forming and preserving. Therefore a national leadership that respects and honors its mothers is on a sound and healthy path. . . . Of course a woman, simply because she is able to cook porridge, sew shirts, and grasp the basic rules of bringing up children, still in no way has the inner aptitude to be a mother, if she does not yet know how to fill her nursery with all the warmth, with the healthy, clean, strong, and cozy atmosphere necessary for growing children to become men and women capable 'of ensuring the continued existence of their people'. . . .

The place that Adolf Hitler assigns to woman in the Third Reich corresponds to her natural and divine destiny. Limits are being set for her, which earlier she had frequently violated in a barren desire to adopt masculine traits. . . . due respect is now being offered to her vocation as mother of the people, in which she can and should develop her rich emotions and spiritual strengths according to eternal laws. This wake-up call of National Socialism to women is one more indication that in Germany today it is not arbitrary laws that are being issued, but rather a nation is returning to essential, eternal rules of order. . . . For the way a mother sees her child, how she cares for, teaches, and forms him, the principles that she instils in him, the attitude that she demands of him, all of this is crucial for the national health, for a German morality, and for the unified overall mind-set of the future nation.

Figure 3.2 Postwar wedding, 1949

3.14 Marriage decline

Alva Myrdal, *Nation and Family* (London: MIT Press, 1945), 35–9, 44–5.

The prudence in marrying, which has become a pattern in Sweden, also results in a high average age at marriage. . . . The average age at first marriage has, however, shown a slight increase for men, from 28.82 to 29.47 years, and a slight decrease for women, from 27.12 to 26.50 years.

A long waiting period before acquiring sufficient economic security to marry has been typical among both the farming and the professional groups in Sweden. . . . Stabilizing one's income and finishing one's studies are some of the ambitions that tend to postpone marriage. As age at marriage is also comparatively high for women, it is logical to conclude that when marriage finally occurs it often joins persons who had selected each other long before. Firsthand knowledge of Swedish culture also reveals the frequency of long engagements, the conventional pattern even being to announce a betrothal years in advance of marriage. This particular matchmaking structure has two important consequences for population problems: it shortens the fertility period within marriage and thus reduces the number of children, and it increases premarital sex relations. . . .

The result of all these tendencies to avoid and postpone marriage obviously is to make Sweden a nation of unwed persons. In the census year of 1930 single persons accounted for 44 per cent of the total population over 15 years of age. In addition nearly 9 per cent were widowed or divorced. . . . At least 20 per cent of Swedish women reaching 50 years of age have never married, while the corresponding figure for Denmark is about 15 per cent and for France about 10 per cent. What this difference in design for living means for the whole cultural, moral, and psychological atmosphere in the different countries should not be overlooked. . . .

In the course of social development, industrialization set in. Its effects did not come primarily through a shift in mores but through increased mobility. . . . Sexual relations within courtship now involved risks. . . . girls did not have at their disposal the impact of the whole society to force men into marriage if relations resulted in issue. Even in the cases where the men could be reached, parents would not look on them with satisfaction unless the men possessed land.

Migration itself thus led to the virtue of daughters becoming a social problem and, consequently, a moral problem as in the more romanticized relations between the sexes among the bourgeoisie. . . . Illegitimacy increased as young women also began to migrate. They were no longer daughters with a parental home which could protect their virtue, if caring much about these things, or at least protect their eventual offspring. To take in a 'natural' child in the maternal grandparents' home became a fairly well-established pattern for a time in all groups but the most proud. As a result the Swedish people have remained relatively tolerant of premarital sex relations. . . .

The interesting fact is that the habit of fairly lax authoritarian inhibitions of the sex life of youth, which stemmed out of the agrarian society, persisted so long that it was paralleled by more modern patterns and thus strengthened before its ultimate decline. One of these patterns was the religious secularization of the Swedish people, diminishing the prohibitive forces of religion. Another was the rise of emancipation ideas, so that even the intellectual upper class accepted a freer outlook on sexual relations. The propaganda for birth control, the discussion of 'free love' in the radical movements toward the close of the last century, the theory of Ellen Key that 'passion is right' and social hypocrisy is the 'sin,' and the influence of psychoanalysis all became widespread before a peasant pattern had vanished. This amalgamation of different designs is offered as a tentative explanation of the apparent frequency of premarital sex relations in Sweden.

3.15 Family rights

The Holy See, *Charte des droits de la famille*, 24 November 1983.

Considering that:

1   The rights, although ex-prime as rights of the individual, have a fundamental social dimension which finds its expression in innate and family life;
II   The family is founded on marriage, that intimate and complementary union of a man and a woman, which is established by the indissoluble bond of marriage freely contracted and publicly affirmed, and is open to the transmission of life;
III   Marriage is a natural institution to which is exclusively entrusted the mission to transmit human life;
IV   The family, natural society, exists before a State or any other community and possesses inherent rights which are inalienable;
V   The family, more than simply a legal, sociological or economic unit, is a community of love and solidarity, able to teach, and . . . transmits cultural values, ethical, social, spiritual and religious, essential to the development and well-being of its members and society;
VI   The family is the place where several generations are fulfilled and help each other grow in human wisdom and to harmonize individual rights with the other requirements of social life. . .
VIII   Society and, we can say particularly, the state and international organizations must protect the family through political, economic, social and legal measures, which aim to strengthen the unity and stability of the family, so that it can exercise its specific function. . .
X   Many families are forced to live in situations of poverty which prevent them from fulfilling their role with dignity;

The Catholic Church, knowing that the good of the individual, society and her own good go through the family, has always considered it part of her mission of proclaiming to all people the plan of God inscribed in human nature, marriage and family, these two institutions to promote and defend against all those who violate them.

Women's realities

Women's reactions to the shifting values and practices of the century were equally varied. While some wished for looser ties and strategies which gave them more personal freedom, others craved the sense of security and responsibility that their idea of the 'traditional' family offered. A Scottish interviewee describing her courtship and impromptu wedding gives us a lens into the lives and views of young working women. Ekaterina Alexandrova describes the role that marriage had come to play in the Soviet Union, a far cry from the communist idyll that Kollontai promoted (3.11). Whilst marriage remained a goal for most women, the soviet government created a situation where marriage was preferable, regardless of the nature of that marriage. Speaking from Estonia, Tiina Jääger explains the mixed impact of soviet rule followed by the heady days of Estonian independence and their impact on marriage and divorce practices. Reflecting on her own situation, she also illustrates some of the shifts identified by Myrdal (3.14).

3.16 A Scottish courtship and marriage

Interview transcript 1901 (1988), Scottish Women's Oral History Project (Smith Art Gallery and Museum, Stirling), 216–18.

Q. What age were you when you got married?

A. Twenty-seven, twenty-five. (laughs) It was the funniest, funniest wedding out, you see we hadn't – there was no money at that time, you didn't have big weddings. And, well I had been going with my husband – well this is good advice for you, you take your time and see and have everything in order before you get married. Don't go for too high things, you'll get that in good time. You see, my husband . . . was a bricklayer, journeyman bricklayer. At that time you were only paid according to what work you were doing, if it was raining you didn't get a guaranteed week, you didn't get paid for that. . . . I worked in the office in King Street . . . And we had been going together on and off, sometimes you had a quarrel, and you know, you made it up again. However, he came this particular night to take me out, we went out every night except a Thursday night, . . . However, he came out this particular Thursday night, and he said – he always whistled, you know and I knew when he was here. So I went out and met him and we went away up, we went away for a walk, we sat up in the King's Park. We had arranged to get married in August, which was . . . the Falkirk Fair when they got their holidays. But he had been shifted to another job which was the Glasgow Fair and he had to take his holidays in July, so we didn't know what to do, we hadn't time to arrange a wedding. So, he said to me on the Thursday night he came, I said, 'What do you want tonight?' He says, 'Let's get married.' So, I thought about it, I said, 'Oh no, I don't think so.' However, we left it at that. So, Friday when I was in the office, the bell went and . . . he went to the little place that they spoke through you see and he asked Mr. Murray [the cashier] if he could speak to me. So, he says, 'Can you get out for a minute?' I said, 'Why?' He says, 'I want you to come with me' up to the Registrar's Office . . . he had it all arranged, I had just to sign my name. We went down and bought the wedding ring and it was at five o'clock at night when the jeweller's was just closing. And on the Saturday morning we were married. We went away to Balloch and had our honeymoon in Balloch, had a lovely honeymoon. . . . So, I came back and I went into Mr. Murray's the cashier. . . . He says, 'What's on?' I says, 'I'm waiting 'til the boss comes in.' So Mr. Simpson the civil engineer came in so I rang the bell, I went in, I had my coat and hat on, and he says, 'Well, did you have a nice holiday?' I says, 'I've something to tell you,' he says, 'Don't tell me you got engaged.' I says, 'No, I got married!' (laughs) So, the reason for that was I didn't know whether he wanted a married woman working, at that time married women didn't work, you see. And I didn't want him to think that I could be – I wondered if I could keep my job on to let you understand, because at that time it wasn't the done thing for a – it's different nowadays, married women didn't get the chance of a job. So, I says, 'I just wondered if it would be alright if I continued work?'. . . So, he says, 'Oh just carry on working.' So I did, took my coat and got on with my work. So, Mr. Murray the cashier said, 'You'll be looking for a house?' I says, 'Yes.' 'Well,' he says, 'I think there'll be one empty soon in Irvine Place.' So, within two or three months I had a house in Irvine Place. So, I carried on working right until, oh, Peter was born in May, so I carried on for nearly a year working. And we just saved up and got the little house furnished and everything.

3.17 Why soviet women want to get married

Ekaterina Alexandrova, in Tatyana Mamnova, ed., *Women and Russia, Feminist Writings from the Soviet Union* (Oxford: Basil Blackwell, 1984), 31–5.

I happened to call an acquaintance of mine in West Germany and she told me that she was getting married in a few days. I started to congratulate her warmly, to wish her happiness, and to express my joy in general on the occasion of her marriage. To this she replied in an everyday, businesslike tone that she saw no cause for joy, on the whole, nothing special in the fact that she was getting married. She has known her husband-to-be for many years; they are living together, they have an excellent relationship, and they are both content with their lot in life. They decided to register their marriage officially because they are expecting a baby and it is easier to deal with the government bureaucracy if the child is listed as the product of a registered marriage. . . . She could not resist making a few caustic remarks about the government bureaucracy and 'this police state'.

My initial reaction to her impending marriage had obviously surprised her and she asked how it was that I, an independent, educated person with a 'male' profession, could attach any significance to such a worthless formality. To this I replied that I had expressed the usual reaction of a Soviet woman. In our country, official or civil marriage is considered a big step for a woman – perhaps the most important achievement in a woman's life, no matter how educated or independent she is and no matter how successful she has been in her profession. The stamp *married* in a passport confers innumerable social benefits, and, perhaps more important, Soviet women need this stamp for their own psychological sense of well-being, for their self-affirmation. This need is created by thousands of little things that are at times imperceptible but nevertheless create a psychological atmosphere. Without that stamp, the Soviet woman feels incomplete. . . .

Yet, my acquaintance was partly right. There really is something to be surprised about and something hard to understand. Here is a society that has proclaimed as its goal the extrication of women from the narrow confines of the family and the inclusion of these women in all forms of public activity. And it would appear that this society had achieved its goal – Soviet women work at the most varied jobs, and many of them are well educated, have a profession, and are financially independent of men. And yet, in this very society, among these very women, a patriarchal social order and its psychology thrive. . . . the most important thing is the psychology . . . that is widespread and typical of the Soviet woman. . . .

What is it that compels the Soviet woman to charge into the pit of marriage Soviet-style of her own free will? For it is precisely of her own free will that she marries, since she is financially independent, has a profession, and has at least some kind of work that gives her a definite social status regardless of the kind of personal life she leads. . . . What makes her prefer, seemingly of her own free will, life in a nightmarish marriage that many married women openly hate and curse? . . . And after the experience of an unsuccessful marriage (or even several), why does she seek with paranoid persistence new attempts to create 'a healthy Soviet family'?

The main cause for this phenomenon lies in the fact that formal civil marriage is supported officially in the USSR to the highest degree. The desire for marriage is actively inculcated in society by the authorities. . . .

To begin with, every Soviet lives with the certainty that the authorities are aware of all the crucial elements of his or her biography and that at any moment the particulars and the most minute details of his or her private life could become the object of the most intense scrutiny. . . . From the outset Soviets know not to relate to their personal lives as if they were strictly their own business, something that, in principle, concerns no one but them.

Figure 3.3 Estonian family, 1930s

3.18 Estonian realities

Tiina Jääger, Programme Manager, Estonian Non-formal Adult Education Association, private correspondence, 2010.

In 1995–1996, the number of divorces jumped up more among the couples that have been married 5–9 years and 10–19 years. 5–7 years had passed after the 'singing revolution', and it became a 'sober' period with a lot of problems and economic crises. Marriages of 10–19 years started 5–10 years before the 'singing revolution'. The situation had changed. Also attitudes.

There weren't too many choices during the Soviet time. You finished education, married, then had children, etc. In the mid 90s, women became more independent and paid much more attention to their career. Estonian women have been always higher educated than men; it was an opportunity for careers but men did not always accept this.

. . . the rate of marriage dropped in 1996. At this time couples lived together without official marriage. In my opinion, this is something to do with female independence. In the Soviet times, living without marriage wasn't very popular. Maybe even socially not accepted. But this wasn't public, more hidden, in people's minds. I think the reason was that our parents and grandparents kept the values and attitudes of the 1930s. The old, good Estonian time as it was called. I remember my mother's stories and photos from this time.

The '70s generation', where I belong, mostly married between ages 18–22. From the mid 1990s young people started more and more often to live together without marriage. For example: I married at age 19; both my daughters are still not officially married.

I thought again also about the divorces in 1995–1996. The number of divorces of these couples who had been married 5–9 years and 10–19 jumped up.

- The first group (5–9y) married on the top the 'ninth wave' of changes: perestroika and the singing revolution. In the mid 90s, after 5–9 years, 'real' life with all its problems finally started: small children, economic problems and women's wish to be more independent. The borders had been open 5 years and people had seen what the life looked like in old Europe (mostly Nordic countries).
- The second group (10–19y). Here it must be something to do with women's independence. This is approximately my age group, married at age 18–22. Their children were young adults, women were well-educated and had become self-confident (plus influence from the Nordic countries) and they started to plan their own career which led to the divorce. Typical question: why do I need a husband? It's easier alone. And men went to the 'second round' and married women 15–20 years younger.

Motherhood

Figure 3.4 Icelandic mother and child, c.1920

If the angel in the house represented the nineteenth-century woman, the perfect mother epitomised the ideal in the twentieth century. Children became valorised in a way they never had been before. And yet, shifting marriage patterns and an increasing tendency for all women to work (see extracts 3.14, 3.25) challenged motherhood while political regimes saw motherhood as a weapon in their arsenal (extracts 3.11, 3.13). These two photographs (Figures 3.4 and 3.5), taken a century apart, depict motherly intimacy as well as the impact of photography on how women visualised their lives. The first is a studio shot in 'best' dress, posed for the camera; the second is a snapshot at a public event, the Estonian Song Festival, which celebrates Estonian culture and nationhood.

Figure 3.5 Estonian mother with daughter and niece, 2010

Singletons

Women from all backgrounds and social classes were single. Some were deliberately so, and, like Madeleine Pelletier, praised it as the 'superior state'. These women may or may not have had sexual relations and intimate friendships, but their self-image and identity was often tied up with their singleness. As always, there were women who simply did not marry, despite wishing to, and in a century with two major and several smaller wars, demographics meant that marriage was not possible for all women. Others found themselves single after divorce or in widowhood. As Tiina Jääger related

(3.18), divorce was sometimes chosen by women who thought a life without men offered a wider range of opportunities. Widowhood did not always leave women 'alone', nor were all widows elderly. Frau J.K, from Marienthal, Austria, describes how she coped and provided for her two small sons after her husband fell in battle in 1917, taking work as she could and prioritising the needs of the sons, who in her older age reciprocated by helping her out. Mary Helen Odie, from Shetland, reflects on how small communities dealt with a variety of singletons, the 'maiden aunt', the implications of living in a seafaring area where females dramatically outnumbered males and the single mother. Some women were attracted to women, and found themselves at odds with society by not marrying men. In twentieth-century Europe, more and more 'came out', but not without personal and social difficulties. E. Krause describes her gradual awareness and acceptance of her 'contrasexuality'. Whilst proud of her sexual orientation she also shows her fear about going public – not surprisingly, as she wrote in 1901.

3.19 Celibacy, the superior state

Madeleine Pelletier, *Le célibat, État supérieur* (Caen: imprimerie Caennaise, 1926), 1–10.

Celibacy is not, as it was to past minds, a brand of immorality, corruption and decadence; it is a consequence of civilisation and modern life in which social unity tends to be not the family, but the individual. . . .

The life of a married man is filled with little success, with petty concerns. The philosopher, scientist, writer, politician marry beneath themselves. In the desire to support the family, for it to hold its own, the idealist intellectual is forced to change into a professional. The love of science or art, devotion to the idea, give way to the desire, the single aim, of getting the most possible money. . . . and well before he ages physically, man is intellectually threadbare . . .

If the superior man demeans the married state, what about the woman? Unless she finds her equal, which is rare, the marriage of an intelligent woman is moral suicide. A number of wives lose all the benefit of a brilliant education in marriage; piano, singing, culture, all are buried in the concern to manage a flat daily life. . . .

For the singleton . . . material concerns are reduced to a minimum. His cerebral life is therefore much greater than the married man's. He has time and energy to spare; next to his profession, he willingly takes a 'hobby': he learns a foreign language, is involved in a science or an art. The worker [has] a cooperative, a union, a fraternal benefit society, he teaches music and is part of a choir, etc.

The singleton remains youthful much longer than a married man. The single woman also retains a young body much longer, because at fifty years she looks thirty, and does not seem to age. She is not worn by maternity and continuous household cares.

. . . today, at the dawn of female emancipation, many young girls, under-standing the realities of marriage, renounce marriage.

The woman no longer expects to find happiness in the sacrifice of her life to a man; the prince has lost his prestige. The man cannot be the god of woman; good or bad, he is a human being, often less intelligent, sometimes vulgar and mean, rude and brutal. . . .

But celibacy does not necessarily mean chastity. The old girl parrot does not belong to our time and is a victim of social prejudice. Sexuality is no more a shame for a woman than it is for men; it is a physiological function, neither beautiful nor ugly; woman has the right to it, as she has the right to eat and breathe. . . . The liberated woman does not hate the man as sex; she hates servitude, and it is to escape it that she refuses to marry. . . .

However, we choose our friends, which is why celibacy is the higher state when social life is organised not according to the routines of past ignorance, but according to reason.

3.20 A widow with children

Marie Jahoda, Paul Lazarsfeld and Hans Zeisel, *Die Arbeitslosen von Marienthal* (Bonn: Surkampf, 1960), 108–9.

Frau J.K, born 1890 in Erlach near Pitten [Austria] . . . wanted to be a decorator, but her siblings were still small and it did not work out. She joined the factory as a running girl and worked there until 1914. She enjoyed entertainment, danced passionately, often went to Vienna to go to the cinema or the theatre. She married in 1910; her husband also worked in the factory; it was a very good marriage, she never had a sad time with her husband. When the second child came, she stayed at home and thought that she would dedicate herself to her children. Her husband joined the army and fell in 1917. At that time the children were a year and a half, three years and seven years old. She had to go back to work, she joined a can-factory in 1918, then worked in various places in Mitterndorf; when the railway arrived in Marienthal in 1920 she came back and in 1929 was employed by the factory. Now she is on 39s [schilling] benefits. All her sons have made something of themselves. The oldest is a gardener in Marchegg and earns 44s a week, he cannot however give her anything, as he is saving to buy a motorcycle, but the second son . . . gives her 30s every week. She has still to receive something from the youngest. He is being taught in Vienna. She has always done everything for her children. The youngest is musically inclined; she had allowed him to learn music and even during the hardest times she had managed to gather 7s a month for the music teacher. She still likes to spend her spare time on entertainment such as the theatre and cinema. She is always happy, dances now happily 'as an old person'. After the war she became active in the social democratic moment; . . . then active in the Children's Friends movement. . . . Since the Children's Friends let the manager go, she runs the orphanage one afternoon every week.

Figure 3.6
Mothers in the community

Her hardest time was between 1916 and 1918 and then last year (1929) until around August. The War was hard on her, due to her husband being killed and she being left alone with three children. Not until 1918 did things improve again, because she could easily get food from the can-factory. Last year was bad in so far as she was completely dependent on her sons. She did not starve, but you don't want to deprive your sons of everything. Her best time is now, as she sees that her children have become something. They also depend on her, take her to Vienna, to the cinema and show her around. She splits her money, so that she spends the money from her son and from her benefits on food and the 50s monthly pension on clothes. When no new clothes are needed, then she buys better food. She now buys the boys better things, without them knowing it.

3.21 Singletons and pregnancy

Mary Helen Odie, Old Haa, Burravoe, Yell, Shetland, interviewed by Lynn Abrams, 4 April 2001.

LA: going back to young women who might have expected not to marry or their sweetheart died at sea what do you think the options were for them? . . .

MO: That would have been their base and then some went off (south) to service . . . south to Edinburgh. . . . One from my village went to Edinburgh and was the servant to Crawford's family and she came back under a bit of a cloud and a large shawl (laughs) and she had a baby . . . she came back to her uncle and aunt who had no children and a fortnight later she had her baby and she stayed a month and she went away and left Christina to rear her child. Forever after, and yet right up to the time that I was at school they got this huge hamper from the family in Edinburgh. . . .

LA: Looking at the census it looks like a lot of unmarried women ended up living with their sisters who married.

MO: Yes well you see they had many children, it was good to have help with the mothering, for the seventh or eighth child wasn't getting much of a share, with the best mother in the world they don't so I do think the maiden aunt was mmm. . . . But on the whole I think the maiden aunts were good . . . desperately sad for them, but they just, this was their family, they were staying with family. It's nothing new in Shetland, absolutely nothing new. . . . Acceptable, accepted. Nowadays you would sort of 'oh why did she stay' like this but in my young time it was still accepted. But they were a great, it was a great support in an extended family.

LA: And it would have been almost impossible for them to live alone anyway.

MO: Yes. There was just one female that survived alone in the nineteenth century that I know of and that was Janet Russell. And she came to a cousin . . . and he gave her a plot of land just outside the house . . . for her to culti-vate . . . she actually survived like that with help from neighbours. But she couldna have lived without help, impossible. . . .

LA: it seems that women were quite keen to hold on to their reputation.

MO: Oh yes, I think they were afraid of the church . . . I think a bit. . . . But really and truly the kirk session was very judgmental. It was fornication . . . really, the terrors of it were terrible . . . probably appearing on the repentance stool and so on, but one of the worst cases . . ., I'm not sure where in Shetland it happened but it said the elders of the church go to her house they did lay her on the bed and they did milk her. . . . Oh I just felt that mad . . . oh they did have a bad deal. . . . I saw a case like that in Ulster in West Yell where two women and one of them was definitely a howdie [midwife] anyway, and this woman had concealed her pregnancy right up until the end.

3.22 'Contrasexuality'

E. Krause, 'Die Wahrheit über mich: Selbstbiographie einer Konträrsexuellen', *Jahrbuch für sexuelle Zwischenstufen*, 3 (1901), 292, 302–7.

Autobiography – Selfpurification! One should keep their hands off of it. And yet I will do it. Why not? Because I was repeatedly asked to serve the good cause with the truth. Alone – I fear, fear!

I'm definitely not one of those who, unhappy about her condition, hangs her head and would call to everyone: 'Oh, we poor exceptions! Forgive us that we exist in the world.' No, I'm proud of my exceptional orientation. I hold my head up, stamp my foot and say boldly. 'See, that's what I am.' . . .

But it takes courage, a lot of courage. Have the same, my dear sisters, and it shows that you are entitled to as good a livelihood and love as the 'normal' world. – Stand up, and people will tolerate you, will recognise you and will even envy you! Take up arms! It must and will succeed. I've achieved it. Why should all of you not succeed in everything . . .

You poor, poor people! When will you strike the hour of salvation? When will it come for our brothers who like us have the destiny to be exceptions to the daily pattern of the ancient and eternal law of nature? Mother Nature can be wrong then? . . . Can we not be more of a purpose than a 'coincidence'? . . . Throw down the gauntlet to me! I will pick it up and say, 'the answer is not guilty'.

Take up arms! . . . Why, why should the innocent suffer; they were also created with feeling, but expressed in a manner which the everyday world will not understand? Mind you, I do not ask for a moral code just for 'exceptionals'. What I ask is, humanity, impartiality, equal rights for all.

Why can there still be found in our enlightened age, the prejudice against 'the old maid', which causes so much mischief? . . . I was lucky that during my medical studies I came across the works of Krafft-Ebing.

Oh, how I reacted! How my eyes were opened! How easy, how purposeful I felt after reading them! Now it was clear to me that I never, never had to marry a man. In my account of my life so far, I recognised my complete coldness towards the other sex and admitted to myself why many woman with beauty, charm, grace, and by natural reason, enchanted me, . . .

But, oh! How many are still unconscious with no idea of their true condition? And these are the ones for which I tremble. . . . Yes, a friend confessed to me that thus she even had become a mother twice. O . . ., such hypocrisy, such a fraud! –

To speak of my marriage – so I intentionally call my relationship with my beloved girlfriend – I hesitate again and again because the relationship is sacred to me, but it would be wrong to hide something. I got to know 'her' on a forest outing. Nature had intoxicated me. On the shore of the lake I wanted to reach out to calm my inflamed soul. As she lay under an oak tree, all dressed in pink. No further! The whole thing is so fabulous . . . that you could keep the story for a novel.

She was married. I went through all the storms of jealousy, despair, wanted to run away with her, kidnap her, and she had to tell me that I had no right. I learned only after her husband's death, which took place suddenly on a hunt, that she also loved me. From that moment on we have lived together as a couple. My sweet little wife sweeps and reigns in our cozy home like a real German housewife, and I work for both of us.

8   The transitional community

Work and identity

The world of work contained many of the tensions found in twentieth-century family life. Louise-Marie Compain examines the phenomenon of middle-class women and work, describing its positive factors in terms of self-esteem and intellectual challenge, but she is also aware of the difficulties, acknowledging that women may suffer bruises along the way. In contrast, Gina Lombroso, a physicist who wrote extensively on women, juxtaposes women's new working pleasures with her perceptions of the drawbacks. The extracts from German sociologists Elisabeth Pfeil and Helge Pross mark the passage of time, with Pfeil's study capturing women's views of house and home in 1961 and Pross's in 1975. This short period tangibly marked significant differences in women's expectations and perceptions of their roles as housewives and workers.

3.23 Consequences of woman's work

Louise-Marie Compain, 'Les consequences du travail de la femme', *La Grande Revue*, 10 (1913), 364–76, in Jennifer Waelti-Waters and Steven Hause, eds, *Feminisms of the Belle Epoque*, trans. Lydia Willis and Jennifer Waelti-Waters (Omaha: University of Nebraska Press, 1994), 134–7.

We shall pay particular attention to the transformations that occur in the middle classes, because it is mainly in this milieu that feminine evolution is taking place at present. The woman of the lower classes has been working for her bread for a long time. As for the women of the upper classes, they play but an insignificant role in social evolution, in view of their small numbers; besides we see some of their most interesting representatives following the present movement. . . .

   The possession of a working skill assures the young girl of material independence and brings her at the same time a new moral independence with respect to marriage. This certainly does not mean that the modern young girl does not want love and does not desire marriage; but she no longer perceives marriage, or perceives it less and less, as a state one has to acquire at any price. She wants to love the man she marries, and she is not ready to marry the first comer who finds her pretty, because she has less time to lose in debilitating dreams and because she is more aware of reality. In a word, she has almost always conquered what we would call freedom of choice, and one can say that this freedom is the most considerable gain the conquest of an occupation has brought her, and its value by far exceeds the material benefits.

Engaging in an occupation ensures the moral dignity of the young woman and at the same time puts her in more direct contact with life. The lawyer who has received the painful confessions of the guilty and the oppressed, the woman doctor who has spent the most beautiful hours of her youth with the sick and the dead, the employee who is in contact with the public, the secretary who is in charge of the mail of a large business or a member of parliament, a teacher, or a nurse will know life better than the young girl of old who only went out accompanied by her mother or her maid to take courses in literature or music.

Certainly, contact with reality does not happen without bruises, and it is possible that the young girl arrives at marriage with so few illusions that her mother is astounded and afflicted by this precocious experience. One young woman told us the other day: 'I have watched men too closely; I know that the best of them are unfaithful to their wives; I know what to expect and I suffer ahead of time.' This lucidity is perhaps exaggerated, but it is certainly a lesser evil than the evil of ignorance that gripped the inactive girl of twenty years ago and aroused in a brain deprived of stimuli a love of the romantic that deformed her judgment and later on kept it from tasting the bitter but invigorating flavors of reality. . . .

The growth of a sense of her dignity as a woman, a loftier ideal of love, a deeper knowledge of life and more zest for it, these seem to us to summarize the moral gains for the female mentality that come from the material independence won by working.

Could one place on the other side of the scale the loss of those special qualities that seem more particularly feminine (sweetness, goodness, grace) or the acquisition of faults that seemed until now to be reserved for men? . . .

Now let us discuss the domestic and social consequences of feminine evolution.

There are two choices: upon marriage, the woman will leave the occupation that she had pursued (and this will not always depend on the husband's income, but also on the love that the woman had for her work), or she will continue to exercise her profession.

In the first case the moral gain the young girl acquired remains intact and adds to the family's happiness. There is no doubt that the woman whose spirit has developed in contact with life is, as a wife, more comprehending of her husband's work and of the struggles he will have to face. It is also certain that as a mother she will be better suited to direct the education of her children, perhaps more aware of the differences in their natures, more apt to become their friend.

If the moral gain remains intact, the material gain also persists in part as a precious insurance in case of sickness, financial misfortunes, or the husband's death. If one of those misfortunes should strike the developing family, the woman would not only find indispensable resources in the profession she exercises, but the previous apprenticeship would find her better equipped for the brutal assault of adverse circumstances.

However, will this woman, who has left paid employment to devote herself completely to her family, have no other ideal but to live in her home sheltered from the outside world? . . . We believe that this could happen, but that it will become more and more rare. The appeal of life outside the home is felt even in the hearts of happy women who have not studied for any practical purpose. Thus, one sees more and more young women who, after the initial tasks of motherhood are over, feel the need for activity outside the home. She returns to or enters the world outside her home by way of social activity. She becomes involved with charity, education, or propaganda.

3.24 Women's happiness

Gina Lombroso, *La Donna Nella Vita* (Bologna: Zanichetti, 1923), 15, 24–7.

The young ladies who wrote to me raise one of the most serious and striking problems that exist in the present world of women. The young ladies of the middle classes have all acquired work and through this both freedom and esteem. . . .

From the day when marriage and starting a family ceased to be the only avenue open to the young woman, all the habits and ideas that are attached to this notion lost their meaning. . . .

The house seems an empty future in the eyes of young girls, even in their mothers' eyes, and they seek to abandon it at all cost. Those women of the aristocracy and the bourgeoisie who are not bound by any profession that requires their activity all day are often on the lookout for those empty occupations and pastimes on useless boards and in even more useless charity organisations, just to have something to do outside of the home. . . .

Despite all [the] advantages, I will not hesitate to assert that life in the past, even with all its unpleasantness, better created the happiness of women based on the holiest of female instincts, than life nowadays, . . .

The woman could not study a century ago, but on the other hand she did not have the duty of submitting to a wide number of exams, which now plagues her from earliest youth. The woman could not travel back then as she can now; but she could depend on her home; she could avoid the eternal contact with foreign and unimportant people to which her current position condemns her.

The woman of the last century could not flirt like the young modern girl, but she could love and be loved much more than nowadays. Men amused themselves much less with her back then, but they did not grow tired of her so early either. The relationship is similar to cakes and bread. The cakes delight more in the beginning, but you soon grow tired of them, while bread never gets tiresome.

The woman of the past could not aspire to any honour or independence, but on the other hand her brain was not under continuous stress; the duties that were entrusted her matched her instincts precisely. She did not find it necessary to venture outside her centre to become happy, and she could instead achieve this with a minimum of favourable conditions.

The life of the woman back then was no picnic, and the emotions she went through were not always pleasant. Children, brothers and husbands presented her with greater challenges than now in regards to care; but this care was in itself an enrichment of her mind and heart.

Love, hate, illusions, disillusionment, joys and sorrow, emotions of all kinds filled her life, not always in a pleasant way, but in continuous interaction and without ever leaving the soul empty.

Today, where we are so eager to pursue amusements, we often forget that worries are part of happiness and an intellectual life which is deprived of emotion is more difficult to live for a woman than an emotional life, despite it being full of pain. . . .

The woman of today can proclaim her independence as loudly as she wants, she can further her mind as much as she wants, think about herself, her merits, her position, her glory; but she cannot do anything else, she cannot follow her altruistic instincts. In throwing herself in the arms of a job or a profession, she now enters the competition, where she must defend herself with tooth and claw, like the man. She can no longer mix her thoughts with the man, and add her own cheerful intuitions to the discussion. She can no longer be generous, modest, devoted. These are all qualities that competition does not allow, that the career does not allow.

3.25 Mothers' occupations

Elisabeth Pfeil, *Die Berufstätigkeit von Müttern* (Tübingen: JCB Mohr, 1961), 97–9.

[Relatives] advise for or against [going to work], depending. They appear as tempters and encouragers. . . . But also the mother or the mother-in-law, who wants to keep the child to themselves, urges the young woman into work; the housewives who complain that they 'would like to get out', the friends who admired the talented young woman – they all encourage the young woman in her plans and will, if necessary, lead the encounter against the husband.

The decision to work must be justified both to herself and to a critical world. Those women who have continued to work and now have made something of themselves, however, are not as self-assured as they appear to envious women. In order to justify their own decision, they are inclined to proselytise. Thus women who are not working and who hesitantly ask if they are doing well, often forget how demanding and difficult it is and what unsolved issues there are. . . . The woman faces the decision and approaches it with eagerness, but often she must also find that it is not so simple: 'in the beginning it all appears so easy . . .'

Until now, we have seen the young couple as a unit, inspired by the same desire for domesticity, but the decision to cooperate, even with young people, is frequently the result of a dispute between the spouses. The formation of the will of the couple only results from a gradual consultation or through one of them prevailing. . . .

'My husband did not agree, I went to work against his will, to him it was not right. I also only wanted to do this for a year.' (Apparently she told him it would be short-term.) 'And now three years have already passed', and seeing that she is thinking about doing another three years, it will be at least six years. And after 17 years of marriage she still wanted to improve the household a little! (35-year-old spinner, one child . . .)

A 32-year-old female worker with two children said that in the beginning her husband would not allow her to work at all, but she had asked and begged. She also wanted to be able to buy what her neighbours could . . .

'My husband was actually not really of the opinion that I should work, especially after our child was born' (. . . 26-year-old stenographer, one child).

An example of where the husband prevails – a driver who took us to a factory and asked us what our plan was – should be cited:

'My wife one day came up with the idea that she wanted to earn a living too, so that we could afford more. She said that she did not have enough to do at home. Then I went and bought a garden lot and told her: So, now you can get yourself something' (He meant fruit and vegetables) 'and have enough to do.' He had then, he added good-naturedly, bought a new hat as consolation, and he was always a bit more generous when it came to her clothes. . . .

One reason why women hesitate about the opportunity to achieve a beautiful home by going to work: It is the issue of child-care, . . . 'a lot more mothers would work, if they knew where they could place their children' (Her 1-year-old son is with his grandmother during the day . . . 26-year-old storage-worker, one child). It is therefore crucial whether or not she can find a childcare solution.

In young married couples' conversations, which precede the decision to go ahead, all possibilities are discussed; giving away the child, if it is even mentioned, is rejected, crèches are not readily available, and many mothers will not entrust their babies to a crèche. Basically, all women would rather that a close relative came to help. . . . almost four-fifths of our young female workers and employees have some kind of help from relatives to rely on, . . . If the help of the relatives falls through, the woman will stop working . . . Specifically the mother and mother-in-law indirectly allow the construction of the young household!

3.26 Housewives' realities

Helge Pross, *Die Wirklichkeit der Hausfrau* (Hamburg: Rowholt Verlag, 1975), 13–14. (emphasis in original)

The role of the housewife has become problematic. She is criticised from a psychological as well as a scientific and political point of view. This is noteworthy when you consider that a couple of decades ago it was the noblest role of the woman, as it was the only truly feminine one, . . . Many women had to and were allowed to enter employment, but claimed that they also had the right to refuse to focus completely on family duties, and would regularly be branded as 'unfeminine'. Such a woman was seen as unnatural, almost as a monster, who neither could nor should be seen as a role model. A real rivalry between the pure housewife and the working woman did not exist. The former would be seen and saw herself as superior. If the working woman was also unmarried then she had no claim whatsoever to the same assessment.

Much of this has since changed. Today the role of the housewife and not the working woman is subjected to low estimation and criticism. An uncertainty is spreading amongst housewives and a new confidence is growing in working women. You can see it almost every day. When working and non-working women are together, the latter become very defensive, and the former make it more or less politely clear that they are carrying the banner of progress. *In many groups the household and the family are synonymous with backwardness, and employment and a personal income are synonymous with emancipation.* Sometimes you almost get the impression that working women now take revenge on the non-working women and pay them back for what they used to suffer in contempt.

The new difficulties of housewives are also visible to others. Even the most common use of language reflects their low status. Well we all know that the housewife also works. However in the familiar distinction between women 'who go to work' and others who stay at home, this is omitted. The customary nature of this distinction shows how much we have dwelt on it, only seeing occupations as work, and thus accepting commercial norms on a personal level. No reasonable person, however, will deny the work nature of housewifely duties. Nor can one deny that the educational functions of woman of the home are just as important to the community as are the creation of goods and services for the market. Finally, it is also clear that the acquisition of external services of men and women presently is only possible through the domestic work of women. *The housewife provides services for the working part of society (including the domestic workload of working women) from 45 to 50 billion hours per year. It is thus almost as large as the amount of work in the labour economy of around 54 billion hours. However one assesses household chores, it is still work in any case. Nevertheless, she is still not rewarded socially, as she is not part of the workforce. While they are still respectable, they are looked down upon. Such contempt is undermining the confidence of the housewife.*

War work

The two world wars are often credited with permanent improvements in women's work opportunities. While they did open new fields to women, they also built on existing patterns of employment, and many women were forced to leave in peacetime. War work was also contentious. These two extracts from Germany show the shift in approaches and the implications of 'total war'. Hindenburg's letter makes the link between political and occupational agitation by women and emphasises the necessity to protect the concept of the family. The all-out effort called for in the Second World War is evident in the passage from Hitler's Germany, when not only were women marshalled to replace men in occupations, but their work was explicitly coupled with propaganda and psychological work. The level of commitment implied was similar across Europe.

3.27 Employing women in war

Letter, Chief of Staff General Paul von Hindenburg to Chancellor Bethmann Hollweg, October 1916, in Ute Daniel, *The War from Within: German Working-class Women in the First World War* (Oxford: Berg, 1997), 68–9.

It is also my opinion that women's work should not be overestimated. Almost all intellectual work, heavy physical labour, as well as all real manufacturing work will still fall on men – in addition to the entire waging of the war. It would be good if clear, official expression were given to these facts and if a stop were put to women's agitation for parity in all professions, and thereby, of course, for political emancipation. I completely agree with your Excellency that compulsory labour for women would be an inappropriate measure. After the war, we will need the woman as spouse and mother. I thus strongly support those measures, enacted through law, prerogative, material aid, etc., aimed at that effect. In spite of the strong opposition to such measures, it is here that vigorous action needs to be taken in order to extinguish the influence of this female rivalry, which disrupts the family. . . .

If I *nevertheless* urge that the requirement to work be extended to all women who are either unemployed or working in trivial positions, now and for the duration of the war, I do so because, in my opinion, women can be employed in many areas to a still greater degree than previously and men can thereby be freed for other *work*. But first industry and agriculture must be urged even more to employ women. . . . In particular, I want to stress again that I consider it especially wrong to keep secondary schools and universities, which have been almost completely emptied of men by conscription, open only for women. It is valueless, because the scholarly gain is minimal; furthermore, because precisely that rivalry with the family that needs to be combated would be promoted; and finally, because it would represent the coarsest injustice if the young man, who is giving everything for his Fatherland, is forced behind the woman.

3.28 The woman's front

Reichsorganisationsleiter der NSDAP, No. 14 (1943), in Stackelberg and Winkle, eds, *The Nazi Germany Sourcebook*, 308–10.

For many women today increased educational and job-related duties are being added to their household responsibilities. In many cases the children have to do without their father, which requires the mother to double her care, prudence, and effort. But in other matters as well she often has to represent her husband and act independently. In the absence of the farmer, many a farmer's wife is running the farm with foreign workers and prisoners of war, i.e. under especially difficult conditions; many a businesswoman is managing the business under similar difficulties in the place of the husband who is serving in the army. A certain degree of strength is called for in order to persevere in unaccustomed circumstances and not to become tired or frustrated. . . . A pronounced characteristic of total war is the increased employment of women in the war economy. As much as one would have liked to spare women this harsh situation – the necessities of war compel us. We cannot wage war against three great powers that are nearly the strongest industrially and richest in natural resources and at the same time allow our own economy to run at half speed. Realizing this, years ago many women party members voluntarily answered the call of the Führer and reported to work. This effort must now be expanded. It is a matter of honor for every woman party member not to shirk her duty under any circumstances, . . .

An important task falls to the woman party member with regard to the formulation of opinion and resolve. Not only the currency of national wealth passes through the hands of women, but also the currency of national morals. The current war has presented us with a completely new situation, it has created a front of women. . . . In this front of women created by the force of circumstances the party member has her responsibility: she is the designated leader. The others look up to her; her psychological power of resistance comforts her companions; from her conviction they draw courage. Even in critical moments she keeps a clear head and maintains her determination, for she has so much political instinct and insight that she knows what's at stake. She will demonstrate the necessary calm and steadfastness even in the face of legitimate human apprehensions. She understands the need and the longing of women for peace, but she knows that for us victory is crucial, not peace. . . . The woman party member has a special responsibility with regard to public opinion. This is formed in wartime primarily by women, at least when it comes to spoken propaganda. Their more active imagination and the more emotional nature of their mental world make them more susceptible to sensational news, rumors, and exaggeration of facts. Here the party member has to be aware of her special responsibility. As a woman she is often in closer contact with her national comrades than a man, and she has the opportunity while shopping and on similar occasions to hear the conversations of larger or smaller groups. . . . It is not necessary to give big speeches at this time; an appeal to feeling and resolve is more important than an appeal to reason.

The party member is most effective through her personality, her conviction, her calm and certainty, her trust in our army, and her belief in the Führer.

Women at work

The female workforce was far more diverse in the twentieth century, including industrial, rural and whitebloused work, and especially professions. This section concentrates on the voices of women as they describe their experiences and reflect on changes. A French factory woman suggests pride in her accomplishments during the First World War, although she says she will look for different work afterwards. British postwoman Mary Hughes also describes her work with a tinge of pride, but acknowledges the suspicion and distrust women encountered moving into 'men's' work. The interview with Agnes Leask from Shetland shows that for many women, especially in rural areas, there was no real separation between home and work, and a sense of time-lessness.

Shops attracted many young women, especially those without the opportunity to follow higher education, like the young interviewee pleased to have work in a shop. Middle-class women were at the forefront of identifying and claiming whitebloused occupations. A Dutch office worker describes the gendered nature of the office in the 1930s, while Kate Adie, one of the century's most distinguished television journalists and long-time Chief News Correspondent for the BBC, describes challenges young women faced in gaining entry to the media, the perceptions and prejudices that abounded and the difference between local radio and international television news.

The professions were at the forefront of women's battle for higher education at the end of the nineteenth century, and access was not plain sailing even in the twentieth. Margaret Booth, the third woman appointed as a High Court Judge in England, examines the relatively recent character of women's position in the legal profession, highlighting just how important barriers to training and gatekeeping can be in the established professions, as well as in the wide array of male-dominated employment.

3.29 In at the deep end

Anonymous, from L. Dorliat, *Women on the Home Front* (1917), in Margaret R. Higonnet, ed., *Lines of Fire: Women Writers of World War I* (New York: Plume, 1999), 129–31.

I am in a workshop for tempering the steel, or rather I was − . . . At the moment of my accident, . . . I was doing the shop-trial of the steel for the shell, testing or inspecting the casing, of course. Right after the tempering bath, when the steel is still hot and black, the other workers and I had to tap it with a buffing wheel in order to polish the steel on a small surface of the bottom and the ogive of the shell. Doing this we handle at least a thousand shells a day, and as I told you, they are big, very heavy to manipulate. Other workers take these same pieces and make a light mark on the polished area, which must not etch the steel further than a certain depth, in a kind of test; they are equipped with a graduated sheet of metal that lets them evaluate the etched lines. If the mark is too deep, the steel is too soft; if it's too shallow, it is too hard; in either case it can't be used and goes back to be recast. The inspection requires great attentiveness. A final verification is made by a controller and as we are always required to put our number on the pieces that pass through our hands, the imperfections, the errors can be traced to their authors.

There too you don't talk, you don't even think of it. The deafening noise of the machines, the enormous heat of the ovens near which you work, the swiftness of the movements make this precision work into painful labor. When we do it at night, the glare together with the temperature of the furnace exhausts your strength and burns your eyes. In the morning when you get home, you throw yourself on your bed without even the strength to eat a bite.
. . .

Forgetting that my buffing machine does an incalculable number of turns a second, I brushed against it with my arm. Clothing and flesh were all taken off before I even noticed. They had to scrape the bone, bandage me every day. I was afraid of an amputation, which luckily was avoided. Only in the last few days have I been able to go without a sling and use my arm; next week I go back to the workshop. I don't want them to change my job, I'm used to my machine and a fresh apprenticeship would not please me at all. I assure you, the first day I was in this noise, near these enormous blast furnaces, opposite the huge machine at which I had to work for hours, I was afraid. We are all like that, all the more so that we are not given time to reflect. You have to understand and act quickly, those who lose their heads don't accomplish anything, but they are rare. In general, one week suffices to turn a novice into a skilled worker. . . .

Yet among us there are women like myself who had never done anything; others who did not know how to sew or embroider; nothing discouraged us. As for me I don't complain, this strained activity pleases me. I can thus forget my loneliness – and not having any children, what else should I do with all my time?

When the war is over, I will look for a job that corresponds better to my taste. I have enough education to become a cashier in a store. I will then be able to be neater than now, for you can't imagine what care it takes to stay more or less clean if you work in metallurgy.

A woman is always woman; I suffered a lot from remaining for hours with my hands and face dirty with dust and smoke. Everything is a matter of habit; among us there are women who seem fragile and delicate – well! if you saw them at work, you would be stunned: it's a total transformation. As for me, I would never have thought I had so much stamina; when I remember that the least little errand wore me out before, I don't recognize myself. Certainly when the day or the night is over, you go home, the fatigue is great, but we are not more tired than the men are. True, we are more sober because we maintain better hygiene and as a result, our sources of energy are more rational and regular, we don't turn to alcohol for strength.

Our sense of the present need, of the national peril, of hatred for the enemy, of the courage of our husbands and sons – all this pricks us on, we work with all our heart, with all our strength, with all our soul. . . . We are very proud of being workers for the national defence.

3.30 Replacing men

Mary Hughes, 'A Postwoman's Perambulations', in Gilbert Stone, ed., *Women War Workers* (London: Harrap & Co., 1917), 67–9.

We Postwomen are a curiously assorted army, ranging socially from the 'tweeny-maid' to the college-bred woman, but having at least two things in common: the desire to do some necessary work, and the physical strength for negotiating endless steps and stairs and for carrying bulky burdens of varying and uncertain quantity.

As with other pursuits which women have had to take up in this time of stress, we seem to have slipped into the work in a calm, businesslike fashion, without materially disturbing the smooth running of the postal machine. True, we were regarded at first with a certain amount of distrust and suspicion by some of the public we were serving. Old gentlemen of no occupation would stand at their windows on the look-out for some peccadillo committed by the new hands, in order that they might send a ream of protest to the harassed postal authorities or indulge in their favourite pastime of writing complaining letters to the newspapers. Our own sex, too, sometimes took up a critical attitude. One day, when scurrying along with heavily laden bag, delivering letters, I remember well seeing two smart women stop dead to gaze on me with raised pince-nez; regardless of the carrying power of their voices they opined that it was hardly women's work, and, in fact, thought women could not be trusted to do the business properly! As these good women were expending their energies in taking shivering and decrepit-looking little dogs for a matutinal airing, I mentally decided that their opinion of my occupation mattered little. . . . On the whole, though, the Postess (as I once heard myself called) has been received amiably and sympathetically enough, with no derision and little grumbling.

. . . one can frankly say that, though the advent of the women has apparently caused some resentment among certain of the men employed, and it is patent that the Postmen's Federation is all a-bristle to prevent any dominance on the part of the women, still, on the whole, the attitude of the postmen to the new-comers has been pleasant enough but always, be it said, on the understanding

Figure 3.7 The rye harvest, Eastern Europe

that we are only looked on as stop-gaps and not as entering into the work to stay. The present pay of Postwomen (which is at the rate of 6d. per hour, with an infinitesimal weekly war bonus) naturally is no inducement to women of education to take up the work, though in this as in most other careers education is all to the good, such as in the matter of identifying unusual script, . . . In the case of dressmakers, or women following other sedentary callings, who have been engaged in this branch of Post Office labour during the past year, a marked improvement in physique is to be noticed, the exercise being healthful. Many wives of men in khaki have taken up the role of Postwomen, though few of these perhaps from the motive I heard voiced the other day by a woman who was sorting near me. She had been speaking of her husband at the Front to her chum, and finished her confidences by saying, 'Well, poor devil, when he is squatting in trench mud it will be nice for him to think that his wife is not lying comfortably in bed, but turning out at five in the morning to "do her bit"'. Though this may not argue a very chivalrous outlook on the part of the unknown spouse, it certainly does express the pleasant spirit of camaraderie between husband and wife that these days of toil and strain have helped to bring into vogue.

3.31 Home and work

Agnes Leask, Gott, Weisdale, Shetland, interviewed by Lynn Abrams, 20 March 2002.

. . . my grandfather came here surely as a young man I think, a very young man, probably with his family and established his home just along the road and that's where I was born and brought up. . . . it went completely out of the family until we were a young married couple looking for a home of our own and it came on the market then, . . . and we bought it with the help of my Dad – . . . we put our last penny into it and we acquired a rather run down croft, that had been neglected for several years, overrun by dockens and nettles, with the fences, mmm apologies for fences, no roof on the old byre, barn roof you could see the daylight through it, and a little but and ben [two-roomed cottage]. But anyhow we took it on. . . . and by that time we had a daughter. And what we were mostly looking for was to generate money quickly and of course the croft hadn't been cultivated so the land was in pretty good [shape]. . . . we ploughed up quite a bit and planted potatoes, for there was a quite a demand for locally grown potatoes for school canteens. . . . We came here in 1958, and then we got into the swing of it. We planted a few the first year and the chap who had the contract for the school canteen . . . said 'plant more they were good'. So for several years we ploughed up as much as we could, sold about a ton of tatties to the school canteen every year which generated a bit of ready cash, but it was a lot of work . . . so it was a case of getting Joanne into her pram on a nice dry day, wheel her down to the field. . . . It wasn't a great deal of money coming in but we sort of scraped by . . . [nearby farms] were always looking for casual labour, so in amongst weeding me own tatties I'd go there whenever they needed casual labour – cabbages, tatties, single turnips, or working the peats because they used to hire in gangs of women to do the peat work. And it all helped to tide us over. When nothing else was available mother and I would go and gather winkles. . . . and then in the evenings in the wintertime I'd do hand knitting. . . . And then there was a knitwear factory in Voe, I'd worked there before I married. Davy had an insurance coming due – . . . We hummed and hahed, shouldn't we put in the bank or should I buy a knitting machine? So I bought the knitting machine and once I got the knitting machine, got orders, firms were giving out orders because it was sort of cottage industry then. Then we were more or less financially secure, as long as I could churn out about a dozen jumpers in the week. That would put our bread on the table for the week, and then of course we had our own vegetables, our own lamb and mutton, albeit in those days not fresh during the wintertime, every bloomin' thing was salted . . . and me mother kept cattle . . . and we got our milk for nothing and I would do the churning so we had our own butter and we made our own cheese. In some respects we were financially better off then as we are now. Our own water was from the well, it didn't cost us anything. We had to carry it in, washing all done by hand. It was only electricity, the only bill.

3.32 Scottish shopgirl

Interview No. 1899, Scottish Women's Oral History Project, 96–7.

It was a jump, the big ironmongery shop. I went in there and I was up in the showroom. The flat above the shop was the showroom and they kept all the, (pause) oh, the lovely stuff you know, brass and copper and all that kind, ornaments and fancy grates. What they didn't have in that top showroom. And then there was another showroom that I went through, . . . it was more for the kitchen, sold stuff for the kitchen, like plates and teapots and everything like that, prams, pots and pans and everything. Well I learned all that and then the girl left and I went into this fancy showroom and they had rugs and carpets. . . .

Q. Did you sell the items?

A. Yes, I could sell anything yes, and then when I was finished, I only worked there in the morning and forenoon, and then when I came back at dinner time I had to work in the shop, you see, learn all the different parts of the shop. And then at the other side of the shop they had the glass cases and silver, copper, and all these different things. Well you had all that to learn and then you had to keep them all clean. Another girl and I, we did it and then their cases here were fancy knives and all these different things. Oh, some beautiful silver. Oh I loved that shop. (laughs). . .

Q. And how did you get the [job] in the shop?

A. . . . it was all men they had before you see, however when the war started. . . . I knew that one of the young lads was called up for the army so they just

Figure 3.8 May Day outing, 1920, Hackman's Sawmills, Finland. The female workers
may have worked in the office, but they also worked in the mills, finishing
and packing.

engaged me right away. And I got started on Monday because he left on the
Saturday and I started on the Monday, and I worked there, (pause) I cannae
mind how long. I got on well down there. And then right at the bottom there
was a door at the back and you could learn all the farm stuff, you know, what
they sold to farms. And then you'd to know about all the different oils and
paraffin, all the different kinds of paraffin and all that. . . .

Q. So what were your hours in the ironmongers then?

A. The hours? I started at eight and I worked from eight to nine, and then
I had, (pause) that was my breakfast hour. From nine to ten I was at home and
then the shop closed at one o'clock and then we started at two and then we
finished at six o'clock at night. And Saturday, Saturday we finished at one
o'clock, it was a better arrangement you know for me for a while when
mother was ill but,

Q. Was your wage better?

A. I had only five shillings in the laundry, oh yes I had. I had, (pause) did I
have seventeen and sixpence I think? . . . oh I loved that shop, I was back three
times. I left when my mother came back from the Dundee Royal, I left to
look after my mother 'cause she was helpless.

3.33 Dutch invoice clerk

Interview, in Francisca De Haan, *Gender and the Politics of Office Work: the
Netherlands 1860–1940* (Amsterdam: Amsterdam University Press, 1988), 139.

Round about six o'clock, being the junior clerk, you had to take the last letters to the big boss in his private office, and above the door there was a little lamp. If it was green, you knocked and put your ear to the door waiting till you heard 'enter'. The first time he would speak so softly that you just wouldn't hear. So after awhile you knocked again and then he roared so loud that your legs would tremble. I think he enjoyed it, but we were scared stiff. On Saturday he first received the travelling salesmen, so the light was red, and we had to wait for another hour or more.

When I was a little older, I was pluckier, but that nearly ended in disaster. I was twenty and wanted to earn more money. I think I was paid forty guilders a month (around 1938). A friend of mine worked in an office where they also used Burrough invoicing machines, and she advised me to apply for a job with her company. I was bound to get more pay, as they were looking for girls to operate those machines. I sent in my application and thought I was being clever by creating two possibilities to get the raise I wanted. I was going to tell my present boss that I wanted a raise. If not, I would leave them and take a job elsewhere where I would get better money. I will never forget what happened.

Modest knock on the door, no answer, another gentle knock, a big roar and in I went. I summoned up all my courage and said that I would like to have a raise, because . . ., that's all I managed to say. 'What', he hollered, 'a raise? Get out of here.' Which I did. All of that month I was in a blue funk; was I to get the sack or not? Also because I did not hear anything about that application. But nothing happened. A few months later I got an answer to my application. I was to be paid 55 guilders a month for operating the invoicing machine, but I was not to tell anyone, because even the eldest girl of 29 in that department only earned 50 guilders.

3.34 Journalism

Kate Adie, *The Kindness of Strangers* (London: Headline Book Publishing, 2002), 107–9.

Journalistic considerations apart, being a female was also a source of diffidence. In the regions, it had been straightforward. In Plymouth, I had been told, 'You get the health stuff and the fashion and the kiddies . . . obviously, eh?' There'd been no embarrassment in the newsroom when this statement was delivered. Lucky to be in the newsroom, girlie. I might have been seven years in local radio producing politics and farming and social problems – but that was upstart local radio. This was regional telly, where convention was stronger and the image of announcerettes gushing next to a vase of flowers lingered. . . .

In London, the situation was not very clear. There had been mutterings that 'more women were needed' – and there had always been one or two female reporters around. What was exciting for me was that the men who assigned us to stories were all, without exception, completely unconcerned by gender politics. You merely represented a pair of legs to be dispatched as fast as possible to a breaking story; indeed, you were always expected to run out of the newsroom and down the corridor, as a sign of dedication. After years of mutterings from the men in local and regional newsrooms, the jokey put-downs whenever a woman turned in a great interview or an unexpected scoop, Television Centre seemed a New Republic of Equality. And so it was – in some areas.

The last bastion of blokes and jokes about tits on the telly existed in the Crew Room. I wasn't quite ready for this, . . . I thought I'd got it sorted, and I reckoned I was the tolerant sort. I'd been through an almost all-male university and adored every minute – women had to be raffled for some formal occasions, so scarce were we. Local radio had delivered a social life so heterosexually frantic that 'happy exhaustion' was regarded as a legitimate excuse for missing early shifts. And I could still remember being told on my first training course that pregnancy was not a total disaster for unmarried BBC ladies – the Corporation merely moved you discreetly to another BBC establishment – though two pregnancies were considered the limit. So I'd grown to see the BBC as a liberal outfit, one where tolerance was the norm, as long as you didn't frighten the horses. . . .

But I hadn't reckoned on the stubbornly neolithic Crew Room in London, which contained a fair number of beer guts and Old Hands.

Several were openly hostile, and I discovered just how deep this hostility went when, in my first month in London, a cameraman in his large crew car attempted to crush my small Ford Escort into a motorway barrier at 70 mph. In the ensuing minute, I chased after him . . . then drove him off the road. . . . I made myself let these things go. . . . Others complained that it wasn't right for a bird to go on foreign assignments. I suppose I was an embarrassment when they picked up tarts and then had rows about payment prior to the police being called to their bedroom down my corridor. . . .

I had no rules to go by. Any fuss would rebound, and anyway, these were days when women were breaking new ground everywhere, grabbing opportunities, being given such wonderful chances – why wreck them? It would only have been seen as 'not being able to hack it'. So I reasoned. And anyway, there were a great number of cameramen who were terrific – kind and encouraging, fun, and protective without being patronising. Why rock the boat – possibly hole it – while the battle was still being fought? . . .

I've always thought that being a reporter is rather like being a gun dog. You don't know exactly what's going to happen; you're not in charge. You're a bit nervous, but keen. A shot rings out, and off you hare to sniff out something interesting and bring it back. And you bring back something which is part of a much wider scene – a small but pertinent trophy, with smell and colour and texture, and a history – which you lay in front of someone hoping that the way you carried it hasn't changed or damaged it. What I didn't ever fancy was being a poodle chasing after a ball and obediently fetching something already familiar in order to fulfil limited expectations.

3.35 Women as lawyers

Dame Margaret Booth, in Mary R. Masson and Deborah Simonton, eds, *Women and Higher Education* (Aberdeen: Aberdeen University Press, 1996), 267–9.

'Should ladies under any circumstances be allowed to act as judges?' enquired the *Daily Telegraph* of its readers on 28 September 1887. The answer which the paper gave to its own question was, not surprisingly, a firm 'No'. 'The nation is not as yet quite ripe for the reception of matrons as magistrates', it said. The 'ripening' effectively took 68 years, for it was not until 30 September 1965 that England and Wales received its first woman High Court Judge, the late Dame Elizabeth Kathleen Lane. . . .

In England and Wales, . . . women have had a struggle to enter and to succeed in the legal profession. It was, and remains, male-dominated, despite the fact that the symbolism of the female presence has long been acknowledged. The womanly figure of justice, with or without scales, sword or blindfold, but always a woman, is portrayed in many courts and on many legal logos, in particular on law society ties. The first advocate of any significance that a child is likely to come across is Portia and the words of her plea 'The quality of mercy is not strained' must vie with those of Hamlet 'To be or not to be' for first place in the league of quotations. . . . But the reality of women as lawyers has been different.

The presence of women in the legal profession is still a matter of relatively recent history. In 1903 Gray's Inn, having admitted Bertha Cave to its Honourable Society, probably by mistake, refused to call her to the Bar simply because she was a woman. That male monopoly was not broken until 1922. Seventy-five years is not a long time in the history of a collegiate and traditionalist profession as old as the Bar. The solicitors' branch of the profession is a good deal younger, but they too admitted their first woman in 1922. At first the numbers of women in both branches increased slowly. By the mid 1950s only 2% of solicitors and 3.2% of barristers were women. By 1991, 18% of practising barristers were women. By 1993 more than a quarter of the 61,000 practising solicitors were women, their number having trebled since 1983–4. There are now as many women reading for a degree in law and entering the profession as there are men, if not more.

It is not now the number of women . . . that is cause for concern. The problem lies in the fact that still so relatively few reach the top. . . . In 1993 the Law Society's annual statistics revealed that of the solicitors with 10–15 years experience 53% of the women were partners in their firms as opposed to 79% of the men and that it took women on average 2 years longer than men to become partners. Of the barristers, currently only 50 women are Queen's Counsel as against 824 men. Their representation on the judiciary is small. Of the 487 county court judges, 28 are women. There are 6 High Court judges out of a total of approximately 96 and one woman in the Court of Appeal – The Appellate Committee of the House of Lords remains a male preserve. . . .

Women are indeed new to the profession, but that of itself is not sufficient to explain their slow rise to the top. In common with all those who seek careers, they face the conflict of interests and loyalties still inherent in being a daughter, a wife or a mother, and in many cases all three. . . .

And little so far has been done to assist women to cope with the various demands so liberally placed upon them in one capacity or another while at the same time enabling them to pursue their work. The recession and consequent cut-backs have made it difficult for many who have had a career break, or even maternity leave, to retrieve their positions. Adequate facilities for child-minding are thin on the ground. . . .

Many women, too, have a reluctance to promote themselves. The Lord Chancellor has publicly expressed his concern that few women apply for positions as assistant recorders, which is the first step towards judicial appointment, or for Silk or for other appointments for which they would be eligible. Of the 540 applications for Silk this year only 43 were from women, which represented a mere 8% of the total of 540 applicants; however, nine were appointed out of the total of 77 who were successful.

Account must be taken, too, of the arduous nature of the work of the legal profession and the demands it makes upon the individual. A barrister may be required to go to any court in any part of the country. Mastering a brief or writing an opinion may take many hours. The routine of a day spent first in court and then in chambers in conference, followed by an evening of paper-work and the preparation of a brief for the next day can be, and usually is, exhausting and leaves little space or energy for other activities. Virginia Woolf aptly described it when she wrote that the daily toil of the barrister 'leaves very little time for friendship, travel or art. This explains why most success-ful barristers are hardly worth sitting next to at dinner they yawn so'. Even Virginia Woolf did not have in mind the possibility that the success-ful barrister might also have had to fit in the housework and the care of children and, indeed, might even have had to prepare and cook the dinner in question.

Legislation and unemployment

Since the early nineteenth century, politicians increasingly legislated on the workplace. For women this often meant 'protection', protection that could be welcome, but which could also be used to exclude them from lucrative work. Clothilde Dissard makes just this sort of argument, showing how legislation helped to suppress women's wages. The Marienthal study of the unemploy-ment of the 1930s shows how starkly different men's and women's time patterns were, with women still constantly busy despite unemployment and men largely unoccupied. The last two extracts draw on British Parliamentary debates. In 1924, Margaret Bondfield argued that problems of men's unem-ployment were prioritised, while women's were disregarded as unimportant. In 1940, Ellen Wilkinson's contention was much the same, that married women were ill-treated in unemployment insurance legislation, largely because successive government policy promoted male interest and the removal of women from industry. Both were elected in 1924, Bondfield serving as the first female Cabinet minister (Minister of Labour), in the interwar Labour government, and Wilkinson becoming the second female Cabinet minister (Minister of Education), in the Labour government of 1945, marking the gradual incursion of strong female voices into government to speak for women.

3.36 Protection of workers

Clothilde Dissard, 'La Protection du Travail feminine', *La Fronde*, 29 Jan. 1900, trans. Jette Kjær, in *Feminisms of the Belle Epoque*, 120–1.

The new law concerning the work of women and children has yet to be voted on by the Senate, and already protests can be heard from all over the working class and the feminist milieu.

What do feminists have against this law? That it does not put the male and female worker on a perfectly equal footing but wants to protect the woman, whereas the man is already considered pure work muscle, totally insignificant and quite unworthy of care from the State. This hypocritical concern of our legislators for female workers is normally liked and greatly appreciated by the trade unions, who are so preoccupied with the competition between the sexes, so very disposed to eliminating women from the lucrative jobs, and stupidly hostile to female labour, under the pretext that female labour lowers the rate of the salaries. These gentlemen deliberately condemn young and unattached women, widows, and unmarried mothers: all those women who suffer and are prepared to work for a starvation wage and who, consequently, are the cause of the meagre salaries that the men themselves earn. . . .

Whereas the law of November 2, 1892, which was voted on at the instigation of the unions, authorizes women to fold newspapers at night – for this work is very poorly paid – it refuses to let women print these same newspapers, since the good wages must be reserved for the men.

Perhaps you imagine that our legislators will make these strange abnormalities disappear in the new law? Think again. If a more equitable clause is written into the code, it will not be applied, because in our society women cannot provoke just treatment, have their rights validated, or obtain the benefit of laws which are in their favour. . . .

Despite the many good reasons that are brought forward concerning the necessity of protecting female labour, and the possibility of protecting the mother and pregnant woman against the demands of her employer, the law is enforced only in cases where men demand it, believing that it will protect their salaries. As for children, adolescents, girls, and minors, nobody worries about them, because they share with women the privilege of not placing a vote in the ballot box.

Hausangestellten Zeitung

Nummer 4 • April 1932 • 9. Jahrgang

Organ der Haus- und Wachangestellten, Reichsfachgruppe im Gesamtverband der Arbeitnehmer der öffentlichen Betriebe und des Personen- und Warenverkehrs

Zeitschrift für die Interessen der Hausgehilfen, Hausangestellten, Portiers, Hausmeister, Fahrstuhlführer, Wächter, Wasch- und Reinemachefrauen in Bureau- und Privathäusern, Angestellten der Wach- und Schließgesellschaften

Erscheint monatlich. Bezugspreis für Nichtmitglieder vierteljährlich 50 Pf. Einzelnummer 20 Pf. Zu beziehen durch die Post. Redaktion und Expedition: Berlin SO 16. Michaelkirchplatz 4. Redaktionsschluß am 20. jeden Monats. Zuschriften und Reklamationen sind an die Schriftleitung zu richten.

Bavaria-Verlag, Gauting vor München

LICHT MUSS WIEDER WERDEN NACH DIESEN DUNKLEN TAGEN

Laßt uns nicht fragen,
ob wir es sehen,
es wird geschehen:
Auferstehen wird ein neues Licht.

Waren unsre Besten nicht
ein wanderndes Sehnen, unerfüllt
nach Licht, das da quillt,
von ihnen noch ungesehen?

Es wird geschehen.
Laßt uns nicht zagen.
Licht muß wieder werden
nach diesen dunklen Tagen.

Hermann Claudius

Figure 3.9 Domestic workers' newspaper: 'Light must return after these dark days', 1932

3.37 Gender, time and unemployment

Marie Jahoda, Paul Lazarsfeld and Hans Zeisel, eds, *Arbeitslosen von Marienthal* (Bonn: Surkampf, 1960), 84–5, 90–1.

Time passes twice in Marienthal; it is different for women and for men. For the latter the division into hours has already lost all meaning. Waking up – eating lunch – going to bed are the points of the day they still have left. In between, time passes without one really knowing what has happened.

The usage of time demonstrates this dramatically. A 33-year-old unemployed man writes:

6–6.30	I get up,
7–8	I wake up the boys, as they have to go to school,
8–9	when they have gone, I go to the shed to bring in wood and water,
9–10	when I come back in, my wife always asks what she should cook, to avoid answering this question, I go to the meadow.
10–11	then it is noon
11–12	(empty)
12–13	we eat at 1 o'clock as the children come home from school at that time,
13–14	after lunch look through the newspaper,
14–15	went downstairs,
15–16	went to Treer
16–17	watched tree-felling in the park, shame about the park.
17–18	I went back home
18–19	then we eat dinner, noodles fried in semolina
19–20	go to bed.

From our survey a hundred men spend their time primarily occupied with the following:

Main occupation	Morning	Afternoon
Doing nothing . . .	35	41
Occupied at home (during winter playing chess or cards, if the weather is nice, sitting out, chatting, etc.)	14	16
A little help in the house and doing nothing (fetching water, shopping, etc.)	31	21
A lot of help in the house (gathering and chopping wood, looking after the children, gardening, mending shoes)	12	15

Main occupation	Morning	Afternoon
Occupied with children	6	5
Small jobs (radio, arts and craft, etc.)	2	2
Total	**100**	**100**

All this however only applies to men, since women are only without pay, and not without work in the strictest sense of the word. She has the household to keep, which fills up her day. Her work is set in a solid context, with numerous fixed tasks, functions and regular duties.

That the day passes differently for women as for men is shown in the following survey of the main occupation of 100 women:

Main occupation	Morning	Afternoon
Housekeeping	74	42
Washing	10	8
Child care	6	12
Small housekeeping duties (sewing, children) and doing nothing	9	38
Total	**100**	**100**

The typical course of time usage of a woman looks as follows:

6–7	getting dressed, heating the house, preparing breakfast,
7–8	washing, haircombing, dressing the children and taking them to school,
8–9	washing dishes, and doing the shopping,
9–10	cleaning the room,
10–11	preparing the cooking,
11–12	finish cooking and eating,
12–13	cleaning dishes, clearing the kitchen,
13–14	helping the children at home,
14–17	darning and sewing,
17–18	picking up the children,
18–19	eating dinner,
19–20	undressing the children, washing and putting them to bed,
20–22	sewing,
22–23	going to bed.

Thus the woman's day is filled with work: She cooks and scrubs, she mends and looks after the children, she worries about the accounts and has only little spare time from domestic work, which in these times is twice as difficult with the limited means of subsistence. . . . The usage of time is so fundamentally different between men and women that the same categories could not even be applied. Sometimes small conflicts make this different meaning of time to the man and the woman with her household work more apparent.

A woman states:

> Despite me now having less to do than before, I am still occupied throughout the entire day and have no distraction. Clothes for children used to be bought, but now one has to spend the entire day mending and darning so that they will look decent. My husband always complains that I haven't finished; he says that other women are out on the street gossiping and I will not finish for the day. He just does not understand how it is to always make sure that the children do not need to be ashamed.

. . . however, the sheer physical effort was much greater before. This is also understood and commented on by the women; in almost all the women's biographies they state that they used to have chores into the night after having worked in the factory. Yet in almost all of the women's biographies the following sentence appears: 'If only we could return to work'; as a purely material wish this is not surprising, but the women always add: even if we disregard the money.

Mrs A. (29 years) says: 'If I could return to the factory, then it would be the best day in my life. It is not just because of the money, but staying here at home, so alone, this is no way to live.'

3.38 Unemployment assistance

Margaret Bondfield, Hansard, House of Commons Debate, 21 January 1924, 169, cc602–3.

The points on which I wish to address this House have very little to do with these intellectual scintillations, but they have a great deal to do with the suffering that is going on in this country at the present time amongst unemployed women. Unemployment amongst women, I recognise, is only a small part of a very large problem, but at the same time those of us who have to face these unemployed women day after day realise that for the unemployed women it is the most vital question before the country, and my criticism of the Government is, that in this small problem there was much that could have been done to mitigate the lot of the women, with very little expense, but with a certain amount of administrative common sense, and they have consistently refused to do that little. We have round about a quarter of a million women who have been unemployed during the last three years. The number has varied from time to time, but some of them have been almost continuously unemployed. There were things that could have been done, extensions of schemes that were already in operation, but what is the record of the Government?

Small grants were given conditional upon certain training schemes being confined entirely to the development and supply of domestic servants. I am not quarrelling with the necessity for securing domestic work training. . . . But the Central Committee could have enormously extended the classes for what we call the homemakers. We were not permitted to have any money at all for that category, which would have been so helpful . . . we have been able to help a certain number of women, but this had to be done entirely out of the funds raised voluntarily and controlled by the Central Committee on Women's Unemployment.

The War made an enormous difference to the position of women in this respect. I do not think hon. Members realise quite what it means to-day, for example, to be in the clothing trades, compared with what it was 15 years ago. In the clothing trades mass production has developed enormously, and the War accentuated that development. Power machines are the rule rather than the exception, and the specialisation of processes has gone on to such an extent that women who have devoted years to the clothing trade are now in the position of having an option of doing only a thirtieth or even an eightieth part of a garment, and they are kept at that task. Here is a great avenue for helpfulness. The unemployed women in the clothing trade could have been helped by the immediate development of technical classes under the education authorities, . . . That would strengthen the efficiency of the labour supply in the clothing trades and would be an enormous advantage not only to the individual but to the general efficiency of the clothing trade as a whole.

3.39 Unemployment insurance

Ellen Wilkinson, Hansard, House of Commons Debate, 4 April 1940, 359 cc373–74.

The married woman worker has always been very badly treated under the Unemployment Insurance scheme. I remember very well what may be called the stampede circumstances in which the anomalies regulations were tightened up in regard to married women. Tremendous pressure was put upon Miss Margaret Bondfield, who was then Minister of Labour, . . . In those days there was a pernicious doctrine that married women in work kept men with families out of work. I have never subscribed to that doctrine, for I do not believe that statistically it is the case; but at that time, there was a growing body of unemployment and a tremendous prejudice against the married woman worker. . . . Since that time, the situation has entirely altered. The married women are being called upon to come back into industry, instead of pressure being exerted to push them out of industry. That being the case, it may be said that there is no problem because all of them can get jobs; but there is the difficulty of women who get a job, then lose it, and are then subjected to the full rigour of the anomalies regulations. . . .

There has been an unfortunate tendency to assume that the mere fact of marriage would render it more improbable that a woman would again get work in her own job. There have been clerical workers, for example, who have been denied standard benefit because a number of employers in the area in question have ruled that they would not employ married women. . . . I want to suggest that this would be a very good time to put women in industry on the same basis as men, to say that the woman stands on her own feet, that she is a worker, that she pays into an insurance fund, and that she has a right to exactly the same privileges of insurance as a man. From that point of view, the fact of marriage is an irrelevant consideration. . . . it would use only a very small amount of the money, but it would do away with what is felt very widely to be a very considerable injustice.

9   The wider stage

Feminism

Throughout the twentieth century varieties of feminism coloured women's thought and lives. Juliet Mitchell's 1966 article in *New Left Review* is one of the seminal broadsides in the feminism of the 1960s and 1970s marking the rise of a radical feminist movement that changed the context for women's lives across Europe. Inge Dahlsgaard's assessment of the movement in Denmark is tangible evidence of the widespread character of action and 'consciousness raising', which figured throughout Europe. The scene in Western Europe was significantly different from Eastern Europe, as the impact of communism defused feminism. Thus the Lila manifesto of East German feminists marks the end of the so-called 'iron curtain' and challenges the form of 'socialist feminism' applied in the DDR.

3.40 Women: the longest revolution

Juliet Mitchell, *New Left Review*, 40 (December 1966), in *Women's Estate* (London: Penguin, 1971), 75–122.

Feminism unites women at the level of their total oppression – it is all-inclusive . . . Its politics match this: it is a total attack. . . .

For feminist revolution we shall need an analysis of the dynamics of sex war as comprehensive as the Marx–Engels analysis of class antagonism was for the economic revolution. More comprehensive. For we are dealing with a larger problem, with an oppression that goes back beyond recorded history to the animal kingdom itself. . . .

We have attempted to take the class analysis one step further to its roots in the biological division of the sexes. We have not thrown out the insights of the socialists; on the contrary, radical feminism enlarges their analysis, granting it an even deeper basis in objective conditions and thereby explaining many of its insolubles.

The material basis for sexual division being the reproductive system, the revolutionary means to its annihilation will be man's scientific ability to transcend it. Science conquers Nature. The ecological revolution will finally put an end to the biological base. Feminism and the new ecological technology arise together, both caused by the contradictions of the primitive and oppressed animal life that mankind lives, within the context of the possibility of vast technological improvement. Both have arisen to protest against man's refusal of what he could do to bring heaven closer to earth. Both, if they are frustrated, will only mean that mankind, in irretrievable conservatism, prefers hell: chronic over-population, famine, wretched hard work, pain, pregnancy, disease. . . . Embracing the feminist and ecological revolution would mean that cybernation and other technological advances would end all joyless labour: the labour of the factory and of the child-bed.

A feminist revolution could be the decisive factor in establishing a new ecological balance: attention drawn to the population explosion, a shifting of emphasis from reproduction to contraception and demands for the full development of artificial reproduction would provide an alternative to the oppressions of the biological family; cybernation, by changing man's relationship to work and wages, by transforming activity from 'work' to 'play' (activity done for its own sake), would allow for a total redefinition of the economy, including the family unit in its economic capacity. The double curse, that man should till the soil by the sweat of his brow, and that woman should bear in pain and travail, would be lifted through technology to make humane living, for the first time, a possibility. . . .

The theory is no more *historical* than it is dialectical. To say that sex dualism was the first oppression and that it underlies all oppression may be true, but it is a general, non-specific truth, it is simplistic materialism, no more. After all we can say there has always been a master class and a servant class, but it does matter *how* these function (whether they are feudal landlords and peasants, capitalists and the working class or so on); there have always been classes, as there have always been sexes, how do these operate within any given, specific society? Without such knowledge (historical materialism) we have not the means of overcoming them. Nothing but this knowledge, and revolutionary action based upon it, determines the fate of technology – towards freedom or towards 1984.

3.41 Commotion on the Left

Inga Dahlsgård, *Women in Denmark, Yesterday and Today* (Copenhagen: Det Danske Selskab, 1980), 271–3.

The new feminist movement first attracted the attention of the public in the spring of 1970 when a group of women, following American examples, publicly removed their brassieres and suspender-belts, discarded false eyelashes, wigs and so on and flung them all together into a large rubbish bag. Beauty contests and the commercial exploitation of women's efforts to live up to the currently-advertised female ideal were the first bastion against which the new assault was launched. Other actions, imaginative or more traditional, soon followed and made it clear that the Danish feminist movement had taken on a new aspect. The mass media were deeply interested and soon found easy victims.

In principle the *Rødstrømper* (Redstockings), as they call themselves in Denmark, are not essentially different from similar movements in other western countries . . . where the new feminist movement first manifested itself, the Dolle Mina movement in Holland or Women's Lib in Britain. They all have roots in the leftist movements that emerged in the late 1960s among the hippies, student rioters, anti-nuclear campaigners and the anti-Vietnam War movements. In all of them there were active girls who little by little began to rebel against merely being on hand to serve their male comrades, to hand out leaflets, duplicate documents, type out speeches for the men, but never themselves to mount the rostrum. These girls were not content simply to make tea and biscuits for the revolution.

The Redstocking movement soon spread all over Denmark and, as in Copenhagen, groups of five or ten were formed for mutual discussion of every kind of issue affecting women, including such highly personal matters as their sex lives. The first objective of the movement, . . . is to raise the consciousness of its supporters, and this is best done in small groups where the participants trust one another and no men are present. Very great importance is attached to these basic discussion-groups. Through them there is created a feminist comradeship or 'sisterly solidarity' to buttress the self-confidence of the individual and foster at the same time a sense of fellowship with other women. The relating of personal experiences in the groups reveals how women are oppressed both in private life and at work, and those present join together to devise means of standing firm against oppression and lend each other strength and courage to do it.

This is a movement in fact, not a society with chairmen, secretaries and treasurers. In the basic groups the various functions are shifted around, and no one is given the opportunity of sitting passively on the sidelines. Yet despite such anarchistic features, which are a source both of weakness and of strength, the groups have managed to work together and their cooperation has recently become more formalised. For example the Redstockings have united in disrupting beauty contests all over Denmark so that these are now rare sights; they have taken the initiative in establishing consumer protection groups, arranged women's camps, notably on the island of Femø where every year now women work, take holidays and hold discussions, with or without children, but always without men. They have inspired courses on feminist subjects in folk high schools, aided the establishment of a special women's folk high school, and one 'Mothers' Day' they built a ramp at an underground station to make it possible to go in and out with perambulators, and so on.

The outward-directed activities of the Redstockings were characterised by three issues in the early years: the equal pay agitation, the campaign against Denmark's affiliation to the EEC, and the fight for free abortion on demand.

The form of action for equal pay that attracted particular attention was occupying a bus and refusing to pay more than 80% of the ticket price – which corresponded more or less to the proportion of female wages to male. Twenty-nine Redstockings were ejected from the bus by the police, and as the mass media had been warned of what was afoot the word went all round Denmark at once.

3.42 'The Lila Manifesto'

Reprinted in *Feminist Studies*, 16/3 (Fall 1990), 627–34.

1 POINT OF DEPARTURE

During this period of radical social change, women are also and increasingly moving 'into action.' Women, as well as men, have been affected by the deforming effects of centralized, administrative socialism. Women, however, are united by the fact that they experience the crisis in a particularly threatening manner.

For in the GDR the formulated rights relating to the women's question could not be fulfilled. On the contrary, misguided policies on women, especially since the 1970s, have led to the reproduction and solidification of patriarchal structures and to retrogression in the emancipation process of women.

In the GDR the ideal of a socialist society of self-determining and self-creating women, men, and children was sacrificed to a social concept in which people were subordinated to economic premises, prescribed from the outside, and finally, made into objects of politics. Policies regarding women were no longer aimed at the goal of women's equality but became an instrument of administrative population and economic policies. With the aim of raising the birth rate, a state-decreed social policy unilaterally assigned the responsibility for family and housework to women. For the sake of a putatively more effective economy, women remained in underpaid, so-called typical women's occupations, and were rarely admitted to higher levels of management. This led to the solidification of a historically antiquated social division of labour on the basis of gender, with particularly weighty consequences:

- Women are expected to assume a double burden through the unilaterally prescribed 'reconcilability of occupation and motherhood' and are thereby enormously overstrained, psychologically and physically.
- Women's orientation to assume primary responsibility for house and family work necessarily relegates them to a secondary position in employment, politics, and social life. . . .
- The undervaluation and depreciation of female competence and capabilities has resulted in the reproduction and solidification of a patriarchal, discriminatory image of women.
- The representation of women's bodies as sexual objects, as well as an increase in violence against women, appears in all areas of social life and is

exaggerated through the media by means of beauty pageants, striptease, and pornography.

- The individuality of women and men is impoverished by an upbringing, which prescribes gender and sexual stereotypes from childhood on.
- As a result of discrimination, feelings of self-worth and the ability to articulate and realize one's own interests are less developed among women than they are among men.

The discrimination of women is characterized as sexism. Sexism is an expression of patriarchal relationships and indicates the oppression, degradation, and discrimination of individuals on the basis of sex.

We women of the 'Lila Offensive' believe that the women's question in the GDR has not been resolved. This means that the elimination of capitalist means of production is indeed a prerequisite, but no guarantee of the cessation of patriarchal repression. This type of repression possesses a general cultural dimension that transcends class and economic organization. Women must become conscious of this fact. The initiative to change this situation must therefore originate with them.

2 GOALS OF THE WOMEN'S INITIATIVE 'LILA OFFENSIVE'

The goal of 'Lila Offensive' is the equality of women and men, which will lead to a qualitatively new self-awareness between the sexes and therefore to a new kind of social relations. Sexual equality is, for us, one of the most basic values of a socialist society. The alternative social model we are striving for takes as its fundamental goal the right of all women, men, and children to a self-determined development of individual potential. . . .

We want to participate in the creation of a socialist society,

- which is ecologically minded, democratic, feminist, multicultural, non totalitarian, and socially just;
- which is not oriented to consumption and competition;
- which is free from social discrimination on the basis of sex, life-style, sexuality, age, skin color, language, and disabilities.

We declare ourselves in favor of an environmentally conscious alternative to the current patriarchal economy, which reduces nature to the object of a quantitatively oriented concept of progress. . . . We are in favor of a radical redefinition of the concept of achievement. Achievement must be based on the abilities and potentials of the individual and not unilaterally determined by considerations of economic efficiency and utility. That is, valuation must take into consideration the person's entire life circumstances.

We women of the 'Lila Offensive' especially want to identify and eliminate the mechanisms and structures that reproduce and dictate the social inequality of women and men:

- We want to contribute to, provoke, and problematize awareness regarding the position and situation of women, i.e., to reveal the details of their current experience.
- We want to demand changes in social conditions aimed at creating actual equality between women and men.
- We want to assist women in recognizing their abilities and (social) position, in articulating their needs and desires, and finally in realizing and decisively raising the resulting objectives and demands.

The elephant in the room

There have been few years during the twentieth century when Europeans were not involved in wars. During that period many more such wars were fought on European soil than was the case from the end of the Napoleonic Wars in 1815 to the outbreak of the Great War in 1914. At the same time there was a strong pacifist movement in which women played a significant and leading part, as Berthe von Suttner shows (3.1). In her trial for treason, Hélène Brion drew attention to the non-status of women as citizens and claims she was a pacifist because she is a feminist. In contrast to Brion, Dolores Ibárruri, 'La Passionaria', was a Basque communist and a leader of the anti-fascist forces in the Spanish Civil War. The speech here is a gentle but nonetheless persuasive positioning of women in the midst of the struggle. Similarly, the photographs of Taro echo this multi-layered approach to propaganda and women.

Women's experience of war shapes this section. Kathe Kollwitz, one of the foremost artists of the century, exposes her deep grief in losing one of her sons in the First World War, grief that resulted in commemorative sculptures. Line Haag's description of concentration camp life in the 1930s is an early account of the horrors that many experienced during the Second World War or in the Stalinist Soviet Union. Similarly, letters written by women in occupied France show the duality of attitudes – a firm hatred of the oppressor nation and stern resistance coupled with a desire and continued striving for normality. Finally, the youngest contribution comes from the diary of Zlata Filipović, a Bosnian girl in Sarajevo, written between 1991 and 1993 as the war began. It captures the attempts at normal living and the disbelief, anger and fear of war, whilst reminding us that not only 'world' wars have a devastating impact on people.

3.43 Cause célèbre

Hélène Brion, 'L'affaire Hélène Brion au 1e Conseil de Guerre', *Revue des Causes Célèbres*, no. 5 (2 May 1918), 152–4.

I appear before this court charged with a political crime; yet I am denied all political rights.

Because I am a woman, I am classified . . . far inferior to all the men of France and the colonies. In spite of the intelligence that has been officially recognised only recently, in spite of the certificates and diplomas that were granted me long ago, before the law I am not the equal of an illiterate black from Guadeloupe or the Ivory Coast. For *he* can participate, by means of the ballot, in directing the affairs of our common country, while *I* cannot. I am outside the law. . . .

I protest against the application of laws that I have neither wished for nor discussed.

This law that I challenge reproaches me for having held opinions of a nature to undermine popular morale. I protest even more strongly and I deny it! My discreet and nuanced propaganda has always been a constant appeal to reason, to the power of reflection, to the good sense that belongs to every human being, however small the portion. . . .

I am first and foremost a *feminist*. All those who know me can attest to it. And it is because of my feminism that I am an enemy of war.

The accusation suggests that under the pretext of feminism I preach pacifism. This accusation distorts my propaganda for its own benefit! I affirm that the contrary is true. . . . I affirm that I have been a militant feminist for many years, well before the war; that since the war began I have simply continued; and that I have never reflected on the horrors of the present without noting that things might have been different if women had had a say in matters concerning social issues. . . .

I am an enemy of war because I am a feminist. War is the triumph of brutal force; feminism can only triumph through moral force and intellectual worth. Between the two there is total contradiction. . . .

You want to offer freedom to enslaved people, you want – whether they like it or not – to call to freedom people who do not seem ready to understand it as you do, and you do not seem to notice that in this combat you carry on for liberty, all people lose more and more what little they possess, from the material freedom of eating what they please and travelling wherever they wish, to the intellectual liberties of writing, of meeting, even of thinking and especially the possibility of thinking straight – all that is disappearing bit by bit because it is incompatible with a state of war.

Take care! The world is descending a slope that will be difficult to remount. . . . if you do not call women to your rescue, you will not be able to ascend the slope, and the new world that you pretend to install will be as unjust and as chaotic as the one that existed before the war!

3.44 Women at the front

Dolores Ibárruri, 4 September 1936, *Speeches and Articles* (Éditions Sociales Internationales, 1938), 22–3.

She was a volunteer, a member of the civilian militia, wearing the blue blouse of a workman. She clasped her rifle with ardour, as though it were not a weapon of death but a much-desired plaything. Amidst the groups of merry

Figure 3.10
'Stop the War', poster from the
International Congress of Women

militiamen who were going smilingly to fight and perhaps to die, she marched in silence, serious and self-engrossed. A light burned in her eyes. They expressed hatred, inflexible determination and courage. I approached her and asked:

'Where are you from?'

'Toledo.'

'Why are you at the front?'

She was silent for a few moments, and then answered:

'To fight fascism, to crush the enemies of the working people and . . . to avenge the death of my brother.'

'Was he killed?'

'Yes, he was a soldier and a communist. When the rebellion broke out they wanted to make him, like many other soldiers, fight our brothers and go against the Republic. He refused and they shot him like a dog. I have come here to join the ranks, to take the place he would have occupied, and to avenge his death, to show the fascist scoundrels that when men die, women take their place. We are fighting with the same enthusiasm and courage as the men. We have learned from them how to die. It is better to die than to live in the fascist hell in which the workers of other countries are suffering, isn't that so, comrade?'. . .

A fighting woman!

She, like the other girls and women who are challenging death, and many of whom are meeting death, is reviving the tradition of the heroines who throughout our history have fought for independence and a constitution. . . . Women have always played a prominent part, supporting the men in the struggle for liberty and showing them by their example that it is better to die than to bow to the butchers and oppressors of the people. . . . They march to death merrily singing. They cheer those who have lost heart, infuse courage into them, and inspire them with the fighting spirit. . . .

Figure 3.11 Women training for a Republican militia outside Barcelona, August 1936, photograph by Gerda Taro

With them will be bound up the revolutionary traditions of our people, with them, the women who are fighting at the front, who are donating their blood to save the wounded, who, forgetting their own fatigue, watch at the bedside of wounded heroes, who died exclaiming: 'Long live liberty!'

We dip our colours in honour of you, dear women comrades, who march into battle together with the men.

All honour to you, women anti-fascists!

3.45 Loss of a child

The Diary and Letters of Käthe Kollwitz, Hans Kollwitz, ed., trans. Richard and Clara Winston (Evanston, IL: Northwestern University Press, 1988), 143, 145, 62–4, 71, 73, 87–88.

(November 1914)

Dear Frau Schroeder and dear Dora! Your pretty shawl will no longer be able to warm our boy. He lies dead under the earth. He fell at Dixmuiden, the first in his regiment. He did not suffer.

At dawn the regiment buried him: his friends laid him in the grave. Then they went on with their terrible tasks. We thank God that he was so gently taken away before the carnage.

Please do not come to see us yet. But we thank you for the sorrow we know, you feel.

Karl and Kaethe Kollwitz and Hans

Sunday, February 21, 1915 [to Hans]

. . . Why does work help me in these times? It is not enough to say that it relaxes me very much. It is simply that it is a task I may not shirk. As you, the children of my body, have been my tasks, so too are my other works. Perhaps that sounds as though I meant that I would be depriving humanity of something if I stopped working. In a certain sense – yes. Because this is my post and I may not leave it until I have made my talent bear interest. Everyone who is vouchsafed life has the obligation of carrying out to the last item the plan laid down in him. Then he may go. Probably that's the point at which most people die. Peter was 'seed for the planting which must not be ground'.

If it had been possible for Father or me to die for him so that he might live, oh how gladly we would have gone. For you as well as for him. But that was not to be.

I am not seed for the planting. I have only the task of nurturing the seed placed in me. And you, my Hans? May you have been born for life after all! You must have been, and you must believe in it.

Diary

August 27 1914

Where do all the women who have watched so carefully over the lives of their beloved ones get the heroism to send them to face the cannon? I am afraid that this soaring of the spirit will be followed by the blackest despair and dejection. The task is to bear it not only during these few weeks, but for a long time – in dreary November as well, and also when spring comes again, in March, the month of young men who wanted to live and are dead. That will be much harder. . . .

December 1, 1914

Conceived the plan for a memorial for Peter tonight, but abandoned it again because it seemed to me impossible of execution. In the morning I suddenly thought of having Reike ask the city to give me a place for the memorial. There would have to be a collection taken for it. It must stand on the heights of Schildhorn, looking out over the Havel. To be finished and dedicated on a glorious summer day. Schoolchildren of the community singing, 'On the way to pray'. The monument would have Peter's form, lying stretched out, the father at the head, the mother at the feet. It would be to commemorate the sacrifice of all the young volunteers.

It is a wonderful goal, and no one has more right than I to make this memorial.

April 27, 1915

I am working on the offering. I had to – it was an absolute compulsion – change everything. The figure bent under my hands of itself, as if obeying its own will – bent over forward. Now it is no longer the erect woman it had been. She bows far forward and holds out her child in deepest humility.

March 19,1918

. . . At the beginning it would have been wholly impossible for me to conceive of letting the boys go as parents *must* let their boys go now, without inwardly affirming it – letting them go simply to the slaughterhouse. That is what changes everything. The feeling that we were betrayed then, at the beginning. And perhaps Peter would still be living had it not been for this terrible betrayal. Peter and millions, many millions of other boys. All betrayed.

That is why I cannot be calm. Within me all is upheaval, turmoil.

Finally I ask myself: What has happened?

After the sacrifice of the boys themselves, and our own sacrifice – will not everything be the same?

All is turbulence.

Figure 3.12 Käthe Kollwitz, *The Parents*

3.46 Concentration camp, 1930s

Lina Haag, *A Handful of Dust*, in Stackelberg and Winkle, eds, *The Nazi Germany Sourcebook*, 146–9.

We are lined up in one of the courtyards. About thirty women: political prisoners, Jews, criminals, prostitutes, and Jehovah's Witnesses. Female guards from the SS circle us like gray wolves. I see this new ideal type of German woman for the first time. Some have blank faces and some have brutal looks, but they all have the same mean expression around their mouths. They pace back and forth with long strides and fluttering gray capes, their commanding voices ring shrilly across the court, and the large wolfhounds with them strain threateningly at their leashes. They are preposterous and terrifying, reminiscent of old sagas, merciless and probably even more dangerous than the brutal SS henchmen, because they are women. Are they women? I doubt it. They could only be unhuman creatures, creatures with gray dogs and with all the instincts, viciousness, and savagery of their dogs. Monsters. . . . The inspections are the worst, or rather the days preceding them. Washing, brushing, scrubbing goes on for hours. Punishment rains down at the slightest infraction. We are bellowed at if there is a wrinkle in the bed sheet, or if a tablespoon is not lying straight in the locker. It's always the same show, no matter who comes. The door is shoved open; we jump up from our seats; the visitor comes in and shouts a cheerful greeting; enthusiasm glows in the eyes of the female warders; the visitor looks benevolently over at us; then he turns to Commandant Kögel with a silly remark, such as 'A very nice room' or 'They seem to be in good health.' Of course Kögel happily agrees and repeatedly gives assurance that no one is subjected to hardships, which the visitor has never doubted. Then with an ebullient 'Heil Hitler' he turns to go. . . . Once even Himmler himself appears, in order to see his German re-education project. He looks insignificant; we had visualized this Satan personified differently, but he is in good spirits and friendly, he laughs a lot and grants several early releases. Acts of mercy by a despot in a good mood. . . . the truth is that we are beaten on the slightest pretext. For the beating we are tied naked to a wooden post, and Warder Mandel flogs us with a dog whip as long as she can keep it up. No one steps forward and says this. Because everyone wants to live. . . . Oh, dear husband, I always thought that after two years of solitary confinement nothing more in this world could frighten me, but I was wrong. I am terribly afraid of the beatings, of the dark cells in which women die so quickly, and of the dreaded chambers in which prisoners are interrogated by Gestapo officials. . . . Fear is torment enough; torment enough is the certainty that these things will happen to us one day. It is absolutely impossible to be here for years without disaster striking one day. It will come. One day it will come.

3.47 Letters from France

Eve Curie, Philippe Barrès, Raoul de Roussy de Sales, eds, *They Speak for a Nation*, trans. Drake and Denise Dekay (New York: Doubleday, Doran & Company, 1941), 7, 101–2.

Wife of a soldier in occupied France to the BBC, London, September 12, 1940.

I am a Frenchwoman in the occupied zone who has suffered terribly over the defection and crushing of her country. I live in a city where every night, powerless and furious, we witness the departure of Henkel IIIs heavy-laden with bombs. Our sole consolation consists in counting the planes and ascertaining with satisfaction that they are always less numerous on returning than when they start out . . . (We are especially happy when we have a visit from the R.A.F. aviators.) We preserve hope and confidence in our English friends. At this moment we share their misfortunes and admire their tenacity. Courage, friends! Hold out, we'll get them!

Even though egotism, prover of defeat, has not lost all its rights in France, many people have already recovered their grip and wish that the war would start again rather than see Germany and Italy plunder our colonies. We hope our government won't consent to further cowardice and will understand that certain French people would prefer to die rather than live permanently under the yoke. If there are those who passively accept the present state of things there are others who revolt at the idea of being bridled all their lives and working for the King of Prussia! Now is the time to recall that old proverb which hasn't lost its veracity!

I regret being unable to give you my address, for my son is young and my husband a soldier, but I would be happy to know if my letter actually reached you. So, if you will, a little signal at nine-thirty one of these evenings. My little one and I will be listening. I'd be very grateful to you. Tell us if sixteen-year-old French boys would be accepted in the R.A.F.?

THERESE

The wife of a Jewish artist, refugee in the Cevennes, to a friend in America. October 5th 1940.

We are getting settled for the winter as best we can. Already the sun shines from 10 A.M. to 3 P.M. It will be bitterly cold, but we hope to have enough wood to keep us reasonably warm. I am knitting heavy gloves and stockings and underwear with a coarse native yarn to keep us from freezing. As for food, I think we shall be able to get along. I have three hundred pounds of potatoes and onions stored in the garret. We have sown spinach on the terrace between the grapevines. With the grapes I have made approximately thirty pounds of grape jam. From the wild bees which have swarmed in one of our windows we got eight pounds of honey. I have bought a female rabbit, and I hope she will be sufficiently prolific so that we can eat a rabbit every ten days. I have no butter nor oil, but I manage with the mutton fat from the meat I get with our meat cards, and I have bought an option on half a pig which is going to be slaughtered in November. This, I suppose, will help us to tide over the winter.

Aside from that, if you can help our son to go to the United States, we ask nothing more. Life for us is finished.

3.48 A child's life in Sarajevo

Zlata Filipović, *Zlata's Diary*, trans. Christina Pribichevich-Zorić (New York: Penguin, 1995), 6–11, 26–35, 41–58, 65–6.

Friday, 11 October 1991
A hard but successful working day. Maths test – A, written test in language – A, biology oral – A. I'm tired, but happy.

Another weekend ahead of me. We're going to Crnotina (our place about fifteen kilometres away) – it has a big orchard with a house that's about 150 years old – a cultural monument under protection of the state. Mummy and Daddy restored it. Grandma and Grandad are still there. . . . I miss the clean air and beautiful countryside.

Saturday, 19 October 1991
Yesterday was a really awful day. . . . when I got home from school, I found my mother in tears and my father in uniform. I had a lump in my throat when Daddy said he had been called up by the police reserve. . . . Mummy and I

were left alone. Mummy cried and phoned friends and relatives. Everyone came immediately. . . . Daddy should be home the day after tomorrow. Thank God!

Tuesday, 22 October 1991

Everything really does seem to have turned out all right. Daddy got back yesterday, on his birthday. He's off again tomorrow, and then every two days. He'll be on duty for ten hours each time. We'll just have to get used to it. I suppose it won't last for long. . . .

Wednesday, 23 October 1991

There's a real war going on in Dubrovnik. It's being badly shelled. People are in shelters, they have no water, no electricity, the phones aren't working. We see horrible pictures on TV. Mummy and Daddy are worried. Is it possible that such a beautiful town is being destroyed? . . .

Wednesday, 30 October 1991

Good news from my piano teacher today. There's going to be a school recital and I'll be playing in it!!! I have to practise. . . . The days are shorter, it's colder, which means it'll snow soon – HOORAY! Jahorina, skiing, two-seaters, one-seaters, ski-lifts – I can hardly wait!!! . . . we've already bought ski tickets for the whole season.

Tuesday, 12 November 1991

The situation in Dubrovnik is getting worse and worse. . . . The pictures on TV are awful. People are starving. . . .

Thursday, 14 November 1991

Daddy isn't going to the reserves any more. Hooray!!! . . . Now we'll be able to go to Jahorina and Crnotina on weekends. But, petrol has been a problem lately. Daddy often spends hours waiting in the queue . . . and often comes home without getting the job done.

. . . Mummy and Daddy keep watching the news on TV. . . . They talk mostly politics with their friends. What is politics? I haven't got a clue. And I'm not really interested. I just finished watching *Midnight Caller* on TV.

Wednesday, 20 November 1991

I've just come home from music school. I had my school recital. I think I was good. . . . I'm tired because it was nerve-racking.

Tuesday, 24 March 1992

There's no more trouble in Sarajevo. But there is in other parts of B-H. . . . Terrible reports and pictures are coming in from all over. . . . The blue helmets (actually, they're blue berets) have arrived in Sarajevo. We're safer now. . . .

Monday, 30 March 1992

Hey, Diary! You know what I think? Since Anne Frank called her diary Kitty, maybe I could give you a name too. . . . I'm going to call you MIMMY . . .

Sunday, 5 April 1992

I'm trying to concentrate so I can do my homework, but I simply can't. Something is going on in town. You can hear gunfire from the hills. . . . You can simply feel that something is coming, something very bad. . . . The radio keeps playing the same song: 'Sarajevo, My Love'. That's all very nice, but my stomach is still in knots and I can't concentrate on my homework any more.

Mimmy, I'm afraid of WAR!!!

Monday, 6 April 1992

Yesterday the people in front of the parliament tried peacefully to cross the Vrbanja bridge. But they were shot at. Who? How? Why? A girl, a medical student from Dubrovnik, was KILLED. Her blood spilled onto the bridge. In her final moments all she said was: 'Is this Sarajevo?' HORRIBLE, HORRIBLE, HORRIBLE.

NO ONE AND NOTHING HERE IS NORMAL! . . .

Thursday, 9 April 1992

All the schools in Sarajevo are closed. There's danger hiding in these hills above Sarajevo. But I think things are slowly calming down. . . . Mummy and Daddy aren't going to work. They're buying food in huge quantities. Just in case, I guess. God forbid! . . .

Saturday, 2 May 1992

Today was truly, absolutely the worst day ever in Sarajevo. The shooting started around noon. . . .

We listened to the pounding shells, the shooting, the thundering noise overhead. We even heard planes. At one moment I realized that this awful cellar was the only place that could save our lives. Suddenly, it started to look almost warm and nice. . . . Almost every window in our street was broken. . . . A terrible day. This has been the worst, most awful day in my eleven-year-old life. I hope it will be the only one. . . .

Thursday, 7 May 1992

Today a shell fell on the park in front of my house, the park where I used to play with my girlfriends. . . . AND NINA IS DEAD. A piece of shrapnel lodged in her brain and she died. She was such a sweet, nice little girl. We . . . used to play together in the park. Is it possible I'll never see Nina again? . . . God, why is this happening?

I'M SO MAD I WANT TO SCREAM AND BREAK EVERYTHING!

Saturday, 23 May 1992

Almost all my friends have left. . . . The phones aren't working, we couldn't even talk to each other. . . . I now spend all my time with Bojana and Maja. . . . I'm lucky to have them, otherwise I'd be all alone among the grown-ups. . . .

Wednesday, 27 May 1992

SLAUGHTER! MASSACRE! HORROR! CRIME! BLOOD! SCREAMS! TEARS! DESPAIR!

. . . Two shells exploded in the street and one in the market. Mummy was nearby at the time. She ran to Grandma's and Grandad's. Daddy and I were beside ourselves because she hadn't come home. . . . HORRIBLE. . . . We didn't know what had happened to her. Was she alive? . . . I looked out the window one more time and . . . I SAW MUMMY RUNNING ACROSS THE BRIDGE. As she came into the house she started shaking and crying. Through her tears she told us how she had seen dismembered bodies. . . . Thank God, Mummy is with us. Thank God.

A HORRIBLE DAY. UNFORGETTABLE. HORRIBLE! HORRIBLE!

Friday, 5 June 1992

There's been no electricity for quite some time and we keep thinking about the food in the freezer. . . .

Daddy found an old wood-burning stove in the attic. . . . We cooked everything, and joining forces with the Bobars, enjoyed ourselves. . . . We even overate. WE HAD A MEAT STROKE. . . .

There's nothing to buy, and even cigarettes and coffee are becoming a problem for grownups. . . . God, are we going to go hungry to boot???

Tuesday, 16 June 1992

Our windows are broken. . . . Suddenly I heard a terrible bang and glass breaking. I was terrified and ran towards the hall. That same moment, Mummy and Daddy were at the door. Out of breath, worried, sweating and pale they hugged me and we ran to the cellar, because the shells usually come one after the other. When I realized what had happened, I started to cry and shake. Everybody tried to calm me down, but I was very upset. I barely managed to pull myself together.

. . . I could have been hit . . . HORRIBLE! I don't know how often I've written that word. HORRIBLE. We've had too much horror. The days here are full of horror. . . .

Wednesday, 24 June 1992

Mimmy, I've just realized that all my friends have left: . . . OHHHH! . . .

These are the books I've read so far: *Mummy, I Love You, . . . Eagles Fly Early*, and the next book I'm going to read is *Little Toto*.

Monday, 29 June 1992
BOREDOM!!! SHOOTING!!! SHELLING!!! PEOPLE BEING KILLED!!!
DESPAIR!!! HUNGER!!! MISERY!!! FEAR!!!

That's my life! The life of an innocent eleven-year-old schoolgirl!! A schoolgirl without a school, without the fun and excitement of school. A child without games, without friends, without the sun, without birds, without nature, without fruit, without chocolate or sweets, with just a little powdered milk. . . . God, will this ever stop, will I ever be a schoolgirl again, will I ever enjoy my childhood again?

Political activism

As women gained political rights and as feminism aided in the battle to gain access to seats of power, women moved from the informal political culture of previous centuries to holding and wielding power themselves. The next two sections demonstrate how women utilised the materials within their grasp. A case study of Irish women in the battle for independence shows the varied activities of women. Arguing the case for women's involvement is Constance Markievicz, first woman elected to the British Parliament, in 1918, though like the rest of Sinn Fein, she did not take her seat. Eily O'Hanrahan O'Reilly describes a moment in the uprising of 1916, at the Jacob's Biscuit Factory, site of the first women's strike in Ireland in 1910. Returning from a mission to Wexford, she reported to Thomas MacDonagh in command. John MacBride was second in command. Michaél, her brother, she only saw again the night before he was hanged, as were the other two. Kathleen O'Callaghan, Sinn Féin *Teachta Dála* [member of Parliament] in 1921, voted against the Anglo-Irish Treaty in accordance with her long-held belief in independence.

3.49 Irish feminism

Constance Markievicz, *Women, Ideals and the Nation*, lecture to the Students' National Literary Society (Dublin: Fergus O'Connor, 1909).

I am not going to discuss the subtle psychological question of why it was that so few women in Ireland have been prominent in the national struggle . . . true, several women have distinguished themselves on the battlefields of '98 and we have the women of the *Nation* newspaper, of the Ladies' Land league, also in our own day the few women who have worked their hardest in the Sinn Féin movement and in the Gaelic League. . . . But for the most part our women, though sincere, steadfast Nationalists at heart, have been content to remain quietly at home, and leave all the fighting and striving to the men.

Lately things seem to be changing. . . . a strong tide of liberty seems to be coming towards us, swelling and growing and carrying before it all the outposts that hold women enslaved and bearing them triumphantly into the life of the nations to which they belong. . . .

'A Free Ireland with No Sex Disabilities in her Constitution' should be the motto of all Nationalist women . . .

Ireland wants her girls to help her build up the national life. Their fresh, clean views of life, their young energies, have been long too hidden away and kept separate in their different homes. Bring them out and organise them, and lo! you will find a great new army ready to help the national cause. . . . No one can help you but yourselves alone; you must make the world look up to you as citizens first, as women after. For each one of you there is a niche waiting – your place in the nation. Try and find it. . . .

In every action we do in life, the idea behind it is the thing that counts – if you go deep enough, to the soul as it were. And so it is only by realising that unless the ideal, the spirit of self-sacrifice and love of country, is at the back of our work for commercial prosperity, sex emancipation, and other practical reforms, that we can hope to help our land. Every little act 'for Ireland's sake' will help to build up a great nation, noble and self-sacrificing, industrious and free . . .

Regard yourselves as Irish, believe in yourselves as Irish, as units of a nation distinct from England, your conqueror, and as determined to maintain your distinctiveness and gain your deliverance. Arm yourselves with weapons to fight your nation's cause. Arm your souls with noble and free ideas. Arm your minds with the histories and memories of your country and her martyrs, her language and a knowledge of her arts, and her industries. And if in your day the call should come for your body to arm, do not shrink from that either. May this aspiration towards life and freedom among the women of Ireland bring forth a Joan of Arc to free our nation!

3.50 The Easter uprising

Eily O'Hanrahan O'Reilly, 'Witness Statement', Bureau of Military History, Jacob's Factory, Irish National Archives, 7–8.

It must have been after 12 o'clock when I got to Dublin (Harcourt street station). A man stepped forward to me and asked me had I been away for the week-end. I said I had been in the country with some friends – I thought he was a detective. He whispered to me, 'It is all right Miss O'Hanrahan. My name is Williams.' . . . It was very late and I was glad when he offered to see me home. We came down by the College of Surgeons and saw the windows barricaded. We were walking over heaps of glass everywhere, especially in O'Connell street. . . .

The next day the two of us (my sister and myself) went to the GPO. We did not know how to contact people. . . . They told me to go to Jacobs. I did and saw some of the men I knew in the window. . . . I called up to them and said I wanted to see Tom MacDonagh. There was a mob outside and when they saw us talking to the Volunteers they called out all sorts insulting remarks to us. MacDonagh told some of the men to put out a ladder for me. I had to climb up. My sister, who stayed outside, was afraid she would be torn to pieces by the mob of women. When I got up to the window I saw the same group and John McBride. The latter did not know me and said he would not let me in but the men vouched that I was Mitchell's sister. I was getting very nervous as there was a lot of sniping outside. I jumped down inside off the window. I was angry with MacBride and told him that he behaved in an unmilitary manner, that he could have placed me under arrest if I was found doing wrong. I told him also that I had business with MacDonagh. I was brought to him to Headquarters, which was a table up a few steps. I told him what had happened in Enniscorthy. I told him, that Seamus Doyle had not been there. 'What did you do with it then?' 'I gave it to Seamus Rafter'. 'Excellent', said he and he took both my hands. . . . I asked him whether I should go back to Wexford. He said that was not necessary. He looked very placid. I said I would remain in Jacobs, but Micheál, who was present during the conversation, said he would prefer that I would go back and look after things in 67 Connaught street, as there were arms still there. Tom MacDonagh then told me to do that and give out any of the stuff that was asked for, and anyway to get rid of all the stuff as we might be raided.

They let me out a side street, and Tom MacDonagh asked me to go to the GPO and tell Pearse they wanted grenades and that he had commissioned McBride in Jacobs. . . . Micheál's eyes were filled with tears and so were mine. Tom MacDonagh said, 'Eily, you'll see Micheál again'. I did the night before his execution.

3.51 Debating the treaty

Kathleen O'Callaghan, Dáil Éireann, Volume 3, 20 December 1921, 59–60.

I rise to support the President's motion for the rejection of these Articles of Agreement, and, lest anybody should afterwards question my right to stand here and criticise and condemn this Treaty, I want it to be understood here and now that I have the clearest right in the world. I paid a big price for that Treaty and for my right to stand here. . . . Since I came up to Dublin for this Session I have been told, with a view to changing my vote, I suppose, that my husband was never a Republican. I challenge any Deputy in this Dáil to deny my husband's devotion to the Republic, a devotion he sealed with his blood. . . . I have been told, too, that I have a duty to my constituents. They, I am told, would vote for this Treaty, and I ought to consider their wishes. Well, my political views have always been known in Limerick, and the people of Limerick who elected me Deputy of this Dáil two months after my husband's murder, and because of that murder, know that I will stand by my convictions and by my oath to the Irish Republic. There is a third point I want to clear up. When it was found that the women Deputies of An Dáil were not open to canvass, the matter was dismissed with the remark: 'Oh, naturally, these women are very bitter'. Well, now, I protest against that. No woman in this Dáil is going to give her vote merely because she is warped by a deep personal loss. The women of Ireland so far have not appeared much on the political stage. That does not mean that they have no deep convictions about Ireland's status and freedom. . . . The women of An Dáil are women of character, and they will vote for principle, not for expediency. For myself, since girlhood I have been a Separatist. I wanted, and I want, an independent Ireland, an Ireland independent of the British Empire, . . . I would like to say here that it hurts me to have to vote against the Minister for Foreign Affairs. He was a friend of my husband. . . . I have the greatest admiration for him, but this is not a matter of devotion to a leader, or devotion to a party, it is a matter of principle, and you may sneer at principle, some of you. It is a matter of principle, a matter of conscience, a matter of right and wrong. . . . Now what have all these hundreds of years of struggle been for? What has it been about? What has been the agony and the sorrow for? Why was my husband murdered? Why am I a widow? Was it that I should come here and give my vote for a Treaty that puts Ireland within the British Empire? Was it that I should take an oath to be a faithful citizen of the British Empire?

Global politics

Women had long been active on the European stage, often proselytising particular causes, like suffrage, pacifism and medical inspection of prostitutes. What increasingly distinguished the twentieth century was women's engage-ment on the European and world stage as recognised political figures and experts. The first extract captures the way several women moved through European and world politics. Medical doctor Gro Harlem Brundtland became Prime Minister of Norway in February 1981, the second female European Prime Minister after Margaret Thatcher, and presided over a world-renowned cabinet with eight women among her eighteen ministers. Her politics always reflected her views on public health and sustainable development, so she moved with a sense of inevitability onto the world stage, invited to establish the World Commission on Environment and Development. These two strands of her career overlapped until she stepped down as Prime Minister in 1996, to become head of the World Health Organization. The second extract relates to women's political standing in Europe itself, and highlights the disquiet of many politically active European women at the persistence of a glass ceiling operating within the European Union.

3.52 Call to action

Gro Harlem Brundtland, Keynote Address, International Conference on Population and Development, Cairo, 5 September 1994.

This conference is really about the future of democracy, how we widen and deepen its forces and scope. Unless we empower our people, educate them, care for their health, allow them to enter economic life – on an equal basis and rich in opportunity, poverty will persist, ignorance will be pandemic and people's needs will suffocate under their numbers. The items and issues of this conference are therefore not merely items and issues, but building blocks in our global democracy. . . .

We make a pledge to change policies. When we adopt the Plan of Action, we sign a promise – a promise to allocate more resources next year than we did this year to health care systems, to education, family planning and the struggle against AIDS. We promise to make men and women equal before the law, but also to rectify disparities, and to promote women's needs more actively than men's until we can safely say that equality is reached. . . .

With 95 per cent of population increase taking place in developing countries the communities that bear the burden of increasing numbers are those least equipped to do so. They are the ecologically fragile areas where current numbers already reflect an appalling disequilibrium between people and earth. . . .

We must all be prepared to be held accountable. That is how democracy works.

It must promise access to education and basic reproductive health services, including family planning as a universal human right for all.

Women will not become more empowered merely because we want them to be, but through change of legislation, increased information and by redirecting resources. It would be fatal to overlook the urgency of this issue. . . . It cannot be repeated often enough that there are few investments that bring greater rewards than investment in women. But still they are being patronized, and discriminated against in terms of access to education, productive assets, credit, income and services, decision-making, working conditions and pay. For too many women in too many countries, real development has only been an illusion.

Women's education is the single most important path to higher productivity, lower infant mortality and lower fertility. . . . So let us pledge to watch over the numbers of school-enrolment for girls. Let us watch also the numbers of girls that complete their education and ask why the numbers differ, also because the girl who receives her diploma will have fewer babies than her sister who does not. . . .

None of us can disregard that abortions occur, and that where they are illegal or heavily restricted, the life and health of the woman is often at risk. Decriminalization of abortions should therefore be a minimal response to this reality, and a necessary means of protecting the life and health of women.

Traditional religious and cultural obstacles can be overcome by economic and social development, with the focus on the enhancement of human resources. For example, Buddhist Thailand, Moslem Indonesia and Catholic Italy demonstrate that relatively sharp reductions in fertility can be achieved in an amazingly short time. . . .

I am pleased to say that the total number of abortions in Norway stayed the same after abortion was legalized, while illegal abortions sank to zero. Our experience is similar to that of other countries, namely that the law has an impact on the decision making process and with the safety of abortion – but not on numbers. . . .

A conference of this status and importance should not accept attempts to distort facts or neglect the agony of millions of women who are risking their lives and health.

3.53 Challenging the male elite

Honor Mahony, 'EU's most powerful women take aim at male elite', EUobserver.com, 18 September 2009, http://euobserver.com/news/28679, accessed 13 February 2013.

BRUSSELS – Some of the most powerful women in the EU are discussing how to bring gender equality to European politics, an arena that continues to be overwhelmingly dominated by men. . . .

The 15-strong gathering, including four EU commissioners, Sweden's Europe minister and seven parliament committee heads, wants women to become better networkers and better at promoting one another in politics.

'There is still a glass ceiling to reach the very top of European politics. It is still very much an old boy's network and men are very good at praising each other and promoting each other,' Finnish Green MEP and head of the human-rights sub-committee, Haidi Hautala, told EUobserver.

'But as there are so few women, this does not really happen.'

Danuta Huebner, the head of the parliament's regional development committee and a former EU commissioner, also stressed the importance of women supporting one another.

'We should do more about networking – that's where we're extremely weak. If we start some networking of women in European institutions, this could have some impact. If you are alone, you just behave as those around you,' said the Polish politician. . . .

Diana Wallis, vice-president of the European Parliament, said the main point of Wednesday's meeting was to say:

'Here we are, a group of women all in fairly high posts in the European institutions, so what's all this chat about there not being women able to do any of the senior jobs either as commissioners, or any other posts that might come up under the treaty of Lisbon.'. . .

Although gender equality is enshrined in EU law, there is often little evidence of it at the top of European politics. The 'family portraits' of the regular gatherings of EU leaders are eloquent witnesses of this – amid a sea of men, German chancellor Angela Merkel is the only woman head of government.

'We talk about gender equality more and more and we have all those laws and everything that is needed to give everyone an equal chance in the political life [yet] when it comes to concrete cases, jobs for taking responsibility in Europe, somehow women disappear,' said Mrs Huebner.

To illustrate her point, she spoke about a 10-minute video to commemorate the 10th anniversary of European Monetary Union. 'There were no women in this, like women did not exist in the history of European integration.'. . .

At the moment, there are eight women commissioners in the 27-member college. Women represent 35 per cent of MEPs in the 736-member strong parliament, with Finland sending the highest proportion . . . (61%) and Malta, with no women for the second legislature running, the least. . . .

One of the main objectives is for the group to drop names of qualified politicians into the EU jobs discussion, with Mrs Hautala mentioning Finnish President Tarja Halonen, former UN human rights commissioner Mary Robinson and communications commissioner Margot Wallstrom for the EU foreign minister or president jobs. . . .

'There are so many good women candidates and we need to get them out there,' she told this website, offering to be a 'mentor' to others seeking EU jobs.

The women's proposals are set to meet resistance among national capitals – even in those countries considered to have a more progressive gender equality policy. Mrs Hautala said she discussed the idea of each government suggesting two candidates for a commission post with Finnish leader Matti Vanhanen.

'Even our prime minister is not convinced,' she said.

Legacies of empire

Gender issues and female sexuality are one of the enduring legacies of the years of colonial occupation and withdrawal. In the first extract, a British member of the Kenyan Legislative Council argues for legislation to protect white women from 'native men'. Katherine Stewart-Murray, Duchess of Atholl and Eleanor Rathbone raise issues dealing with the health and well-being of native women. Both began their political careers in local activism: Stewart-Murray was the first Scottish female Member of Parliament, nicknamed the 'Red Duchess' for her social views though elected as a Unionist, while Rathbone became an independent MP and is remembered as the pioneer of family allowances. Bringing imperial issues home is Myriam Benraad's article on why the burqa should be banned in France. This is paired with historian Joan Scott, who discusses the Europeanisation of immigrant cultures with particular reference to the French 'assimilationist' approach.

3.54 Gender and race

Colony and Protectorate of Kenya, Legislative Council Debates, 1 July 1926, vol. 1 (Nairobi: Government printer), 247–50.

Capt. the Hon. E. M. V. Kenealy: your Excellency, the legislation now before the House is entirely due to increasing assaults on white women by native men. . . .

Twelve or fifteen years ago the natives of Kenya Colony considered an European a half-God; he does not think so to-day. Why? . . . I think I am right in saying . . . the native has changed his view because the principles of intellectual, social and racial equality have been inculcated into him, to his disadvantage and to the disaster of the present relationship between European and Native. . . . Is the native mental attitude in regard to crimes of a sexual nature different to ours? I think it will be generally admitted that it is, and there is a reason for it. . . . In a native woman chastity is often considered unimportant. A European woman would rather lose her life than her chastity – it is the dominating factor in her life; . . . A thing I may state definitely is that a European man is prepared to sacrifice his life for the chastity of his womankind and if once we lose that ideal as a race we perish. I think it is philosophically correct to state that the degree of punishment for any offence lies in its reflex action in the eyes of the sufferer – not in the eyes of some academic person . . .

In this instance we are dealing with the white community. They are the sufferers and they are right in suggesting that their view of punishment is the correct one, and I am here to support that view.

Since nature has made such manifests [*sic*] differences between the races it is futile and hypocritical to ignore them. I maintain that there should be racial discrimination not only in this legislation but in most legislation. . . . It is a cowardly course to ignore the obvious racial differences and it is reasonable to recognize these differences in legislation. We want legislation to protect our womankind against the native; why obfuscate the issue by pretending that there are other factors. . . .

We have heard a great deal of native opinion in regard to these assaults, and yet . . . there has not been an appeal from the native for the death penalty; no such appeal has come from the native. We feel that the natives themselves should have asked for this penalty. The country is grievously disappointed. If these native chiefs cannot recognize the ethical aspect to the case let us instead instruct them by penal legislation that our womenkind must be inviolate. . . .

Let this Council admit, as the civilized world admits, that man's life is a lesser thing than woman's chastity and legislate accordingly.

3.55 Colonial policy in relation to coloured races

Great Britain, House of Commons Debates, 11 December 1929, 233, cc599–608.

Duchess of ATHOLL

I want to bring before the House some reasons why some Members of this House, who have been studying conditions amongst women and children in the Crown Colonies – women and girls particularly – feel that there is urgent need for more consideration to be given to the social well-being, health, and education of women and girls in some of our dependencies than sometimes seems to have been the case. . . .

Figure 3.13 Katherine Stewart-Murray, Duchess of Atholl

In particular, we have been terribly impressed by what we have learned . . ., namely, the existence of a pre-marriage rite among young girls, among many African tribes, a rite which is frequently referred to as the circumcision of girls. We have heard that this obtains in Southern Nigeria and among one tribe in Uganda, but we understand that it exists in its worst form among the Kikuyu tribe in Kenya. I am sure it will be realised that this is not an easy subject to deal with publicly. I venture to bring it before the House, because none of us can afford to forget the responsibility that has been impressed upon us from the benches opposite – the responsibility for that Colonial Empire – which is directly governed from this House . . . particularly when we remember how little native races may be able to express themselves, and how backward they may be in respect of many of their customs.

. . . I doubt very much if, even apart from missionaries and doctors, and perhaps Government officials, there are many white people who realise what this rite is, and what it means to the health and well-being of the girls and women. . . . Our Committee has been assured by medical men, and by missionaries who have attended these women in hospital and in their homes, that the rite is nothing short of mutilation. It consists of the actual wholesale removal of parts connected with the organs of reproduction. The operation is performed publicly before one or two thousand people by an old woman of the tribe armed with an iron knife. No anaesthetic is given, and no antiseptics are used. The old woman goes with her knife from one girl to another, performing the 'operation', returning it may be once or twice to each victim. A lady missionary steeled herself to see this operation not long ago, and has given a description of it verified by photographs which she took. She told us that the girl has a whistle put into her mouth so that her screams will not be heard. A medical man told us that the operation leaves great scarring, contraction, and obstruction; natural eliminating processes are gravely interfered with, and there is reason to believe that much blood poisoning results. The obstruction causes terrible suffering at childbirth, and the first child is rarely born alive. . . . one missionary who has attended many of these young women in hospital in their confinement told me recently that out of 10 cases, affecting 20 lives, only six lives survived. . . .

I ask the House what could be more inhuman than the practice which I have described, and what could be more contrary to what we understand as British justice than that a girl endeavouring to escape from this terrible custom should not have the protection of a British Court.

Miss RATHBONE. . .

The Noble Lady the Member for Kinross has communicated to the House some of the results of the consultations that we have been holding . . . I want very shortly to allude to another aspect of the question. We have had evidence from witnesses which has revealed to us that the position of the native women in many of these tribes – I do not say all – is one of sheer slavery, . . . without let or hindrance from the British authorities – slavery, not to Europeans, but to men of their own race. . . . A girl is sold by her father, often in early infancy, without choice, to the man who is destined to be her husband. Before marriage she undergoes, again without choice, at the age of 10 or 11, the cruel custom that has been described. . . . After marriage she becomes the property of her husband, to be used by him and treated by him as he desires. If he dies, she becomes the absolute property of his next male kin, it may be his brother, his cousin, or even a little boy of her own. She may be sold by her new owner in one direction, her daughter may be sold in another direction; the sons are usually retained as the representatives of the tribe. . . . are those things less hurtful and humiliating and degrading to humanity because the persons who perpetuate them are the blood relations of the women who endure them?

3.56 Burqas and Frenchness

Myriam Benraad, 'Why the burqa should be banned', *The French Paper*, August 2009, 10.

There is something undeniably strange about seeing a woman walk down a street in France covered from head to toe in a burqa. For women of my generation, who was raised in a French environment and educated in a French school, it is unnerving. Our republican model, which depends so much on what we call *laïcité*, or secularism, has tended to erase most cultural and religious differences in the public sphere. When we were at school, for example, we didn't know who was who: Catholic, Muslim or Jew. We weren't used to expressing those differences. To speak in simple terms, it was – and is – very unFrench.

It is because of this – and not because I feel the burqa is necessarily an affront to women's rights – that on a personal level I am disturbed when I see a woman in France in the full veil.

My father is a Muslim, albeit an atheist one, and I have travelled extensively around the Islamic world. If you go to a hairdressers [*sic*] in one of the Gulf countries you'll see women remove their burqas to reveal themselves as the sexy, thoroughly modern women they are underneath. If a woman chooses to wear it, let her wear it. The argument that it is always imposed on them does not wash with me.

However, in the interests of social and political peace, I am in favour of a ban on the burqa in France. Some Muslim leaders are arguing that forbidding women from wearing their garment of choice would lead to more friction between communities and make this six million-strong population feel even more stigmatised than it already does. In fact, putting a ban in place now would avoid huge social problems in the future.

Things are changing in France. Islam is now the second largest religion and our country has become a melting pot of different ethnicities and cultural identities. But tensions between the communities are growing. There is a real malaise, which manifests itself in racism behind closed doors, and discrimination in the workplace.

Of course, most people won't admit to harbouring racist prejudices, but that doesn't mean those prejudices don't exist. The truth is there is a real fear in certain segments of society about what France is becoming.

There is still a strong nationalist sentiment that is rooted in a certain form of self-identity. The vast majority of French people do not identify themselves through women in burqas: It's as simple as that. . . .

So, what can be done to keep the peace? Well, first of all, it is clear that our long-cherished Republican model of citizenship, which emphasises French nationality over any other ethnic or religious ties, needs to be reformed. As France evolves, it is failing to keep pace. . . .

But, despite its failings, the fact is that very few people acknowledge that things need to change. If they admitted it was no longer working, it would imply a need to reform the whole system and that would be political dynamite. It is perhaps hard for those from an Anglo-Saxon background to understand, but *laïcité*, for us, runs straight to the heart of what it means to be French.

3.57 The politics of the veil

Joan Wallach Scott, *The Politics of the Veil* (Princeton: Princeton University Press, 2007), 11–12, 14–16, 18.

I argue that the representation of Muslim sexuality as unnatural and oppressive when compared to an imagined French way of doing sex intensified objections to the veil, grounding these in indisputable moral and psychological conviction.

In France many of those who supported a ban on headscarves insisted they were protecting a nation conceived to be one and indivisible from the corrosive effects of *communautarisme* (which I have translated as 'communalism'). . . . In France *communautarisme* refers to the priority of group over national identity in the lives of individuals; in theory there is no possibility of a hyphenated ethnic/national identity – one belongs either to a group or to the nation. . . . equality is achieved, in French political theory, by making one's social, religious, ethnic, and other origins irrelevant in the public sphere; it is as an abstract individual that one becomes a French citizen. . . .

France insists on assimilation to a singular culture, the embrace of a shared language, history, and political ideology. The ideology is French republicanism. Its hallmarks are secularism and individualism, the linked concepts that guarantee all individuals equal protection by the state against the claims of religion and any other group demands.

French universalism insists that sameness is the basis for equality. To be sure, sameness is an abstraction, a philosophical notion meant to achieve the formal equality of individuals before the law. But historically it has been applied literally: assimilation means the eradication of difference. . . .

North Africans, many of whom are Muslims, claimed that the only way to reverse discrimination against them was to consider their religion on a par with that of Christians and Jews. If individuals with those commitments could be considered fully French, so could Muslims, even if the requirements of their religious beliefs led them to pray and dress differently – women wearing hijabs, for example. . . . But whatever the controversies were among Muslims, what united them as a group was the desire to be considered 'fully French' without having to give up on the religious beliefs, communal ties, or other forms of behavior by which they variously identified themselves.

The reaction of politicians and republican ideologists to these demands for the recognition of difference was swift and uncompromising. They insisted that the way things had always been done was the right way and that the challenges from groups such as women, homosexuals, and immigrants would undermine the coherence and unity of the nation, betraying its revolutionary heritage. Even as they granted that discrimination might exist and allowed some measures to correct it, they did so in ways that would not endanger the bottom line: the need to maintain the unity of the nation by refusing to recognize difference. . . .

As for Muslims, their claims were rebuffed on the ground that satisfying them would undermine *laïcité*, the French version of secularism, which its apologists offer as so uniquely French as to be untranslatable. . . . Muslim headscarves were taken to be a violation of French secularism and, by implication, a sign of the inherent non-Frenchness of anyone who practiced Islam, in whatever form. To be acceptable, religion must be a private matter; it must not be displayed 'conspicuously' in public places, especially in schools, the place where the inculcation of republican ideals began. The ban on headscarves established the intention of legislators to keep France a unified nation: secular, individualist, and culturally homogeneous. They vehemently denied the objection that cultural homogeneity might also be racist. . . .

Worlds of creativity

Women increasingly participated in and reached into more genres as expressive media expanded. The first woman to receive the Nobel Prize for Literature was Swede Selma Lagerlöf, in 1909. Here she describes, in third-person narrative, her first success with what became her most popular work, *Gösta Berlings Saga*. The image of Swede Elin Wägner and friends reading newspapers captures the freedom but also the overlap between politics, pacifism, environmentalism and literature. Alongside Fredrika Bremer, she is seen as one of the foremost influential feminist pioneers in Sweden. The newer worlds of culture and expression, such as journalism, cinema and photography drew women as they did men. Line Morgenstein's late nineteenth-century description of women in German journalism is included, to highlight the early popularity of journalism. It also provides an entrée to the importance of journalism in the twentieth century as women pushed into mainstream media and found intellectual, cultural and occupational outlets through the various media. Ève Curie, younger daughter of physicist Marie Skłodowska-Curie, had a diverse career as a respected musician and pianist, working for the Free French and ultimately in journalism. The extract from *Journey Among Warriors* describes setting off on her mission to study the Second World War, and invites comparison with Kate Adie, who describes her perception of her role as a journalist (see also 3.35). Germaine Dulac began as a socialist feminist journalist but became interested in film, and owned and ran her own film company, initially making commercial films, but moving into impressionist and surreal filmmaking.

Visual media were key to twentieth-century culture and in addition to cinema, television and print media, photography and photojournalism were important fields where women developed their talents. Thus the image of Spanish women training for the Republican militia in 1936, by Gerda Taro, who died while photographing the Spanish Civil War, epitomises the use of photography as art as well as highlighting the potential of photography as news and as propaganda (3.11). Helene Schjerfbeck created a series of some 40 self-portraits between 1878 and 1945 which project an intense range of expression, focusing on the mind, and which capture the viewer in their challenging gaze as she explored her identity and craft. Käthe Kollwitz describes her art above (3.12). Fashion became much more prominent during the century, with haute couture and informality jostling for space, with Coco Chanel in the vanguard. Fashion and freedom combined to inform the clothing of women golfers long before trousers or shorts were permitted. In the final extract Dorothy Campbell Hurd, the first internationally famous woman golfer, describes the shock of women playing on her local golf links.

3.58 'Story of a story'

Harry E. Maule, *Selma Lagerlöf, The Woman, Her Work, Her Message* (New York: Doubleday, Page and Company, 1917), 12–25.

Once there was a story that wanted to be told and sent out in the world. This was very natural, inasmuch as it knew that it was already as good as finished. Many, through remarkable deeds and strange events, had helped create it; others, had added their straws to it by again and again relating these things. What it lacked was merely a matter of being joined together, so that it could travel comfortably through the country. As yet it was only a confused jumble of stories – a big, formless cloud of adventures rushing hither and thither like a swarm of stray bees on a summer's day, not knowing where they will find some one who can gather them into a hive. . . .

It must have been because so many legends and traditions hovered about the farm that one of the children growing up there longed to become a narrator . . . one of the girls – one who was delicate and could not romp and play like other children, and who found her keenest enjoyment in reading and hearing stories about all the great and wonderful things which had happened in the world.

However, at the start it was not the girl's intention to write about the stories and legends surrounding her. She had not the remotest idea that a book could be made of these adventures, which she had so often heard related that to her they seemed the most commonplace things in the world. When she tried to write, she chose material from her books, stringing together stories of the Sultans in 'Thousand and One Nights', Walter Scott's heroes, and Snorre Sturleson's 'Kings of Romance'.

It need hardly be said that what she wrote was the least original and the crudest that has ever been put upon paper. . . . one autumn, when she was two-and-twenty, she went to Stockholm to prepare herself for the vocation of teacher.

The girl soon became absorbed in her work. She wrote no more, but went in for studies and lectures. It actually looked as though the story would lose her altogether.

Then something extraordinary happened. . . . she was walking one day up Malmskillnad Street with a bundle of books under her arm. She had just come from a lecture on the history of literature. . . . She said to herself that Runeberg's jolly warriors and Bellman's happy-go-lucky roisterers were the very best material a writer could have to work with. And suddenly this thought flashed upon her: Värmland, the world in which you have been living, is not less remarkable . . . If you can only learn how to handle it, you will find that your material is quite as good as theirs.

Thus she caught her first glimpse of the story. And the instant she saw it, the ground under her seemed to rock. . . .

Then and there the girl determined that she would write the story of Värmland's Cavaliers, and never for an instant did she relinquish the thought of it; but many long years elapsed before the determination was carried out. . . . During these years things were constantly happening which helped mould it. . . .

The homestead where she had grown up was sold. She journeyed to the home of her childhood to see it once again before strangers should occupy it. As she was leaving, perhaps never more to see the dear old place, she decided in all meekness and humility to write the book in her own way and according to her own poor abilities. . . . It might be a book at which people would laugh, but anyway she would write it – write it for herself, to save for herself what she could still save of the home – the dear old stories, the sweet peace of the care-free days, and the beautiful landscape with the long lakes and the many-hued blue hills.

But for her, who had hoped that she might yet learn to write a book people would care to read, it seemed as if she had relinquished the very thing in life she had been most eager to win. It was the hardest sacrifice she had ever made.

A few weeks later, she was again at her home in Landskrona seated at her desk. She began writing – she did not exactly know what this was to be – but she was not going to be afraid of strong words, of exclamations, of inter-rogations, nor would she be afraid to give herself with all her childishness and

Figure 3.14 Elin Wägner (centre) and friends reading newspapers

all her dreams! After she had come to this decision, the pen began to move almost of itself. This made her quite delirious. She was carried away with enthusiasm. Ah, this was writing!

3.59 Journalism, 1900

Lina Morgenstein, 'German Women in Journalism', in Ishbel Gordon, ed., *Women in Professions* (London: International Council of Women, 1899), 47–51.

A pleasing feature of modern journalism in Germany is the growing respect and kindly attitude towards the woman movement, and the rapid dying out of the cheap jests and gibes of thirty years ago. We owe this to the indefatigable efforts, to the strength and courage displayed by the women who did the pioneer work in the elevation of our sex, and who by their literary productions compelled general and respectful recognition from the press. There is now scarcely one political or general newspaper in Germany without its women contributors.

The advent of the woman journalist dates from the middle of the last century, when Gottsched first issued the magazine *Die philosophischen Tadlerinnen* ('The Philosophical Lady Critics'); this periodical had several eminent women contributors; they belonged to a group of remarkable and intellectual women, on whom several literary and university societies have lavished distinction. . . . The first woman's paper edited by a woman appeared in 1848, when the censorship of the press had been abolished. Frau Louise Otto Peters had the courage to publish it with this motto: 'As citizens in Freedom's Realm I would enrol ye' (Women). . . .

In 1873 I founded the Hausfrauen Verein, and shortly afterwards began to publish the *Deutsche Hausfrauen-Zeitung* ('Married Women's Paper') as its organ. . . . Our object was to prove how great could be the power of womanhood when it was united and concentrated on the solution of such problems as the servants' question, the education of boys and girls at home and at school, domestic hygiene, the regulation of market prices of food stuffs, and kindred subjects. . . .

In 1895 the society Frauenwohl ('Woman's Welfare') added to our list another bi-monthly, *Die Frauen-bewegung* ('The Woman Movement'). Its original editors were Frau Minna Cauer and Frau Lily von Gizycki [Lily Braun]; but the last-named lady resigned shortly afterwards, [a supplement contains] parliamentary news that is of special interest to women, . . .

German women, however, write for many other publications besides those specially intended for their own sex, for they have long ago earned honourable recognition for themselves in every branch of literature and journalism. Step by step, sometimes under masculine pseudonyms, they have entered every department of the press. Everywhere they have found fruitful ground, on which they have laboured diligently and successfully. To the political press they have become welcome contributors, while among the critics of the drama, of art and of literature, we have [several] well-known women . . . Besides being contributors of fiction, poetry, and philosophy, women hold appointments as press representatives and reporters, as proof-readers and compositors, as practical printers, and in other technical capacities. . . .

In conclusion, I am happy to be able to tell you that German women authors and journalists are admitted as members of equal standing to all the literary clubs and associations founded by men; and at their meetings and social gatherings the lady members are freely welcomed, and their stimulating influence is frankly recognised by their male colleagues.

3.60 Foreign correspondent, 1941

Ève Curie, *Journey Among Warriors* (London: Heinemann, 1943), 1–3, 32–5, 494–7.

At five-thirty in the morning, on Monday, November 10, 1941, I was at the Pan-American Airways base at La Guardia Field, New York, inside a trans-atlantic Clipper. There were no lights in the huge seaplane that floated on the calm water, like an anchored ship. I was alone, curled up in one of the seats, with a fur-lined coat on my knees. I was waiting, in the dark, for the departure of the aircraft at sunrise.

For a long time I had been trying to go on this trip – and now I was going. . . . From that Monday morning on, I would move, as fast as planes, ships, cars, and trains could carry me, toward the world's battlefields, toward the countries which were struggling against the Axis, in every continent. I did not know how far I should manage to get, and I was aware that a lone traveller could only catch a glimpse of the general picture of the conflict. Yet I well knew why I was going. . . . I wanted to watch the team of anti-Axis nations gradually tightening the grasp that would, one day, stifle the enemy. What were the real bonds, the ties of solidarity between these Allied warring peoples? . . . What did the great camp of Liberty look like, extending as it did from the African tropics to Russia and the Far East, through heat and frost, through snow and sand? That was what I would try to learn. . . .

I had not gone to bed, that night, and had spent my time kneeling on the floor of my Manhattan hotel room, between a scale, meant to weigh my luggage, and my two travelling bags, made of soft canvas, from which I eliminated one by one the heaviest items. The forty-four pounds allowed by Pan-American Airways were only thirty-five pounds once my typewriter was deducted. The thirty-five pounds became twenty-nine pounds after I had taken into account my papers, stationery, and the thick Anglo-French dictionary with which I could not part: for the first time in my life, I was to write dispatches directly in English, to act as a 'special war correspondent' for the Herald Tribune Syndicate, New York, and for Allied Newspapers, Ltd., London. This intrusion of mine in the Anglo-Saxon press, the best in the world, impressed me frightfully. . . .

I had packed the woollen stockings, the sweaters, the gloves, the woollen underwear meant for Russia – then the three washable dresses, and the lighter shoes that I should wear in the tropics. I had added one brown silk dress, one woollen suit, woollen slacks. No hat, of course: I should wear a snood, or a scarf tied as a turban. The minute make-up case was the smallest I had ever had, . . .

After many hesitations I had taken an evening dress with me – but at the last moment I had left behind the evening shoes and evening bag: they were too heavy. Why an evening dress anyway? The only important things – so I thought at the time – were the strong, low-heeled walking shoes, the whipcord suit, and the typewriter. Only later on was I to discover that, when making a trip to the world's battlefields, one must have evening clothes and visiting cards. . . .

On Friday, November 21st, the Sunderland B.O.A.C. flying boat took off at dawn, while the sun was still red. My Arab porter stopped bothering about my bags and squatted on the mauve-tinted sand for his morning prayers. We soon left the Nile and flew for hours over desert. Coming back to the river again, we landed on its waters in Wadi Halfa. While we had breakfast at the hotel, we listened to the radio: the advancing British troops were ten miles from Tobruk. All morning we raced over pale sand, entirely monotonous except for small dunes, rocks, or clefts. Suddenly we reached the lower valley of the Nile. Looking at it from the sky, I could understand in an instant everything that had been written and said about it in thousands of years. It was miraculous fertility versus dry desert – it was life versus death. . . .

[On her return home] What I had seen was an association of very different peoples – different in race, colour, religion, political regime, standard of living, wealth, and form of civilization – which fought side by side, but not 'together,' the same global war against the same enemies. . . .

We all wanted to win – but we did not yet rub shoulders as friends, as war comrades. We had not really sworn to be faithful to each other in victory or in defeat, in peace as in war. We all went the same way – but each at our own step, each singing a different tune.

3.61 Foreign correspondent, 1990s

Kate Adie, *The Kindness of Strangers*, 419–20, 425.

Unless you focus all your wits on the unexpected and complex and baffling and frightening events which happen daily, the audience is not well served. . . .

I've wondered if reporting is like putting together one of those irritating jigsaw puzzles which builds a scene out of a thousand tiny scenes . . . And all the time, you must not let one of those tiny images knock the bigger picture out of focus. If you're injured or intimidated in a nasty and jarring moment, you have to stop it from informing your entire view. . . .

I never expected to be a reporter, nor, when I found myself embroiled in journalism, did I see it as a crusade. It's an honourable trade, whose practitioners exchange a privileged position at significant events for the obligation of telling others exactly what happens. How we see our world and tell others about it will always be changing. Fashion and commerce modify the menu and the style, and technology galvanises the speed of delivery and the spread of information. The printing press and the satellite alter the means; education regulates the understanding. Interest in the further corners of the earth ebbs and flows, while the sound of conflict resonates continually. . . .

You witness other people's grief and anger and excitement and joy, and you also feel it; however, rather than becoming part of the scene, you take away with you a sense of wonder that survival and humanity are stronger than violence and suffering. You're a bystander, a witness, and although you alight very briefly on other people's lives, there is fascination and delight to be found.

Occasionally you get a little too close to stories and your fellow man tries to swat you out of existence. I've been very lucky – three bullets doing little damage and a fourth fired by a Libyan army commander who was in two minds (both of them drunk). . . . Eventually he shot at me from point-blank range, nicked my collar bone and demolished a sizeable slab of his drawing-room wall. I stalked off as best I could and – sounding like a British nanny delivering a ticking-off – announced: 'We don't behave like that in my country – and anyway, I'm only a reporter.'

I just stick to the facts.

3.62 Cinema as movement

Germaine Dulac, 'Les Esthetique, les entraves, la cinegraphie integrale,' *L'Art cinematographique*, vol. 2 (1927), in *Framework* 19, trans. Stuart Liebman (1982), 6–8.

When it appeared, the cinema, a mechanical invention created to capture life's true continuous movement, and also the creator of synthetic movements, surprised the intellects, the imaginations, and the sensibilities of artists whom no course prepared for this new form of expression, and who believed that literature, the art of written thoughts and feelings, that sculpture, the art of plastic expression, that painting, the art of color, that music, the art of sound, that dance, the art of gestural harmonies, and that architecture, the art of proportion, were adequate forms with which to create and to unbosom themselves. If many minds appreciated the singular significance of the cinematograph, very few grasped its aesthetic truth. . . . This required a new sense, parallel to the literary, musical, sculptural, or pictorial senses in order to be understood. . . .

It is rather disturbing to recount the simplistic way in which we greeted its manifestations. At first, the cinema was for us nothing but a photographic means to reproduce the mechanical movement of life; the word 'movement' evoked in our minds only the banal vision of animated people and things, going, coming, or shaking with no other concern than to let them develop within the borders of the screen, when it was instead necessary to consider movement in its mathematical and philosophical essence. . . .

Human existence is movement because it changes position, lives, acts, and reflects successive impressions. Rather than studying the concept of movement in its plain and mechanical visual continuity as an end in itself, unaware that the truth might lay therein, we moved from deduction to deduction, from confusion to confusion to assimilate the cinema with the theater. . . .

Figure 3.15 Helen Schjerfbeck, *Self-portrait with pink spot*, 1944

The meaning of the word 'movement' was entirely lost sight of, and in the cinema it (movement) was made subservient to succinctly recollected stories whose series of images, too obviously animated, were used to illustrate the subject. . . .

Cinegraphic movement, in which visual rhythms corresponding to musical rhythms give the overall movement its meaning and power, and which is composed of values analogous to note values, had to be completed, if I may put it thus, by the sonorities constituted by the feeling contained in the image itself. Here the architectural proportions of the set, the flickering of artificial light, the density of shadows, the balance or imbalance of lines, and the resources of perspective could play a role. . . . A responsive chord, a baroque chord, a dissonant chord within the larger movement of the succession of images.

In this way, despite our ignorance, the cinema, by freeing itself from its initial mistakes and transforming its aesthetics, drew nearer in technique to music, leading to the claim that a rhythmic visual movement could provoke a feeling analogous to that aroused by sounds.

By slow degrees, narrative structure and the actor's performance assumed less importance than the study of the images and of their juxtaposition. Just as a musician works on the rhythm and the sonorities of a musical phrase, the filmmaker sets himself to work on the rhythm and the sonorities of images. Their emotional effect became so great and their interrelationships so logical that their expressiveness could be appreciated in its own right without the assistance of a text.

This was the ideal that guided me recently when composing *La Folie des vaillants* (1925). I avoided acted scenes in order to stick to the song of the images alone, exclusively to the song of emotions within a diminished, almost nonexistent, but always dynamic action.

3.63 Fashion icon

Micheline Sandrel, *Interview with Coco Chanel*, c. 20 July 1969, http://fashion abecedaire.tumblr.com/post/16695026717/interview-translation-coco-chanel-on-fame-trousers (accessed 1 May 2013).

These girls, you dress them in trousers, they become vulgar, I don't know why. Maybe because they feel they need to waddle. I stop her, tell her not to walk like that, take the trousers off her, put them on another girl, exactly the same result.

In the countryside you wear trousers, it's the most useful thing, you don't get cold, you can get a bit wet it doesn't matter. I came up with them nearly 20 years ago. I came up with them by modesty, because I find wearing a swimsuit on the beach similar to walking around naked. Once you've bathed, even if you want to stay on the beach, putting on trousers isn't that difficult. A skirt isn't pretty, a robe is awful, trousers are the best option. You can roll around in the sand all day long. But from this usage to it becoming a fashion, having 70% of women wearing trousers at evening dinner is quite sad. . . .

It suits very young people. After a certain age, it looks like you put them on to look younger. Nothing is more aging than trying to look younger, it's the stupidest thing a woman can do, thinking 'if I'm wearing trousers, I'll look younger than if I'm wearing a skirt'. We live in a weird period. Women are becoming I don't know what . . . the other sex . . . I don't know how you do that. Wearing trousers doesn't change their face. You need trousers, I'll make trousers. We don't like skirts anymore, we like trousers so I'll make some. This shows how much I've changed because two years ago I would have said: 'to hell with what they need, they can do whatever they want, I won't make trousers'. . . .

If you move away from style, you have to start over and over again, it's impossible. Unfortunately, this is what is happening at the moment. Some couturiers are really good couturiers but they change every week, and this is the reason why I've created my own style. I couldn't do it if I had to come up with something new every week, you end up creating very ugly things. . . .

I've been fighting all couturiers for the past two years on those short dresses [mini-skirts]. I find them indecent. . . . To show one's knees, they need to be perfect, they are an articulation, it's like showing your elbow. Yes, that's it, you'd be showing your elbows all day, look how nice my elbows are. It's awful. Do you know what's been happening to me? When I walk into restaurants men look at me and applaud me because I've spoken against showing one's knees, that it was awful, pointless and hardly ever pretty and that if they had any idea of what the body is like, they'd know if you have bad knees you also have bad hips, too large, you're built to have children. . . . Oh no it's awful. And I believe that if you show everything off, you don't want anything anymore. . . .

I've got a really, really beautiful *clientèle*. This is the only thing I'm truly proud of. I'm convinced there isn't a house in France with a *clientèle* like mine. From all around the world you understand, the best from all around the world and I don't blush saying so, it's bold to say so with such confidence but it's the truth. You can check it, I believe anyone who dresses well in the world dresses here. There are few houses you see where women come from the US to order their dresses. They want to rest, they've been to a spa, they don't want to hear about going out, no, they're here to order their dresses, they know how to dress. Perfect. . . .

3.64 A sporting life

Dorothy Campbell Hurd, 'Plump in the middle of the Congregation', *Golf Illustrated* (August 1915).

I believe that the first woman who played on the links at North Berwick was Miss Violet Chambers and I have often heard my mother say that she was

Figure 3.16
Golf fashion, 1903, 1929
and 1935, marking the
shift from long, 'feminine'
attire to short, sporty
skirts, to more practical
trousers

almost mobbed when she first started as the sight was such a surprise to the conservative people of the town.

Later on the daughters of the English Church clergyman took it up and gradually enough people became interested to warrant the making of a ladies' course: which was shortly afterwards laid out in a field of a few acres, to the west of the Marine Hotel. I was not made a member until I was twelve years old and until then had to be contented to play with our faithful nurse, Marion McSwan, on the small links relegated to the caddies. This was a course of the roughest description, with holes innocent of tins or even of flags and whose only caretakers were the cows who occasionally condescended to browse there. Sometimes we would mark out a little course of our own on the wet sand after the tide had gone out, . . .

I have only got a very indistinct recollection of the first real match I ever played which is not surprising as I was only five years old at the time. It was a two ball foursome in which I had as partner a Mr. Arthur Dewar, who was afterwards member of Parliament for some place in Scotland, I forget exactly where.

The course was considerably shorter than it is now as its Western boundary was the Eel Burn but before the end it seemed painfully long to me, as I was so weary that I had to be carried on my partner's shoulder between shots. Even so, with the inherent stubbornness of the Scots we finished our round and actually won the match on the eighteenth green. Somehow this performance did not find favor in the eyes of our nurse, for after I was tucked up in my crib that night I heard her confide in the under nurse that she would like to take the nose of my recent partner and 'gie it a guid pull through his hair for such daft-like capers!'

Further reading

Selected sourcebooks

Albistur, Maïté and Daniel Armogathe, eds, *Le Grief des femmes: Anthologie de textes féministes du Moyen Âge à la Seconde République*. Paris: Éditions Hier et demain, 1978.

Bell, Susan Groag and Karen Offen, eds, *Women, Family and Freedom*, 2 vols. Stanford University Press, 1983.

Bonnell, Victoria E., ed., *The Russian Worker*. Berkeley: University of California Press, 1983.

DiCaprio, Lisa and Merry Wiesner, eds, *Lives and Voices: Sources in European Women's History*. Boston: Houghton Mifflin, 2001.

Dülmen, Andrea van, ed. *Frauen: ein historisches Lesebuch*. München: Verlag C. H. Beck, 1991.

Engel, Barbara, ed., *A Revolution of Their Own: Voices of Women in Soviet History*. London: Perseus, 1997.

Folger Collective on Early Women Critics, *Women Critics, 1660–1820, An Anthology*. Bloomington: Indiana University Press, 1995.

Hellerstein, Erna Olafson, Leslie Parker Hume and Karen Offen, eds, *Victorian Women, A Documentary Account of Women's Lives in Nineteenth-century England, France and the United States*. Brighton: Harvester Press, 1981.

Herminghouse, Patricia A. and Magda Mueller, eds, *German Feminist Writings*. The German Library. New York/London: Continuum, 2001.

Iggers, Wilma A., ed, *Women of Prague, Ethnic Diversity and Social Change from the Eighteenth Century to the Present*. Oxford: Berghan Books, 1995.

Levy, Darline Gay, Harriet Branson Applewhite, and Mary Durham Johnson, *Women in Revolutionary Paris, 1789–1795*. Urbana: University of Illinois Press, 1979.

Riemer, Eleanor S. and John Fout, eds, *European Women, A Documentary History, 1789–1945*. New York: Schocken Books. 1980.

Surveys

Abir-Am, Pnina G. and Dorinda Outram, *Uneasy Careers and Intimate Lives: Women in Science, 1789–1979*. New Brunswick, NJ: Rutgers University Press, 1987.

Abrams, Lynn, *The Making of Modern Woman*. London: Longman, 2002.

Allen, Ann Taylor, *Women in Twentieth-century Europe*. London: Palgrave, 2008.

Anderson, Bonnie S. and Judith Zinsser, *A History of Their Own, Women in Europe from Prehistory to the Present*. 2 vols. London: Penguin, 1988.

Arnot, Margaret L. and Cornelie Usborne, eds, *Gender and Crime in Modern Europe*. London: UCL Press, 1999.

Bock, Gisela, *Women in European History*. Oxford: Blackwell, 2002.

Boxer, Marilyn and Jean Quataert, eds, *Connecting Spheres. European Women in a Globalizing World, 1500 to the Present*. Oxford: Oxford University Press, 2000.

Bridenthal, Renate, Susan Moser Stuard and Merry E. Wiesner, eds, *Becoming Visible, Women in European History*, 3rd ed. Boston, MA: Houghton, Mifflin Company, 1998. See also 1977 edition.

Caine, Barbara and Glenda Sluga, *Gendering European History, 1780–1920*. London: Continuum, 2000.

Duby, Georges and Michelle Perrot, eds, *A History of Women in the West*, 5 vols. Cambridge, MA: Harvard University Press, 1993–96.

Fuchs, Rachel G. and Victoria E. Thompson, *Women in Nineteenth-century Europe*. London: Palgrave, 2005.

Hufton, Olwen, *The Prospect before Her, A History of Women in Western Europe*. London: Fontana Press, 1995.

Hunt, Margaret, *Women in Eighteenth-century Europe*. London: Pearson/Longman, 2009.

Kalof, Linda, ed., *A Cultural History of Women*, 6 vols. London: Bloomsbury, 2013.

Montgomery, Fiona and Christine Collett, eds, *The European Women's History Reader*. London: Routledge, 2002.

Simonton, Deborah, *A History of European Women's Work, 1770 to the Present*. London: Routledge, 1998.

Simonton, Deborah, ed., *The Routledge History of Women in Europe since 1700*. London: Routledge, 2006.

Simonton, Deborah, *Women in European Culture and Society: Gender, Skill and Identity from 1700*. London: Routledge, 2011.

Smith, Bonnie, *Changing Lives: Women in European History since 1700*. Lexington, MA: D. C. Heath and Company, 1989.

Tilly, Louise and Joan Scott, *Women, Work and Family*. London: Routledge, 1987.

Wunder, Heide, *He is the Sun, She is the Moon*. Cambridge, MA: Harvard University Press, 1998.

Index

Note: page numbers in italics indicate figures